# SUPERGIRL

# FRIENDS & FUGITIVES

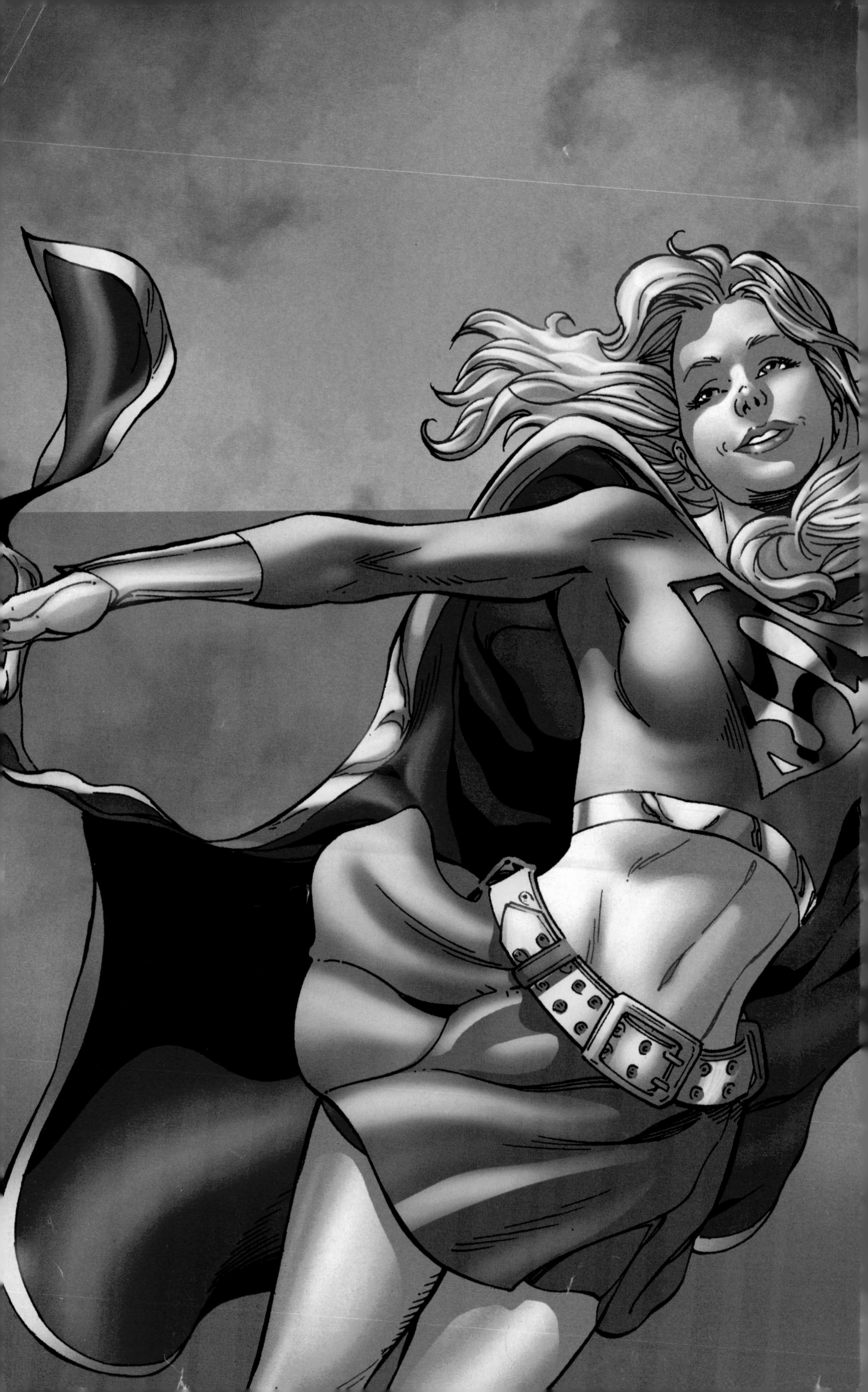

# SUPERGIRL

## FRIENDS & FUGITIVES

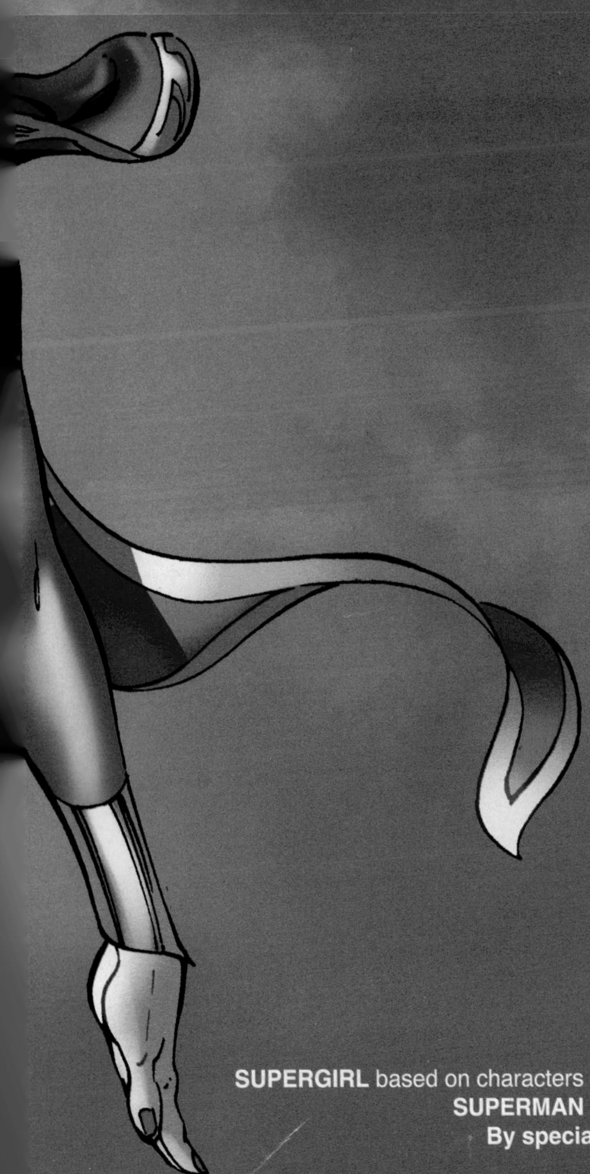

**STERLING GATES**
**GREG RUCKA**
writers

**JAMAL IGLE**
**PERE PÉREZ**
**FERNANDO DAGNINO**
**EDUARDO PANSICA**
**MATT CAMP**
pencillers

**JON SIBAL**
**PERE PÉREZ**
**RAÚL FERNÁNDEZ**
**JÚLIO FERREIRA**
**MATT CAMP**
inkers

**NEI RUFFINO**
**PETE PANTAZIS**
**JAVIER MENA**
**BLOND**
colorists

**JARED K. FLETCHER**
**ROB LEIGH**
**JOHN J. HILL**
letterers

**JOSHUA MIDDLETON**
collection cover artist

**SUPERGIRL** based on characters created by **JERRY SIEGEL** and **JOE SHUSTER**
**SUPERMAN** created by **JERRY SIEGEL** and **JOE SHUSTER**
**By special arrangement with the JERRY SIEGEL family**

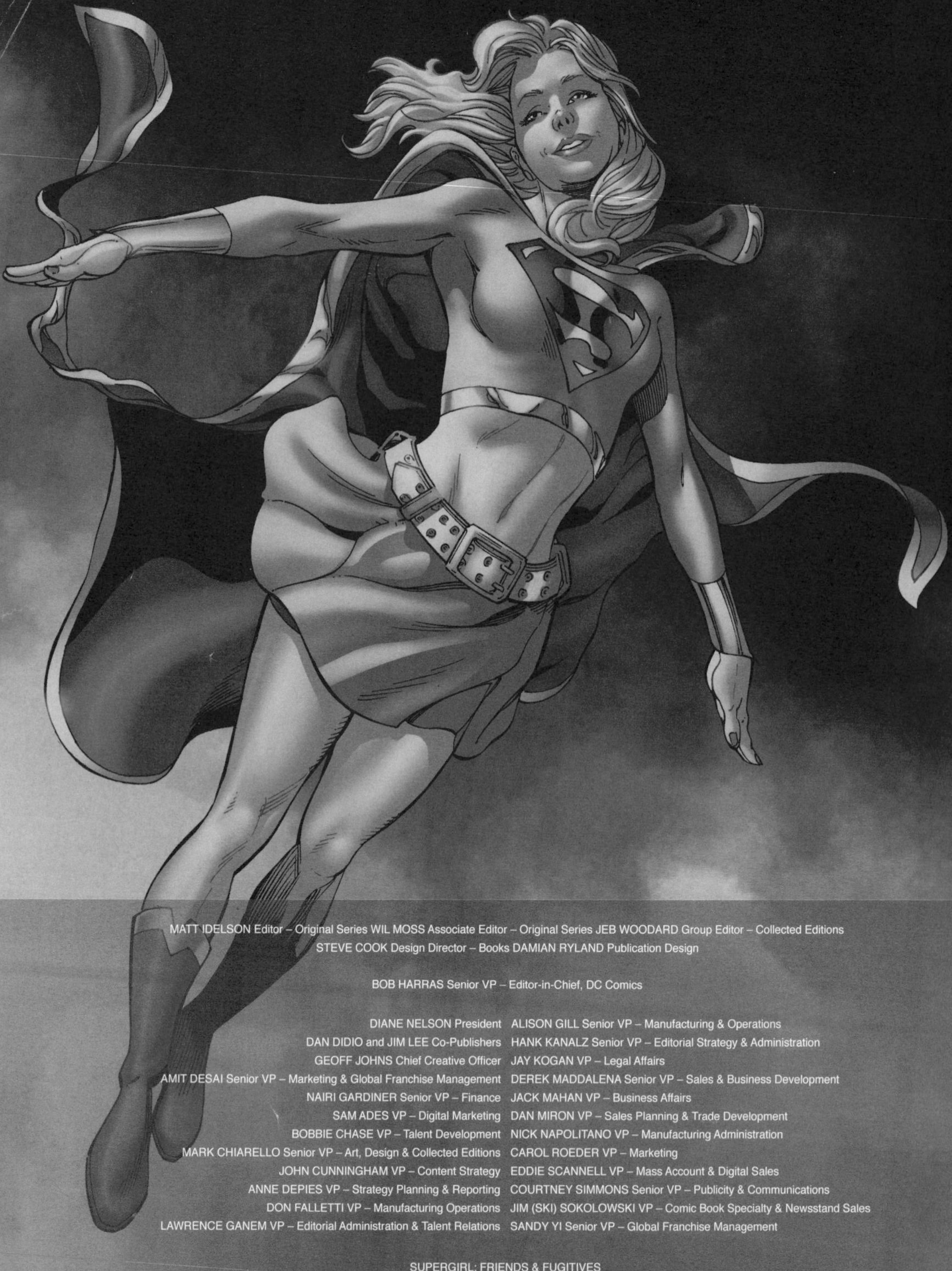

MATT IDELSON Editor – Original Series WIL MOSS Associate Editor – Original Series JEB WOODARD Group Editor – Collected Editions
STEVE COOK Design Director – Books DAMIAN RYLAND Publication Design

BOB HARRAS Senior VP – Editor-in-Chief, DC Comics

DIANE NELSON President
DAN DIDIO and JIM LEE Co-Publishers
GEOFF JOHNS Chief Creative Officer
AMIT DESAI Senior VP – Marketing & Global Franchise Management
NAIRI GARDINER Senior VP – Finance
SAM ADES VP – Digital Marketing
BOBBIE CHASE VP – Talent Development
MARK CHIARELLO Senior VP – Art, Design & Collected Editions
JOHN CUNNINGHAM VP – Content Strategy
ANNE DEPIES VP – Strategy Planning & Reporting
DON FALLETTI VP – Manufacturing Operations
LAWRENCE GANEM VP – Editorial Administration & Talent Relations
ALISON GILL Senior VP – Manufacturing & Operations
HANK KANALZ Senior VP – Editorial Strategy & Administration
JAY KOGAN VP – Legal Affairs
DEREK MADDALENA Senior VP – Sales & Business Development
JACK MAHAN VP – Business Affairs
DAN MIRON VP – Sales Planning & Trade Development
NICK NAPOLITANO VP – Manufacturing Administration
CAROL ROEDER VP – Marketing
EDDIE SCANNELL VP – Mass Account & Digital Sales
COURTNEY SIMMONS Senior VP – Publicity & Communications
JIM (SKI) SOKOLOWSKI VP – Comic Book Specialty & Newsstand Sales
SANDY YI Senior VP – Global Franchise Management

SUPERGIRL: FRIENDS & FUGITIVES



DC Comics, 2900 West Alameda Ave., Burbank, CA 91505
Printed by RR Donnelley, Salem, VA, USA. 8/5/16. First Printing.
ISBN: 978-1-4012-7015-5

Library of Congress Cataloging-in-Publication Data is available.

PEFC Certified
Printed on paper from sustainably managed forests and controlled sources
PEFC
PEFC/29-31-75
www.pefc.org

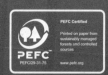

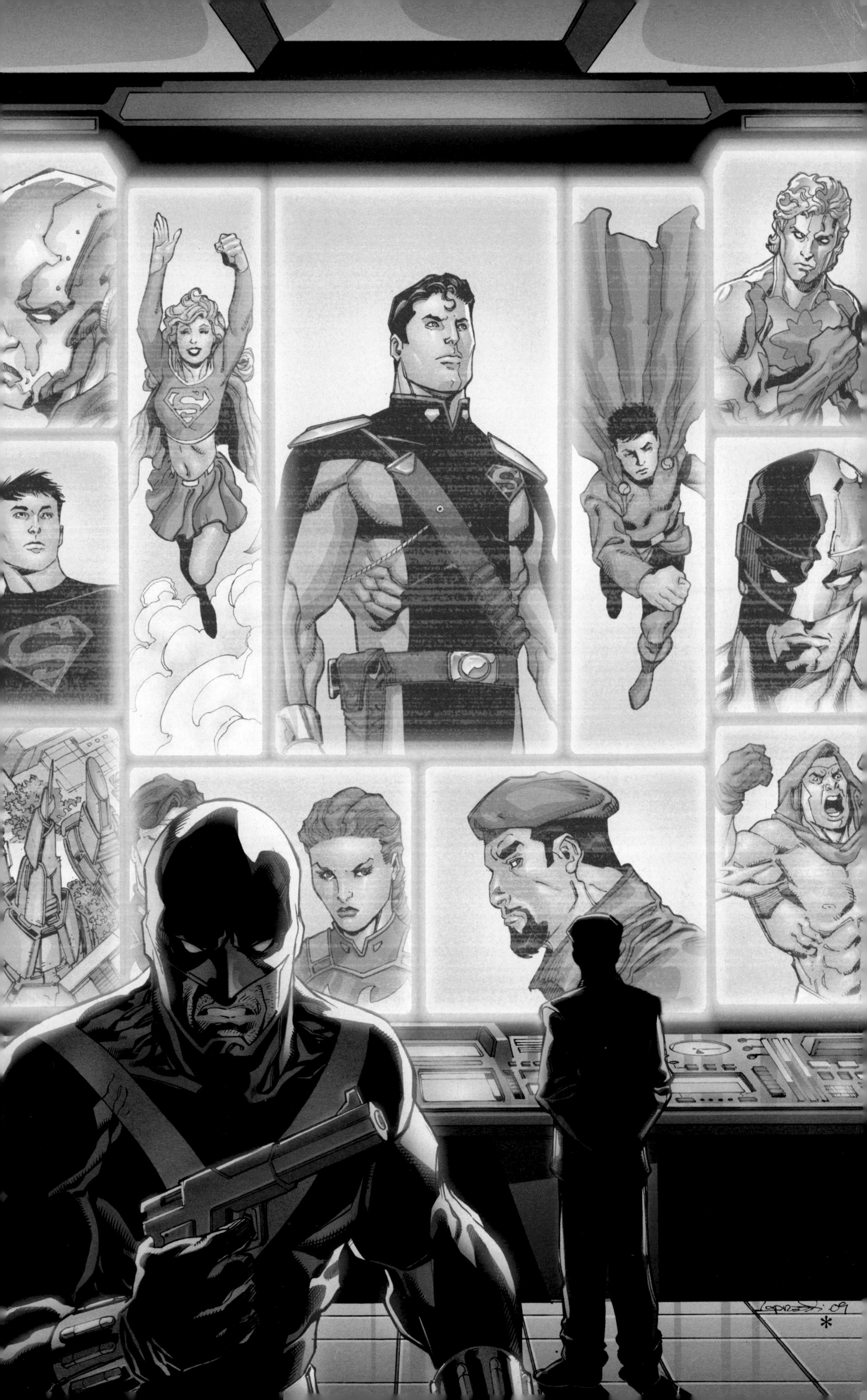

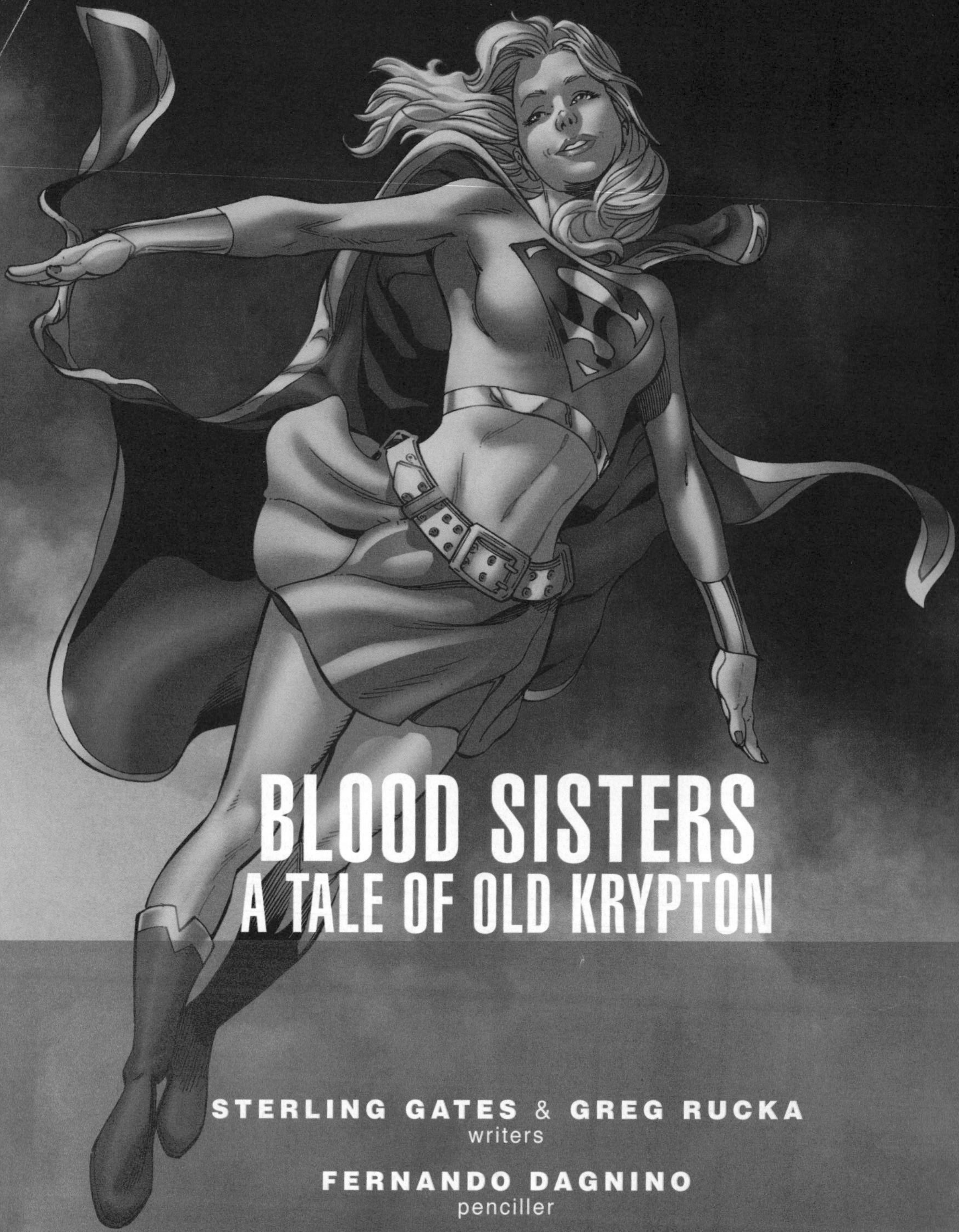

# BLOOD SISTERS
## A TALE OF OLD KRYPTON


**STERLING GATES & GREG RUCKA**
writers

**FERNANDO DAGNINO**
penciller

**RAÚL FERNÁNDEZ**
inker

**BLOND**
colorist

**JOHN J. HILL**
letterer

**AARON LOPRESTI with HI-FI**
cover

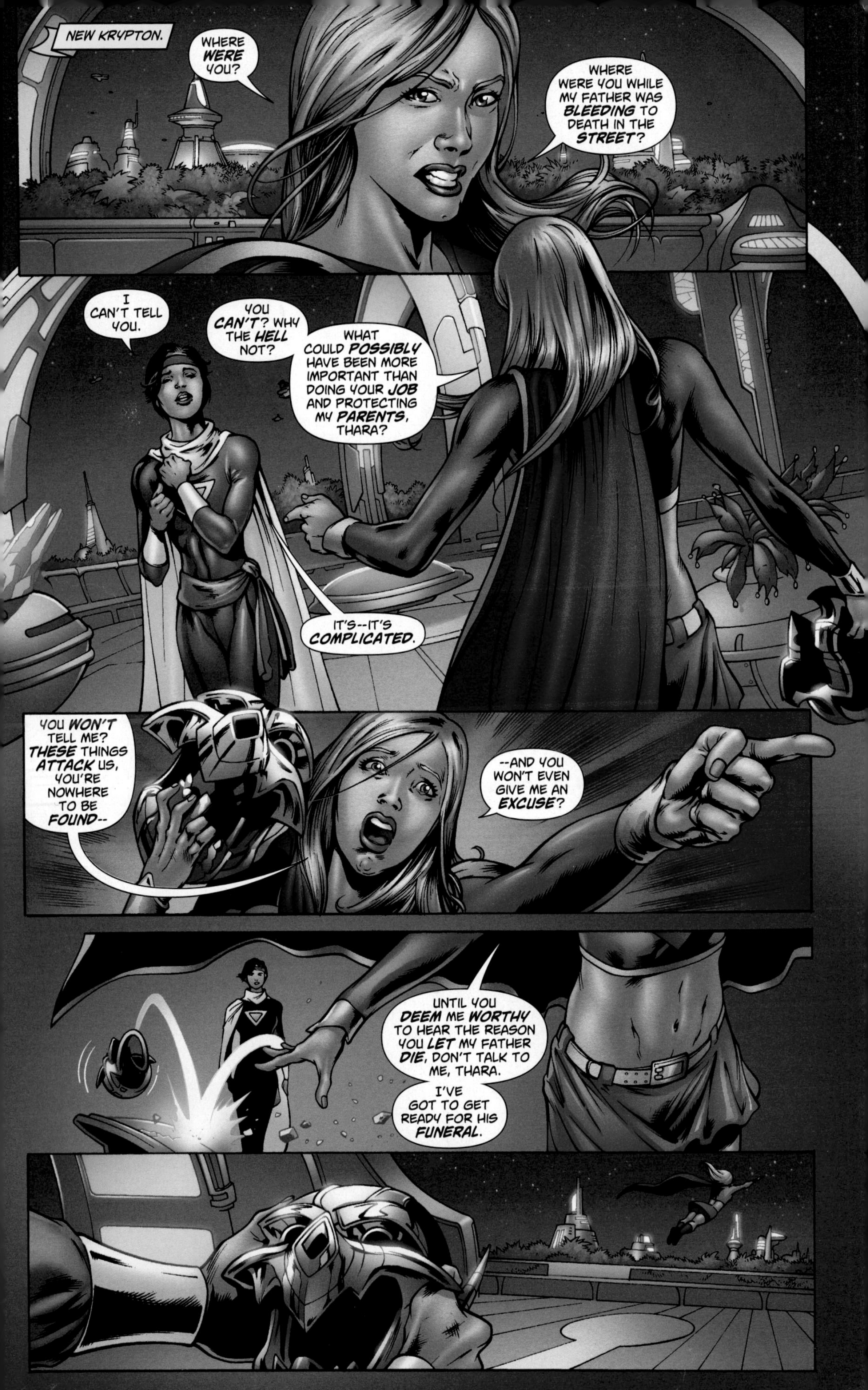
NEW KRYPTON.
WHERE WERE YOU?
WHERE WERE YOU WHILE MY FATHER WAS BLEEDING TO DEATH IN THE STREET?
I CAN'T TELL YOU.
YOU CAN'T? WHY THE HELL NOT?
WHAT COULD POSSIBLY HAVE BEEN MORE IMPORTANT THAN DOING YOUR JOB AND PROTECTING MY PARENTS, THARA?
IT'S--IT'S COMPLICATED.
YOU WON'T TELL ME? THESE THINGS ATTACK US, YOU'RE NOWHERE TO BE FOUND--
--AND YOU WON'T EVEN GIVE ME AN EXCUSE?
UNTIL YOU DEEM ME WORTHY TO HEAR THE REASON YOU LET MY FATHER DIE, DON'T TALK TO ME, THARA.
I'VE GOT TO GET READY FOR HIS FUNERAL.

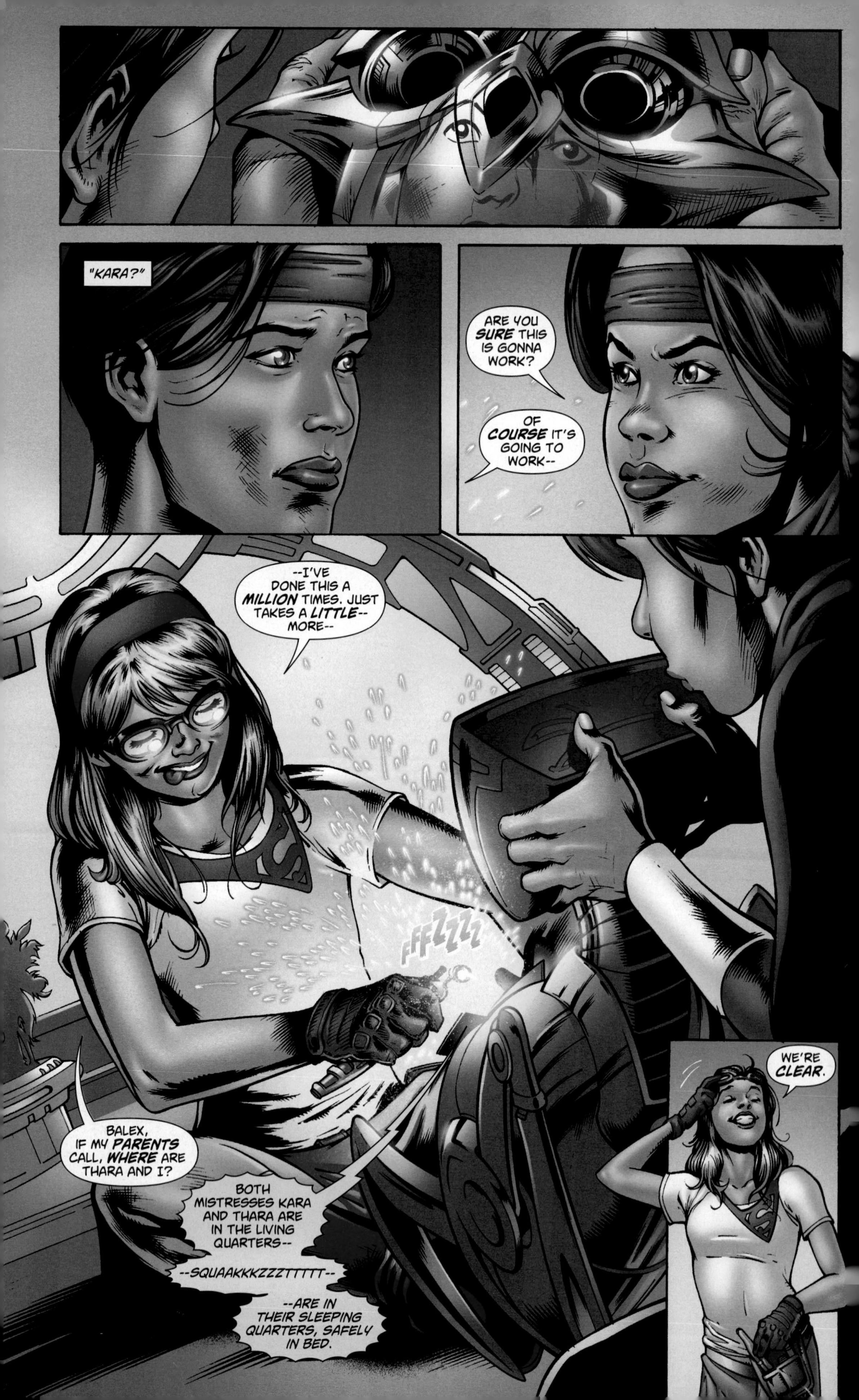
"KARA?"
ARE YOU SURE THIS IS GONNA WORK?
OF COURSE IT'S GOING TO WORK--
--I'VE DONE THIS A MILLION TIMES. JUST TAKES A LITTLE-- MORE--
FFZZZZZ
BALEX, IF MY PARENTS CALL, WHERE ARE THARA AND I?
BOTH MISTRESSES KARA AND THARA ARE IN THE LIVING QUARTERS--
--SQUAAKKKZZZTTTTT--
--ARE IN THEIR SLEEPING QUARTERS, SAFELY IN BED.
WE'RE CLEAR.

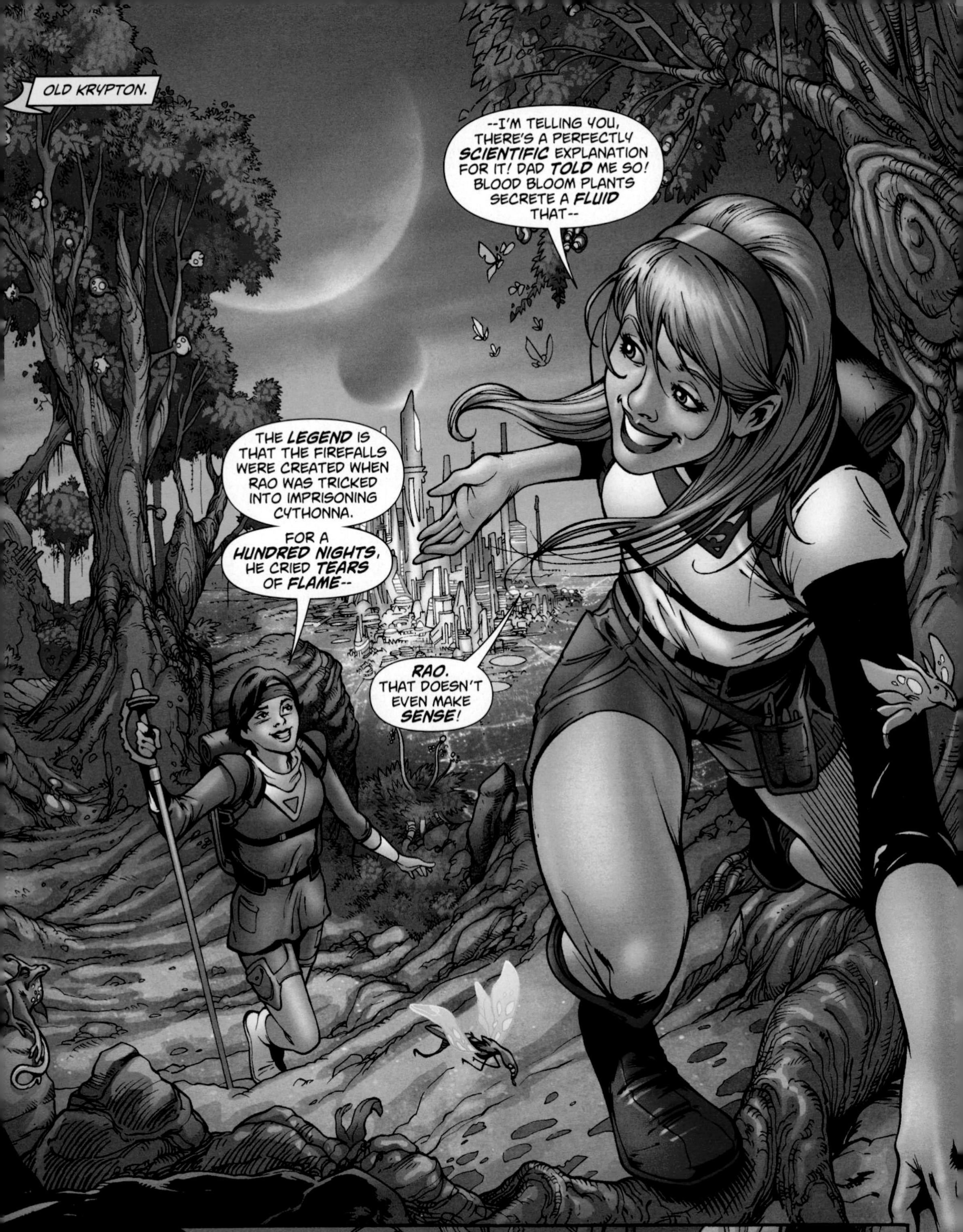
OLD KRYPTON.
--I'M TELLING YOU, THERE'S A PERFECTLY SCIENTIFIC EXPLANATION FOR IT! DAD TOLD ME SO! BLOOD BLOOM PLANTS SECRETE A FLUID THAT--
THE LEGEND IS THAT THE FIREFALLS WERE CREATED WHEN RAO WAS TRICKED INTO IMPRISONING CYTHONNA.
FOR A HUNDRED NIGHTS, HE CRIED TEARS OF FLAME--
RAO. THAT DOESN'T EVEN MAKE SENSE!

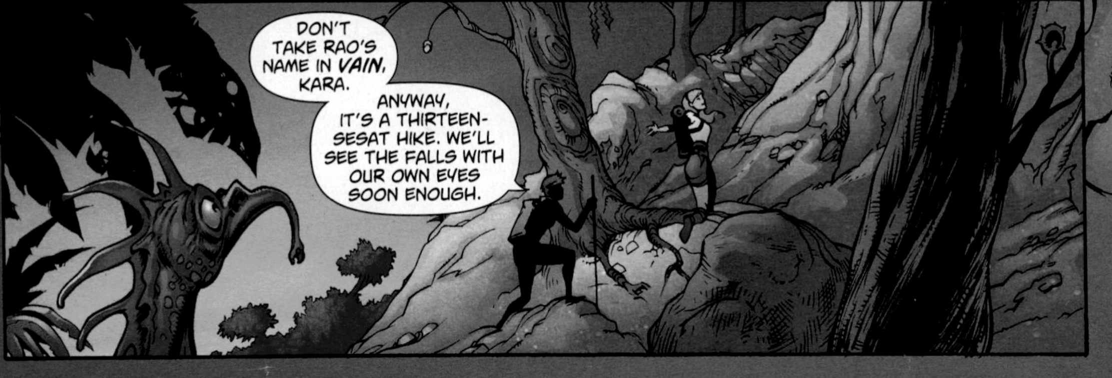
DON'T TAKE RAO'S NAME IN VAIN, KARA.
ANYWAY, IT'S A THIRTEEN-SESAT HIKE. WE'LL SEE THE FALLS WITH OUR OWN EYES SOON ENOUGH.

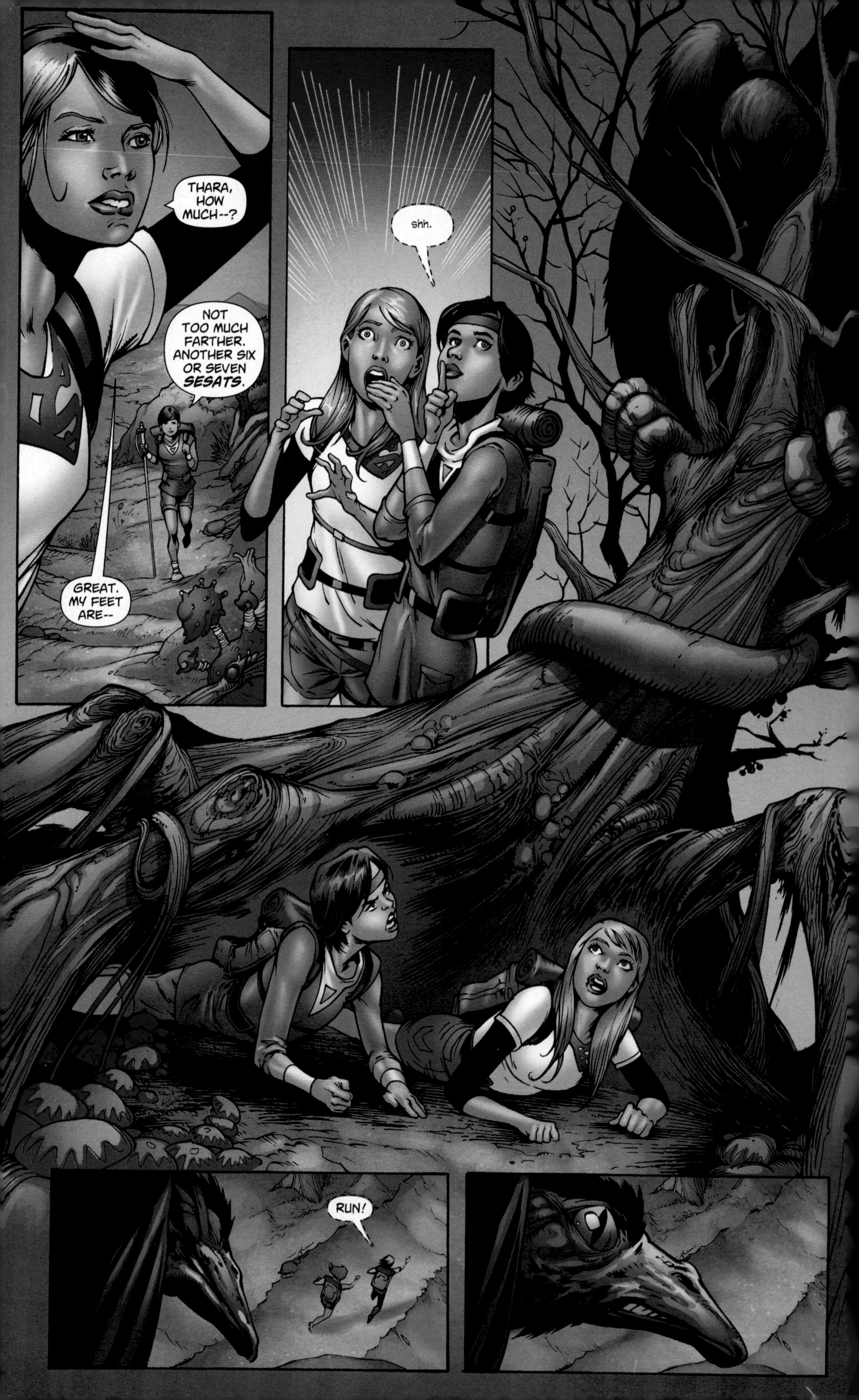
THARA, HOW MUCH--?
NOT TOO MUCH FARTHER. ANOTHER SIX OR SEVEN SESATS.
GREAT. MY FEET ARE--
shh.
RUN!

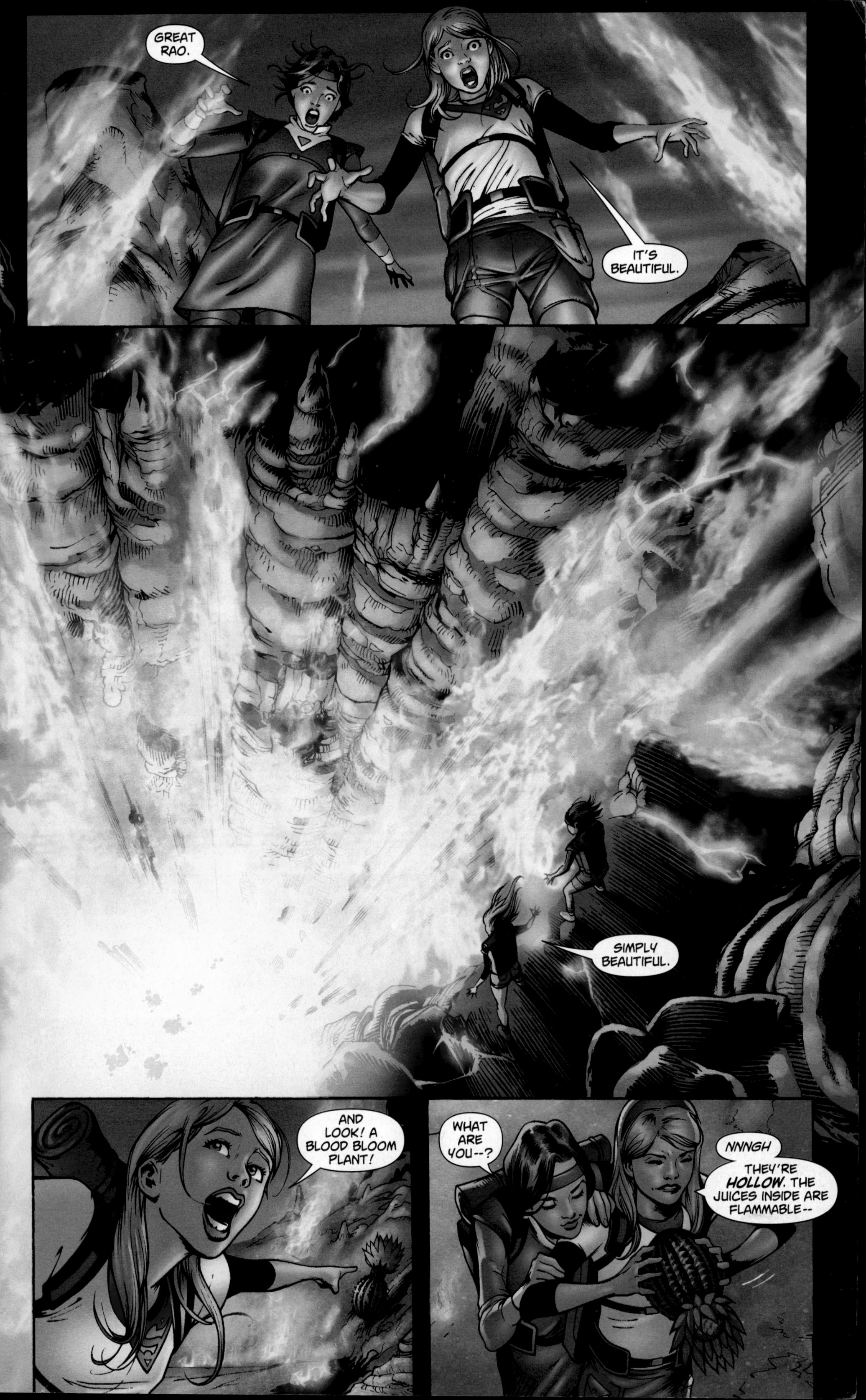
GREAT RAO.
IT'S BEAUTIFUL.
SIMPLY BEAUTIFUL.
AND LOOK! A BLOOD BLOOM PLANT!
WHAT ARE YOU--?
NNNGH
THEY'RE HOLLOW. THE JUICES INSIDE ARE FLAMMABLE--

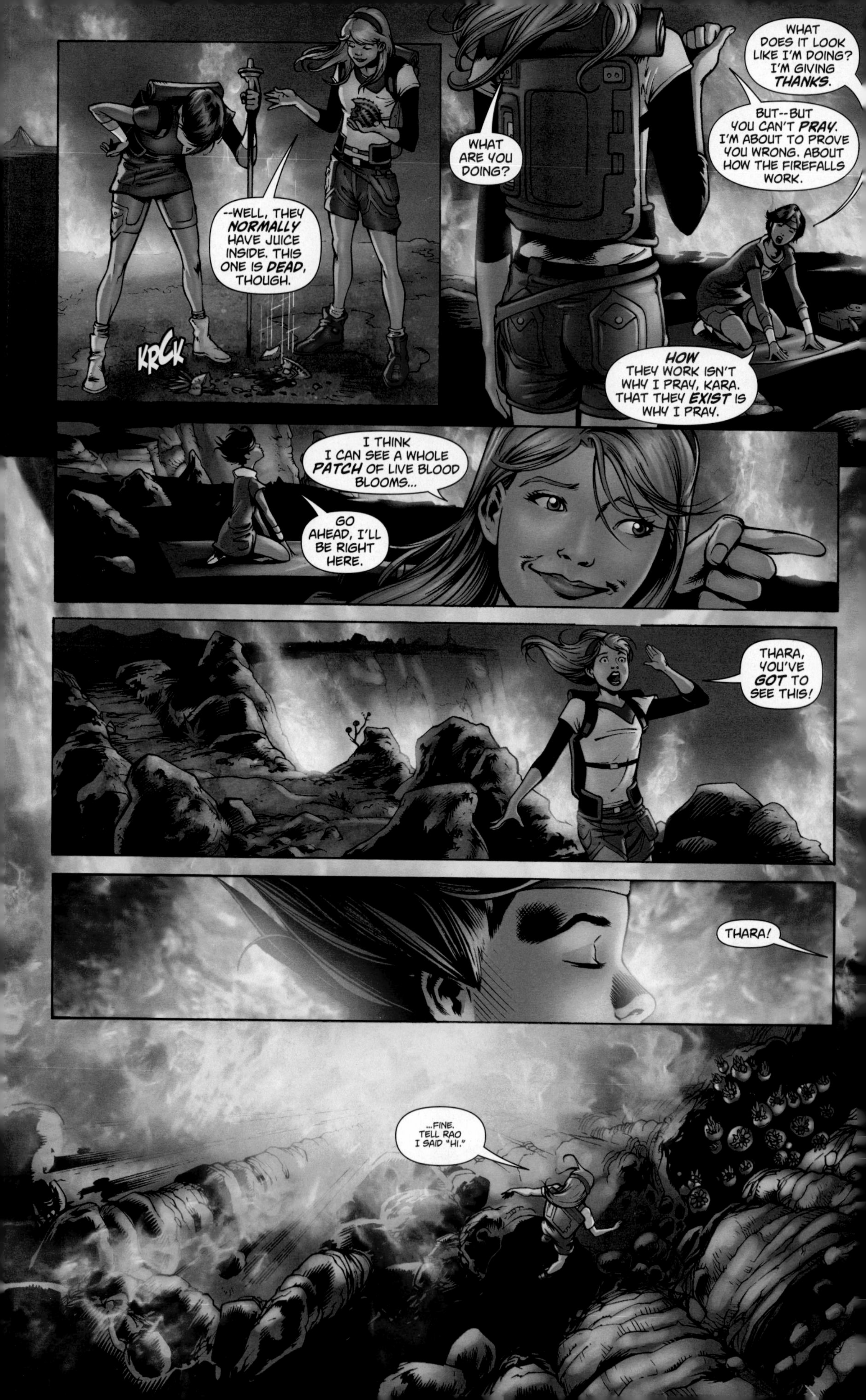
--WELL, THEY NORMALLY HAVE JUICE INSIDE. THIS ONE IS DEAD, THOUGH.
KRCK
WHAT ARE YOU DOING?
WHAT DOES IT LOOK LIKE I'M DOING? I'M GIVING THANKS.
BUT--BUT YOU CAN'T PRAY. I'M ABOUT TO PROVE YOU WRONG. ABOUT HOW THE FIREFALLS WORK.
HOW THEY WORK ISN'T WHY I PRAY, KARA. THAT THEY EXIST IS WHY I PRAY.
I THINK I CAN SEE A WHOLE PATCH OF LIVE BLOOD BLOOMS...
GO AHEAD, I'LL BE RIGHT HERE.
THARA, YOU'VE GOT TO SEE THIS!
THARA!
...FINE. TELL RAO I SAID "HI."

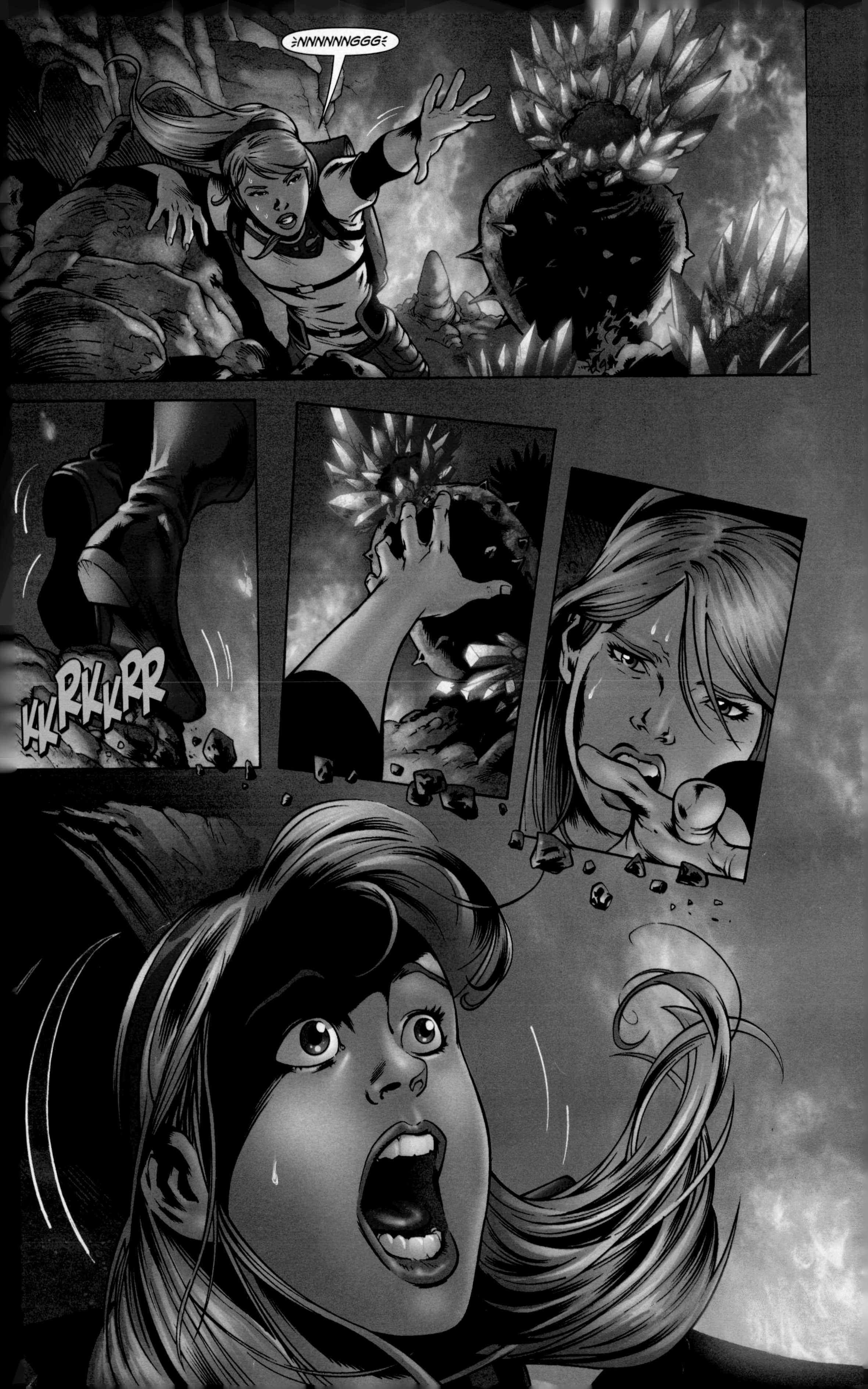
NNNNNNGGG
KKRKKRR

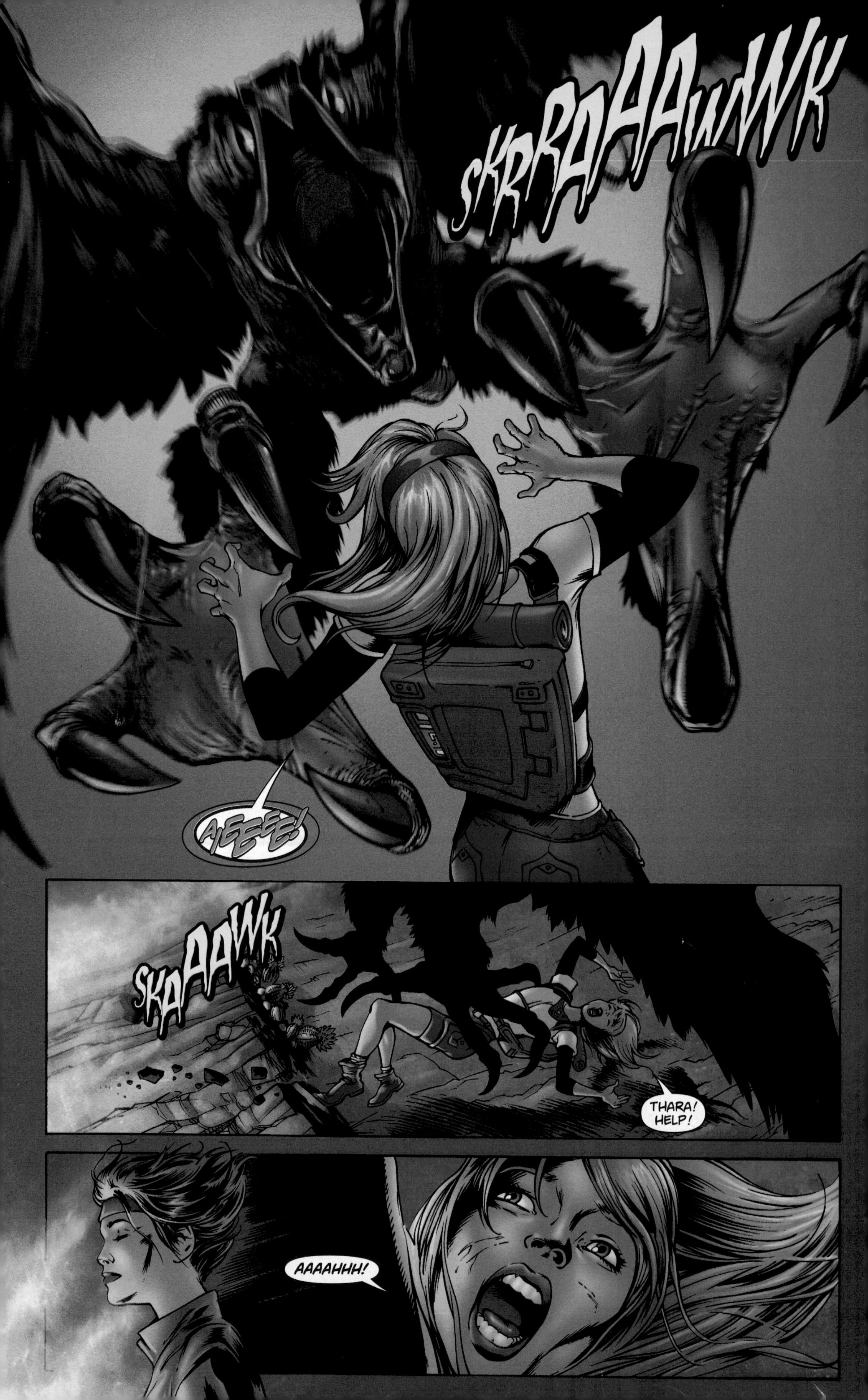
SKRRAAAWWK
AIEEEEE!
SKAAAWK
THARA! HELP!
AAAAHHH!

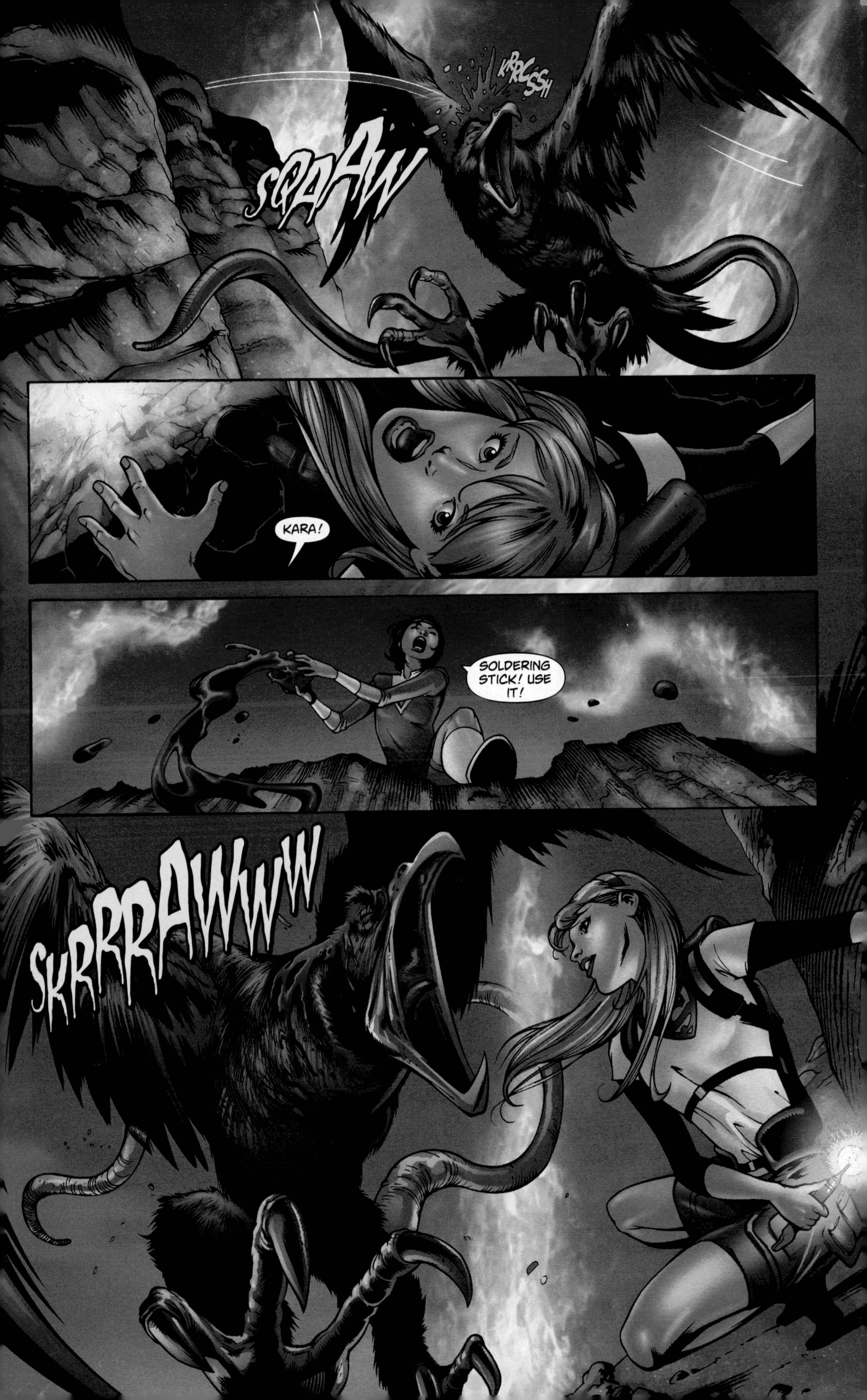
KRRCSSH
SQAAW
KARA!
SOLDERING STICK! USE IT!
SKRRRAWWW

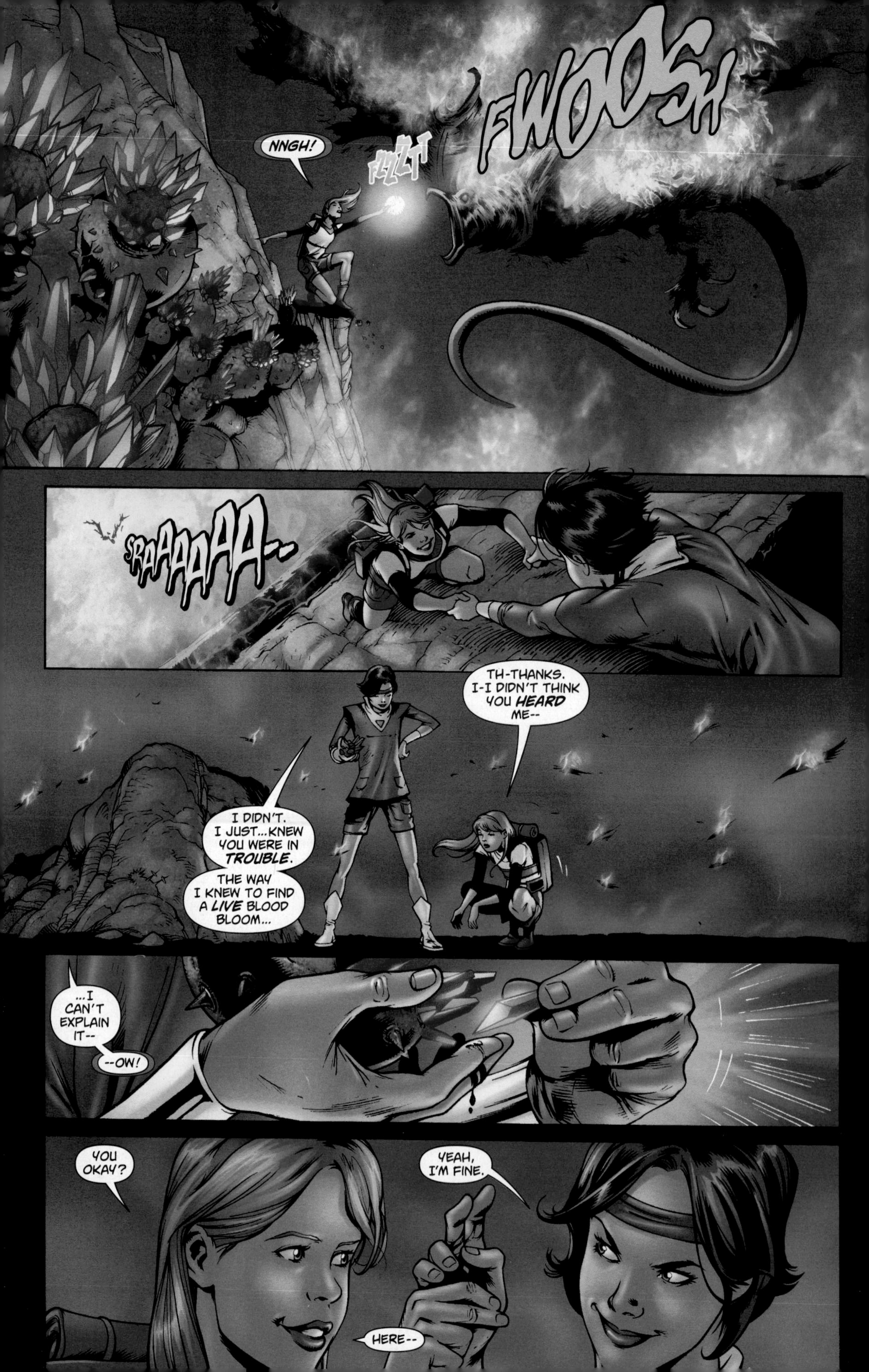
NNGH!
FZZZT
FWOOSH
SRAAAAAA--
TH-THANKS. I-I DIDN'T THINK YOU HEARD ME--
I DIDN'T. I JUST...KNEW YOU WERE IN TROUBLE.
THE WAY I KNEW TO FIND A LIVE BLOOD BLOOM...
...I CAN'T EXPLAIN IT--
--OW!
YOU OKAY?
YEAH, I'M FINE.
HERE--

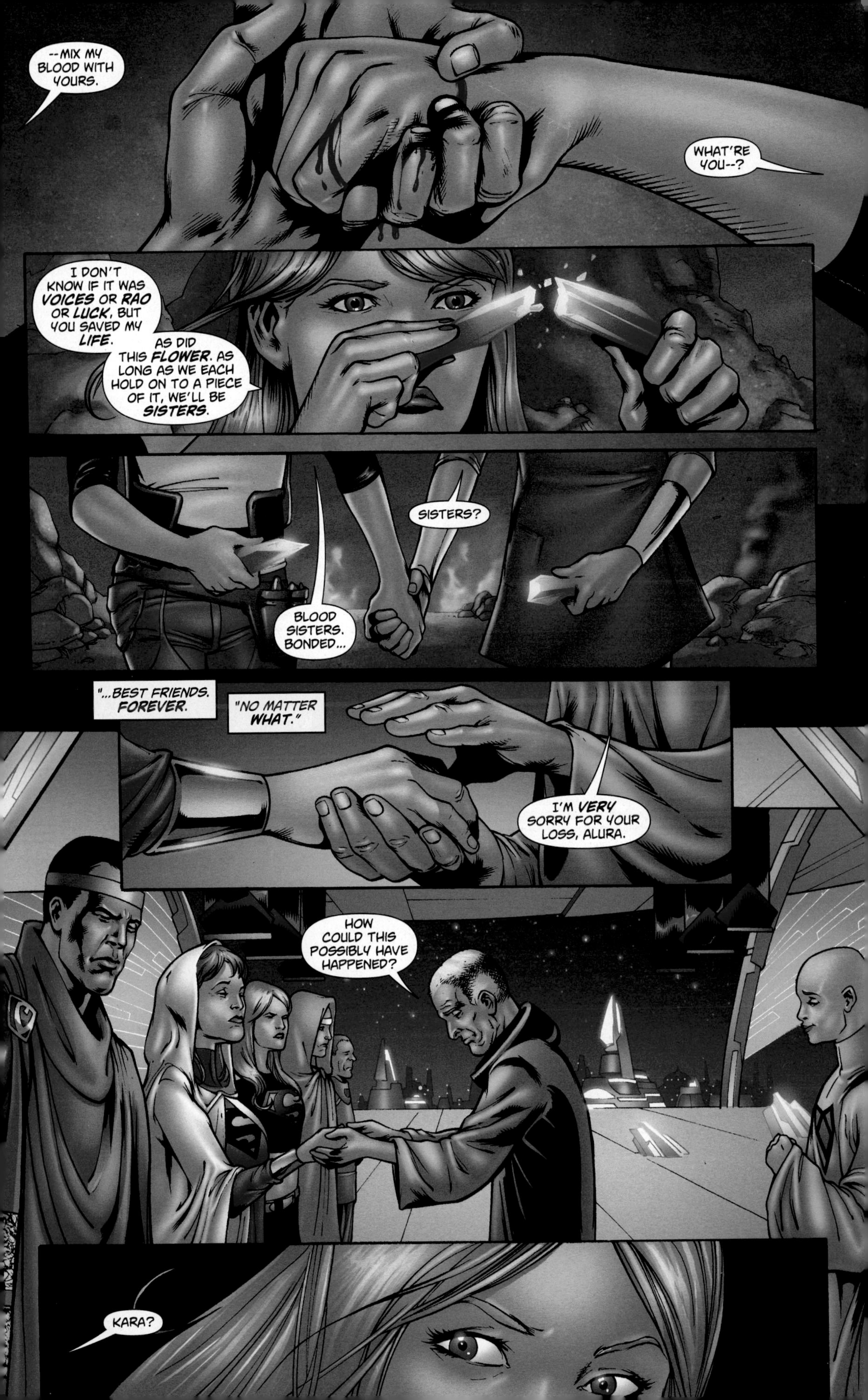
--MIX MY BLOOD WITH YOURS.
WHAT'RE YOU--?
I DON'T KNOW IF IT WAS VOICES OR RAO OR LUCK, BUT YOU SAVED MY LIFE.
AS DID THIS FLOWER. AS LONG AS WE EACH HOLD ON TO A PIECE OF IT, WE'LL BE SISTERS.
SISTERS?
BLOOD SISTERS. BONDED...
"...BEST FRIENDS. FOREVER.
"NO MATTER WHAT."
I'M VERY SORRY FOR YOUR LOSS, ALURA.
HOW COULD THIS POSSIBLY HAVE HAPPENED?
KARA?

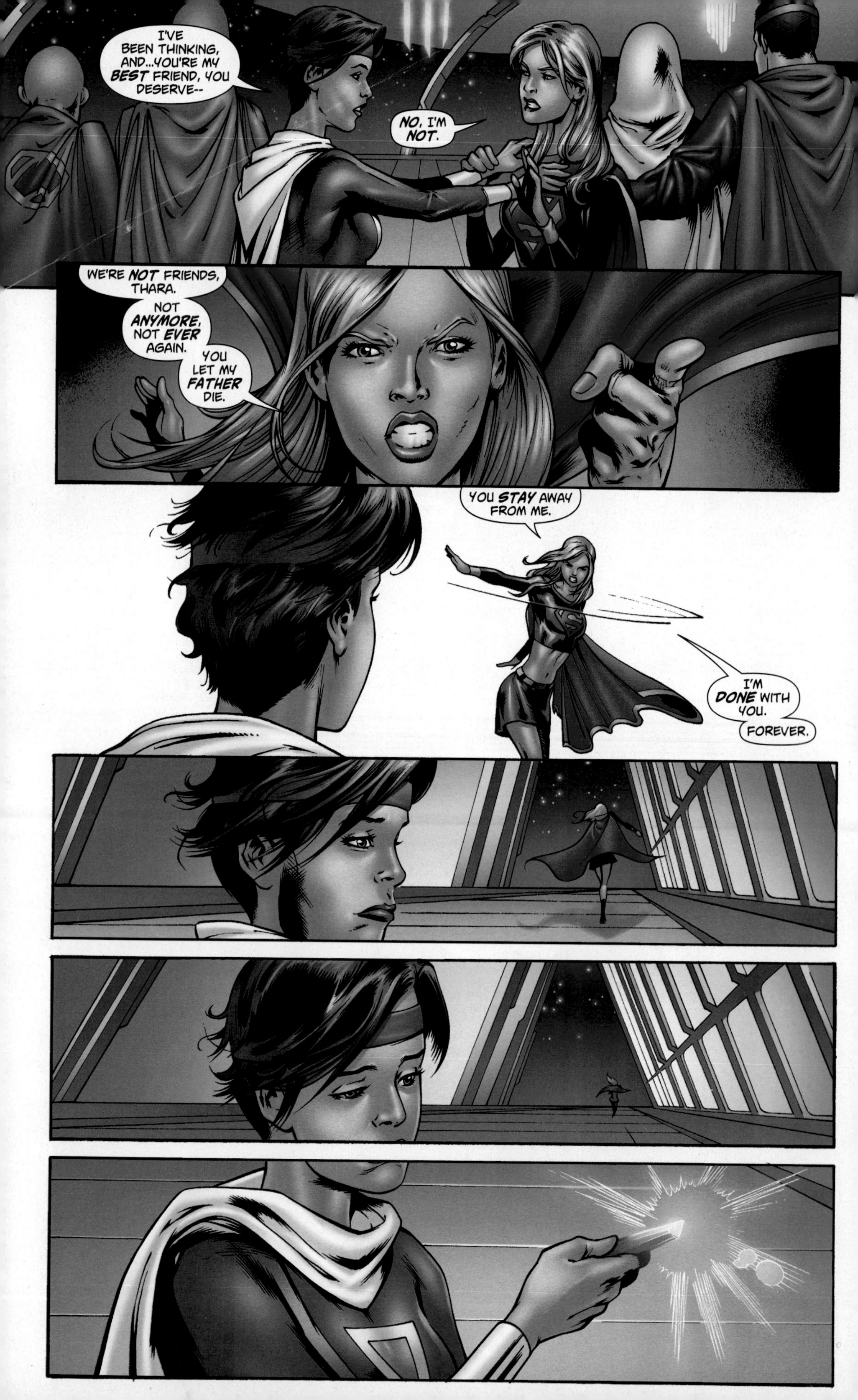
I'VE BEEN THINKING, AND...YOU'RE MY BEST FRIEND, YOU DESERVE--
NO, I'M NOT.
WE'RE NOT FRIENDS, THARA.
NOT ANYMORE, NOT EVER AGAIN.
YOU LET MY FATHER DIE.
YOU STAY AWAY FROM ME.
I'M DONE WITH YOU.
FOREVER.

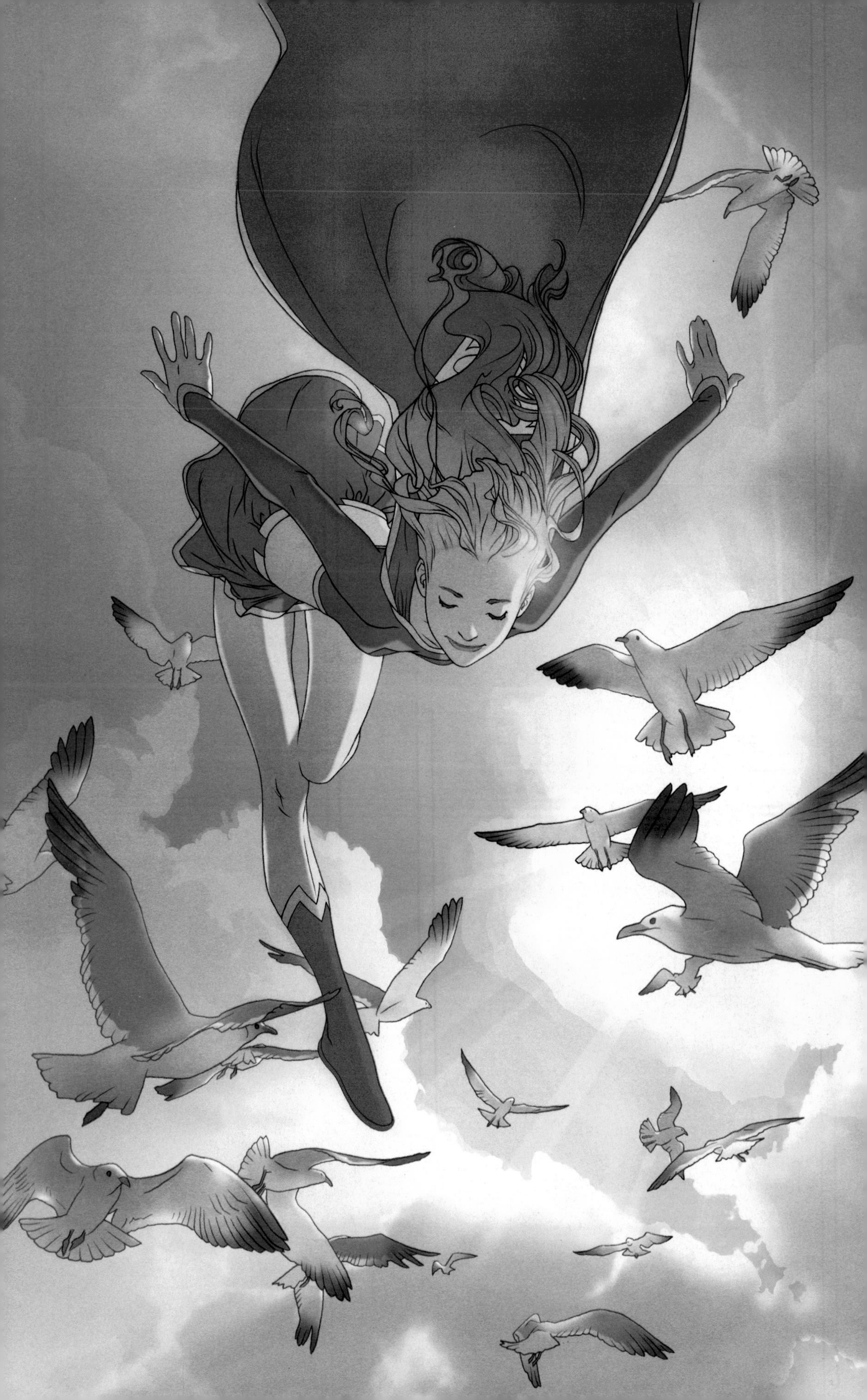

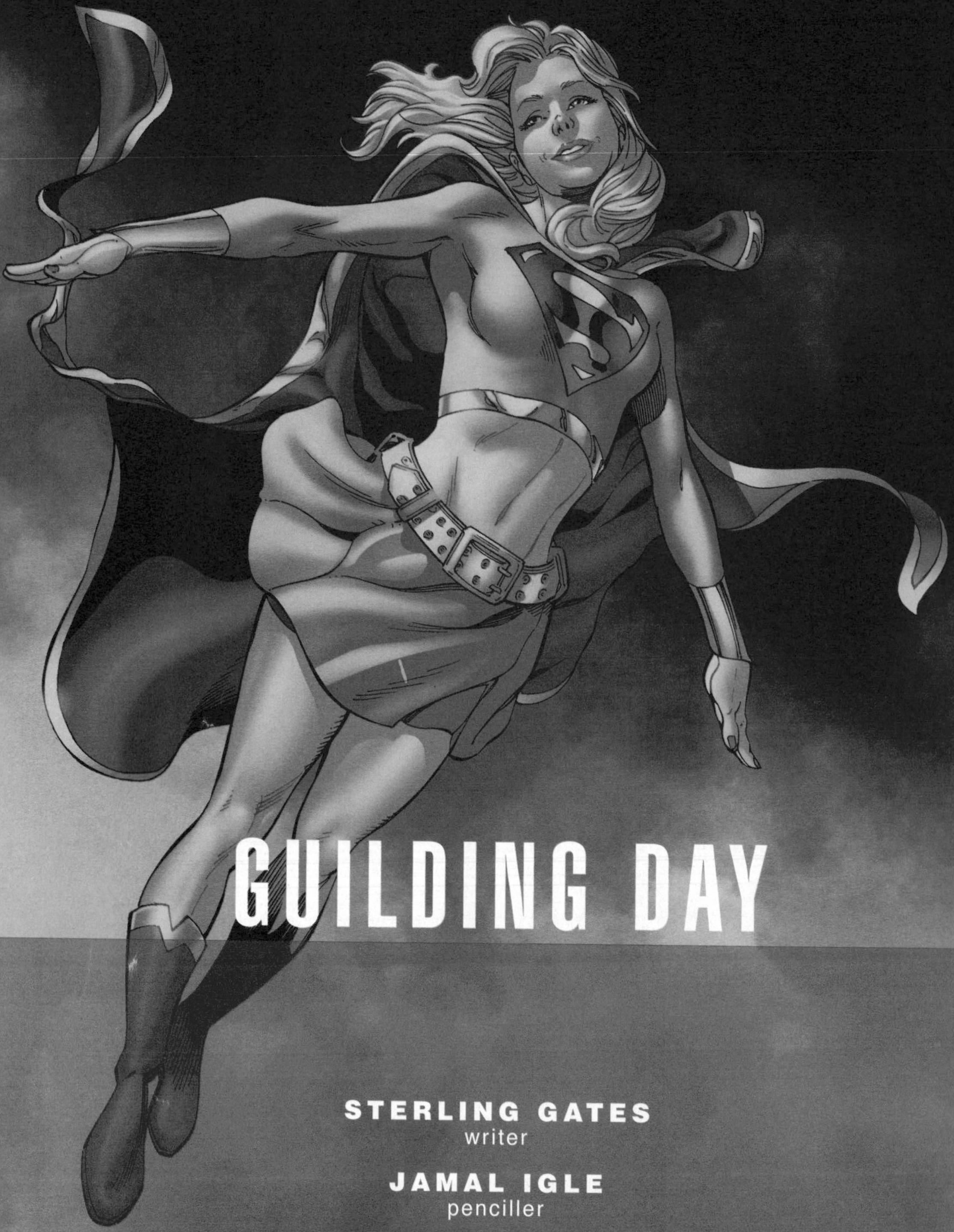

# GUILDING DAY

**STERLING GATES**
writer

**JAMAL IGLE**
penciller

**JON SIBAL**
inker

**PETE PANTAZIS**
colorist

**JARED K. FLETCHER**
letterer

**JOSHUA MIDDLETON**
cover

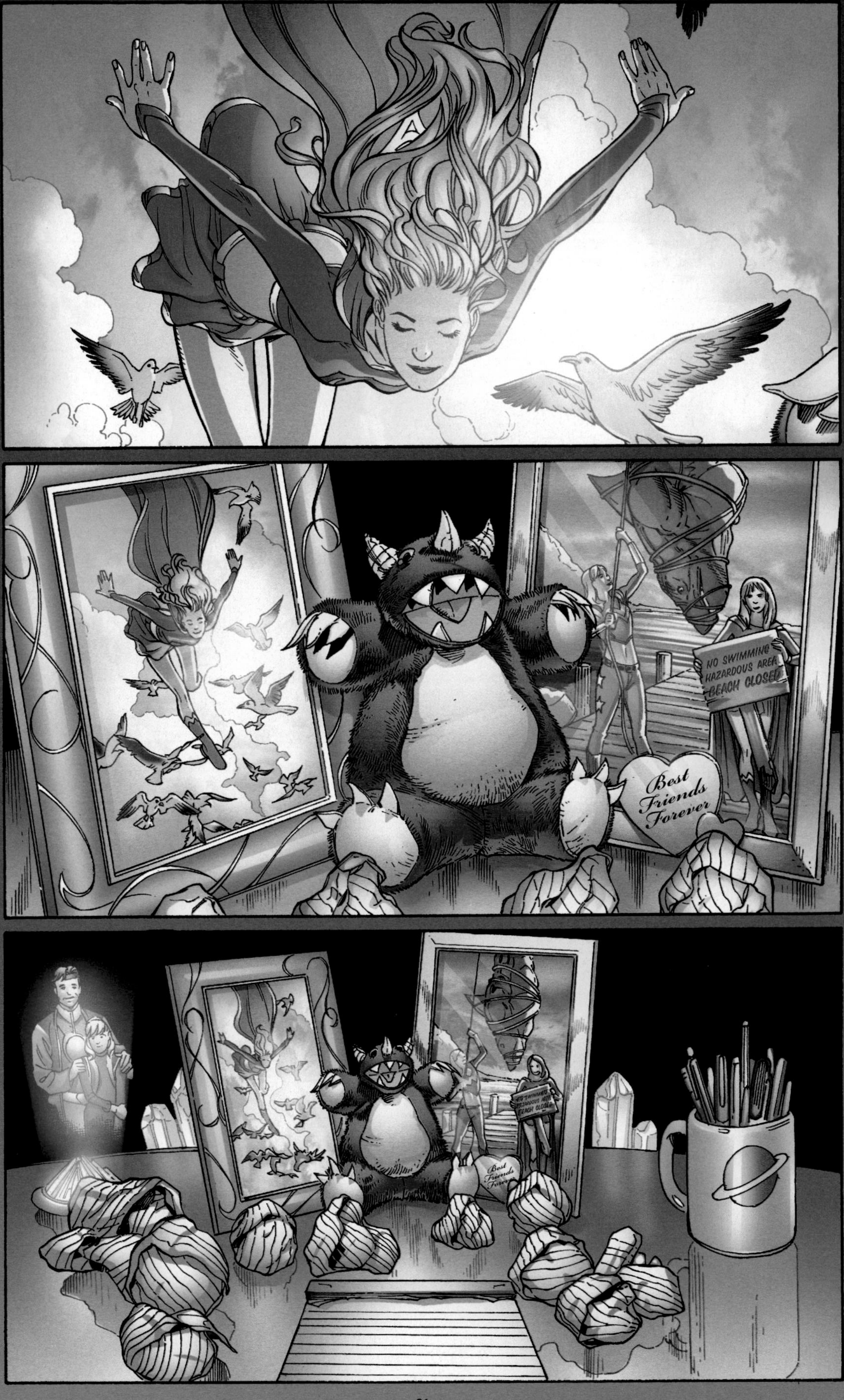

NO SWIMMING
HAZARDOUS AREA
BEACH CLOSED
Best Friends Forever

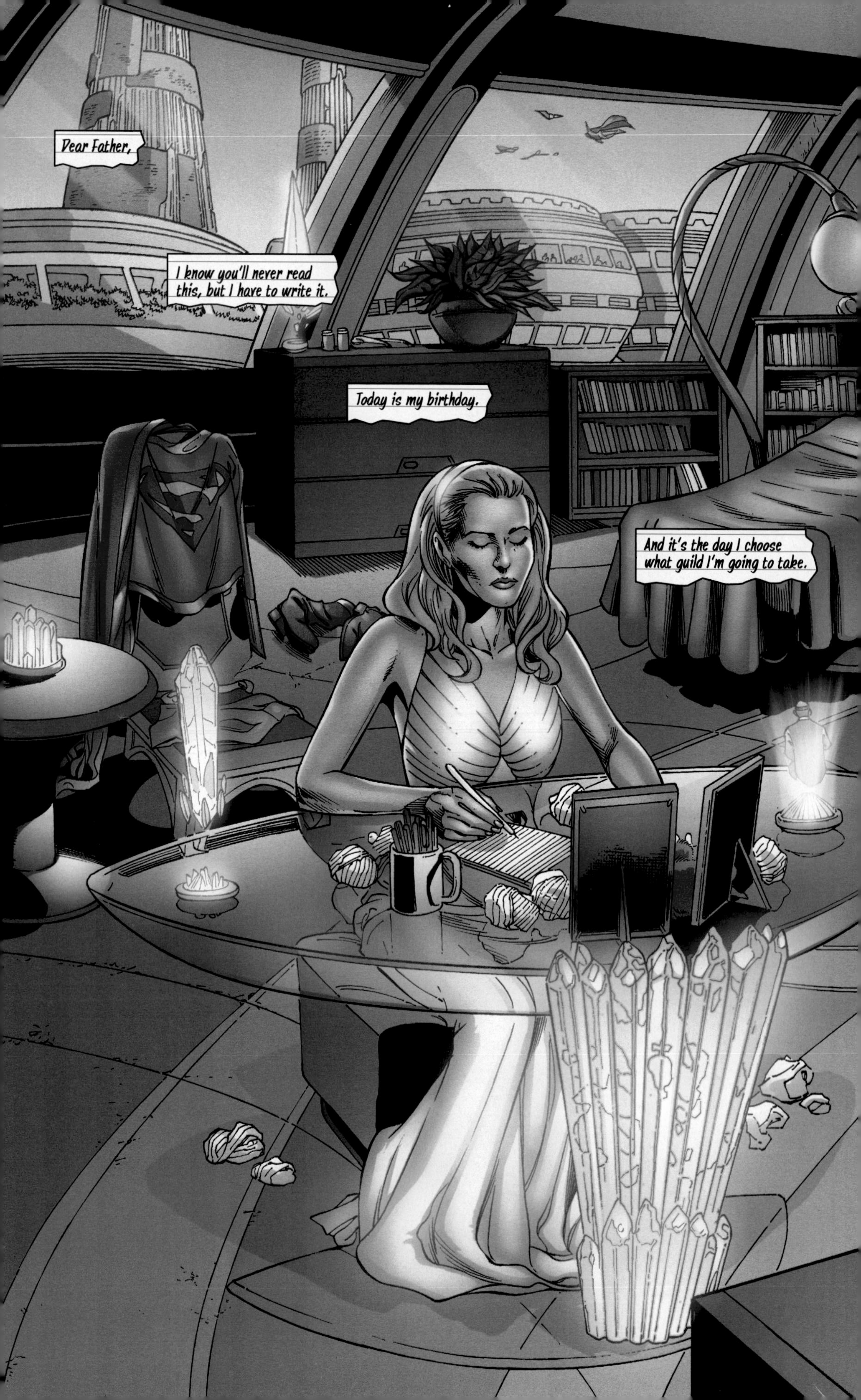
Dear Father,
I know you'll never read this, but I have to write it.
Today is my birthday.
And it's the day I choose what guild I'm going to take.

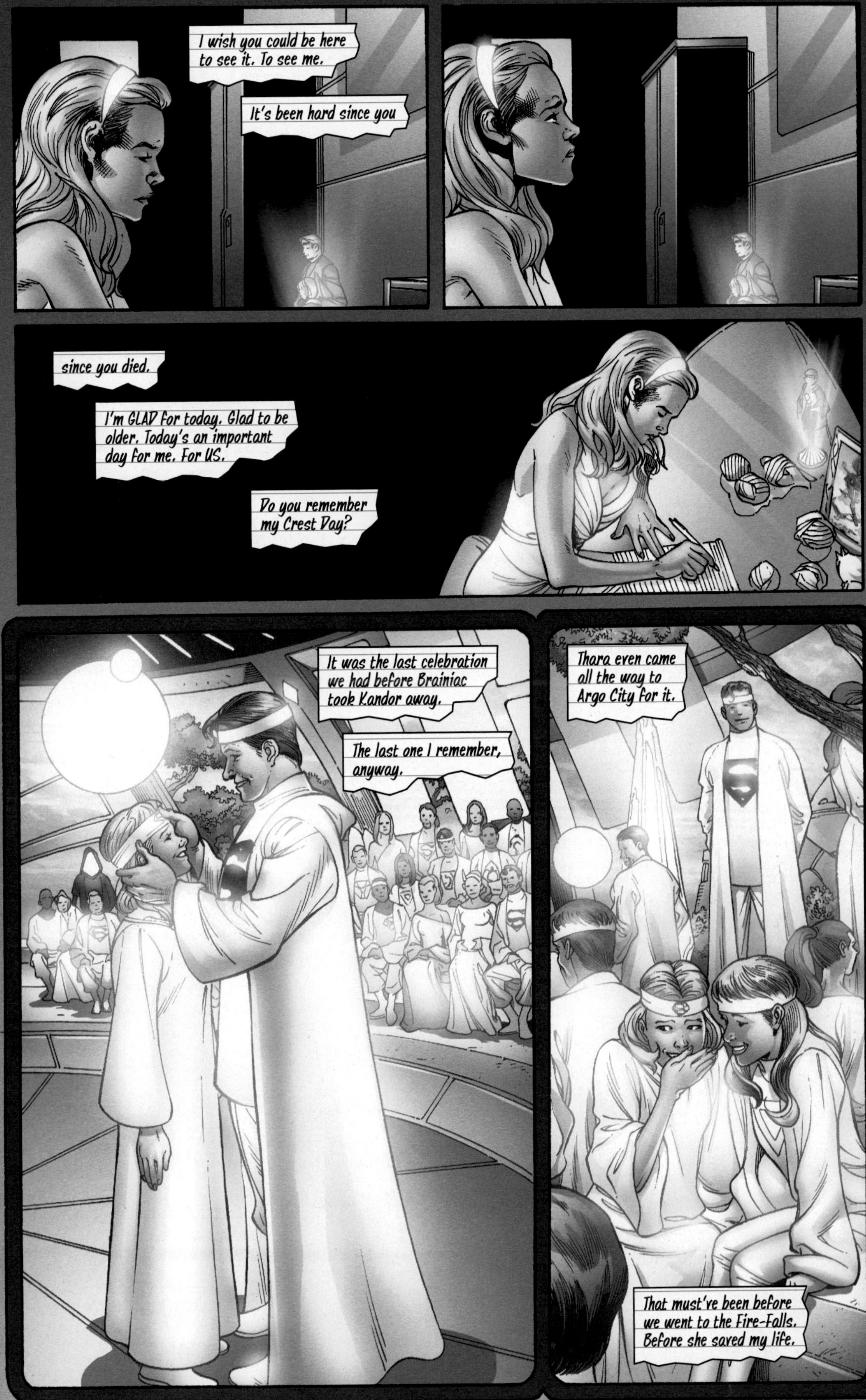
I wish you could be here to see it. To see me.
It's been hard since you
since you died.
I'm GLAD for today. Glad to be older. Today's an important day for me. For US.
Do you remember my Crest Day?
It was the last celebration we had before Brainiac took Kandor away.
The last one I remember, anyway.
Thara even came all the way to Argo City for it.
That must've been before we went to the Fire-Falls. Before she saved my life.

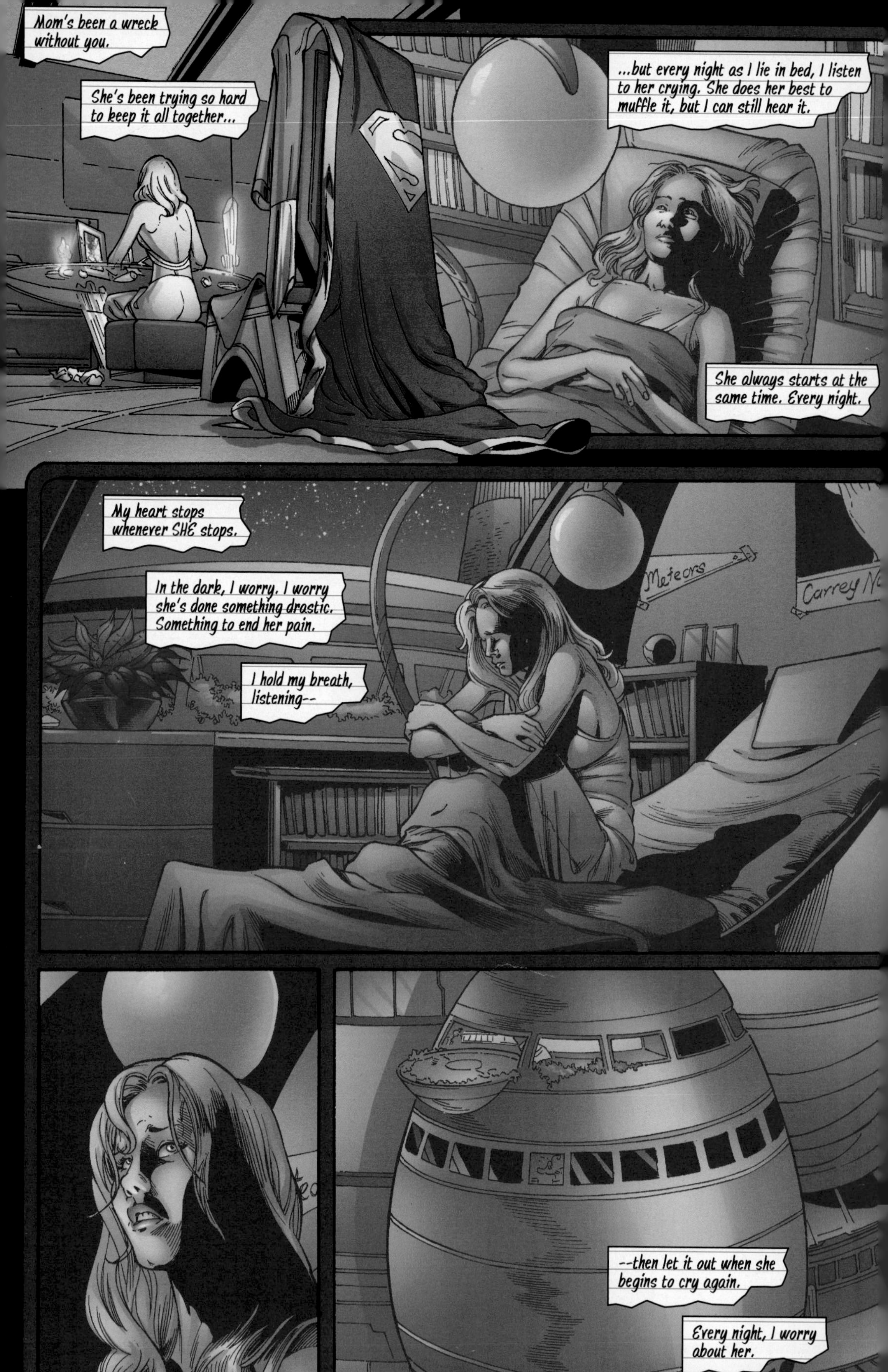
Mom's been a wreck without you.
She's been trying so hard to keep it all together...
...but every night as I lie in bed, I listen to her crying. She does her best to muffle it, but I can still hear it.
She always starts at the same time. Every night.
My heart stops whenever SHE stops.
Meteors
In the dark, I worry. I worry she's done something drastic. Something to end her pain.
I hold my breath, listening--
--then let it out when she begins to cry again.
Every night, I worry about her.

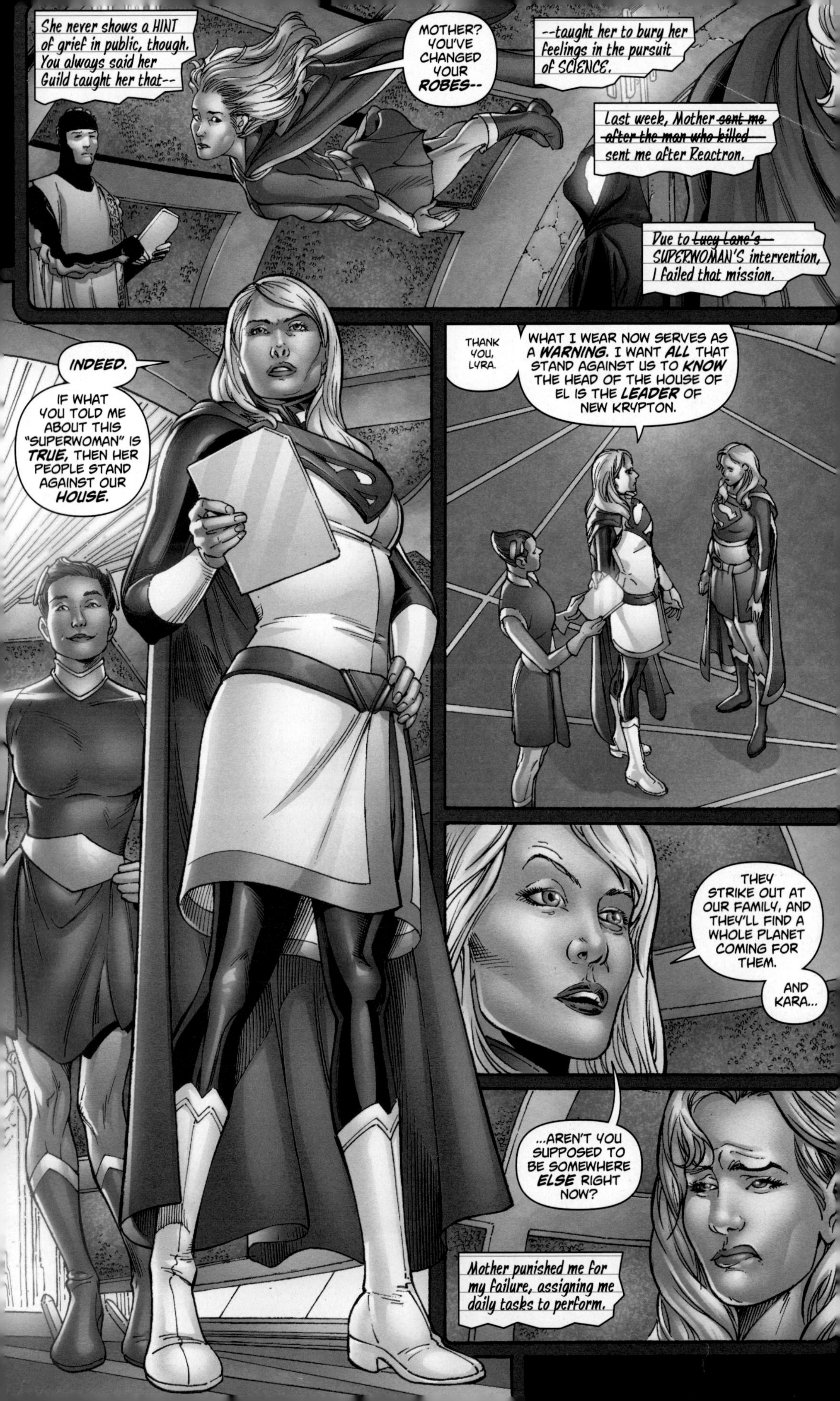

She never shows a HINT of grief in public, though. You always said her Guild taught her that--
MOTHER? YOU'VE CHANGED YOUR ROBES--
--taught her to bury her feelings in the pursuit of SCIENCE.
Last week, Mother ~~sent me after the man who killed~~ sent me after Reactron.
Due to ~~Lucy Lane's~~ SUPERWOMAN'S intervention, I failed that mission.
INDEED.
IF WHAT YOU TOLD ME ABOUT THIS "SUPERWOMAN" IS TRUE, THEN HER PEOPLE STAND AGAINST OUR HOUSE.
THANK YOU, LYRA.
WHAT I WEAR NOW SERVES AS A WARNING. I WANT ALL THAT STAND AGAINST US TO KNOW THE HEAD OF THE HOUSE OF EL IS THE LEADER OF NEW KRYPTON.
THEY STRIKE OUT AT OUR FAMILY, AND THEY'LL FIND A WHOLE PLANET COMING FOR THEM.
AND KARA...
...AREN'T YOU SUPPOSED TO BE SOMEWHERE ELSE RIGHT NOW?
Mother punished me for my failure, assigning me daily tasks to perform.

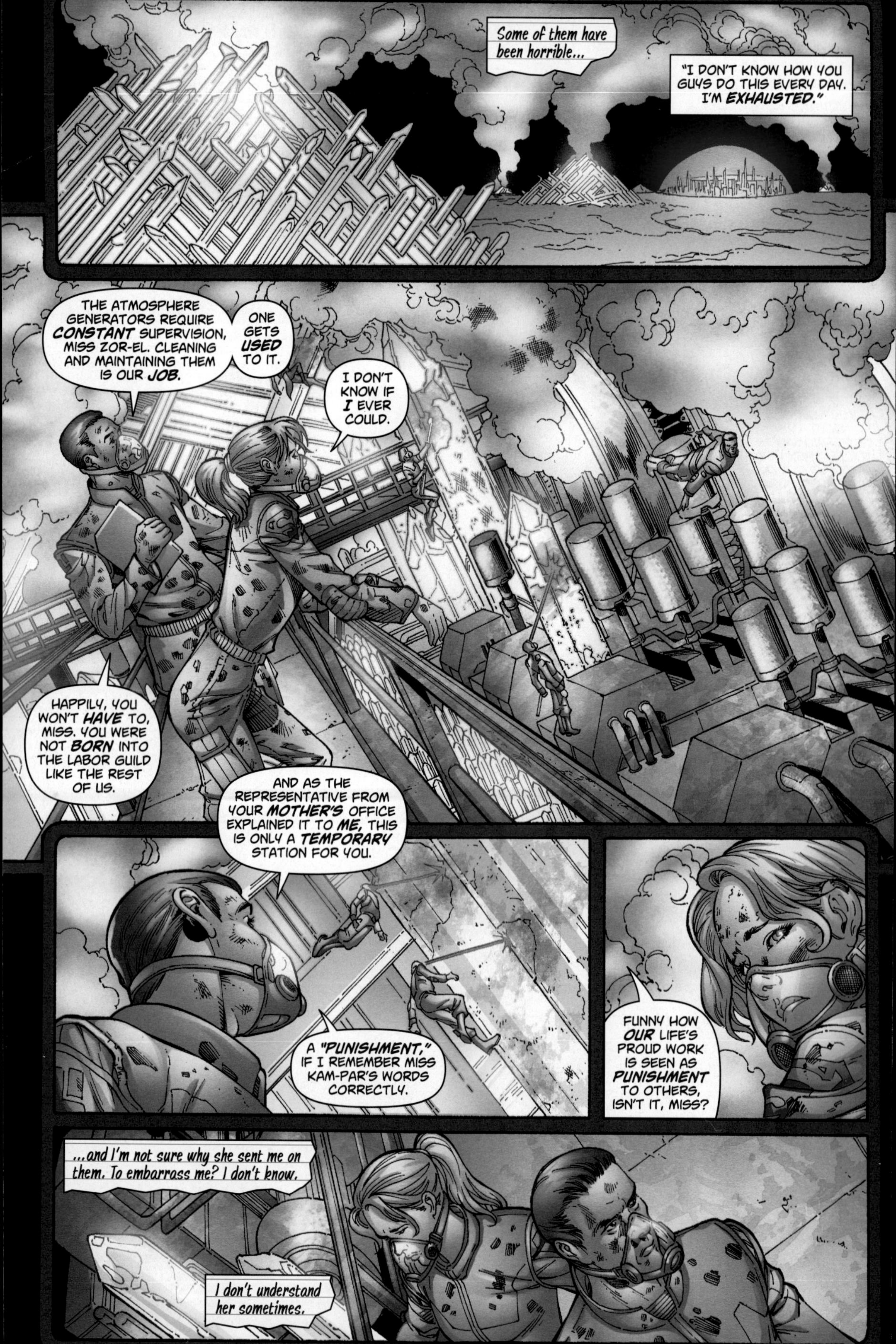
Some of them have been horrible...
"I DON'T KNOW HOW YOU GUYS DO THIS EVERY DAY. I'M EXHAUSTED."
THE ATMOSPHERE GENERATORS REQUIRE CONSTANT SUPERVISION, MISS ZOR-EL. CLEANING AND MAINTAINING THEM IS OUR JOB.
ONE GETS USED TO IT.
I DON'T KNOW IF I EVER COULD.
HAPPILY, YOU WON'T HAVE TO, MISS. YOU WERE NOT BORN INTO THE LABOR GUILD LIKE THE REST OF US.
AND AS THE REPRESENTATIVE FROM YOUR MOTHER'S OFFICE EXPLAINED IT TO ME, THIS IS ONLY A TEMPORARY STATION FOR YOU.
A "PUNISHMENT," IF I REMEMBER MISS KAM-PAR'S WORDS CORRECTLY.
FUNNY HOW OUR LIFE'S PROUD WORK IS SEEN AS PUNISHMENT TO OTHERS, ISN'T IT, MISS?
...and I'm not sure why she sent me on them. To embarrass me? I don't know.
I don't understand her sometimes.

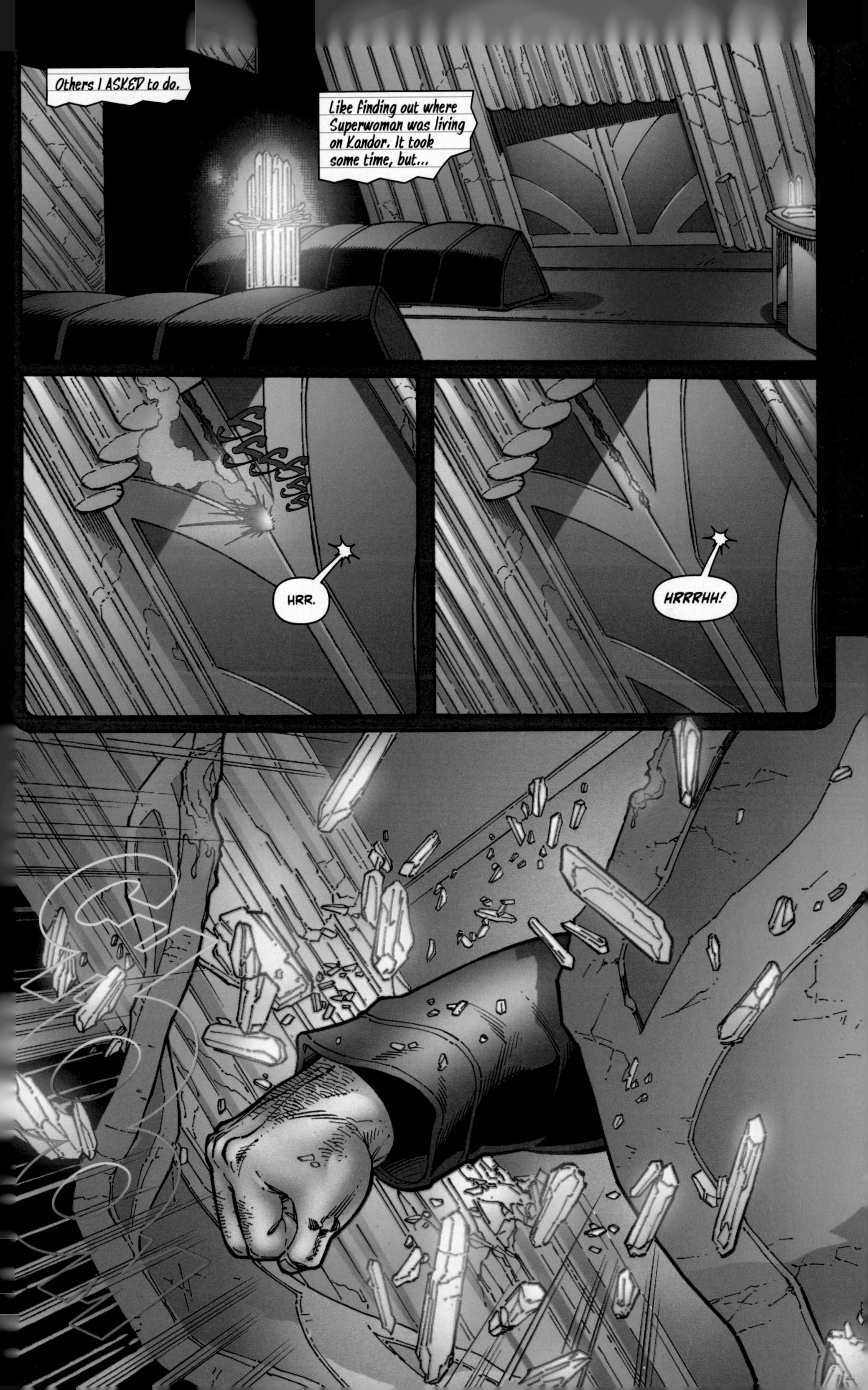
Others I ASKED to do.
Like finding out where Superwoman was living on Kandor. It took some time, but...
HRR.
HRRRHH!

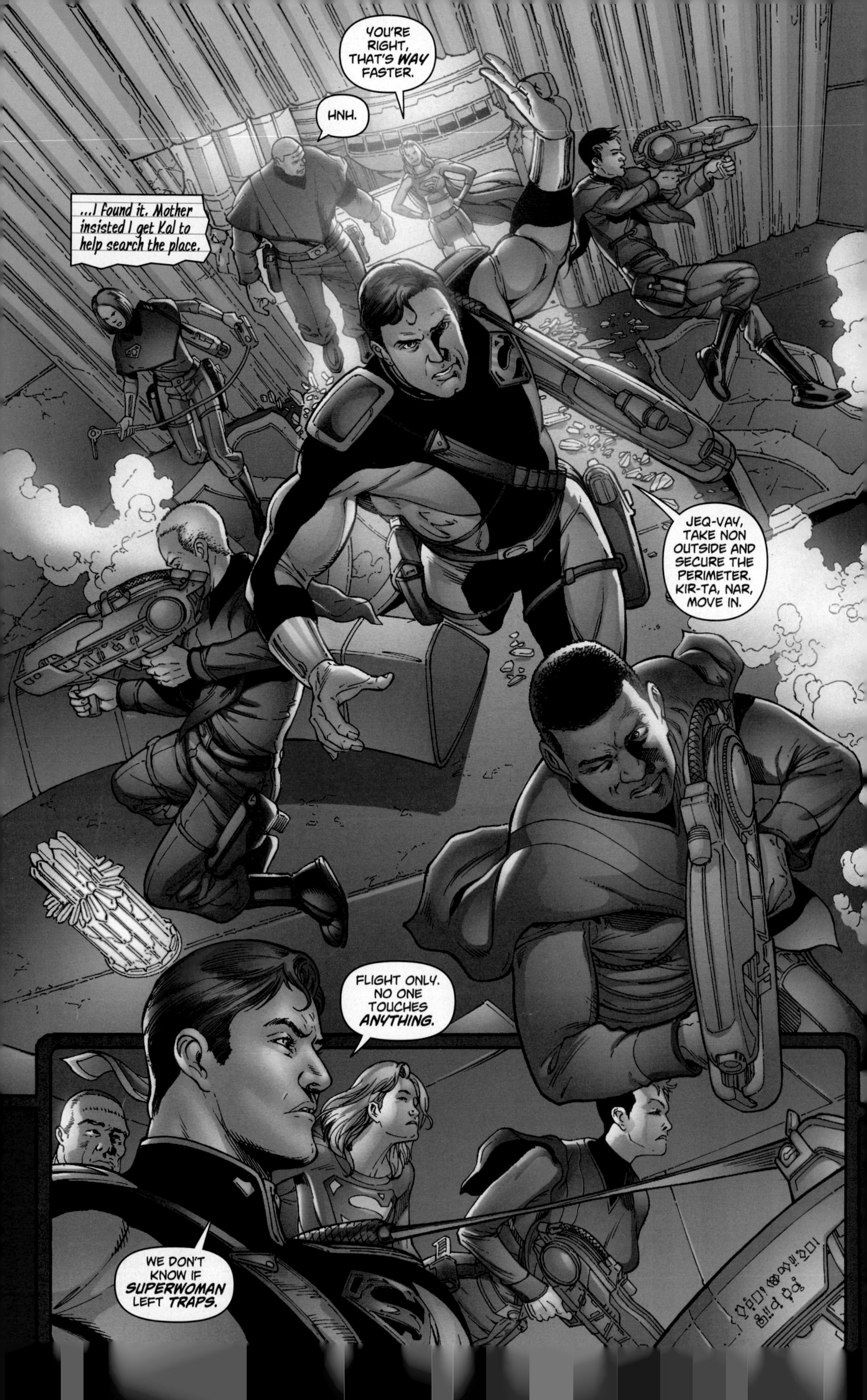
...I found it. Mother insisted I get Kal to help search the place.
HNH.
YOU'RE RIGHT, THAT'S WAY FASTER.
JEQ-VAY, TAKE NON OUTSIDE AND SECURE THE PERIMETER. KIR-TA, NAR, MOVE IN.
FLIGHT ONLY. NO ONE TOUCHES ANYTHING.
WE DON'T KNOW IF SUPERWOMAN LEFT TRAPS.

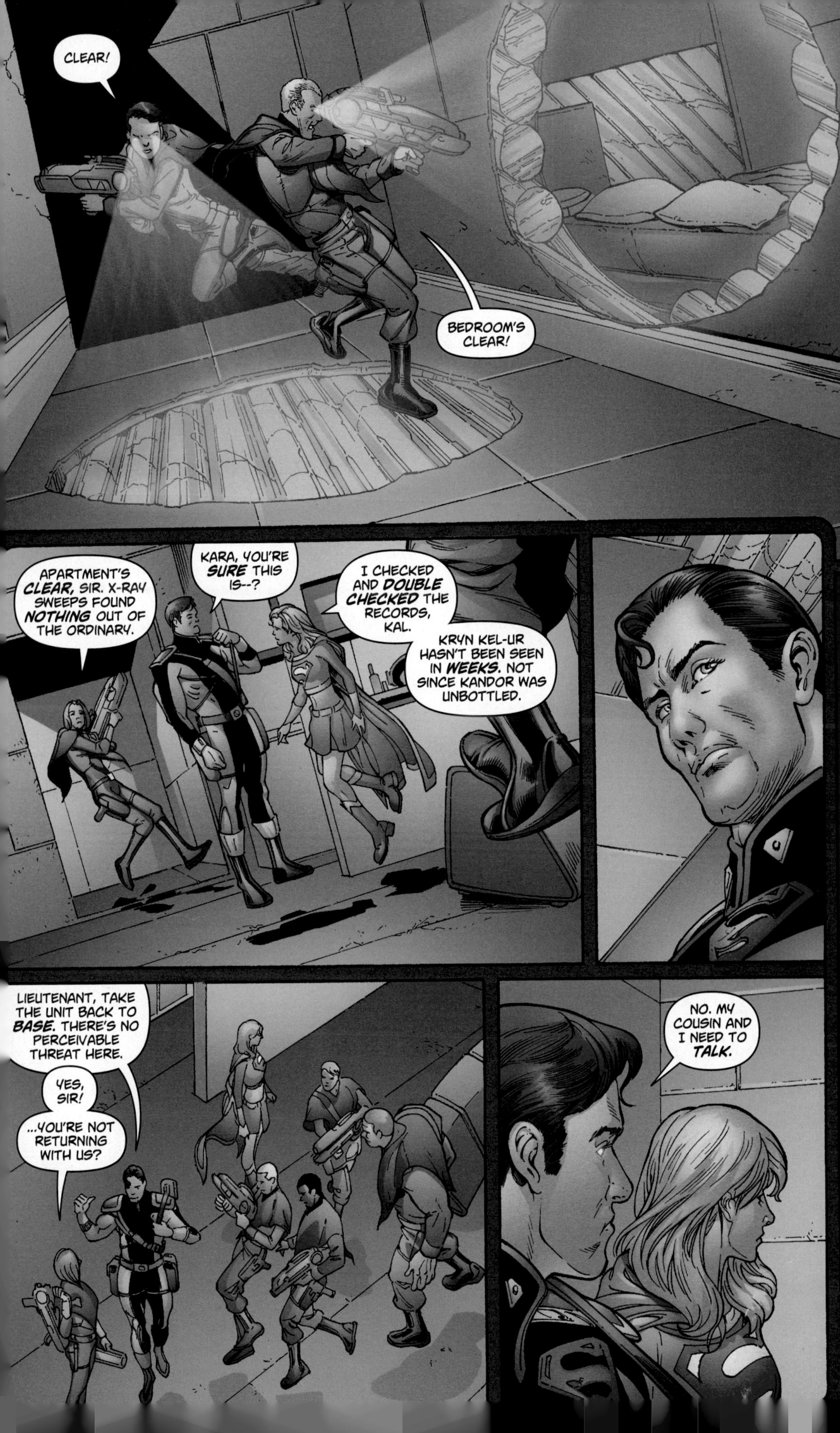
CLEAR!
BEDROOM'S CLEAR!
APARTMENT'S CLEAR, SIR. X-RAY SWEEPS FOUND NOTHING OUT OF THE ORDINARY.
KARA, YOU'RE SURE THIS IS--?
I CHECKED AND DOUBLE CHECKED THE RECORDS, KAL.
KRYN KEL-UR HASN'T BEEN SEEN IN WEEKS. NOT SINCE KANDOR WAS UNBOTTLED.
LIEUTENANT, TAKE THE UNIT BACK TO BASE. THERE'S NO PERCEIVABLE THREAT HERE.
YES, SIR!
...YOU'RE NOT RETURNING WITH US?
NO. MY COUSIN AND I NEED TO TALK.

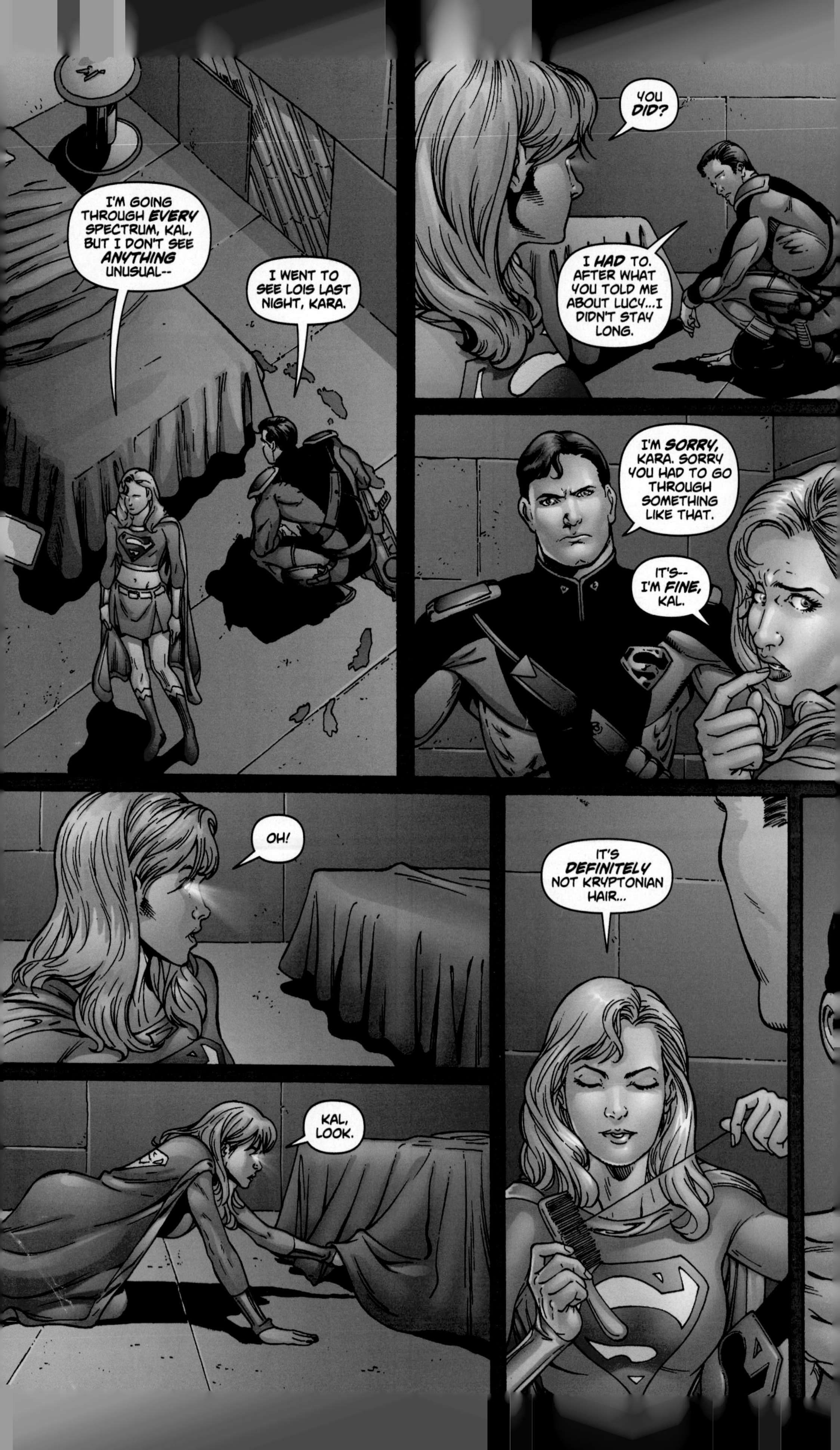
I'M GOING THROUGH EVERY SPECTRUM, KAL, BUT I DON'T SEE ANYTHING UNUSUAL--
I WENT TO SEE LOIS LAST NIGHT, KARA.
YOU DID?
I HAD TO. AFTER WHAT YOU TOLD ME ABOUT LUCY...I DIDN'T STAY LONG.
I'M SORRY, KARA. SORRY YOU HAD TO GO THROUGH SOMETHING LIKE THAT.
IT'S-- I'M FINE, KAL.
OH!
KAL, LOOK.
IT'S DEFINITELY NOT KRYPTONIAN HAIR...

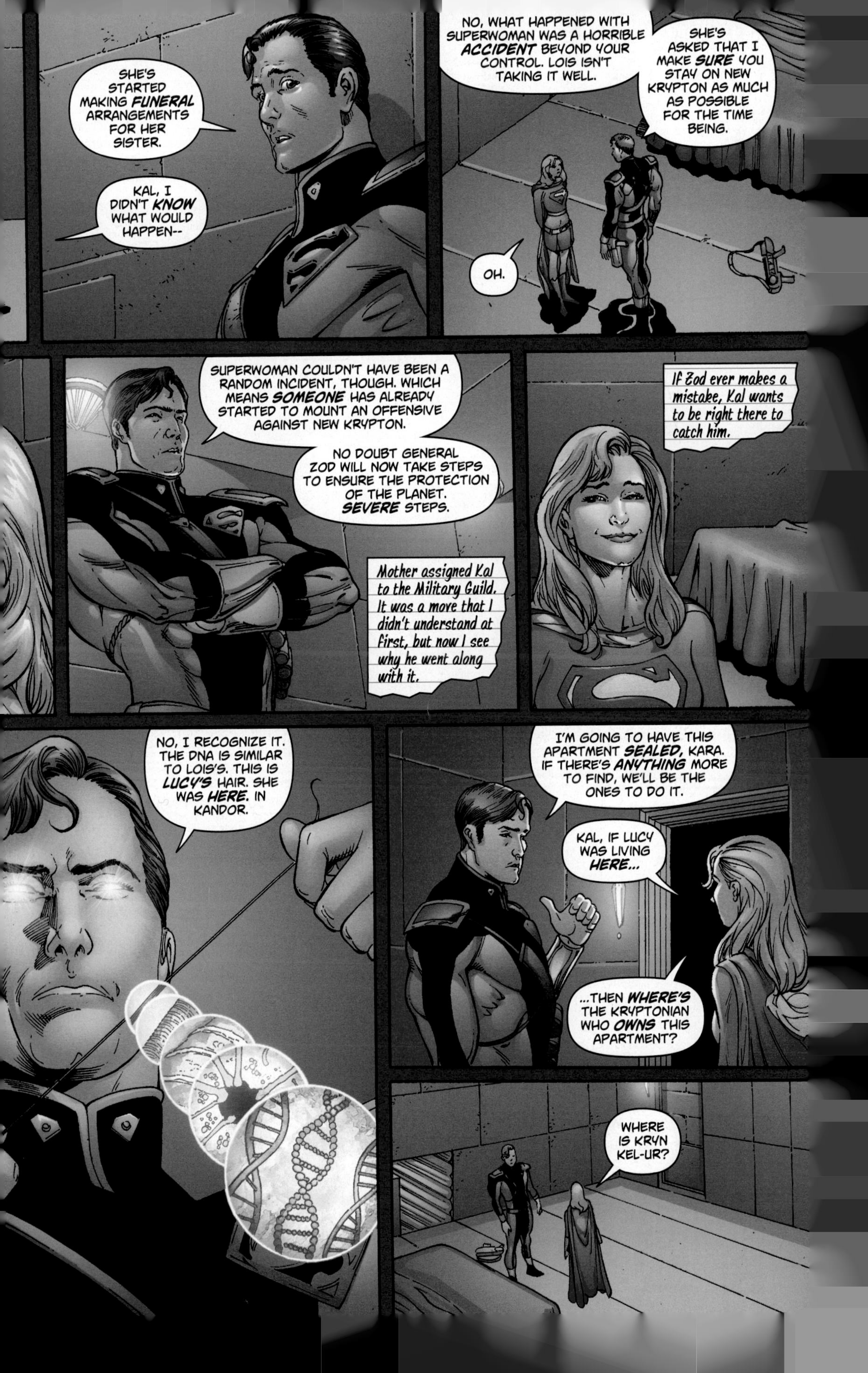
SHE'S STARTED MAKING FUNERAL ARRANGEMENTS FOR HER SISTER.
KAL, I DIDN'T KNOW WHAT WOULD HAPPEN--
NO, WHAT HAPPENED WITH SUPERWOMAN WAS A HORRIBLE ACCIDENT BEYOND YOUR CONTROL. LOIS ISN'T TAKING IT WELL.
SHE'S ASKED THAT I MAKE SURE YOU STAY ON NEW KRYPTON AS MUCH AS POSSIBLE FOR THE TIME BEING.
OH.
SUPERWOMAN COULDN'T HAVE BEEN A RANDOM INCIDENT, THOUGH. WHICH MEANS SOMEONE HAS ALREADY STARTED TO MOUNT AN OFFENSIVE AGAINST NEW KRYPTON.
NO DOUBT GENERAL ZOD WILL NOW TAKE STEPS TO ENSURE THE PROTECTION OF THE PLANET. SEVERE STEPS.
Mother assigned Kal to the Military Guild. It was a move that I didn't understand at first, but now I see why he went along with it.
If Zod ever makes a mistake, Kal wants to be right there to catch him.
NO, I RECOGNIZE IT. THE DNA IS SIMILAR TO LOIS'S. THIS IS LUCY'S HAIR. SHE WAS HERE. IN KANDOR.
I'M GOING TO HAVE THIS APARTMENT SEALED, KARA. IF THERE'S ANYTHING MORE TO FIND, WE'LL BE THE ONES TO DO IT.
KAL, IF LUCY WAS LIVING HERE...
...THEN WHERE'S THE KRYPTONIAN WHO OWNS THIS APARTMENT?
WHERE IS KRYN KEL-UR?

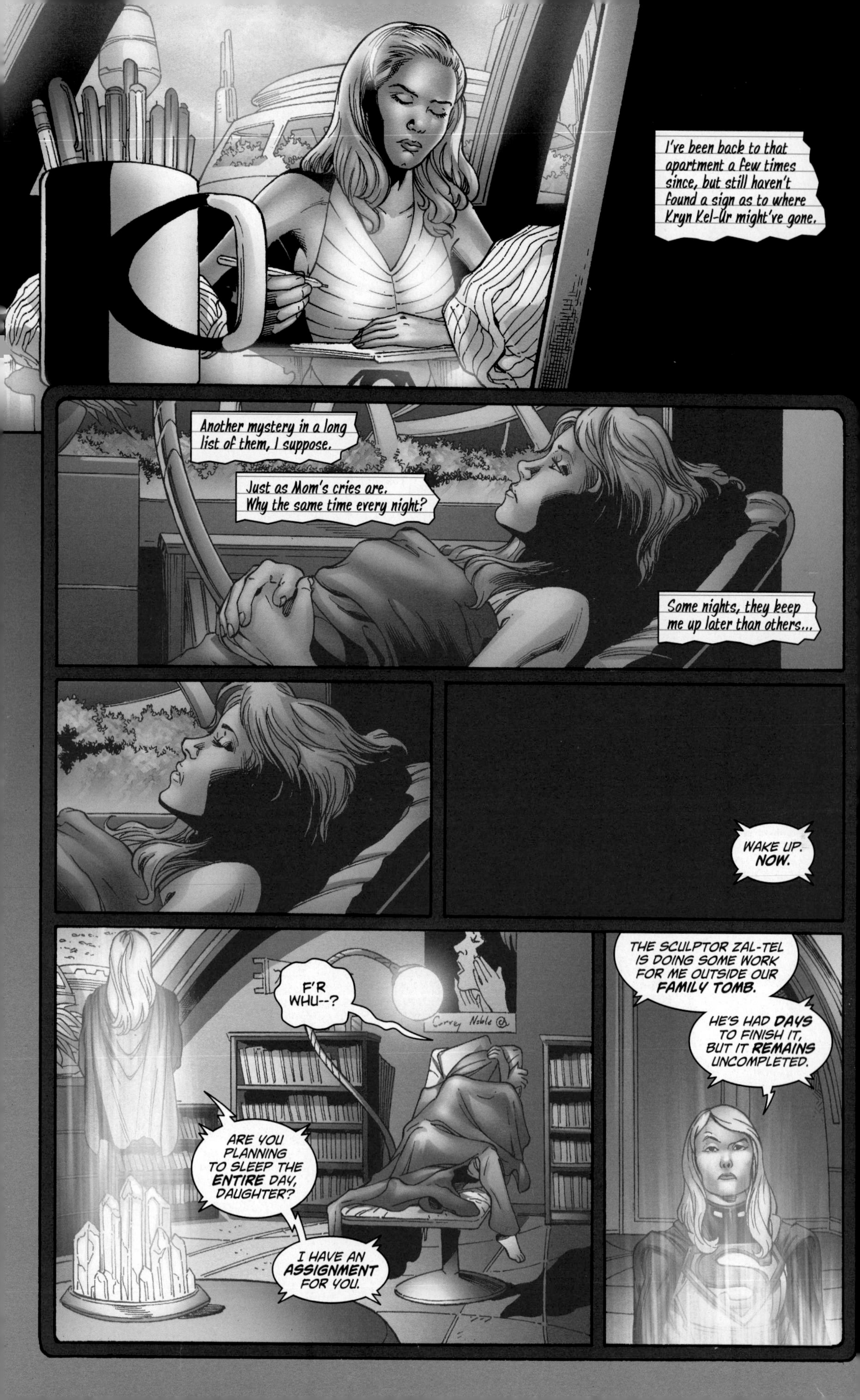
I've been back to that apartment a few times since, but still haven't found a sign as to where Kryn Kel-Ur might've gone.
Another mystery in a long list of them, I suppose.
Just as Mom's cries are. Why the same time every night?
Some nights, they keep me up later than others...
WAKE UP. NOW.
F'R WHU--?
Correy Noble
ARE YOU PLANNING TO SLEEP THE ENTIRE DAY, DAUGHTER?
I HAVE AN ASSIGNMENT FOR YOU.
THE SCULPTOR ZAL-TEL IS DOING SOME WORK FOR ME OUTSIDE OUR FAMILY TOMB.
HE'S HAD DAYS TO FINISH IT, BUT IT REMAINS UNCOMPLETED.

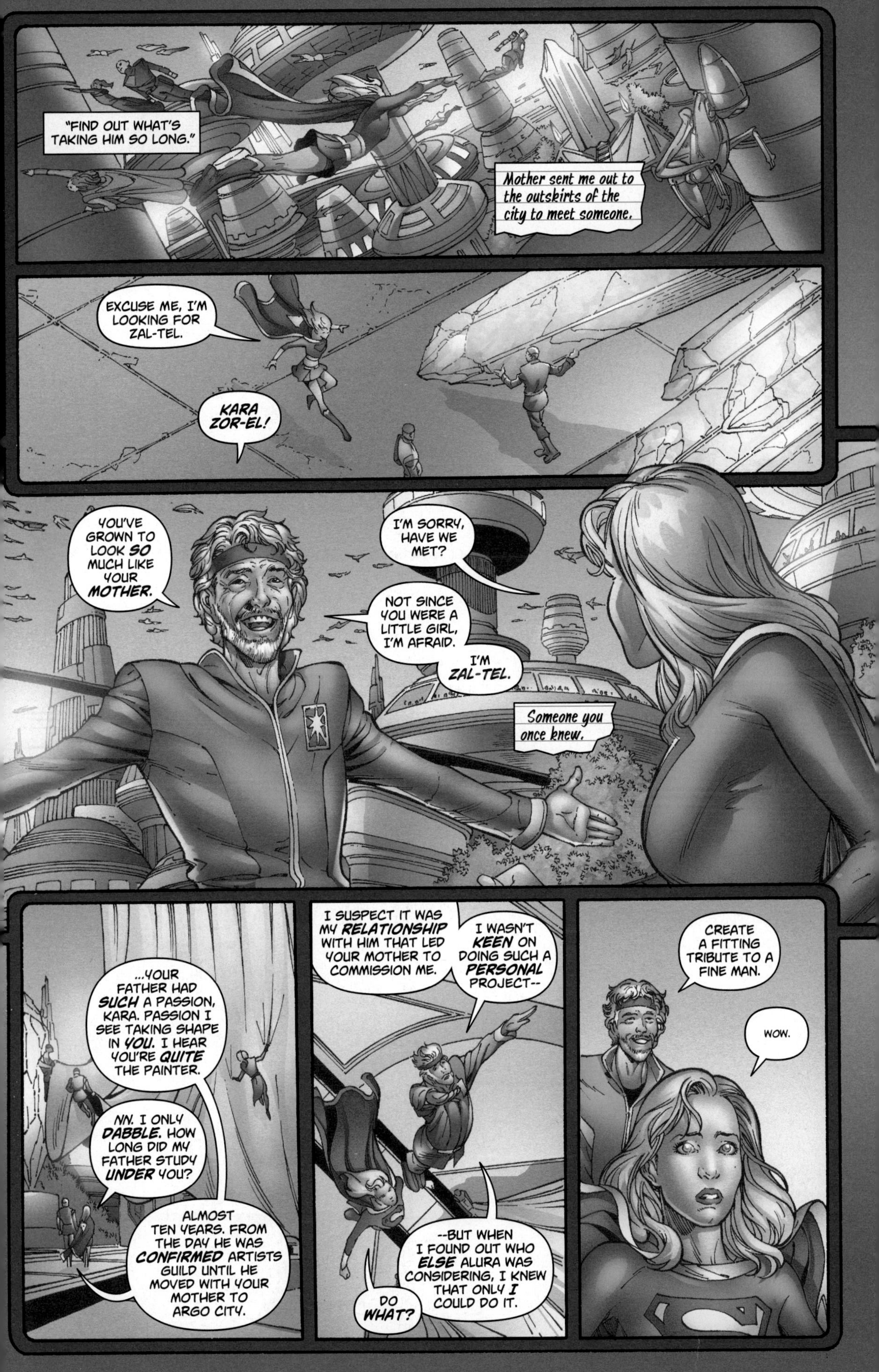
"FIND OUT WHAT'S TAKING HIM SO LONG."
Mother sent me out to the outskirts of the city to meet someone.
EXCUSE ME, I'M LOOKING FOR ZAL-TEL.
KARA ZOR-EL!
YOU'VE GROWN TO LOOK SO MUCH LIKE YOUR MOTHER.
I'M SORRY, HAVE WE MET?
NOT SINCE YOU WERE A LITTLE GIRL, I'M AFRAID.
I'M ZAL-TEL.
Someone you once knew.
...YOUR FATHER HAD SUCH A PASSION, KARA. PASSION I SEE TAKING SHAPE IN YOU. I HEAR YOU'RE QUITE THE PAINTER.
NN. I ONLY DABBLE. HOW LONG DID MY FATHER STUDY UNDER YOU?
ALMOST TEN YEARS. FROM THE DAY HE WAS CONFIRMED ARTISTS GUILD UNTIL HE MOVED WITH YOUR MOTHER TO ARGO CITY.
I SUSPECT IT WAS MY RELATIONSHIP WITH HIM THAT LED YOUR MOTHER TO COMMISSION ME.
I WASN'T KEEN ON DOING SUCH A PERSONAL PROJECT--
--BUT WHEN I FOUND OUT WHO ELSE ALURA WAS CONSIDERING, I KNEW THAT ONLY I COULD DO IT.
DO WHAT?
CREATE A FITTING TRIBUTE TO A FINE MAN.
WOW.

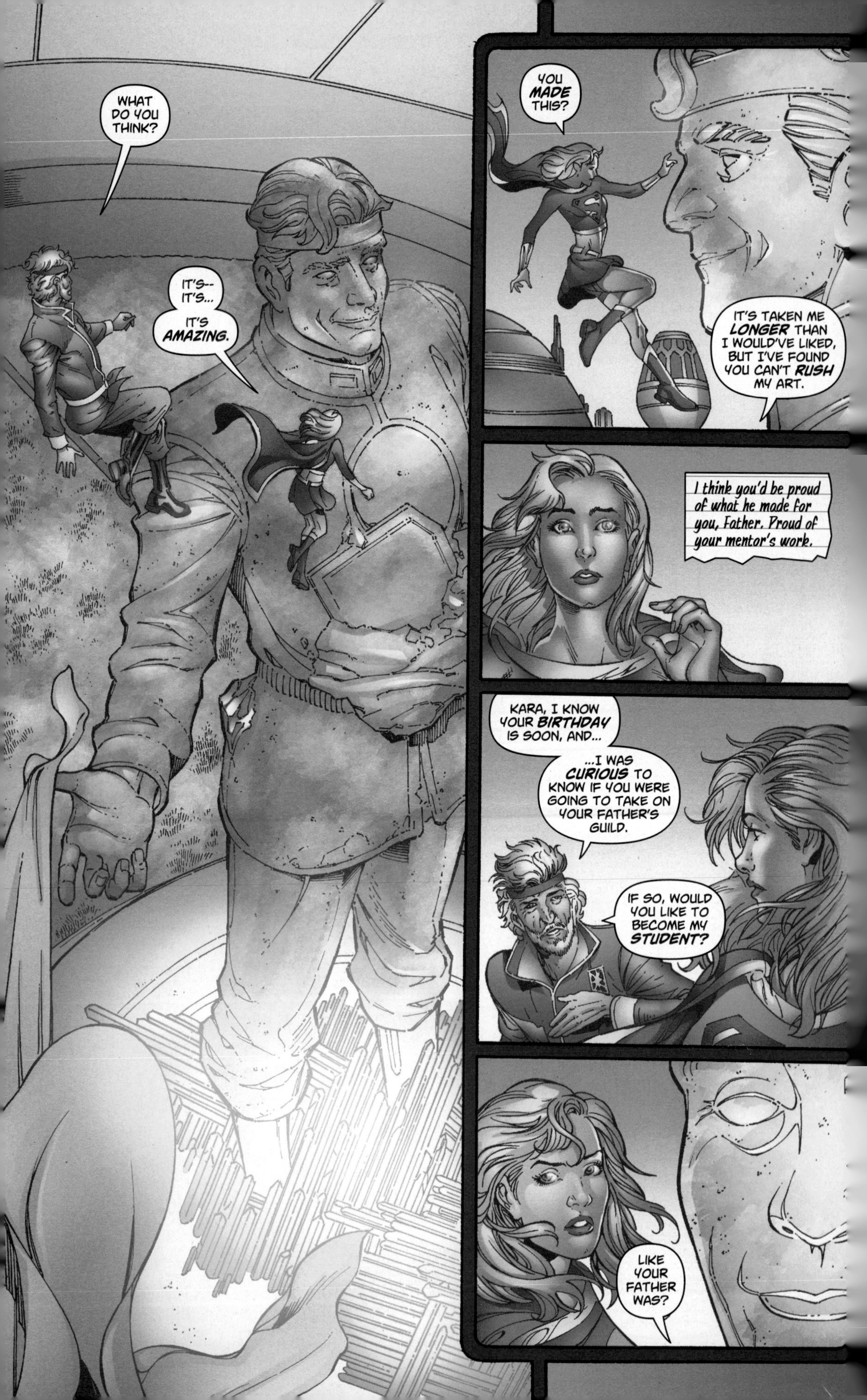
WHAT DO YOU THINK?
IT'S-- IT'S...
IT'S AMAZING.
YOU MADE THIS?
IT'S TAKEN ME LONGER THAN I WOULD'VE LIKED, BUT I'VE FOUND YOU CAN'T RUSH MY ART.
I think you'd be proud of what he made for you, Father. Proud of your mentor's work.
KARA, I KNOW YOUR BIRTHDAY IS SOON, AND...
...I WAS CURIOUS TO KNOW IF YOU WERE GOING TO TAKE ON YOUR FATHER'S GUILD.
IF SO, WOULD YOU LIKE TO BECOME MY STUDENT?
LIKE YOUR FATHER WAS?

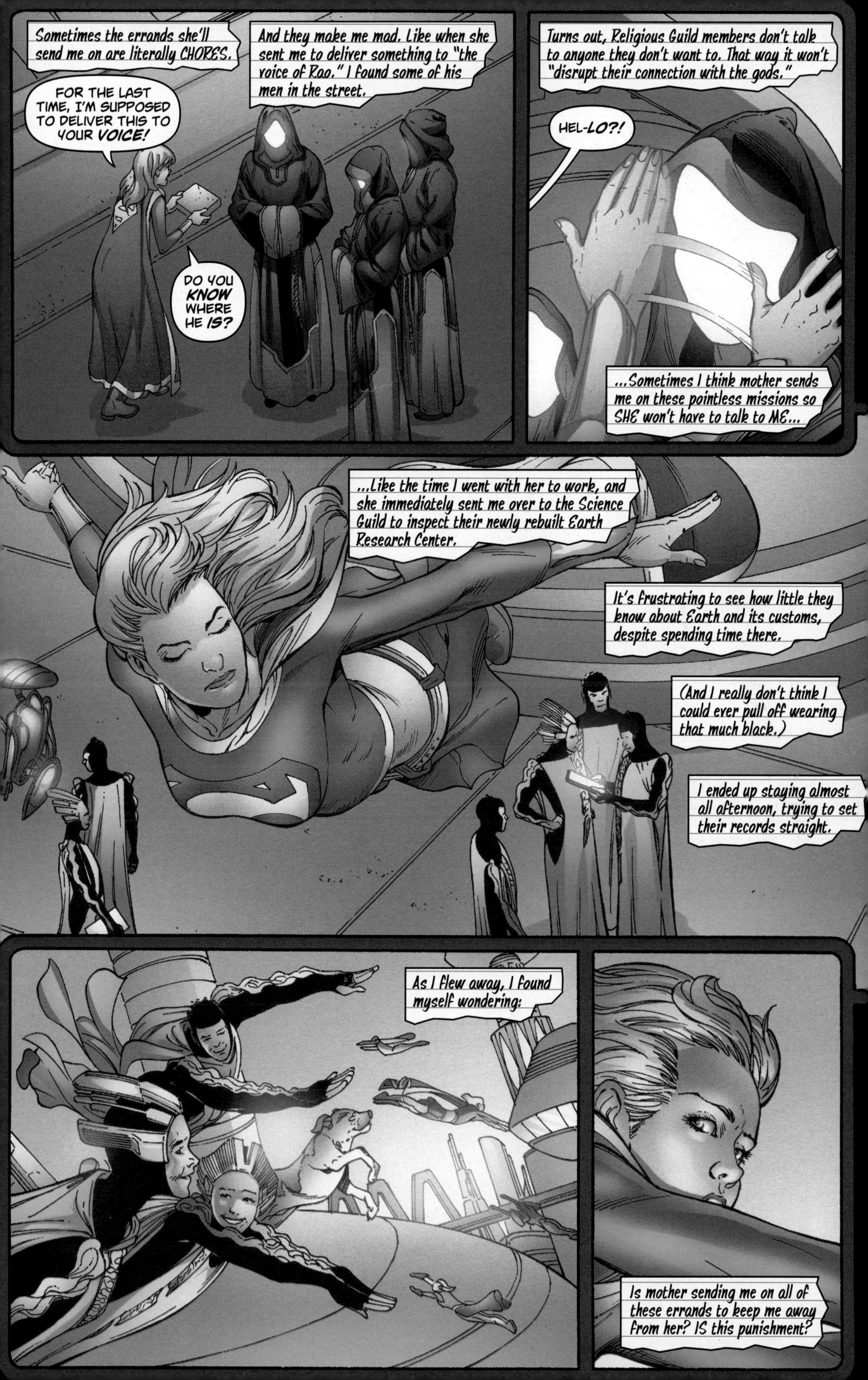

Sometimes the errands she'll send me on are literally CHORES.
FOR THE LAST TIME, I'M SUPPOSED TO DELIVER THIS TO YOUR VOICE!
And they make me mad. Like when she sent me to deliver something to "the voice of Rao." I found some of his men in the street.
DO YOU KNOW WHERE HE IS?
Turns out, Religious Guild members don't talk to anyone they don't want to. That way it won't "disrupt their connection with the gods."
HEL-LO?!
...Sometimes I think mother sends me on these pointless missions so SHE won't have to talk to ME...
...Like the time I went with her to work, and she immediately sent me over to the Science Guild to inspect their newly rebuilt Earth Research Center.
It's frustrating to see how little they know about Earth and its customs, despite spending time there.
(And I really don't think I could ever pull off wearing that much black.)
I ended up staying almost all afternoon, trying to set their records straight.
As I flew away, I found myself wondering:
Is mother sending me on all of these errands to keep me away from her? IS this punishment?

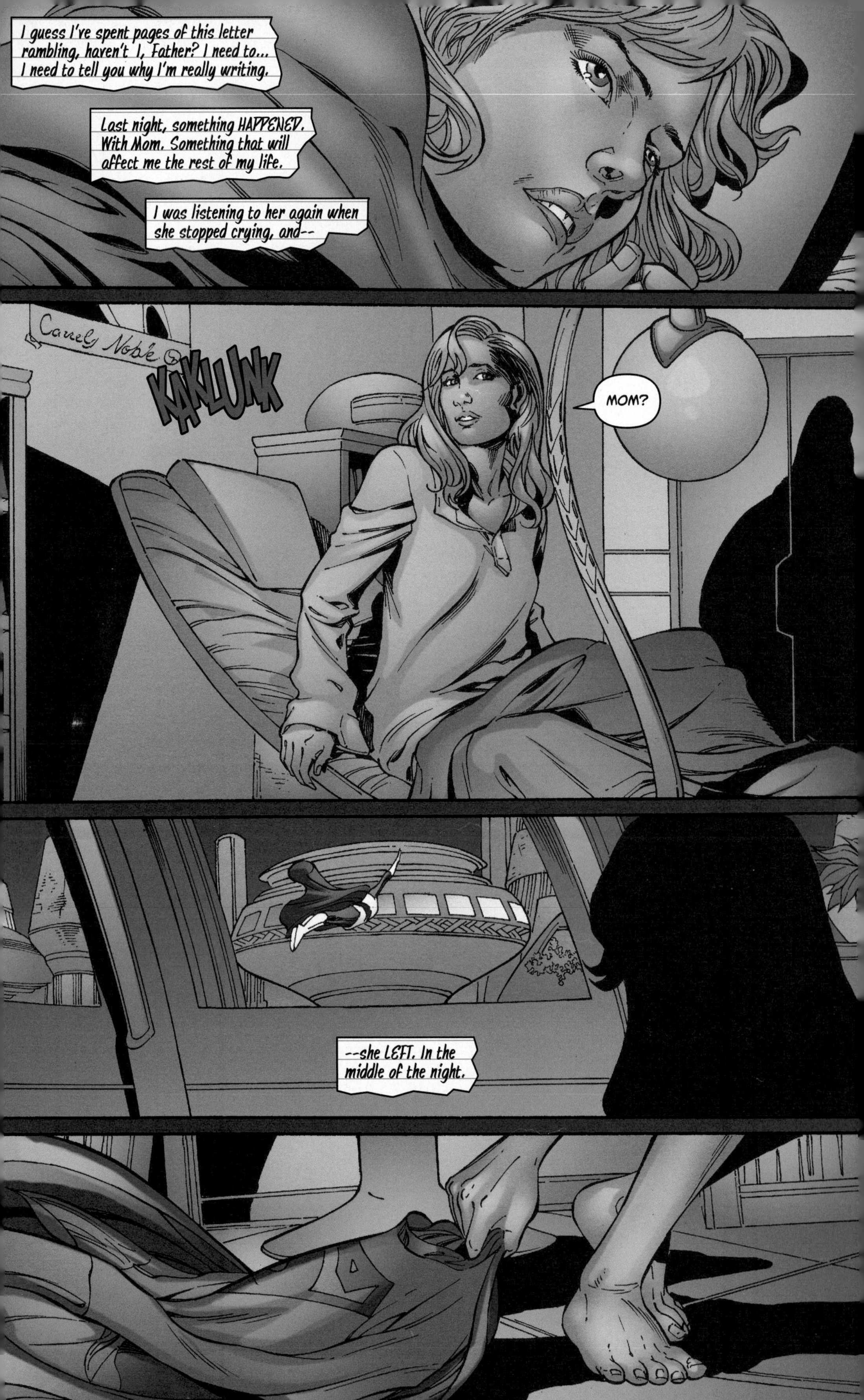
I guess I've spent pages of this letter rambling, haven't I, Father? I need to... I need to tell you why I'm really writing.
Last night, something HAPPENED. With Mom. Something that will affect me the rest of my life.
I was listening to her again when she stopped crying, and--
KAKLUNK
MOM?
--she LEFT. In the middle of the night.

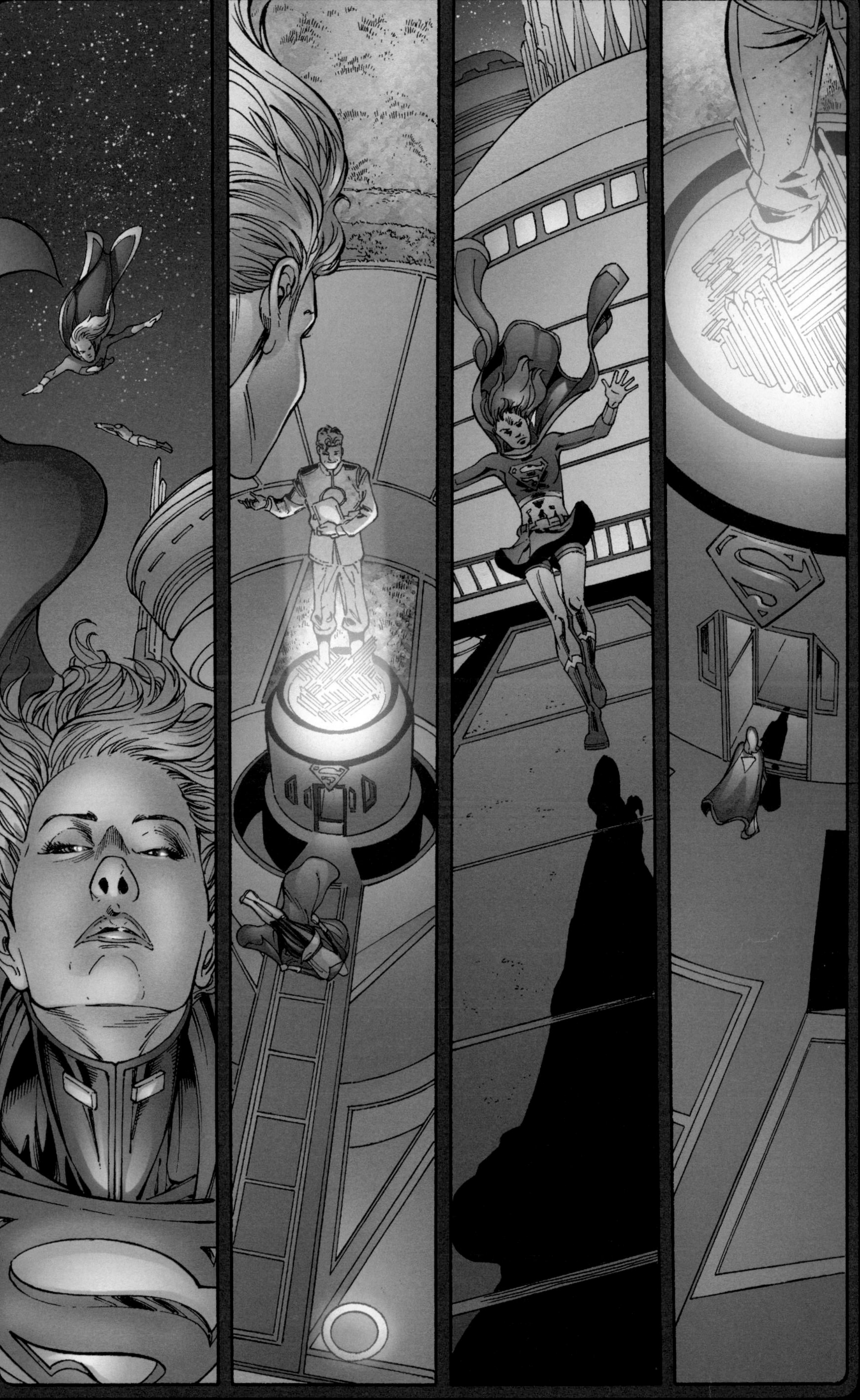

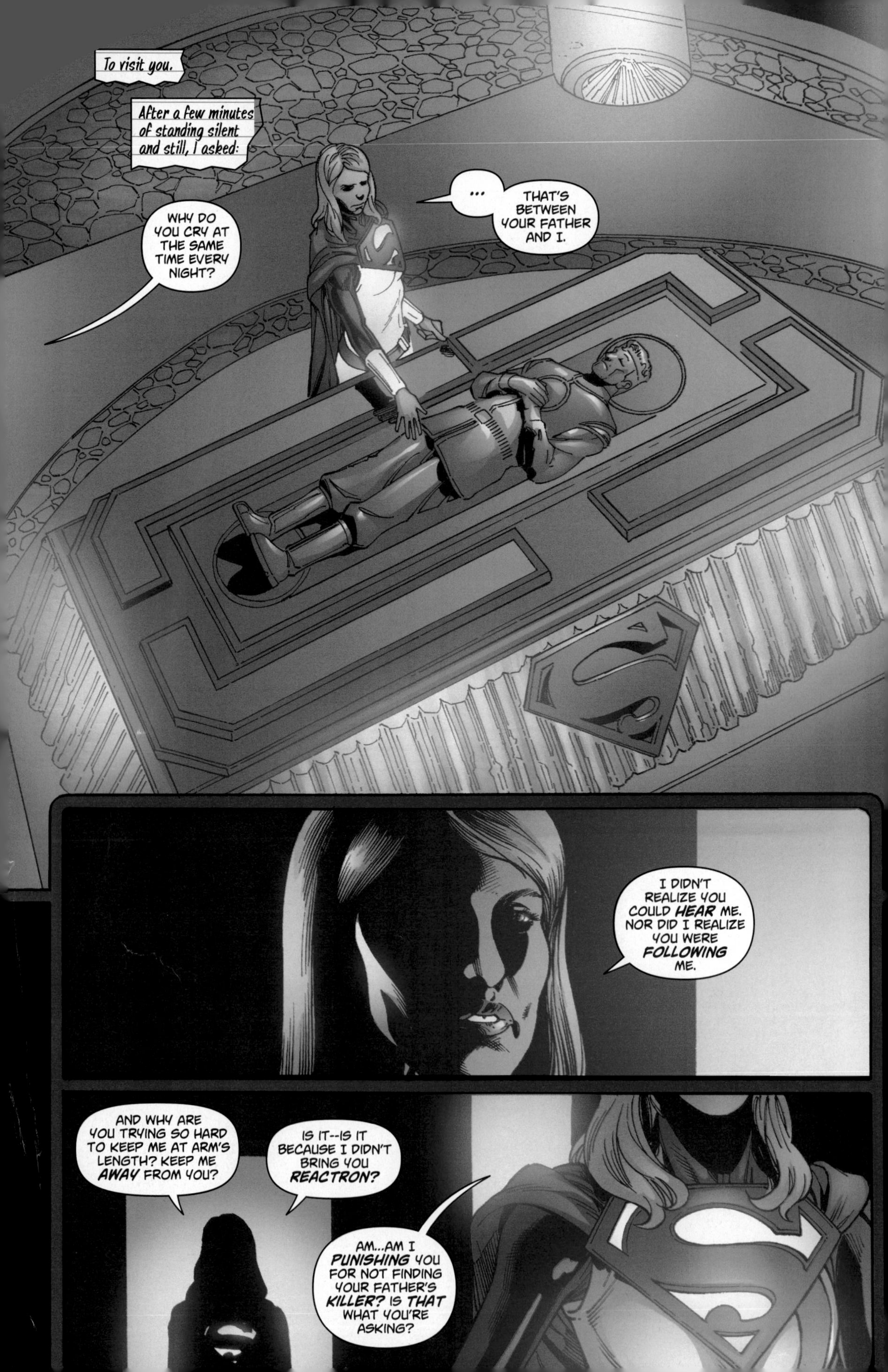
To visit you.
After a few minutes of standing silent and still, I asked:
WHY DO YOU CRY AT THE SAME TIME EVERY NIGHT?
... THAT'S BETWEEN YOUR FATHER AND I.
I DIDN'T REALIZE YOU COULD HEAR ME. NOR DID I REALIZE YOU WERE FOLLOWING ME.
AND WHY ARE YOU TRYING SO HARD TO KEEP ME AT ARM'S LENGTH? KEEP ME AWAY FROM YOU?
IS IT--IS IT BECAUSE I DIDN'T BRING YOU REACTRON?
AM...AM I PUNISHING YOU FOR NOT FINDING YOUR FATHER'S KILLER? IS THAT WHAT YOU'RE ASKING?

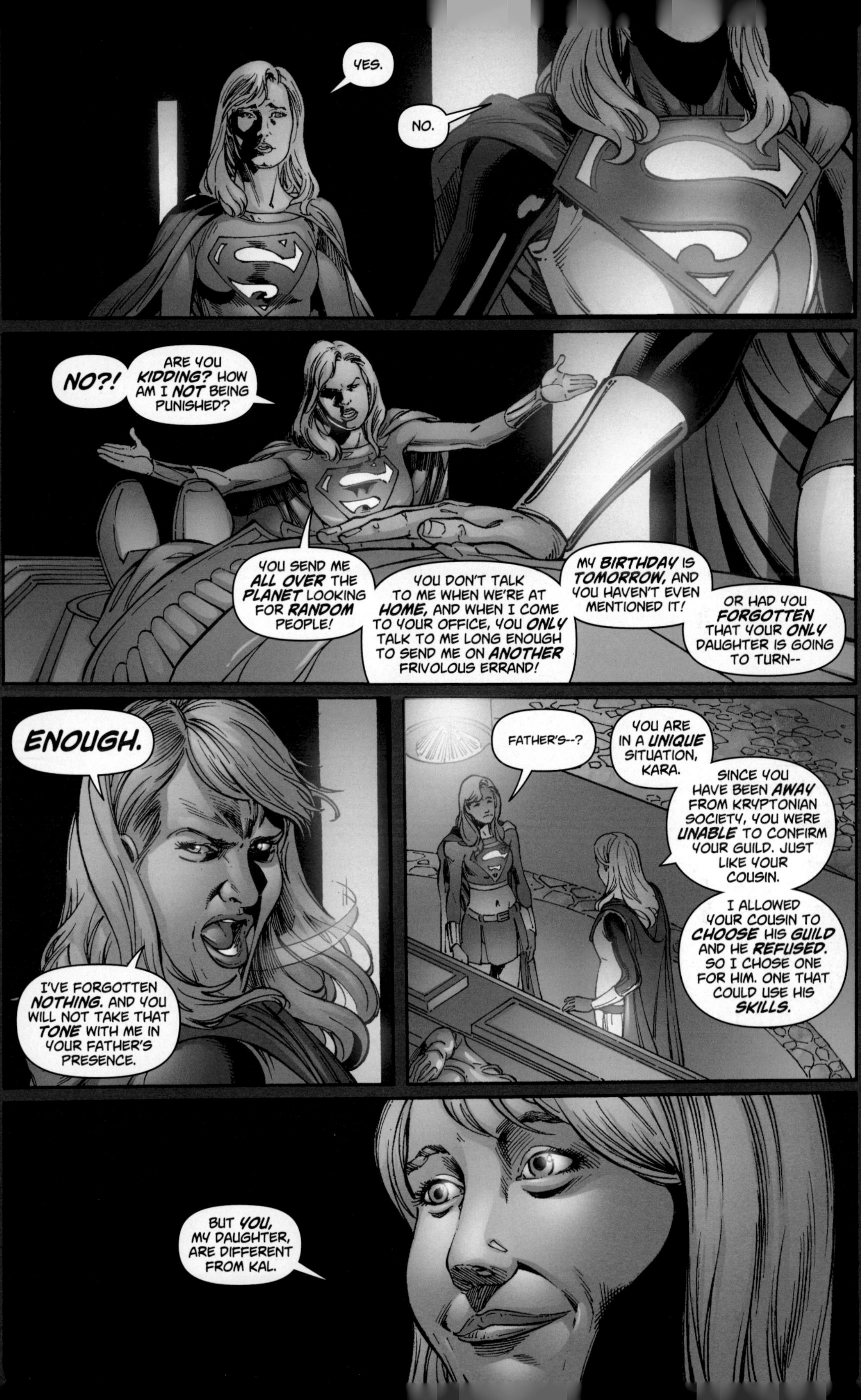
YES.
NO.
NO?!
ARE YOU KIDDING? HOW AM I NOT BEING PUNISHED?
YOU SEND ME ALL OVER THE PLANET LOOKING FOR RANDOM PEOPLE!
YOU DON'T TALK TO ME WHEN WE'RE AT HOME, AND WHEN I COME TO YOUR OFFICE, YOU ONLY TALK TO ME LONG ENOUGH TO SEND ME ON ANOTHER FRIVOLOUS ERRAND!
MY BIRTHDAY IS TOMORROW, AND YOU HAVEN'T EVEN MENTIONED IT!
OR HAD YOU FORGOTTEN THAT YOUR ONLY DAUGHTER IS GOING TO TURN--
ENOUGH.
I'VE FORGOTTEN NOTHING. AND YOU WILL NOT TAKE THAT TONE WITH ME IN YOUR FATHER'S PRESENCE.
FATHER'S--?
YOU ARE IN A UNIQUE SITUATION, KARA.
SINCE YOU HAVE BEEN AWAY FROM KRYPTONIAN SOCIETY, YOU WERE UNABLE TO CONFIRM YOUR GUILD. JUST LIKE YOUR COUSIN.
I ALLOWED YOUR COUSIN TO CHOOSE HIS GUILD AND HE REFUSED. SO I CHOSE ONE FOR HIM. ONE THAT COULD USE HIS SKILLS.
BUT YOU, MY DAUGHTER, ARE DIFFERENT FROM KAL.

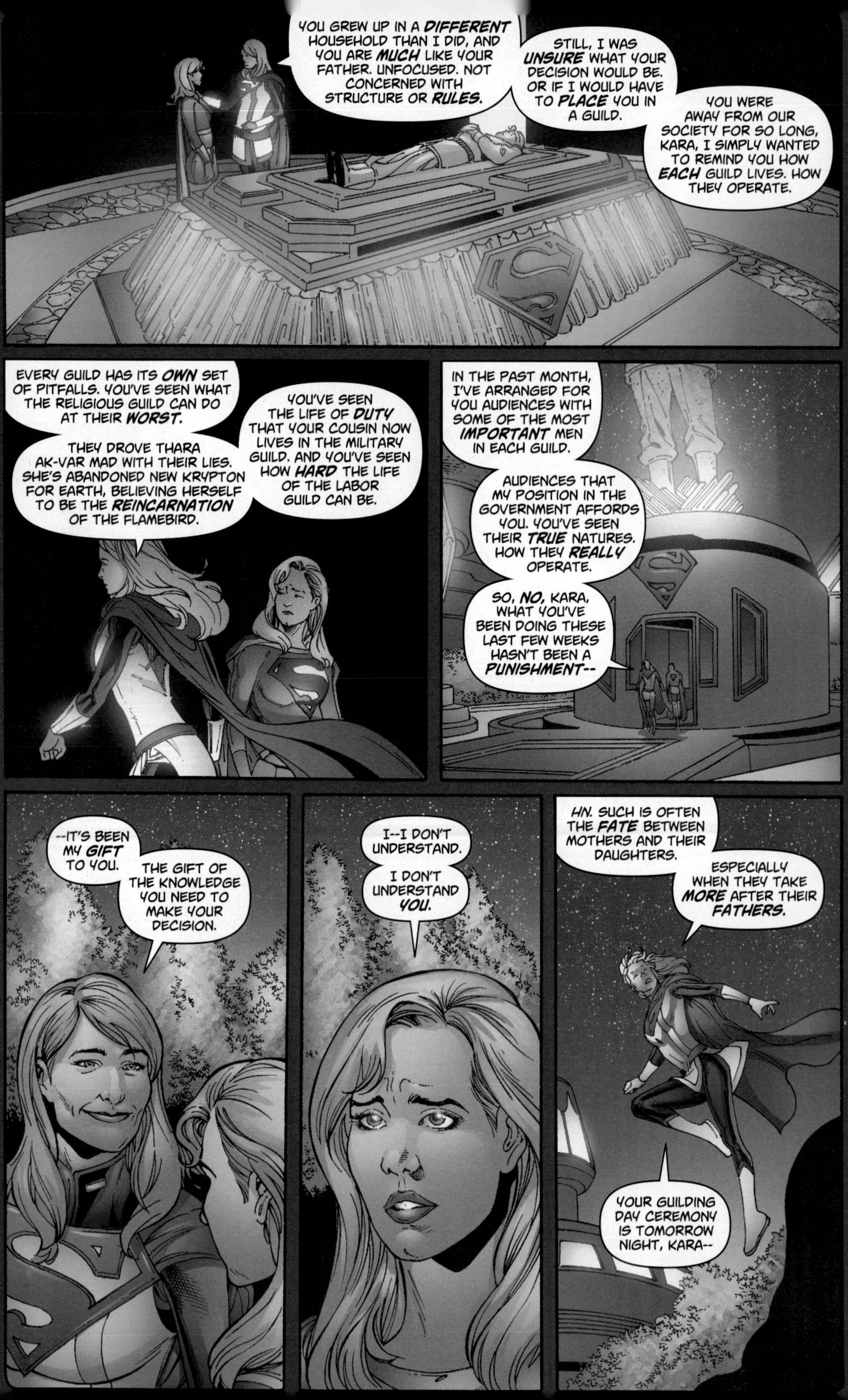
YOU GREW UP IN A DIFFERENT HOUSEHOLD THAN I DID, AND YOU ARE MUCH LIKE YOUR FATHER. UNFOCUSED. NOT CONCERNED WITH STRUCTURE OR RULES.
STILL, I WAS UNSURE WHAT YOUR DECISION WOULD BE. OR IF I WOULD HAVE TO PLACE YOU IN A GUILD.
YOU WERE AWAY FROM OUR SOCIETY FOR SO LONG, KARA, I SIMPLY WANTED TO REMIND YOU HOW EACH GUILD LIVES. HOW THEY OPERATE.
EVERY GUILD HAS ITS OWN SET OF PITFALLS. YOU'VE SEEN WHAT THE RELIGIOUS GUILD CAN DO AT THEIR WORST.
THEY DROVE THARA AK-VAR MAD WITH THEIR LIES. SHE'S ABANDONED NEW KRYPTON FOR EARTH, BELIEVING HERSELF TO BE THE REINCARNATION OF THE FLAMEBIRD.
YOU'VE SEEN THE LIFE OF DUTY THAT YOUR COUSIN NOW LIVES IN THE MILITARY GUILD. AND YOU'VE SEEN HOW HARD THE LIFE OF THE LABOR GUILD CAN BE.
IN THE PAST MONTH, I'VE ARRANGED FOR YOU AUDIENCES WITH SOME OF THE MOST IMPORTANT MEN IN EACH GUILD.
AUDIENCES THAT MY POSITION IN THE GOVERNMENT AFFORDS YOU. YOU'VE SEEN THEIR TRUE NATURES. HOW THEY REALLY OPERATE.
SO, NO, KARA, WHAT YOU'VE BEEN DOING THESE LAST FEW WEEKS HASN'T BEEN A PUNISHMENT--
--IT'S BEEN MY GIFT TO YOU.
THE GIFT OF THE KNOWLEDGE YOU NEED TO MAKE YOUR DECISION.
I--I DON'T UNDERSTAND.
I DON'T UNDERSTAND YOU.
HN. SUCH IS OFTEN THE FATE BETWEEN MOTHERS AND THEIR DAUGHTERS.
ESPECIALLY WHEN THEY TAKE MORE AFTER THEIR FATHERS.
YOUR GUILDING DAY CEREMONY IS TOMORROW NIGHT, KARA--

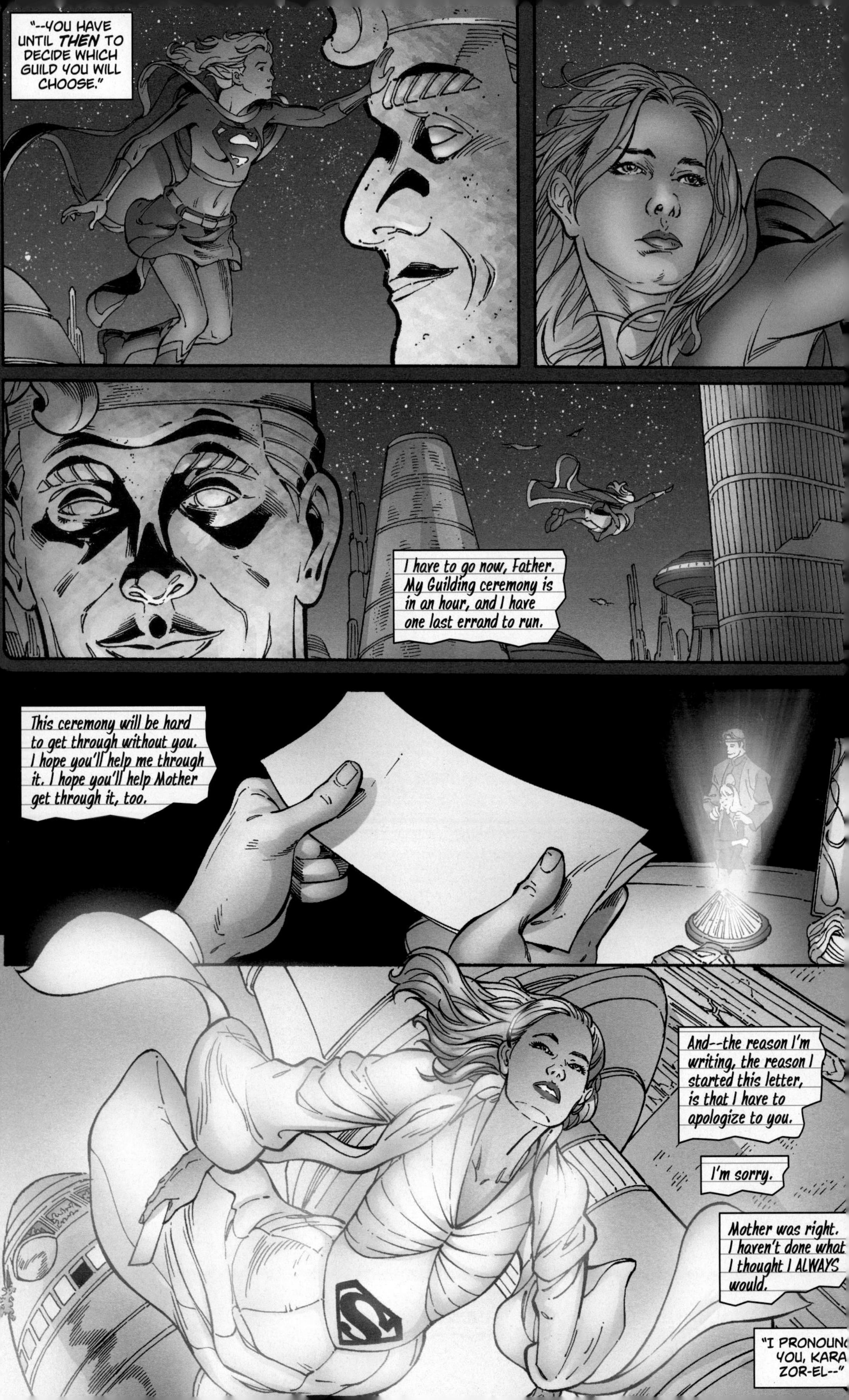
"--YOU HAVE UNTIL THEN TO DECIDE WHICH GUILD YOU WILL CHOOSE."
I have to go now, Father. My Guilding ceremony is in an hour, and I have one last errand to run.
This ceremony will be hard to get through without you. I hope you'll help me through it. I hope you'll help Mother get through it, too.
And--the reason I'm writing, the reason I started this letter, is that I have to apologize to you.
I'm sorry.
Mother was right. I haven't done what I thought I ALWAYS would.
"I PRONOUNC YOU, KARA ZOR-EL--"

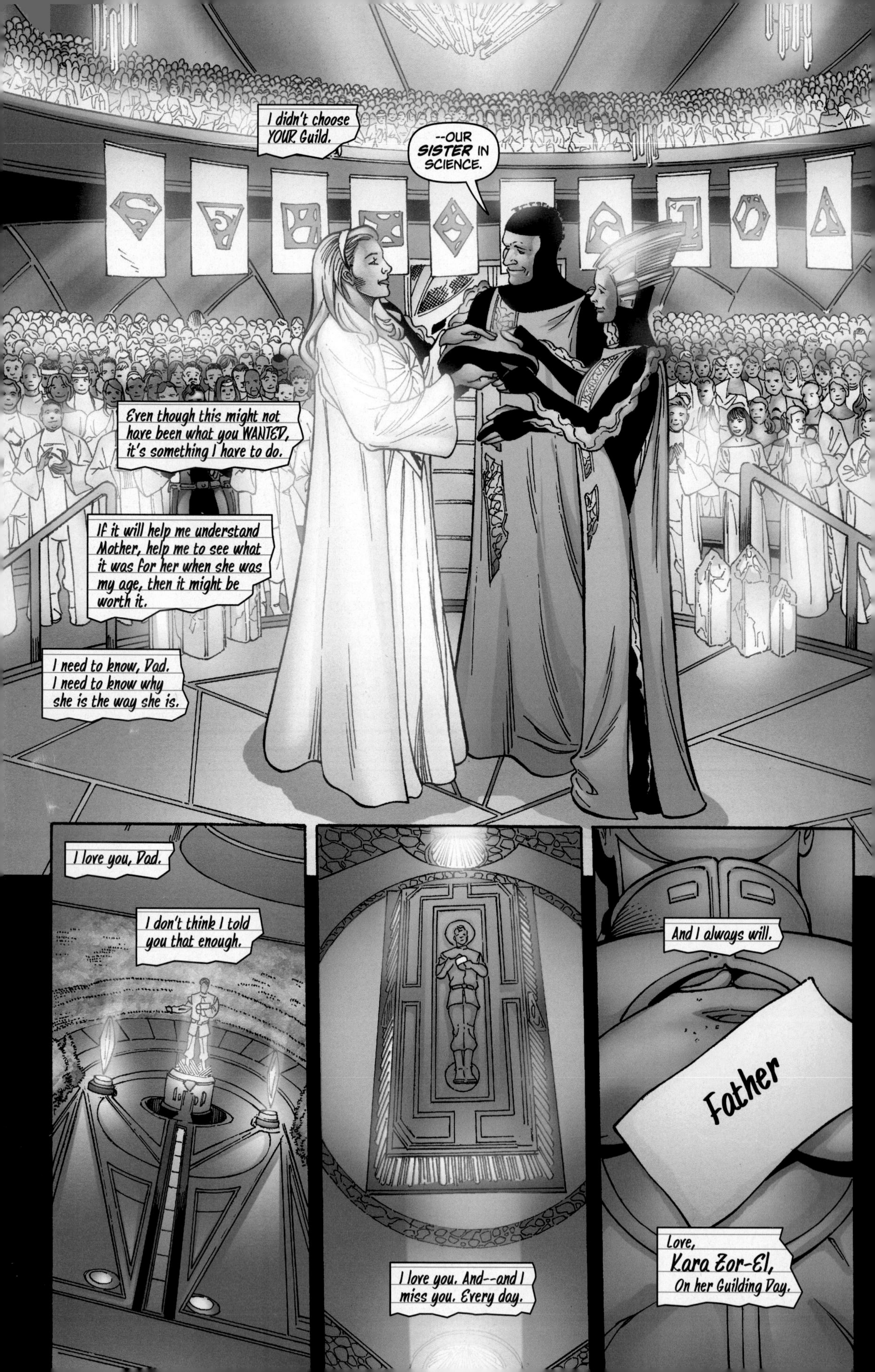
I didn't choose YOUR Guild.
--OUR SISTER IN SCIENCE.
Even though this might not have been what you WANTED, it's something I have to do.
If it will help me understand Mother, help me to see what it was for her when she was my age, then it might be worth it.
I need to know, Dad. I need to know why she is the way she is.
I love you, Dad.
I don't think I told you that enough.
I love you. And--and I miss you. Every day.
And I always will.
Father
Love, Kara Zor-El, On her Guilding Day.

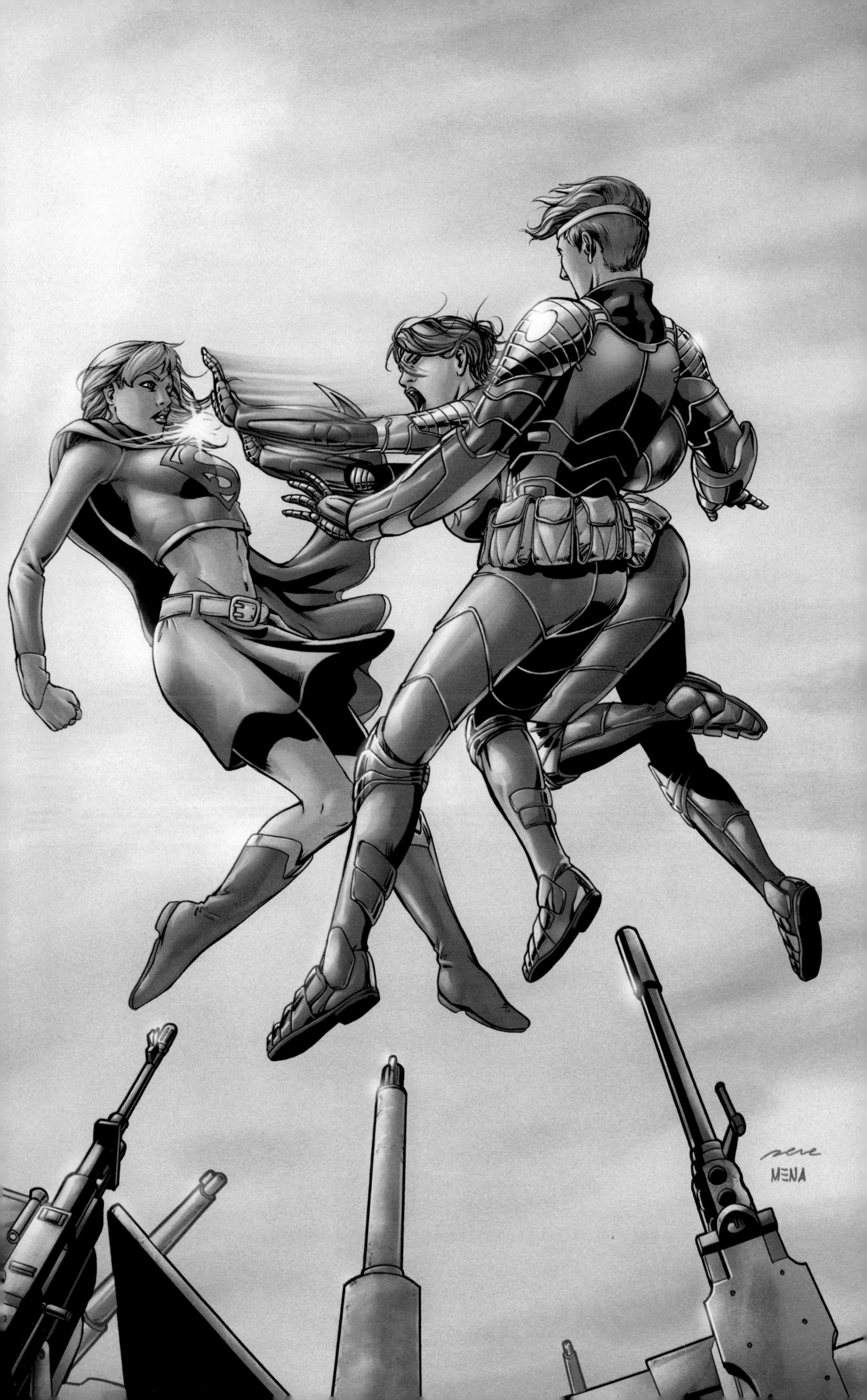
MENA

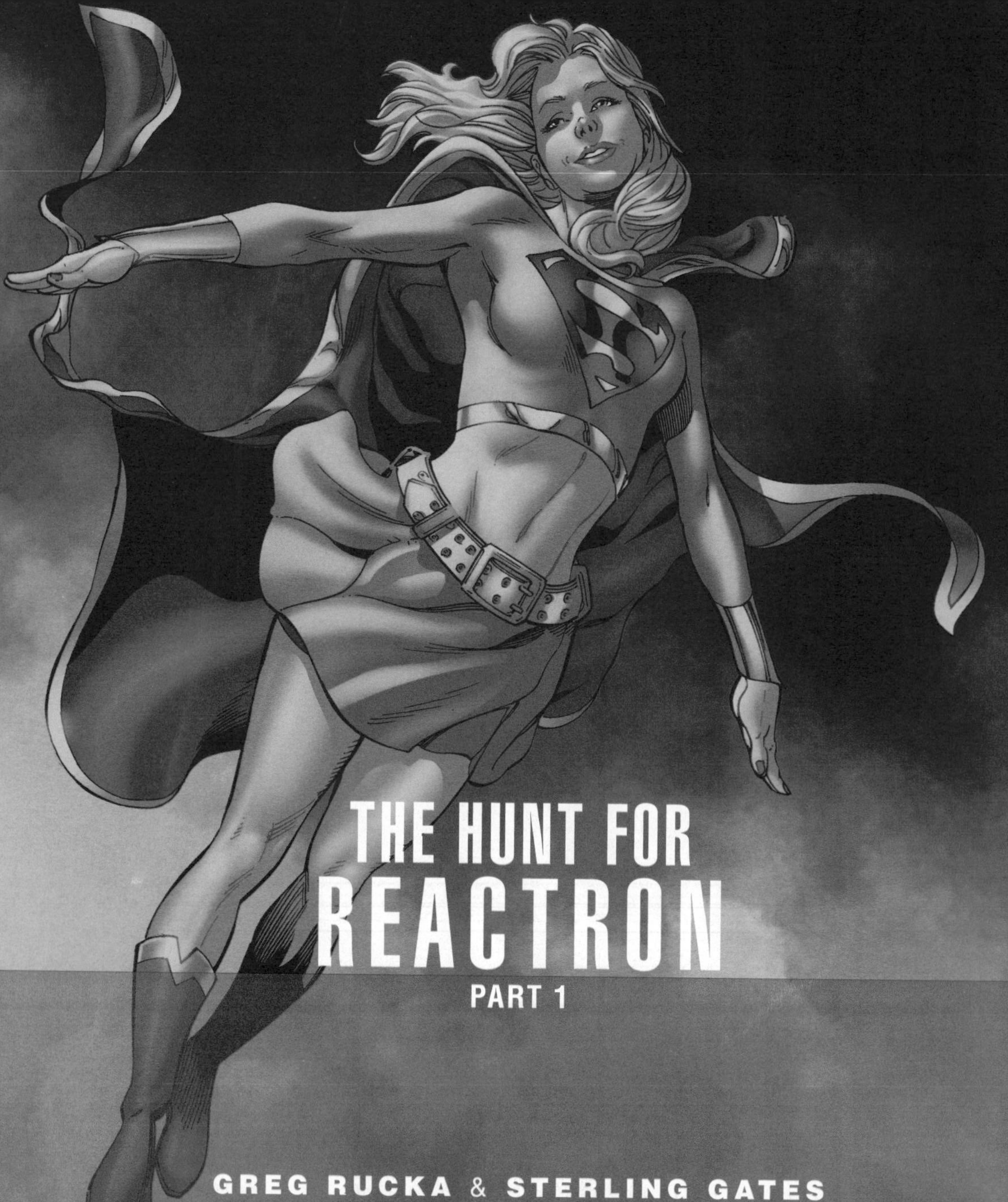

# THE HUNT FOR REACTRON

PART 1

**GREG RUCKA** & **STERLING GATES**
writers

**PERE PÉREZ**
artist

**JAVIER MENA**
colorist

**ROB LEIGH**
letterer

**PERE PÉREZ** with **JAVIER MENA**
cover

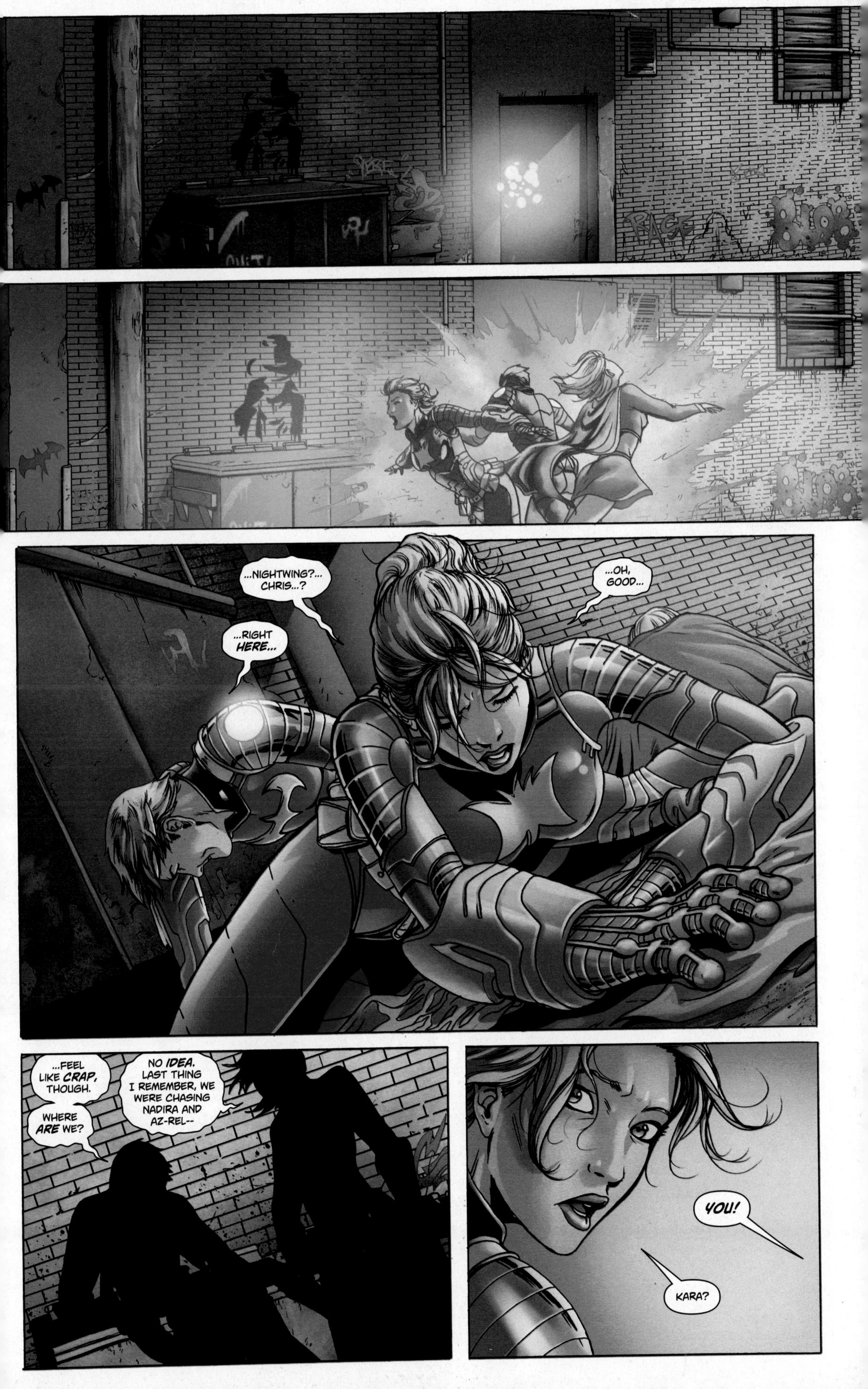
...NIGHTWING?... CHRIS...?
...RIGHT HERE...
...OH, GOOD...
...FEEL LIKE CRAP, THOUGH.
WHERE ARE WE?
NO IDEA. LAST THING I REMEMBER, WE WERE CHASING NADIRA AND AZ-REL--
YOU!
KARA?

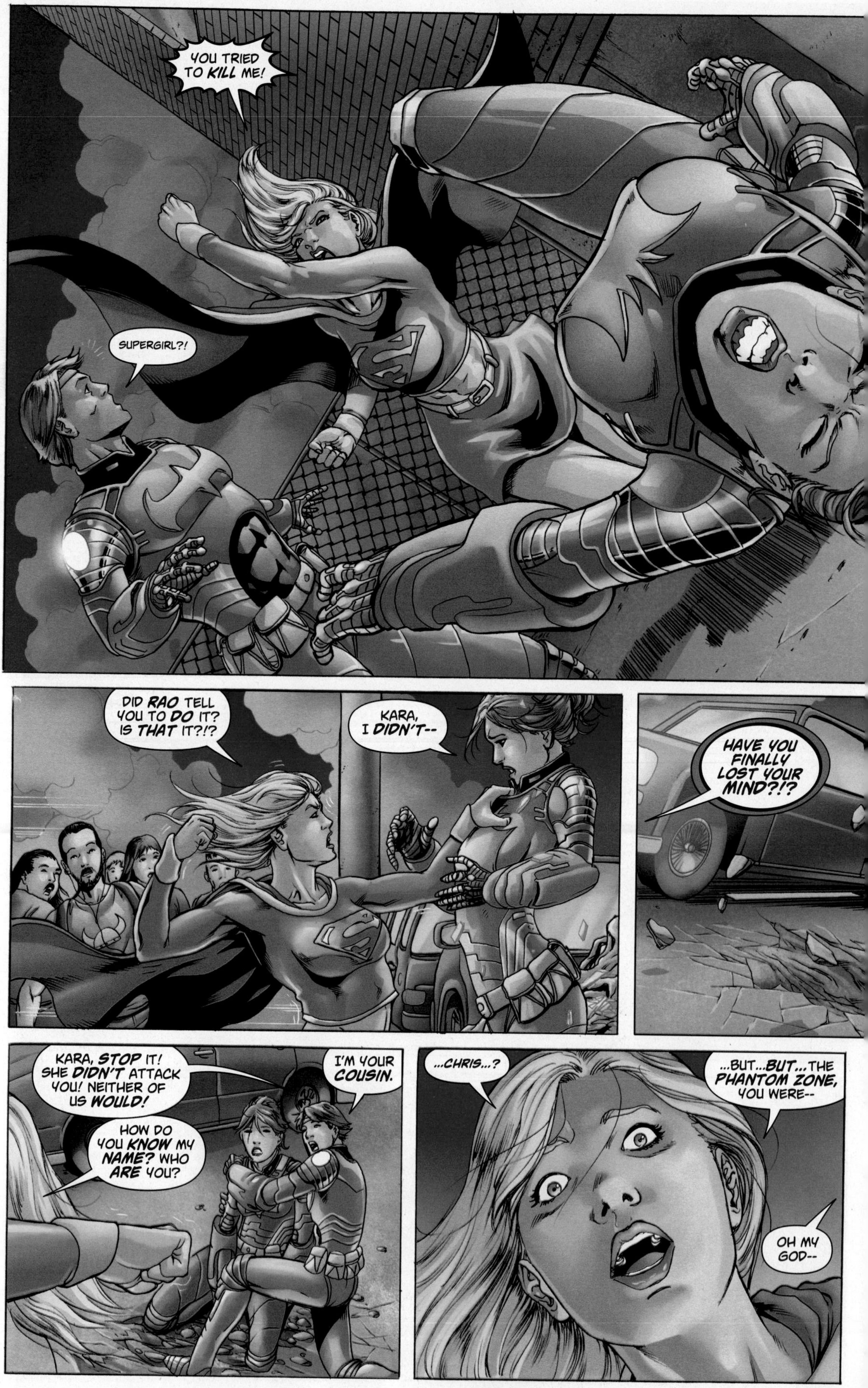
YOU TRIED TO KILL ME!
SUPERGIRL?!
DID RAO TELL YOU TO DO IT? IS THAT IT?!?
KARA, I DIDN'T--
HAVE YOU FINALLY LOST YOUR MIND?!?
KARA, STOP IT! SHE DIDN'T ATTACK YOU! NEITHER OF US WOULD!
I'M YOUR COUSIN.
HOW DO YOU KNOW MY NAME? WHO ARE YOU?
...CHRIS...?
...BUT...BUT...THE PHANTOM ZONE, YOU WERE--
OH MY GOD--

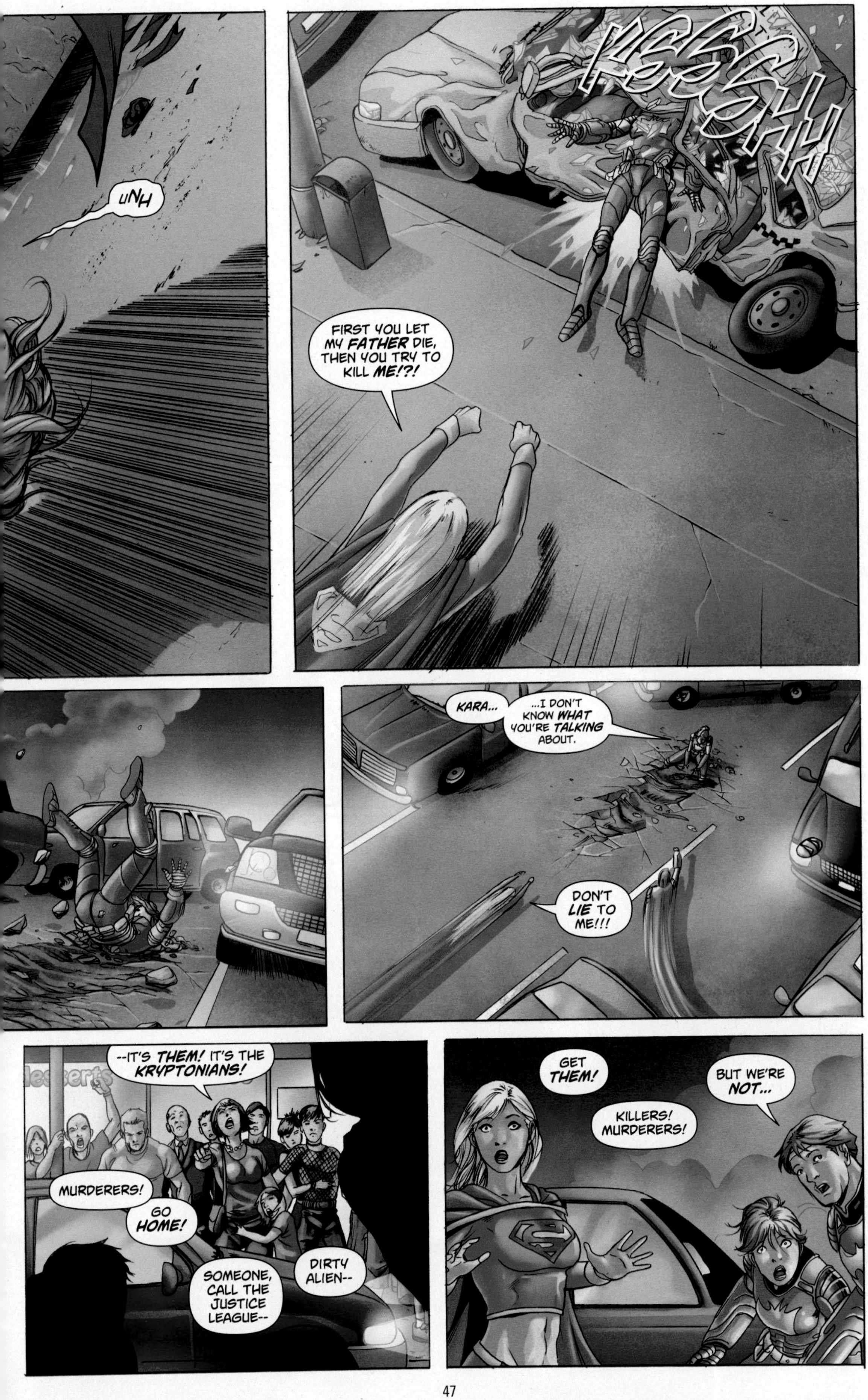
uNH
KSSSHH
FIRST YOU LET MY FATHER DIE, THEN YOU TRY TO KILL ME!?!
KARA...
...I DON'T KNOW WHAT YOU'RE TALKING ABOUT.
DON'T LIE TO ME!!!
--IT'S THEM! IT'S THE KRYPTONIANS!
MURDERERS!
GO HOME!
SOMEONE, CALL THE JUSTICE LEAGUE--
DIRTY ALIEN--
GET THEM!
KILLERS! MURDERERS!
BUT WE'RE NOT...

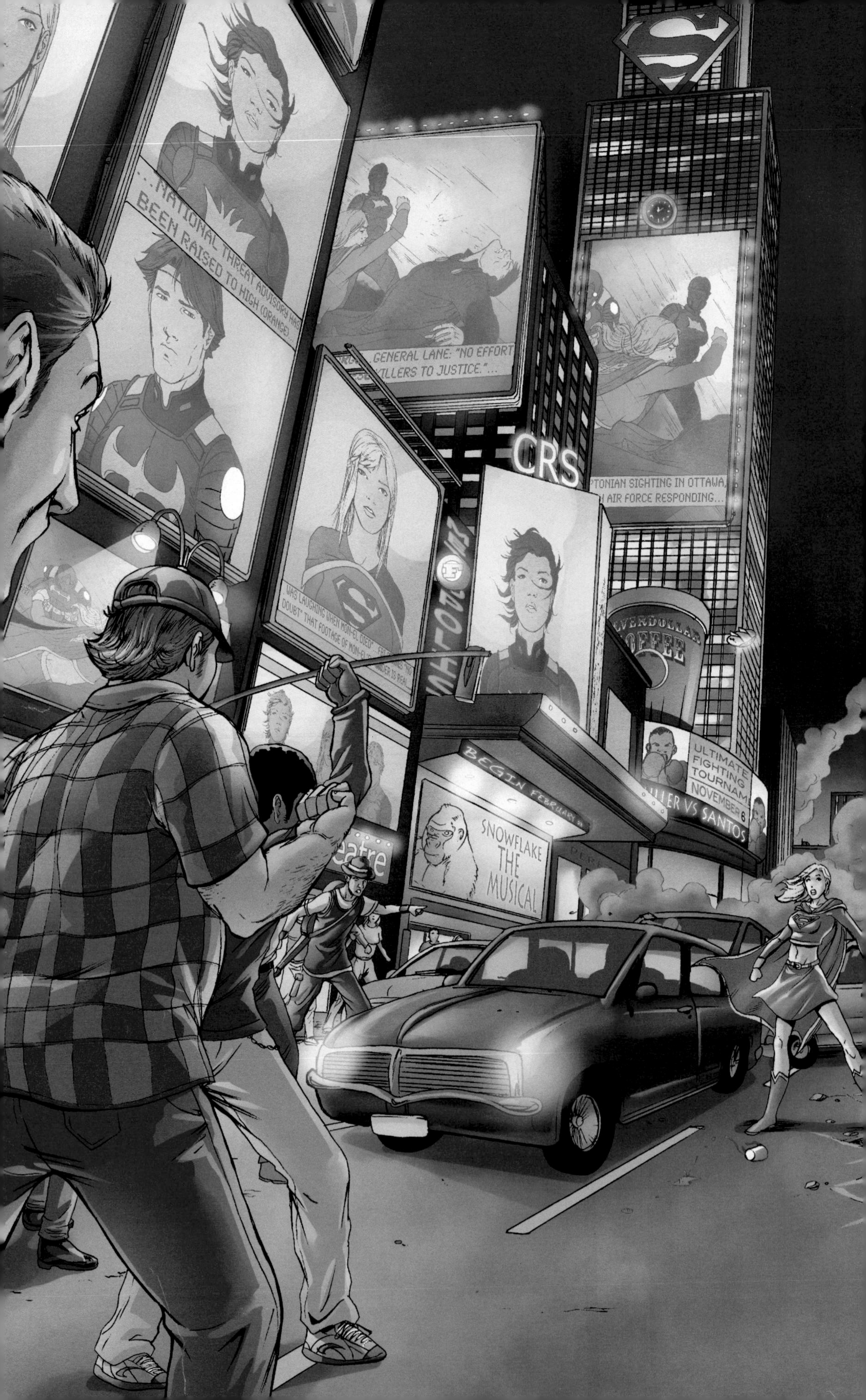
...NATIONAL THREAT ADVISORY HAS BEEN RAISED TO HIGH (ORANGE).
...GENERAL LANE: "NO EFFORT
KILLERS TO JUSTICE."...
CRS
PTONIAN SIGHTING IN OTTAWA,
H AIR FORCE RESPONDING...
WAS LAUGHING WHEN MON-EL DIED" ...FBI
DOUBT" THAT FOOTAGE OF MON-EL
ER IS REAL...
EVERDOLLAR
OFFEE
ULTIMATE FIGHTING TOURNAM
NOVEMBER 6
LLER VS SANTOS
BEGIN FEBRUARY
SNOWFLAKE THE MUSICAL
eatre

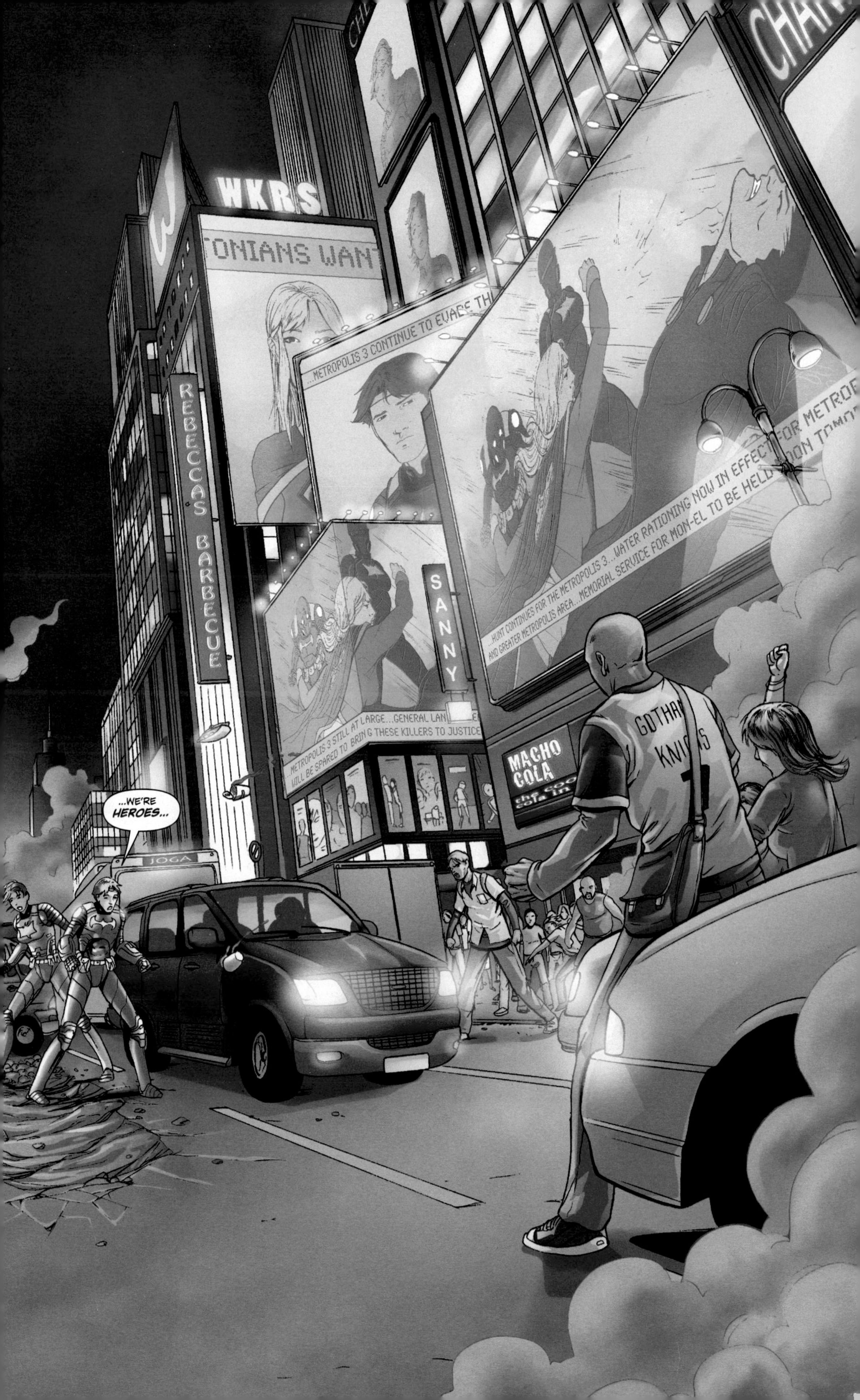

WKRS
TONIANS WANT
...METROPOLIS 3 CONTINUE TO EVADE TH
REBECCAS BARBECUE
SANNY
...METROPOLIS 3 STILL AT LARGE...GENERAL LAN
WILL BE SPARED TO BRING THESE KILLERS TO JUSTICE
...HUNT CONTINUES FOR THE METROPOLIS 3...WATER RATIONING NOW IN EFFECT FOR METRO
AND GREATER METROPOLIS AREA...MEMORIAL SERVICE FOR MON-EL TO BE HELD
MACHO COLA
GOTHAM KNIGHTS
JOGA
...WE'RE HEROES...

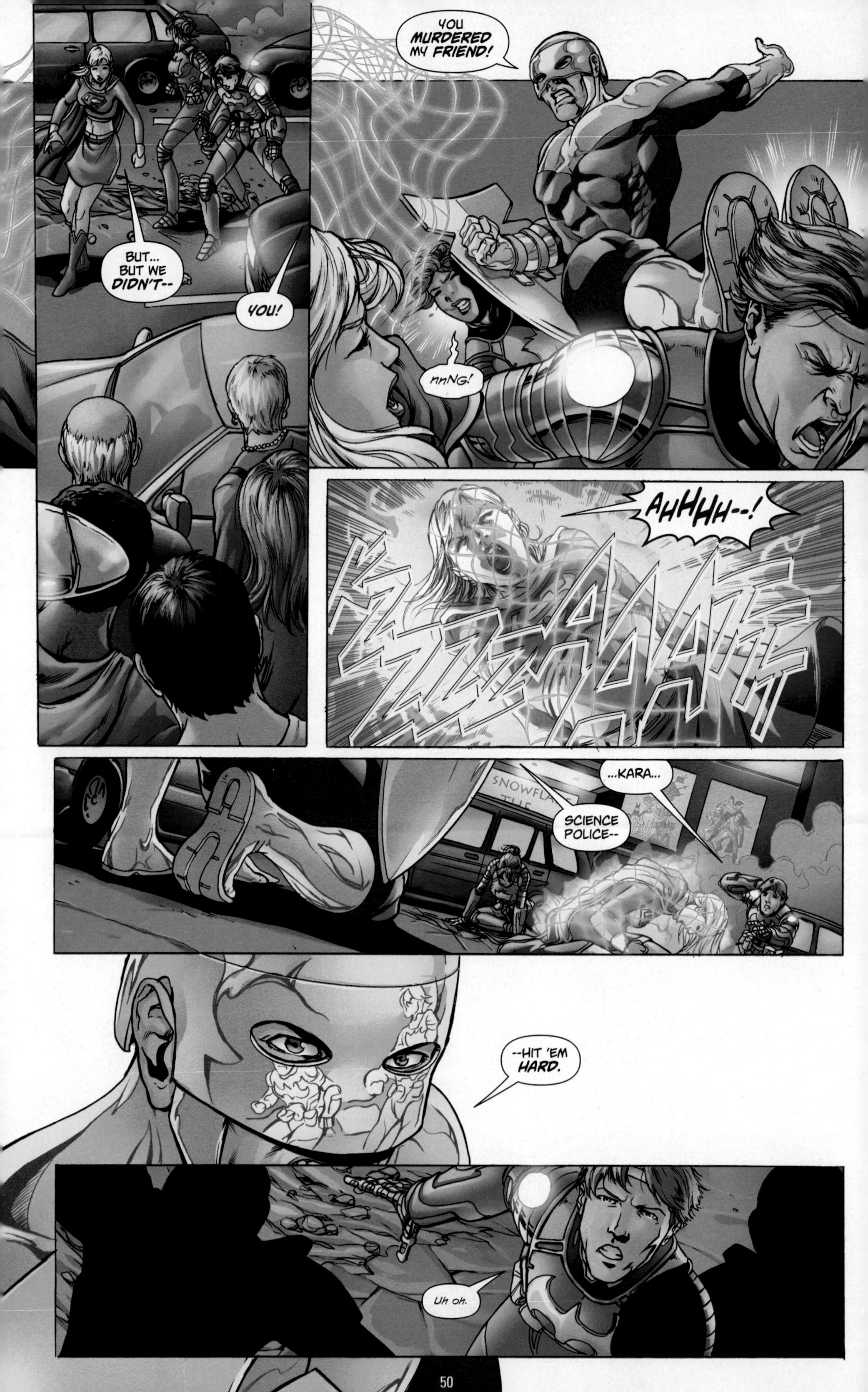
BUT... BUT WE DIDN'T--
YOU!
YOU MURDERED MY FRIEND!
nnNG!
AHHHH--!
KZZZZAAAKK
...KARA...
SCIENCE POLICE--
--HIT 'EM HARD.
Uh oh.

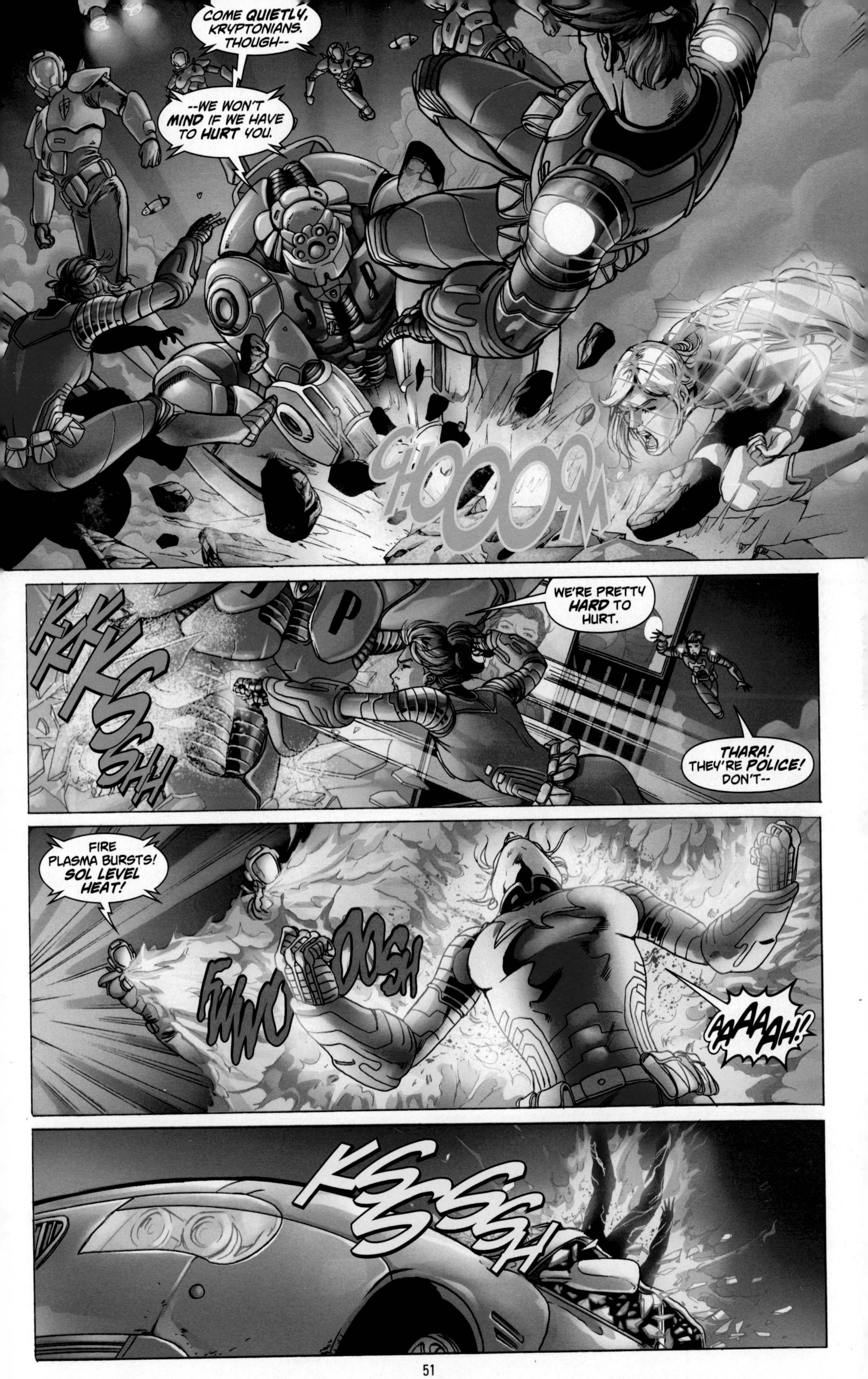
COME QUIETLY, KRYPTONIANS. THOUGH--
--WE WON'T MIND IF WE HAVE TO HURT YOU.
CHOOOOM
KKKKSSSHH
WE'RE PRETTY HARD TO HURT.
THARA! THEY'RE POLICE! DON'T--
FIRE PLASMA BURSTS! SOL LEVEL HEAT!
FWWOOOSH
AAAAAH!!
KSSSSSH

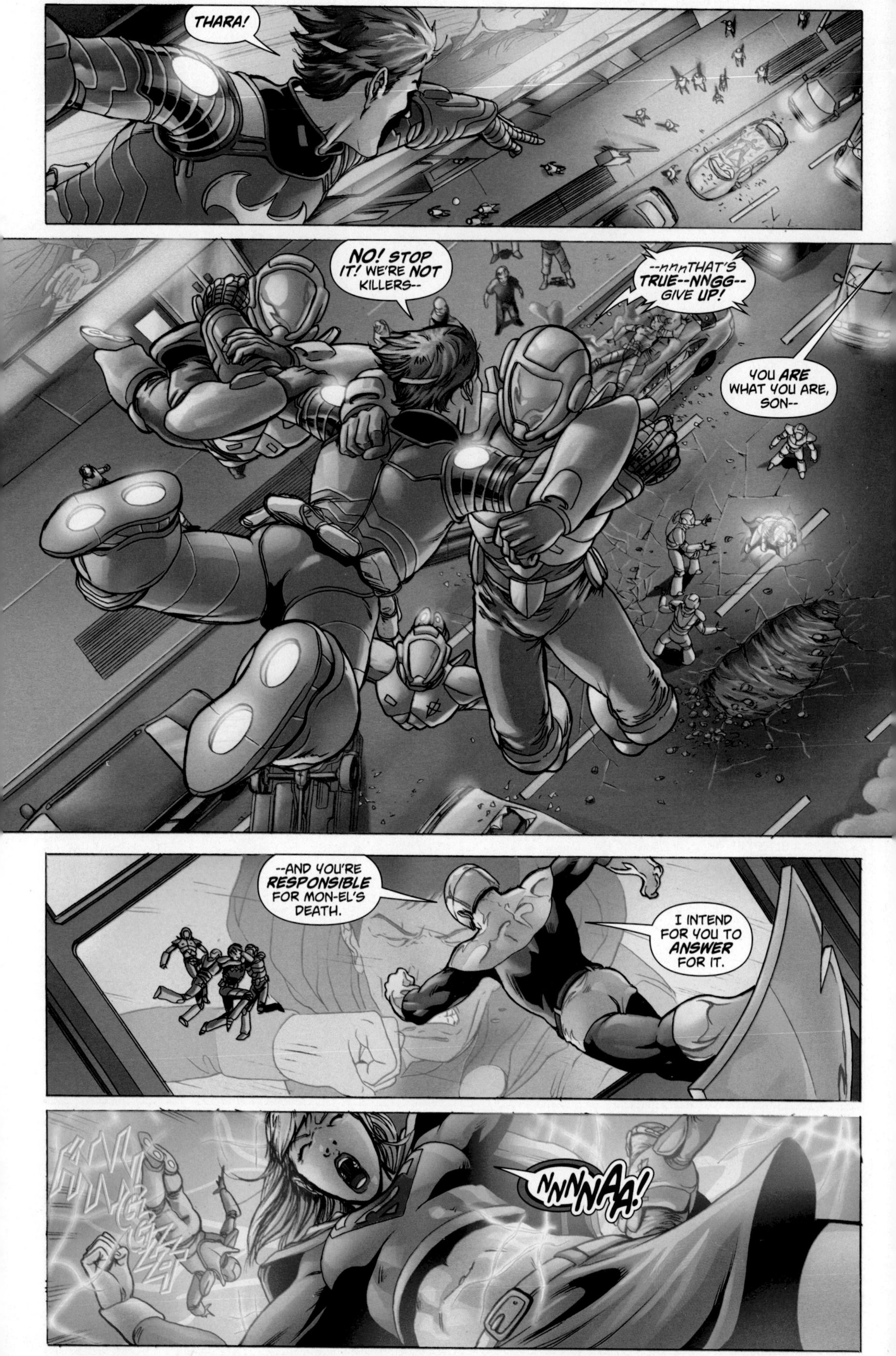
THARA!
NO! STOP IT! WE'RE NOT KILLERS--
--nnnTHAT'S TRUE--NNGG-- GIVE UP!
YOU ARE WHAT YOU ARE, SON--
--AND YOU'RE RESPONSIBLE FOR MON-EL'S DEATH.
I INTEND FOR YOU TO ANSWER FOR IT.
NNNNAA!

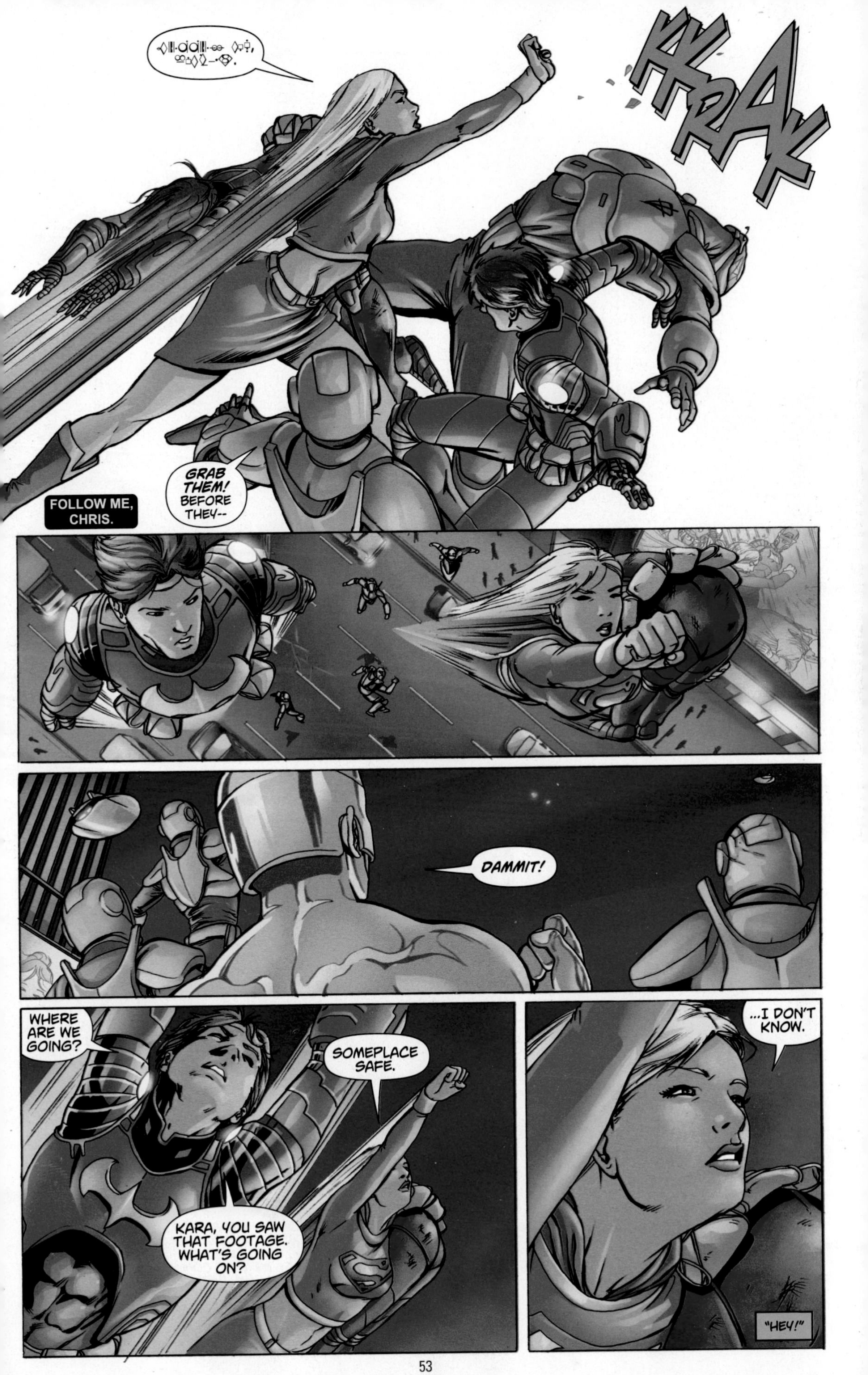
KKRAK
GRAB THEM! BEFORE THEY--
FOLLOW ME, CHRIS.
DAMMIT!
WHERE ARE WE GOING?
SOMEPLACE SAFE.
KARA, YOU SAW THAT FOOTAGE. WHAT'S GOING ON?
...I DON'T KNOW.
"HEY!"

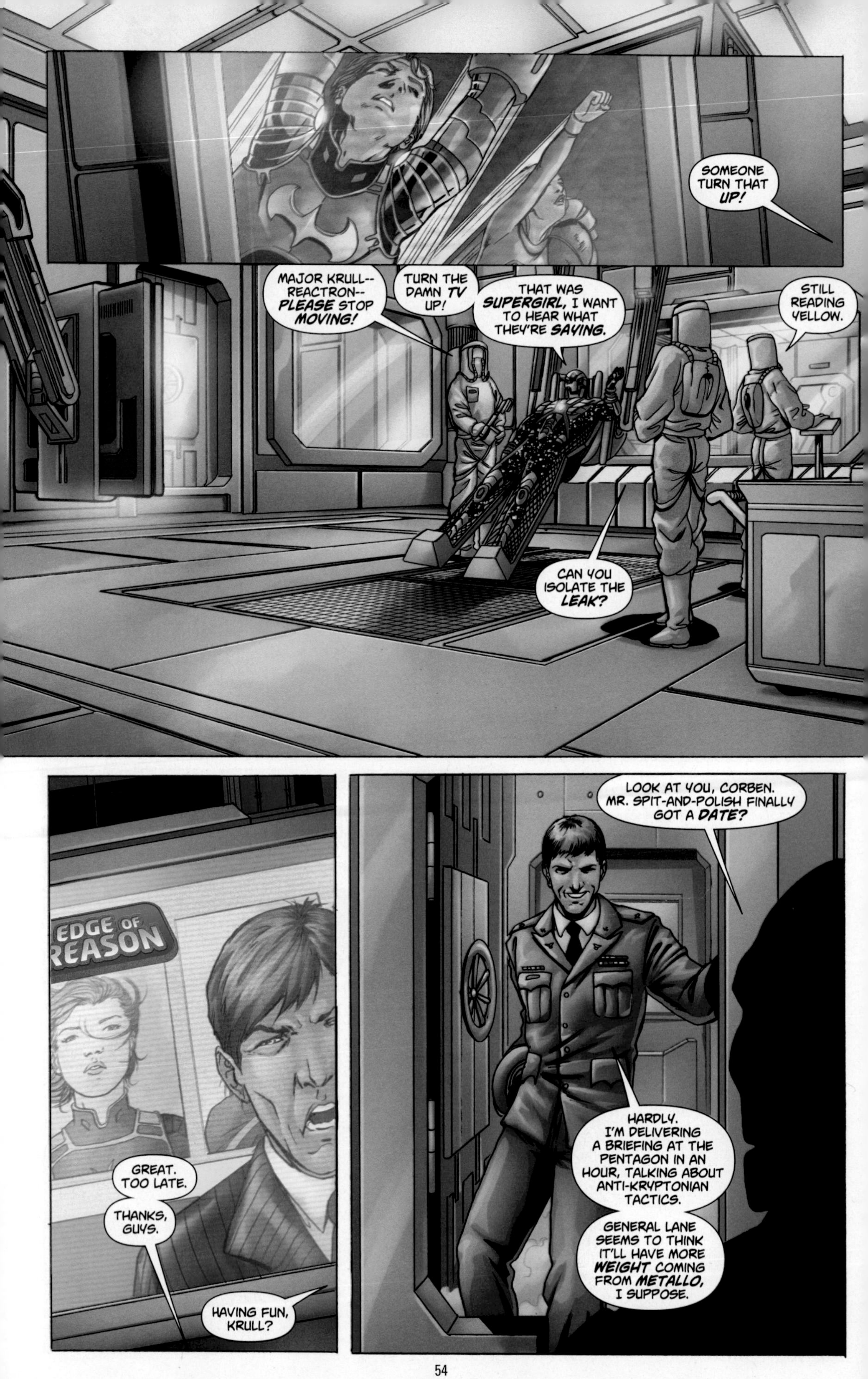
SOMEONE TURN THAT UP!
MAJOR KRULL-- REACTRON-- PLEASE STOP MOVING!
TURN THE DAMN TV UP!
THAT WAS SUPERGIRL, I WANT TO HEAR WHAT THEY'RE SAYING.
STILL READING YELLOW.
CAN YOU ISOLATE THE LEAK?
EDGE OF REASON
GREAT. TOO LATE.
THANKS, GUYS.
HAVING FUN, KRULL?
LOOK AT YOU, CORBEN. MR. SPIT-AND-POLISH FINALLY GOT A DATE?
HARDLY. I'M DELIVERING A BRIEFING AT THE PENTAGON IN AN HOUR, TALKING ABOUT ANTI-KRYPTONIAN TACTICS.
GENERAL LANE SEEMS TO THINK IT'LL HAVE MORE WEIGHT COMING FROM METALLO, I SUPPOSE.

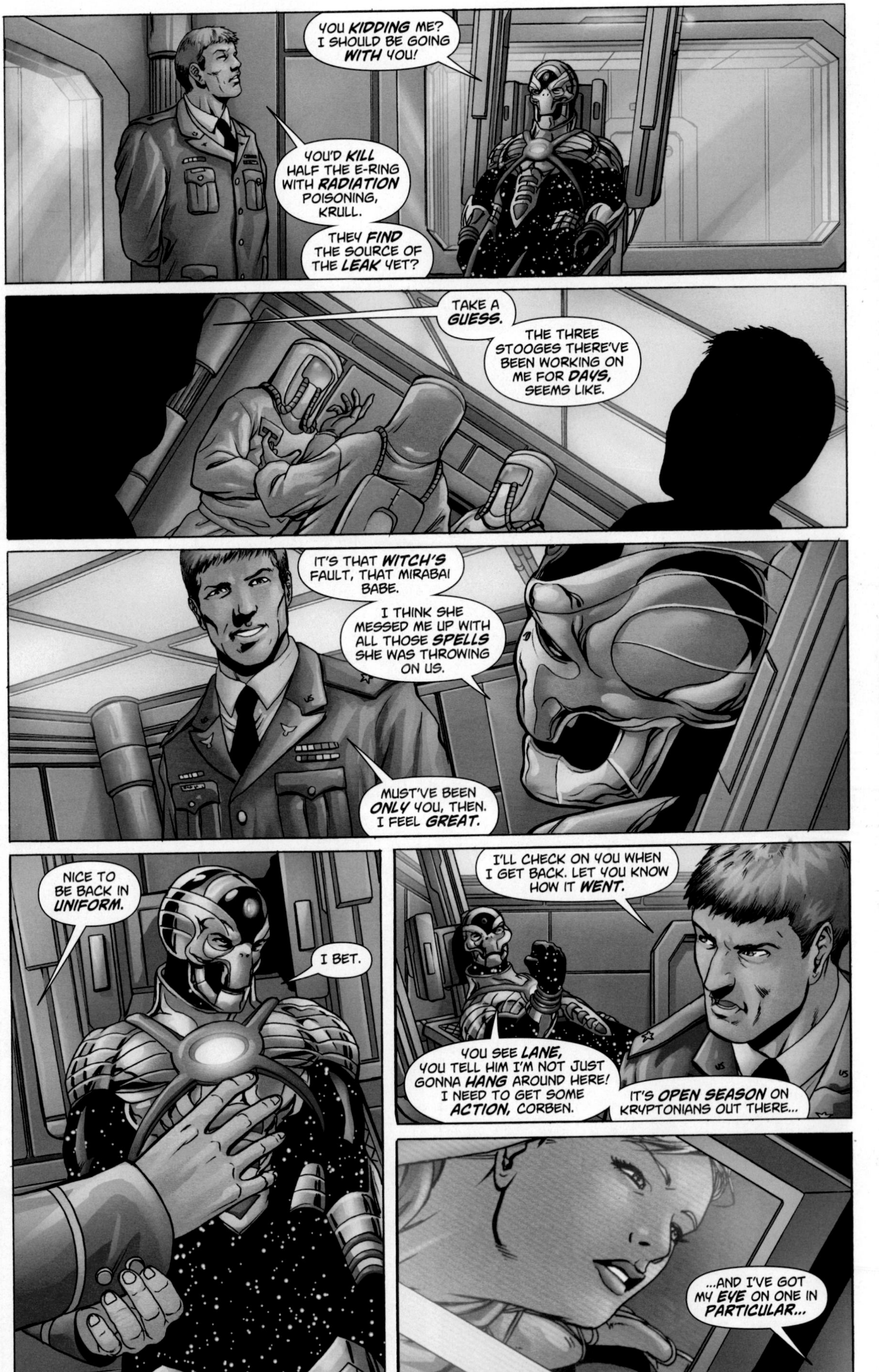
YOU KIDDING ME? I SHOULD BE GOING WITH YOU!
YOU'D KILL HALF THE E-RING WITH RADIATION POISONING, KRULL.
THEY FIND THE SOURCE OF THE LEAK YET?
TAKE A GUESS.
THE THREE STOOGES THERE'VE BEEN WORKING ON ME FOR DAYS, SEEMS LIKE.
IT'S THAT WITCH'S FAULT, THAT MIRABAI BABE.
I THINK SHE MESSED ME UP WITH ALL THOSE SPELLS SHE WAS THROWING ON US.
MUST'VE BEEN ONLY YOU, THEN. I FEEL GREAT.
NICE TO BE BACK IN UNIFORM.
I BET.
I'LL CHECK ON YOU WHEN I GET BACK. LET YOU KNOW HOW IT WENT.
YOU SEE LANE, YOU TELL HIM I'M NOT JUST GONNA HANG AROUND HERE! I NEED TO GET SOME ACTION, CORBEN.
IT'S OPEN SEASON ON KRYPTONIANS OUT THERE...
...AND I'VE GOT MY EYE ON ONE IN PARTICULAR...

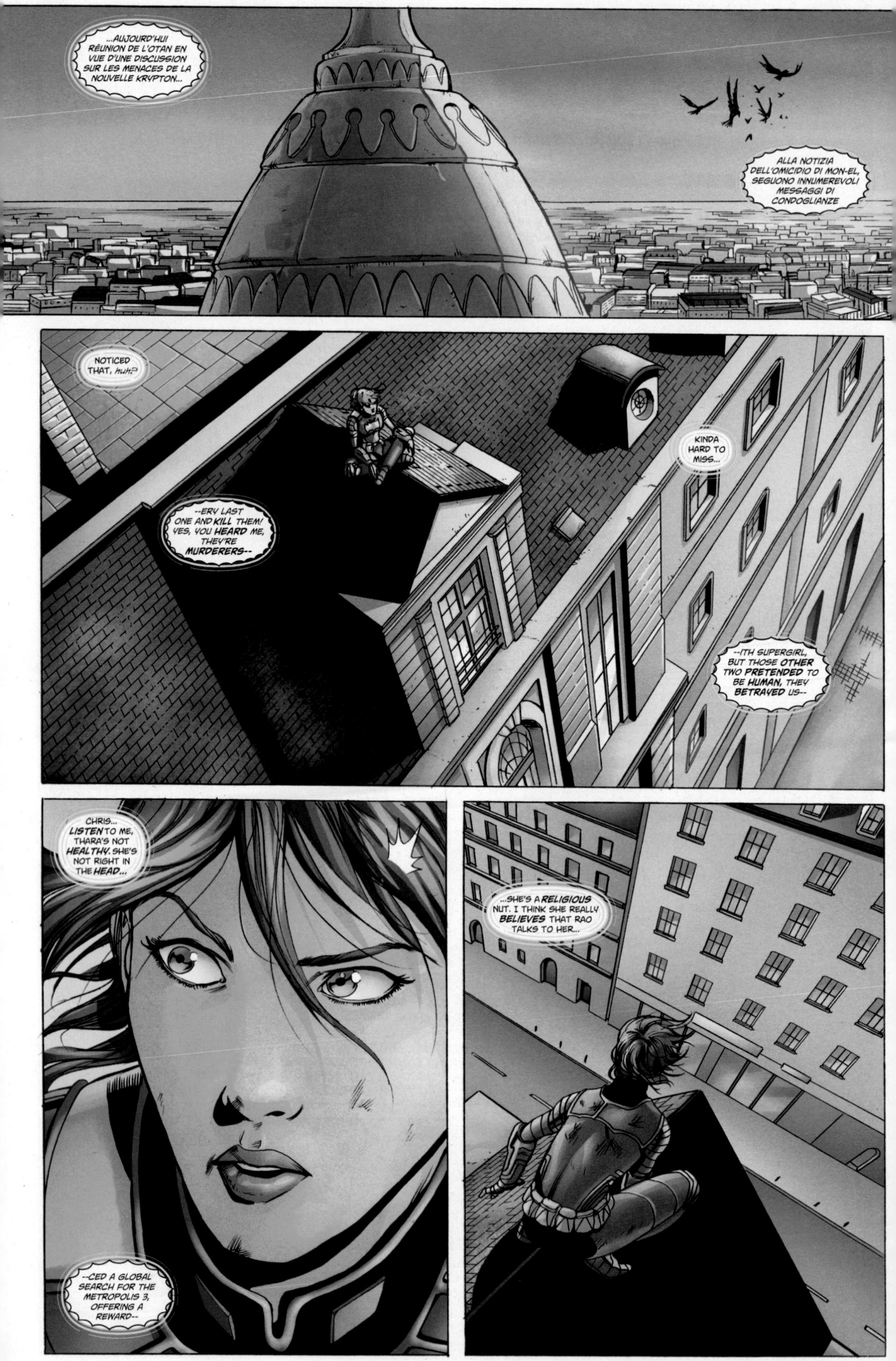
...AUJOURD'HUI RÉUNION DE L'OTAN EN VUE D'UNE DISCUSSION SUR LES MENACES DE LA NOUVELLE KRYPTON...
ALLA NOTIZIA DELL'OMICIDIO DI MON-EL, SEGUONO INNUMEREVOLI MESSAGGI DI CONDOGLIANZE
NOTICED THAT, huh?
KINDA HARD TO MISS...
--ERY LAST ONE AND KILL THEM! YES, YOU HEARD ME, THEY'RE MURDERERS--
--ITH SUPERGIRL, BUT THOSE OTHER TWO PRETENDED TO BE HUMAN, THEY BETRAYED US--
CHRIS... LISTEN TO ME, THARA'S NOT HEALTHY. SHE'S NOT RIGHT IN THE HEAD...
...SHE'S A RELIGIOUS NUT. I THINK SHE REALLY BELIEVES THAT RAO TALKS TO HER...
--CED A GLOBAL SEARCH FOR THE METROPOLIS 3, OFFERING A REWARD--

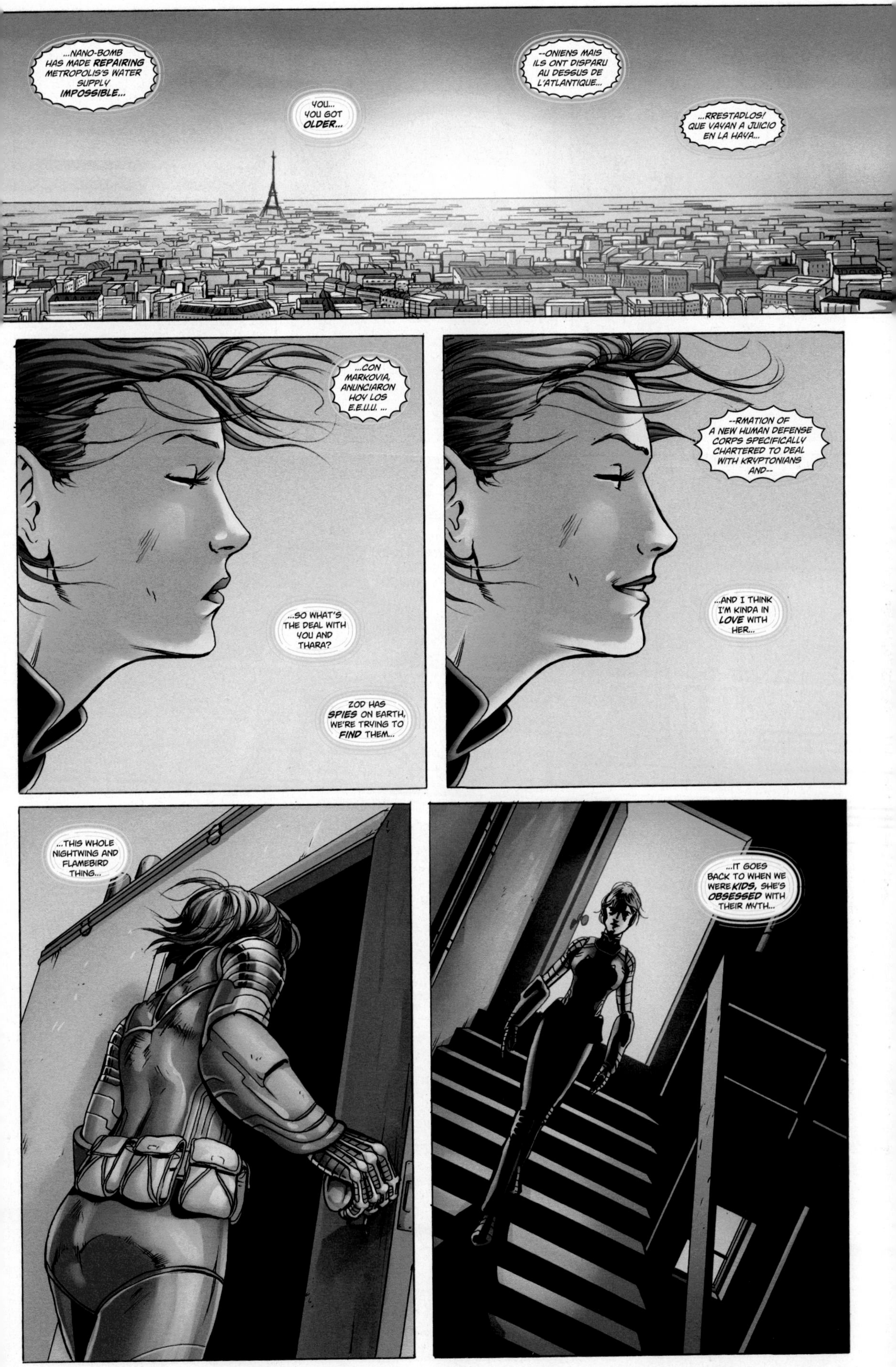
...NANO-BOMB HAS MADE REPAIRING METROPOLIS'S WATER SUPPLY IMPOSSIBLE...
YOU... YOU GOT OLDER...
--ONIENS MAIS ILS ONT DISPARU AU DESSUS DE L'ATLANTIQUE...
...RRESTADLOS! QUE VAYAN A JUICIO EN LA HAYA...
...CON MARKOVIA, ANUNCIARON HOY LOS E.E.U.U. ...
...SO WHAT'S THE DEAL WITH YOU AND THARA?
ZOD HAS SPIES ON EARTH, WE'RE TRYING TO FIND THEM...
--RMATION OF A NEW HUMAN DEFENSE CORPS SPECIFICALLY CHARTERED TO DEAL WITH KRYPTONIANS AND--
...AND I THINK I'M KINDA IN LOVE WITH HER...
...THIS WHOLE NIGHTWING AND FLAMEBIRD THING...
...IT GOES BACK TO WHEN WE WERE KIDS, SHE'S OBSESSED WITH THEIR MYTH...

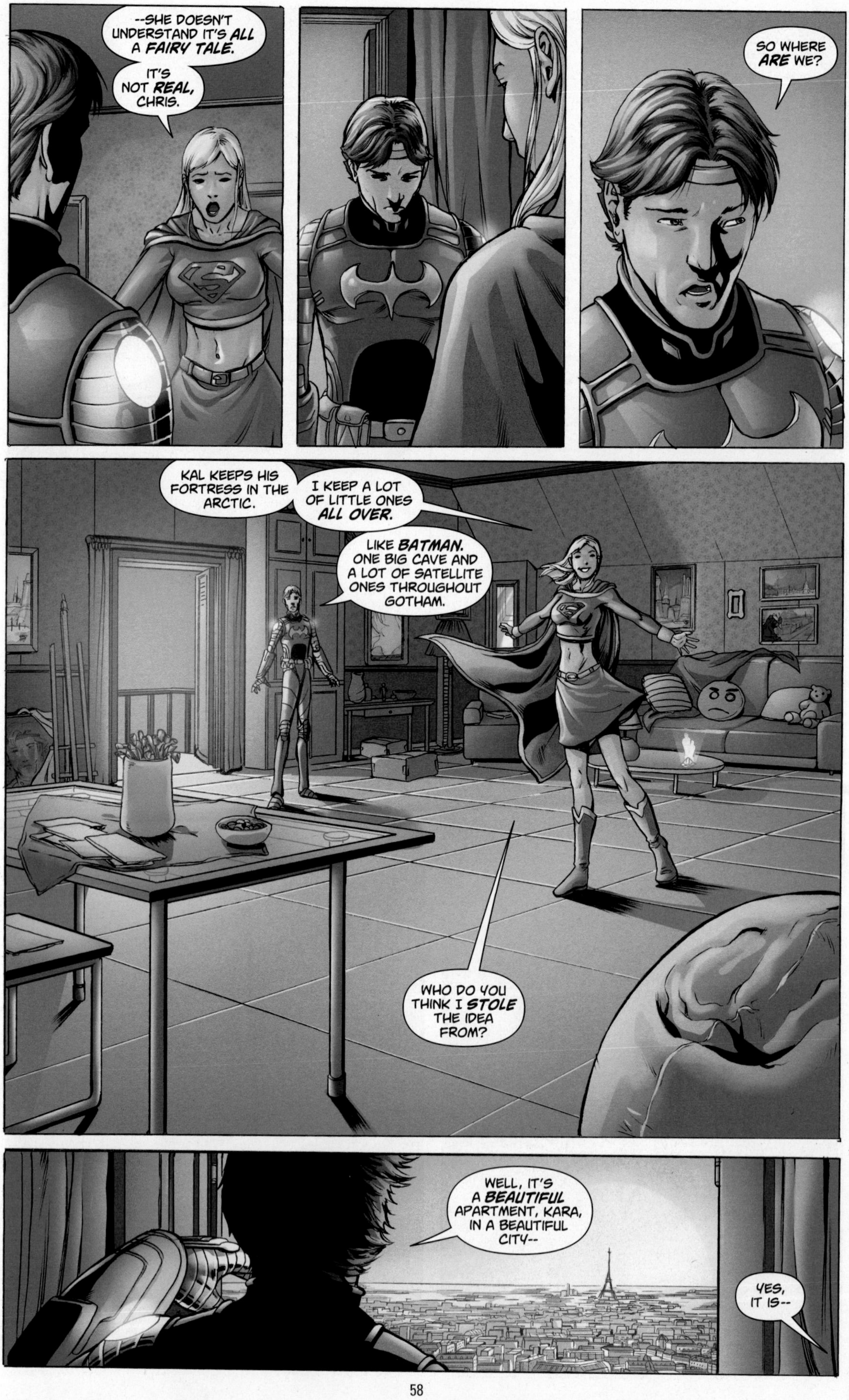
--SHE DOESN'T UNDERSTAND IT'S ALL A FAIRY TALE.
IT'S NOT REAL, CHRIS.
SO WHERE ARE WE?
KAL KEEPS HIS FORTRESS IN THE ARCTIC.
I KEEP A LOT OF LITTLE ONES ALL OVER.
LIKE BATMAN. ONE BIG CAVE AND A LOT OF SATELLITE ONES THROUGHOUT GOTHAM.
WHO DO YOU THINK I STOLE THE IDEA FROM?
WELL, IT'S A BEAUTIFUL APARTMENT, KARA, IN A BEAUTIFUL CITY--
YES, IT IS--

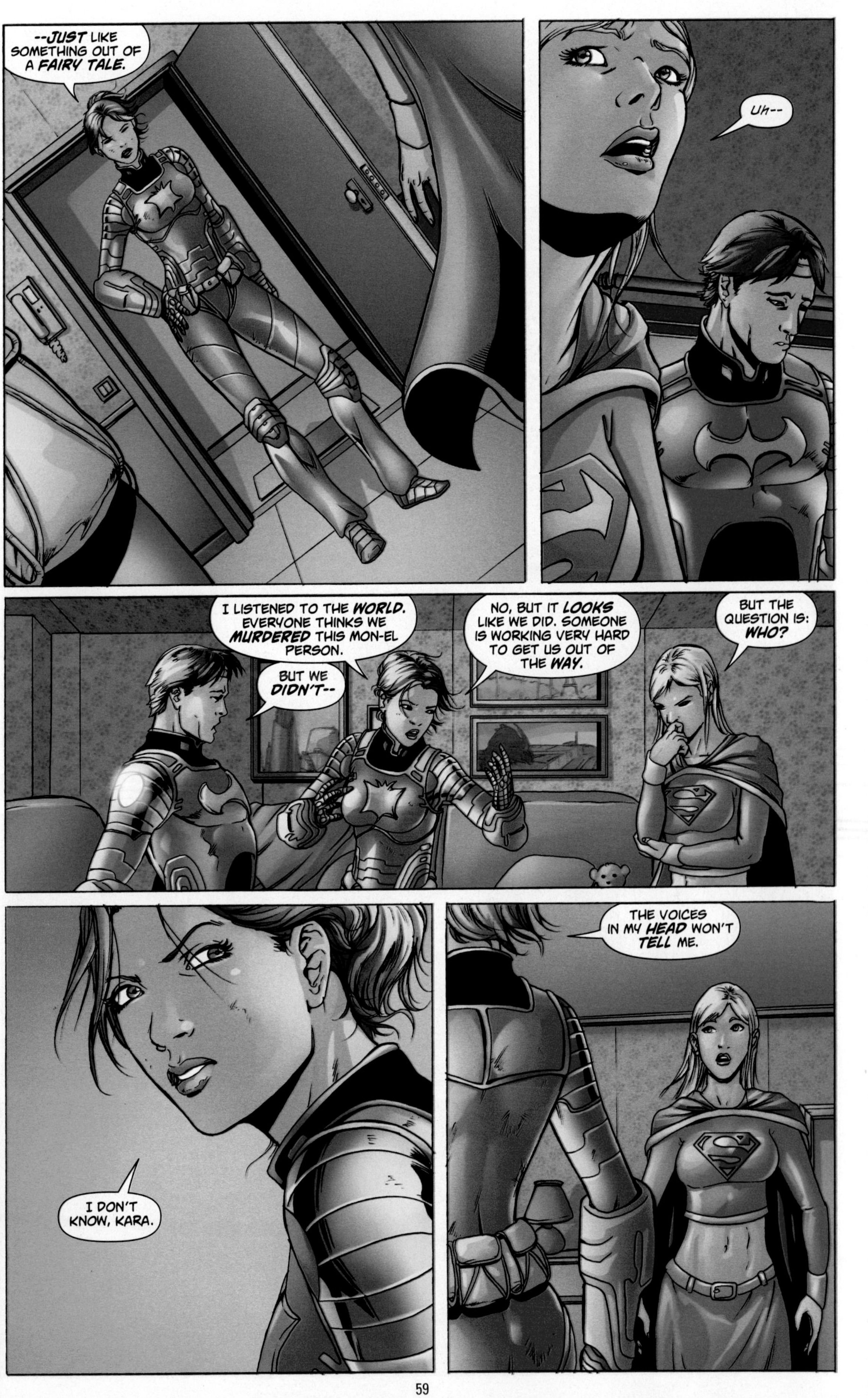
--JUST LIKE SOMETHING OUT OF A FAIRY TALE.
Uh--
I LISTENED TO THE WORLD. EVERYONE THINKS WE MURDERED THIS MON-EL PERSON.
BUT WE DIDN'T--
NO, BUT IT LOOKS LIKE WE DID. SOMEONE IS WORKING VERY HARD TO GET US OUT OF THE WAY.
BUT THE QUESTION IS: WHO?
I DON'T KNOW, KARA.
THE VOICES IN MY HEAD WON'T TELL ME.

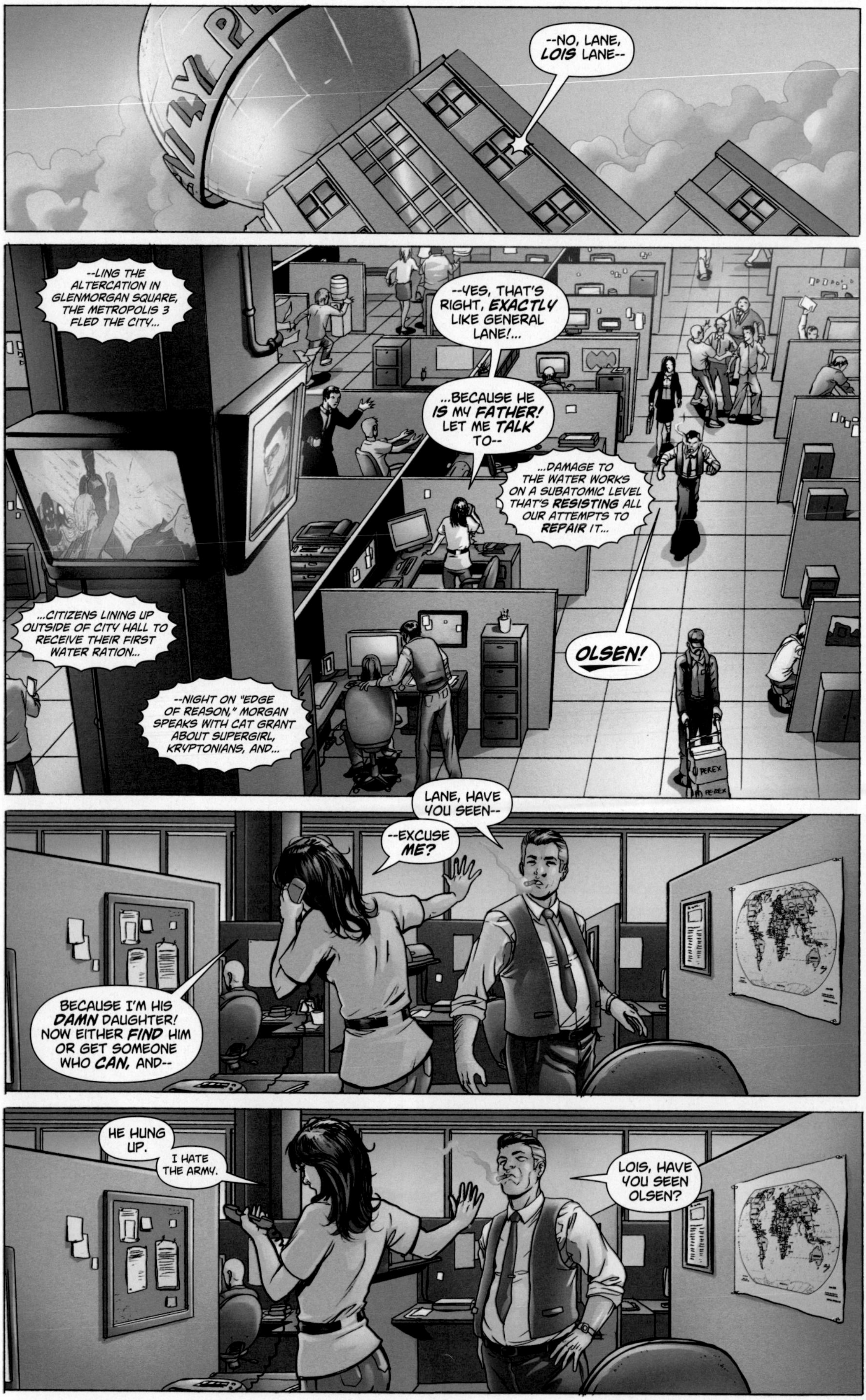
--NO, LANE, LOIS LANE--
--LING THE ALTERCATION IN GLENMORGAN SQUARE, THE METROPOLIS 3 FLED THE CITY...
--YES, THAT'S RIGHT, EXACTLY LIKE GENERAL LANE!...
...BECAUSE HE IS MY FATHER! LET ME TALK TO--
...DAMAGE TO THE WATER WORKS ON A SUBATOMIC LEVEL THAT'S RESISTING ALL OUR ATTEMPTS TO REPAIR IT...
...CITIZENS LINING UP OUTSIDE OF CITY HALL TO RECEIVE THEIR FIRST WATER RATION...
--NIGHT ON "EDGE OF REASON," MORGAN SPEAKS WITH CAT GRANT ABOUT SUPERGIRL, KRYPTONIANS, AND...
OLSEN!
PEREX
LANE, HAVE YOU SEEN--
--EXCUSE ME?
BECAUSE I'M HIS DAMN DAUGHTER! NOW EITHER FIND HIM OR GET SOMEONE WHO CAN, AND--
HE HUNG UP.
I HATE THE ARMY.
LOIS, HAVE YOU SEEN OLSEN?

NO, SORRY, CHIEF.

GIMME A SEC?

CAT! CAT, *WAIT!*

I'M LATE, LOIS. CAN YOU SHOUT AT ME *LATER?*

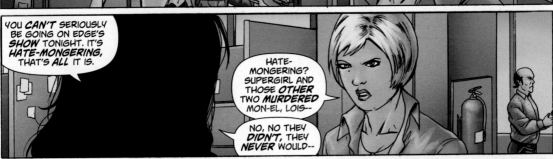

YOU *CAN'T* SERIOUSLY BE GOING ON EDGE'S *SHOW* TONIGHT. IT'S *HATE-MONGERING*, THAT'S *ALL* IT IS.

HATE-MONGERING? SUPERGIRL AND THOSE *OTHER* TWO *MURDERED* MON-EL, LOIS--

NO, NO THEY *DIDN'T*, THEY *NEVER* WOULD--

LOOK AT THE *TELEVISION!* THE WHOLE *WORLD* SAW IT!

VIDEO CAN BE *FAKED!*

THEY'VE *CONFIRMED* THAT THE *FOOTAGE* IS *UNALTERED!*

FACE IT, LOIS! THESE *ALIENS* THAT YOU'VE *CHAMPIONED* ALL THESE YEARS ARE *NOT* OUR FRIENDS...

...THEY'RE THE *ENEMY*, AND THE PEOPLE WHO *STAND* WITH THEM, WHO *DEFEND* THEM...

...THEY MIGHT WANT TO START *WATCHING* WHAT THEY SAY AND WHAT THEY *WRITE...*

...OR *SOMEONE* MIGHT THINK *THEY'RE* THE ENEMY, TOO....

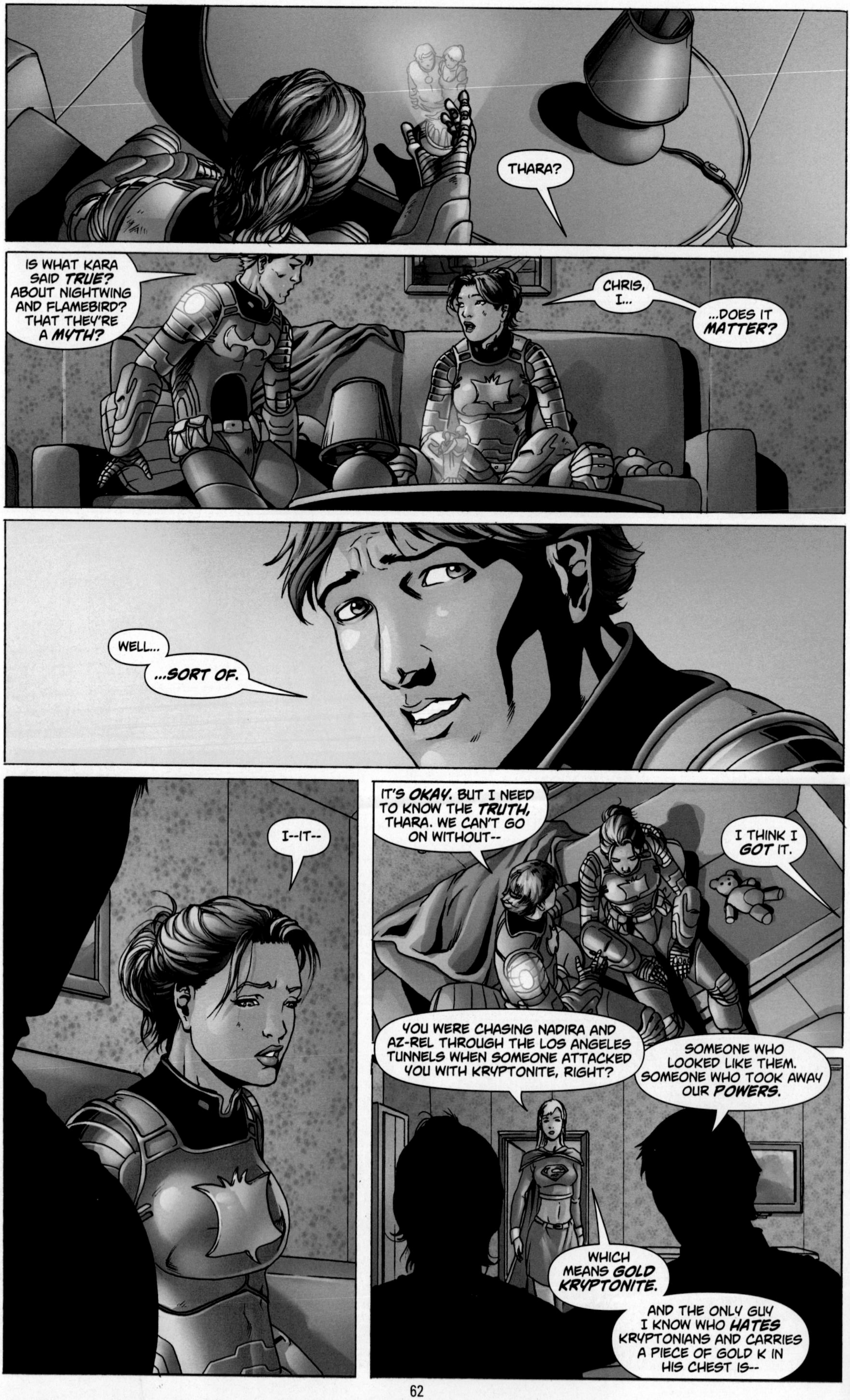

THARA?
IS WHAT KARA SAID TRUE? ABOUT NIGHTWING AND FLAMEBIRD? THAT THEY'RE A MYTH?
CHRIS, I...
...DOES IT MATTER?
WELL...
...SORT OF.
I--IT--
IT'S OKAY. BUT I NEED TO KNOW THE TRUTH, THARA. WE CAN'T GO ON WITHOUT--
I THINK I GOT IT.
YOU WERE CHASING NADIRA AND AZ-REL THROUGH THE LOS ANGELES TUNNELS WHEN SOMEONE ATTACKED YOU WITH KRYPTONITE, RIGHT?
SOMEONE WHO LOOKED LIKE THEM. SOMEONE WHO TOOK AWAY OUR POWERS.
WHICH MEANS GOLD KRYPTONITE.
AND THE ONLY GUY I KNOW WHO HATES KRYPTONIANS AND CARRIES A PIECE OF GOLD K IN HIS CHEST IS--

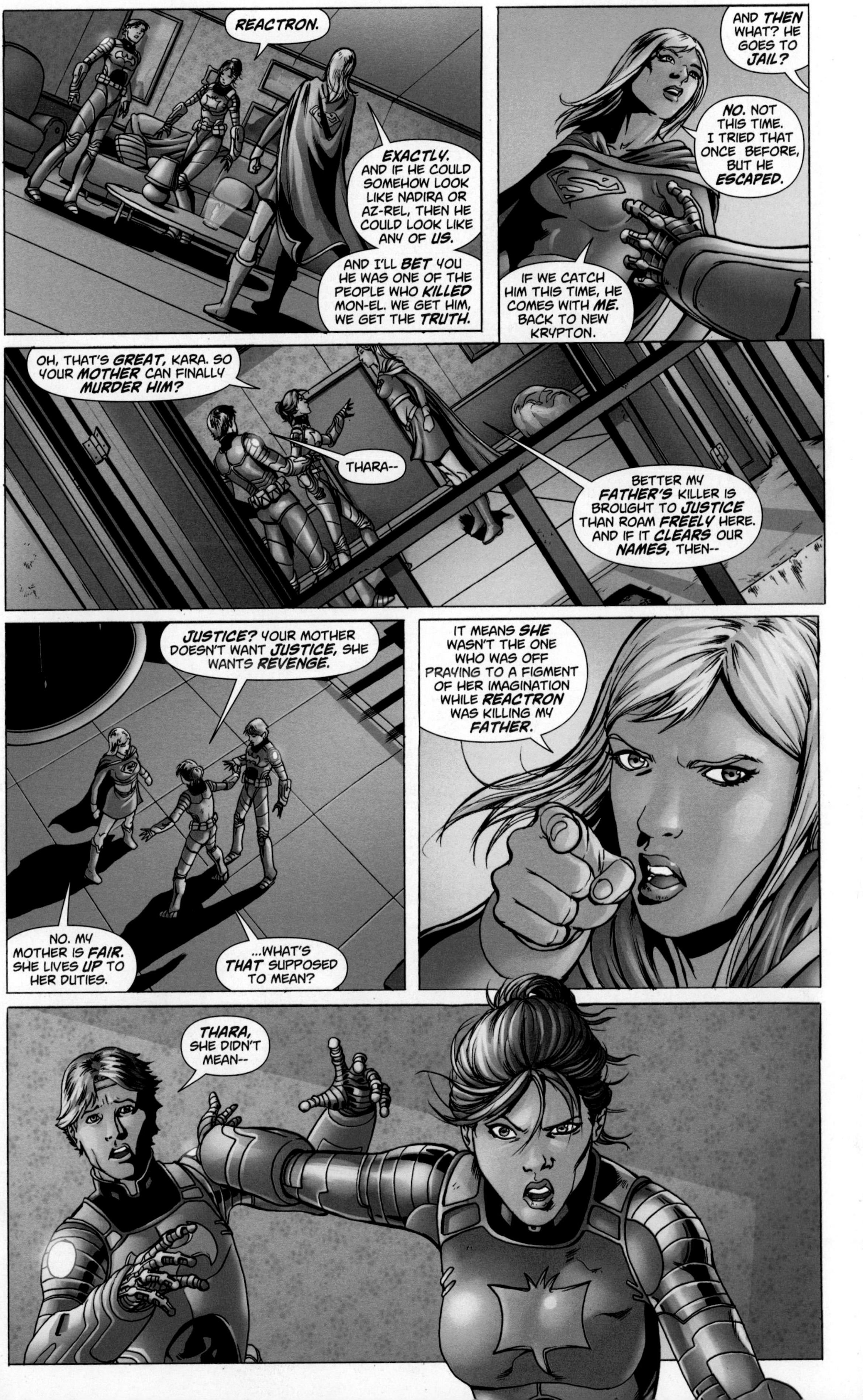

REACTRON.
EXACTLY. AND IF HE COULD SOMEHOW LOOK LIKE NADIRA OR AZ-REL, THEN HE COULD LOOK LIKE ANY OF US.
AND I'LL BET YOU HE WAS ONE OF THE PEOPLE WHO KILLED MON-EL. WE GET HIM, WE GET THE TRUTH.
AND THEN WHAT? HE GOES TO JAIL?
NO. NOT THIS TIME. I TRIED THAT ONCE BEFORE, BUT HE ESCAPED.
IF WE CATCH HIM THIS TIME, HE COMES WITH ME. BACK TO NEW KRYPTON.
OH, THAT'S GREAT, KARA. SO YOUR MOTHER CAN FINALLY MURDER HIM?
THARA--
BETTER MY FATHER'S KILLER IS BROUGHT TO JUSTICE THAN ROAM FREELY HERE. AND IF IT CLEARS OUR NAMES, THEN--
JUSTICE? YOUR MOTHER DOESN'T WANT JUSTICE, SHE WANTS REVENGE.
NO. MY MOTHER IS FAIR. SHE LIVES UP TO HER DUTIES.
...WHAT'S THAT SUPPOSED TO MEAN?
IT MEANS SHE WASN'T THE ONE WHO WAS OFF PRAYING TO A FIGMENT OF HER IMAGINATION WHILE REACTRON WAS KILLING MY FATHER.
THARA, SHE DIDN'T MEAN--

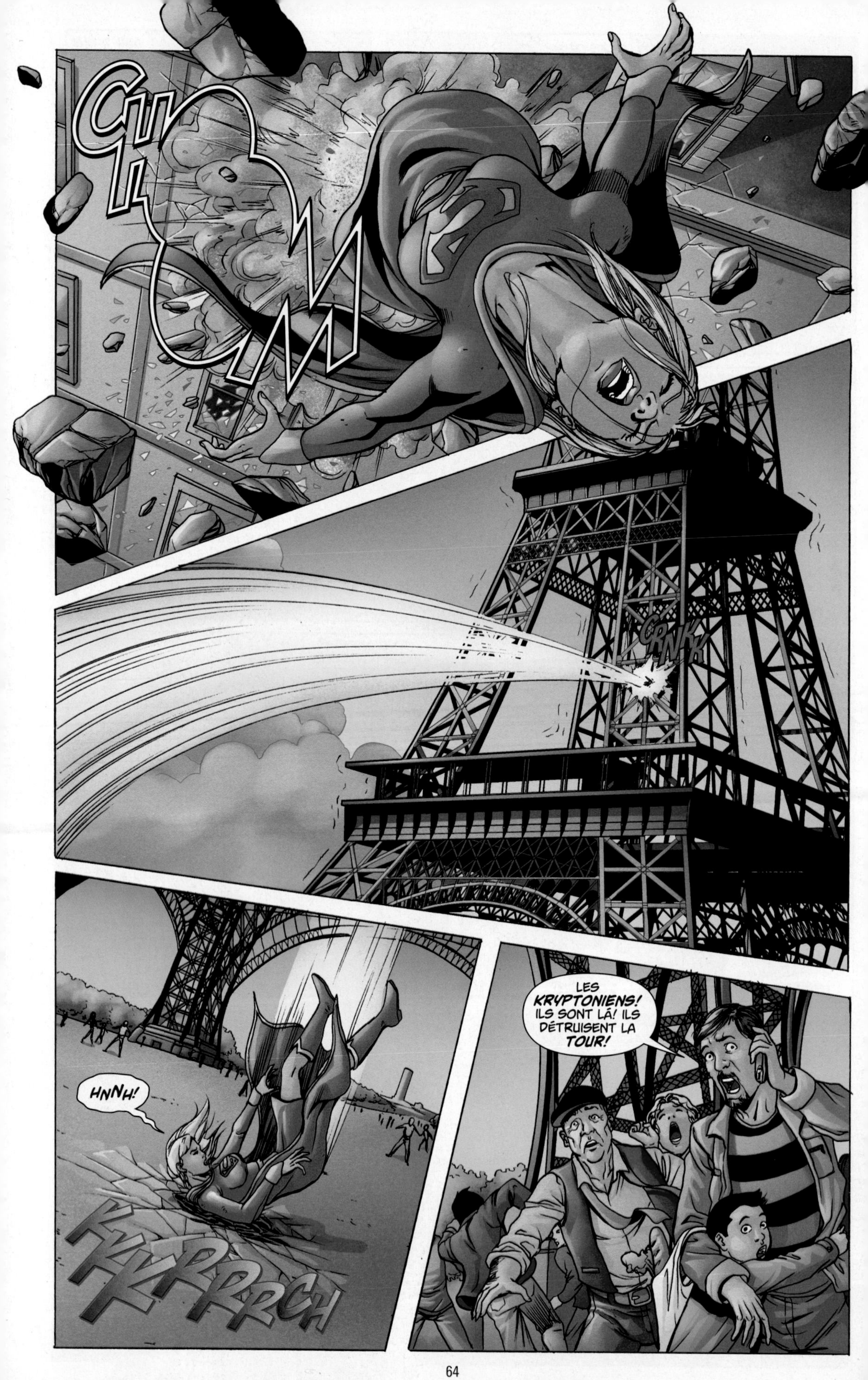
CRNKK
HNNH!
KKRRRCH
LES KRYPTONIENS! ILS SONT LÀ! ILS DÉTRUISENT LA TOUR!

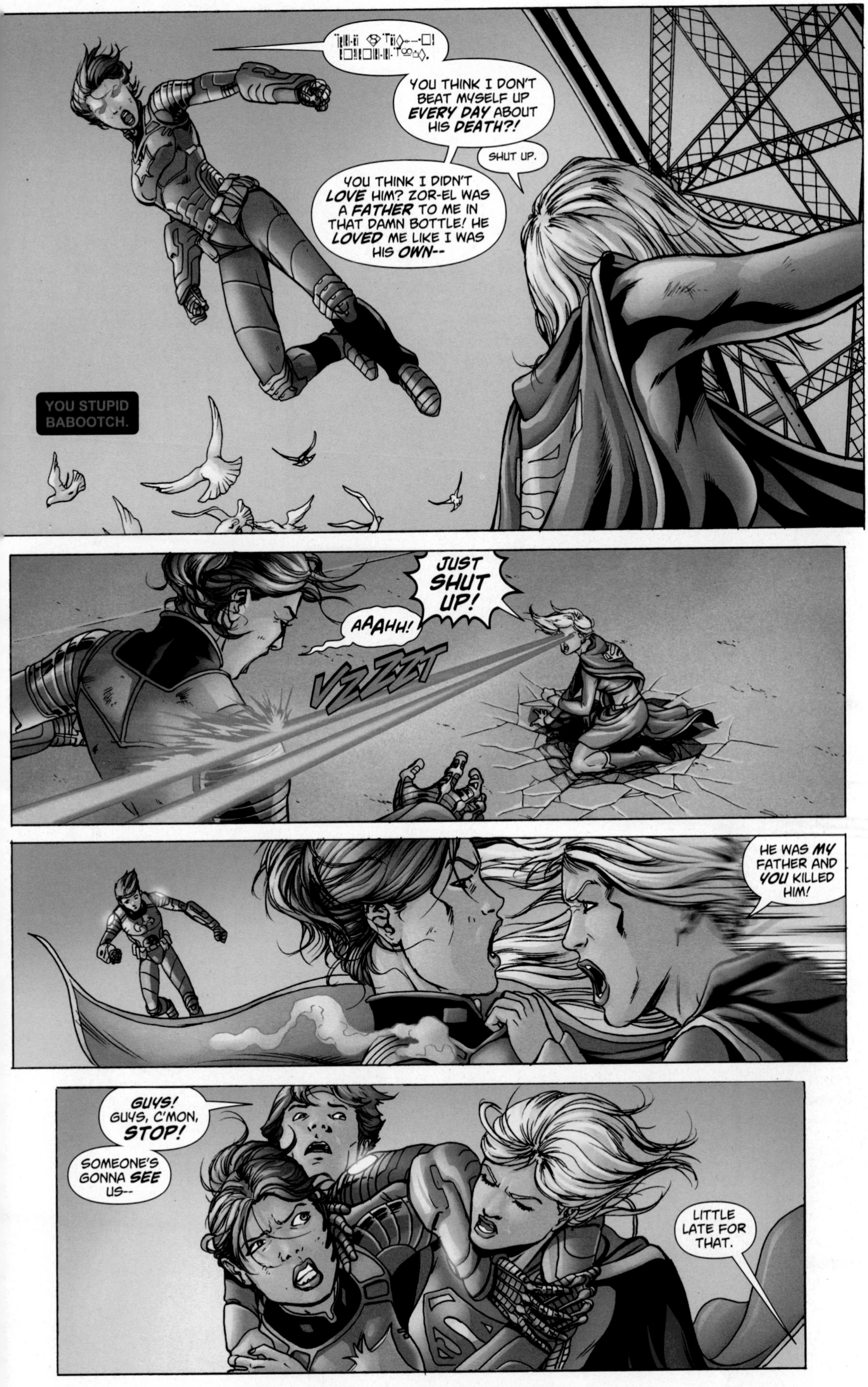
YOU THINK I DON'T BEAT MYSELF UP EVERY DAY ABOUT HIS DEATH?!
SHUT UP.
YOU THINK I DIDN'T LOVE HIM? ZOR-EL WAS A FATHER TO ME IN THAT DAMN BOTTLE! HE LOVED ME LIKE I WAS HIS OWN--
YOU STUPID BABOOTCH.
JUST SHUT UP!
AAAHH!
VZZZT
HE WAS MY FATHER AND YOU KILLED HIM!
GUYS! GUYS, C'MON, STOP!
SOMEONE'S GONNA SEE US--
LITTLE LATE FOR THAT.

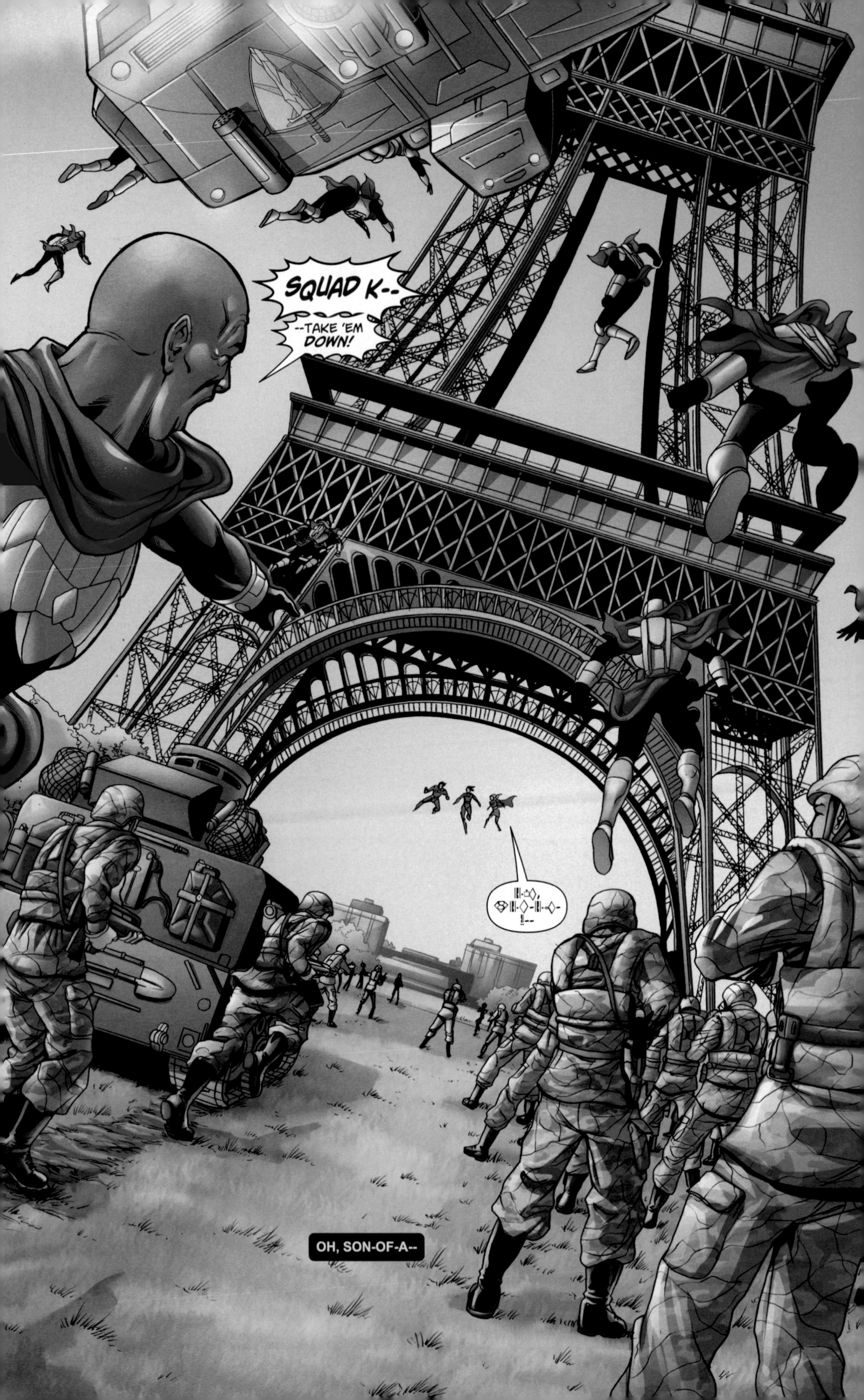
SQUAD K--
--TAKE 'EM DOWN!
OH, SON-OF-A--

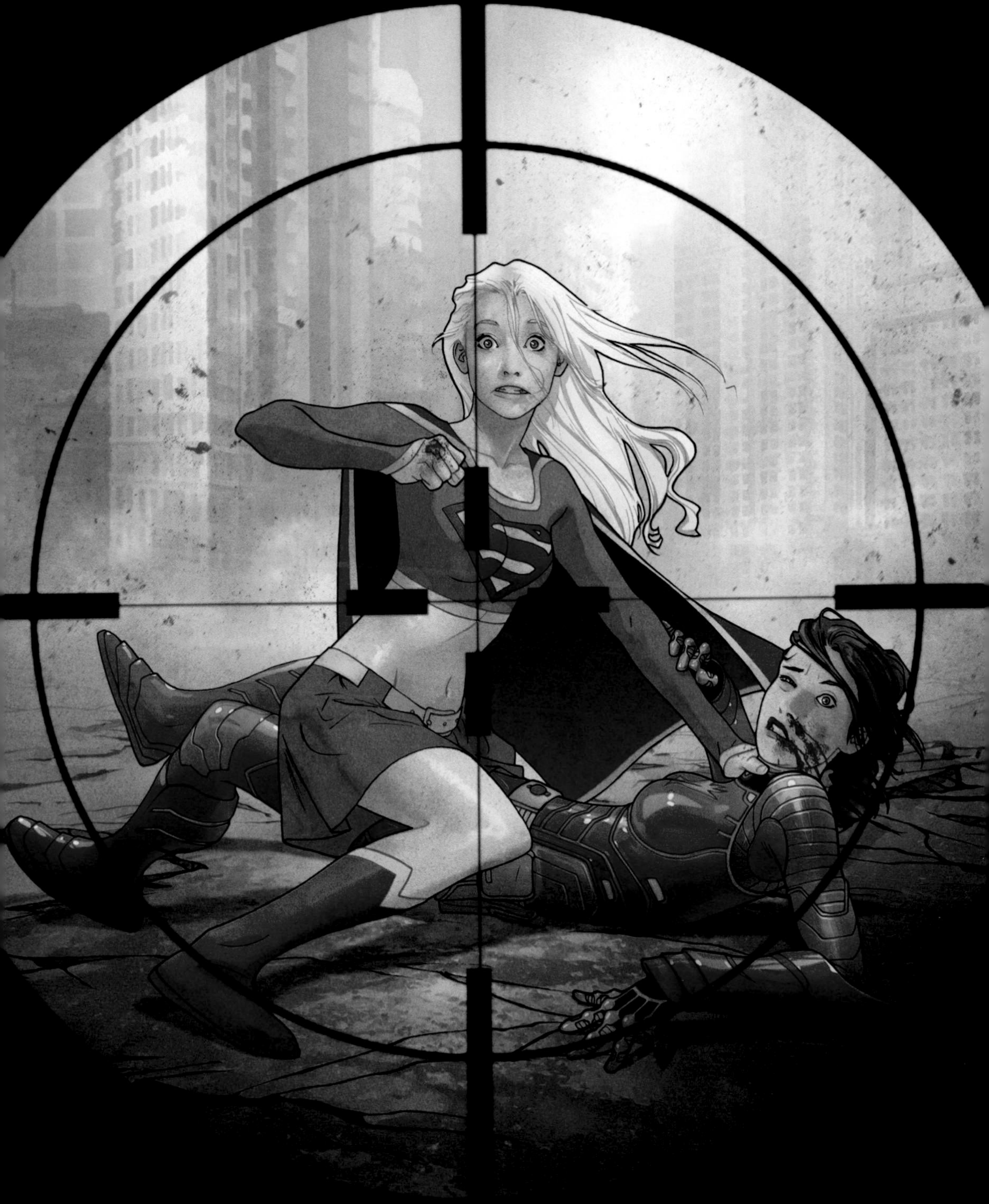

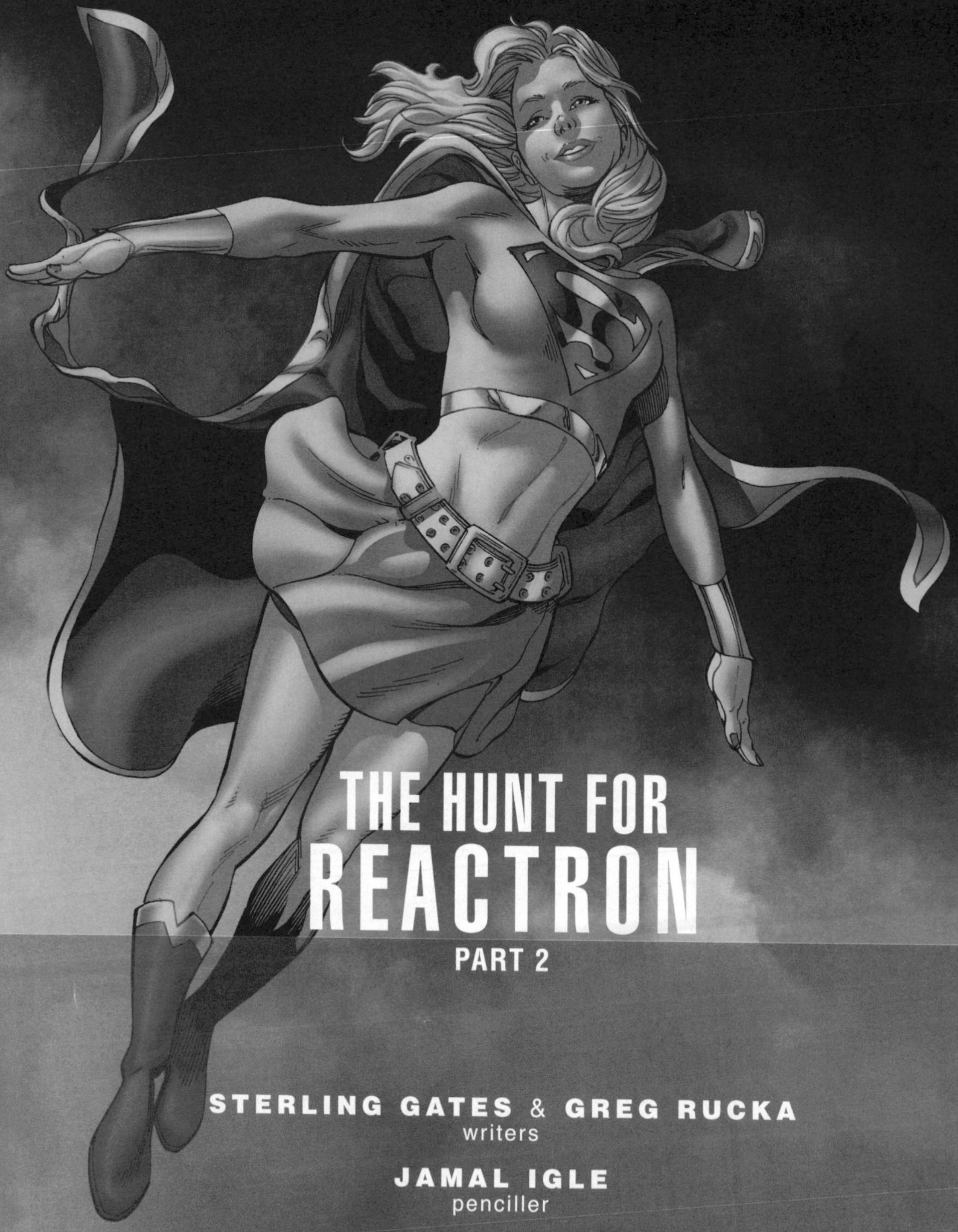

# THE HUNT FOR REACTRON

## PART 2

**STERLING GATES** & **GREG RUCKA**
writers

**JAMAL IGLE**
penciller

**JON SIBAL**
inker

**NEI RUFFINO**
colorist

**JARED K. FLETCHER**
letterer

**JOSHUA MIDDLETON**
cover

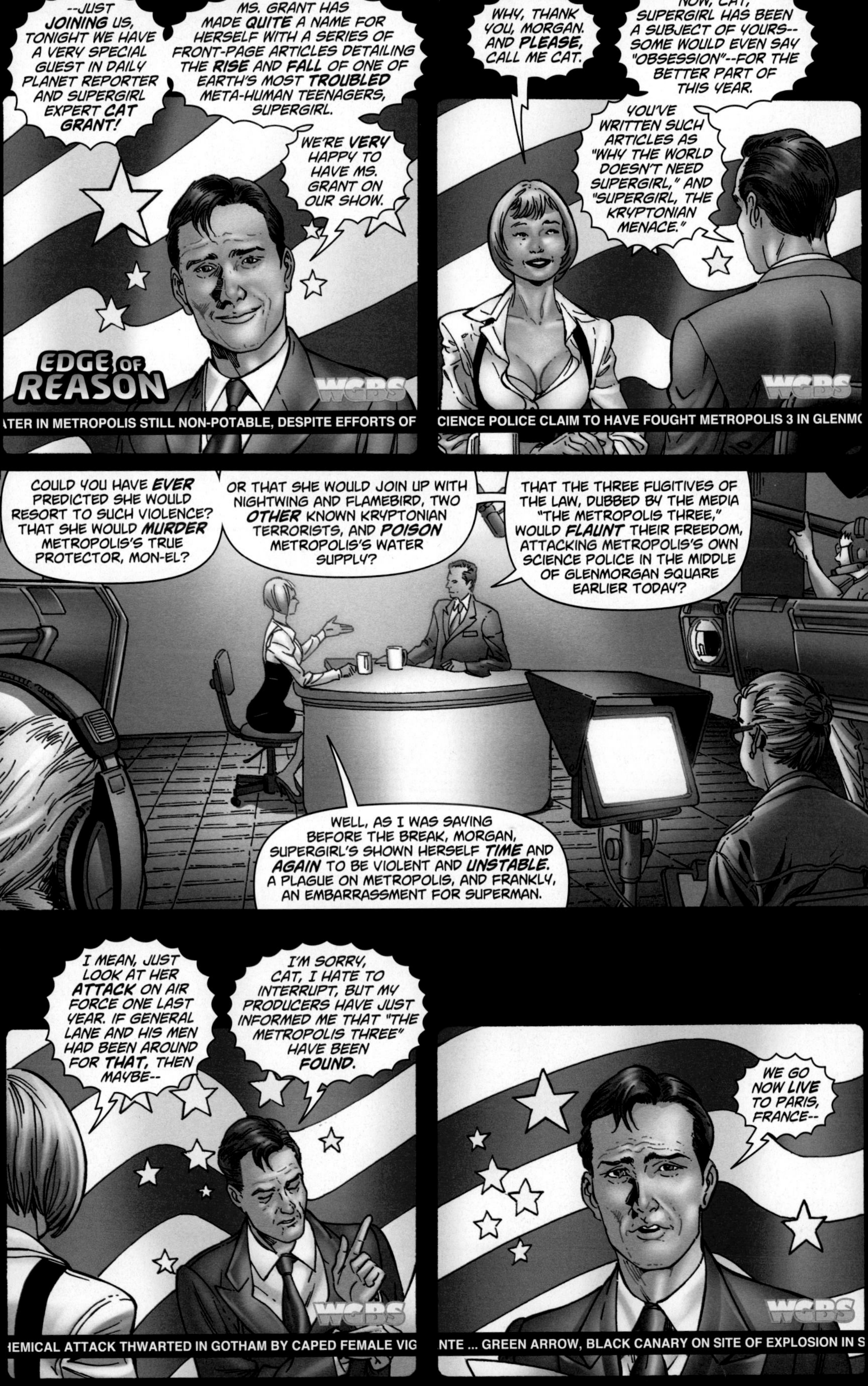

--JUST JOINING US, TONIGHT WE HAVE A VERY SPECIAL GUEST IN DAILY PLANET REPORTER AND SUPERGIRL EXPERT CAT GRANT!
MS. GRANT HAS MADE QUITE A NAME FOR HERSELF WITH A SERIES OF FRONT-PAGE ARTICLES DETAILING THE RISE AND FALL OF ONE OF EARTH'S MOST TROUBLED META-HUMAN TEENAGERS, SUPERGIRL.
WE'RE VERY HAPPY TO HAVE MS. GRANT ON OUR SHOW.
EDGE OF REASON
WGBS
ATER IN METROPOLIS STILL NON-POTABLE, DESPITE EFFORTS OF
WHY, THANK YOU, MORGAN. AND PLEASE, CALL ME CAT.
NOW, CAT, SUPERGIRL HAS BEEN A SUBJECT OF YOURS--SOME WOULD EVEN SAY "OBSESSION"--FOR THE BETTER PART OF THIS YEAR.
YOU'VE WRITTEN SUCH ARTICLES AS "WHY THE WORLD DOESN'T NEED SUPERGIRL," AND "SUPERGIRL, THE KRYPTONIAN MENACE."
WGBS
CIENCE POLICE CLAIM TO HAVE FOUGHT METROPOLIS 3 IN GLENMO
COULD YOU HAVE EVER PREDICTED SHE WOULD RESORT TO SUCH VIOLENCE? THAT SHE WOULD MURDER METROPOLIS'S TRUE PROTECTOR, MON-EL?
OR THAT SHE WOULD JOIN UP WITH NIGHTWING AND FLAMEBIRD, TWO OTHER KNOWN KRYPTONIAN TERRORISTS, AND POISON METROPOLIS'S WATER SUPPLY?
THAT THE THREE FUGITIVES OF THE LAW, DUBBED BY THE MEDIA "THE METROPOLIS THREE," WOULD FLAUNT THEIR FREEDOM, ATTACKING METROPOLIS'S OWN SCIENCE POLICE IN THE MIDDLE OF GLENMORGAN SQUARE EARLIER TODAY?
WELL, AS I WAS SAYING BEFORE THE BREAK, MORGAN, SUPERGIRL'S SHOWN HERSELF TIME AND AGAIN TO BE VIOLENT AND UNSTABLE. A PLAGUE ON METROPOLIS, AND FRANKLY, AN EMBARRASSMENT FOR SUPERMAN.
I MEAN, JUST LOOK AT HER ATTACK ON AIR FORCE ONE LAST YEAR. IF GENERAL LANE AND HIS MEN HAD BEEN AROUND FOR THAT, THEN MAYBE--
I'M SORRY, CAT, I HATE TO INTERRUPT, BUT MY PRODUCERS HAVE JUST INFORMED ME THAT "THE METROPOLIS THREE" HAVE BEEN FOUND.
WGBS
HEMICAL ATTACK THWARTED IN GOTHAM BY CAPED FEMALE VIG
WE GO NOW LIVE TO PARIS, FRANCE--
WGBS
NTE ... GREEN ARROW, BLACK CANARY ON SITE OF EXPLOSION IN S

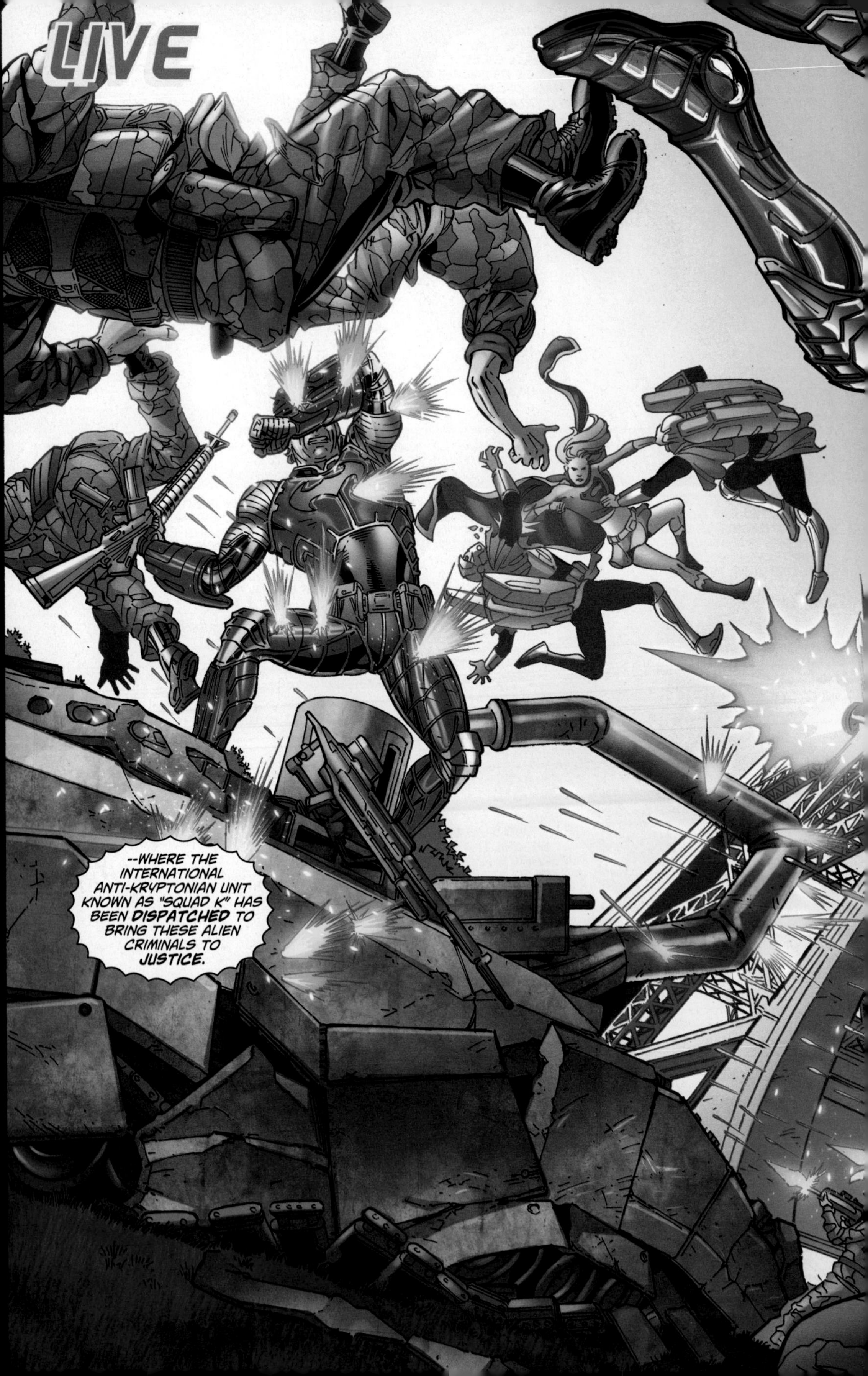
LIVE
--WHERE THE INTERNATIONAL ANTI-KRYPTONIAN UNIT KNOWN AS "SQUAD K" HAS BEEN DISPATCHED TO BRING THESE ALIEN CRIMINALS TO JUSTICE.

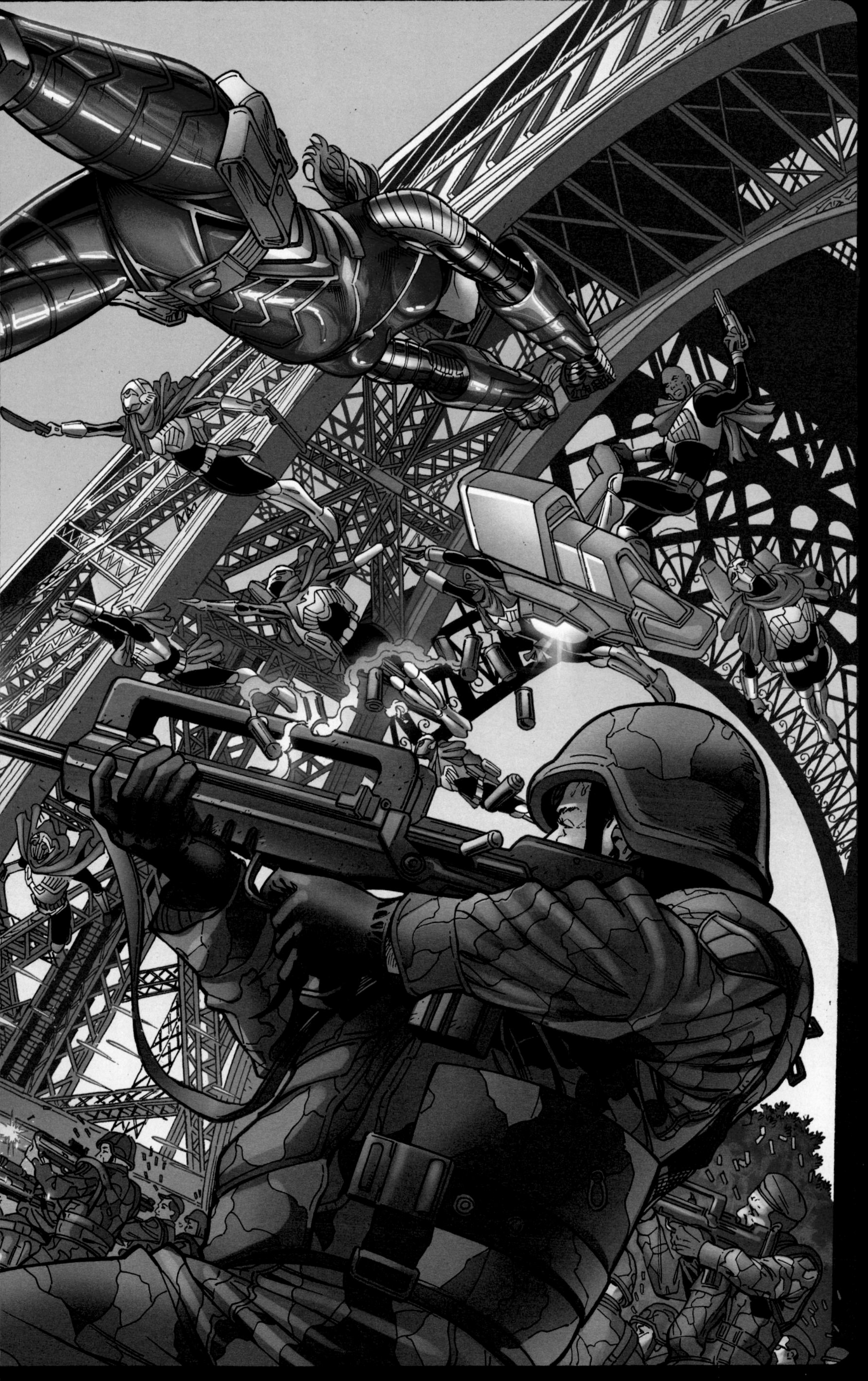

LIVE

CLEARLY A DESPERATE STRUGGLE, CAT...

ARIS. THREAT LEVEL IS: ORANGE. MET 3 BATTLING SQUAD K AT

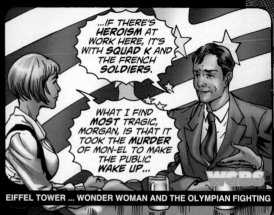

...IF THERE'S HEROISM AT WORK HERE, IT'S WITH SQUAD K AND THE FRENCH SOLDIERS.

WHAT I FIND MOST TRAGIC, MORGAN, IS THAT IT TOOK THE MURDER OF MON-EL TO MAKE THE PUBLIC WAKE UP...

EIFFEL TOWER ... WONDER WOMAN AND THE OLYMPIAN FIGHTING

LIVE

...IT'S KNOWN THAT SUPERGIRL IS THE DAUGHTER OF ALURA ZOR-EL, THE RULER-- OR SHOULD WE SAY QUEEN?--OF NEW KRYPTON.

THAT'S CORRECT, MORGAN. WHICH GOES TO WHAT I'VE BEEN SAYING...

...THAT SUPERGIRL, PERHAPS MORE THAN ANY OTHER KRYPTONIAN, IS AN ENEMY OF EARTH...

CEPTED OFFER OF NATO SUPPORT. BBC REPORTS THREE FIGHTER SQUADRONS

LIVE

SQUAD K SEEMS TO BE HOLDING THEIR OWN FOR THE MOMENT...

...AND I'M FRANKLY TERRIFIED BY WHAT THEY'LL DO TO US NEXT IF THEY CAN'T BE STOPPED.

MOBILIZING AT THE BORDER. GEN. LANE, "UNBRIDLED FAITH IN SQUAD K." PRESI

LIVE

...THOUGH THE MILITARY FORCES SEEM LESS--

DENT CONFIRMS FBI TO PURSUE

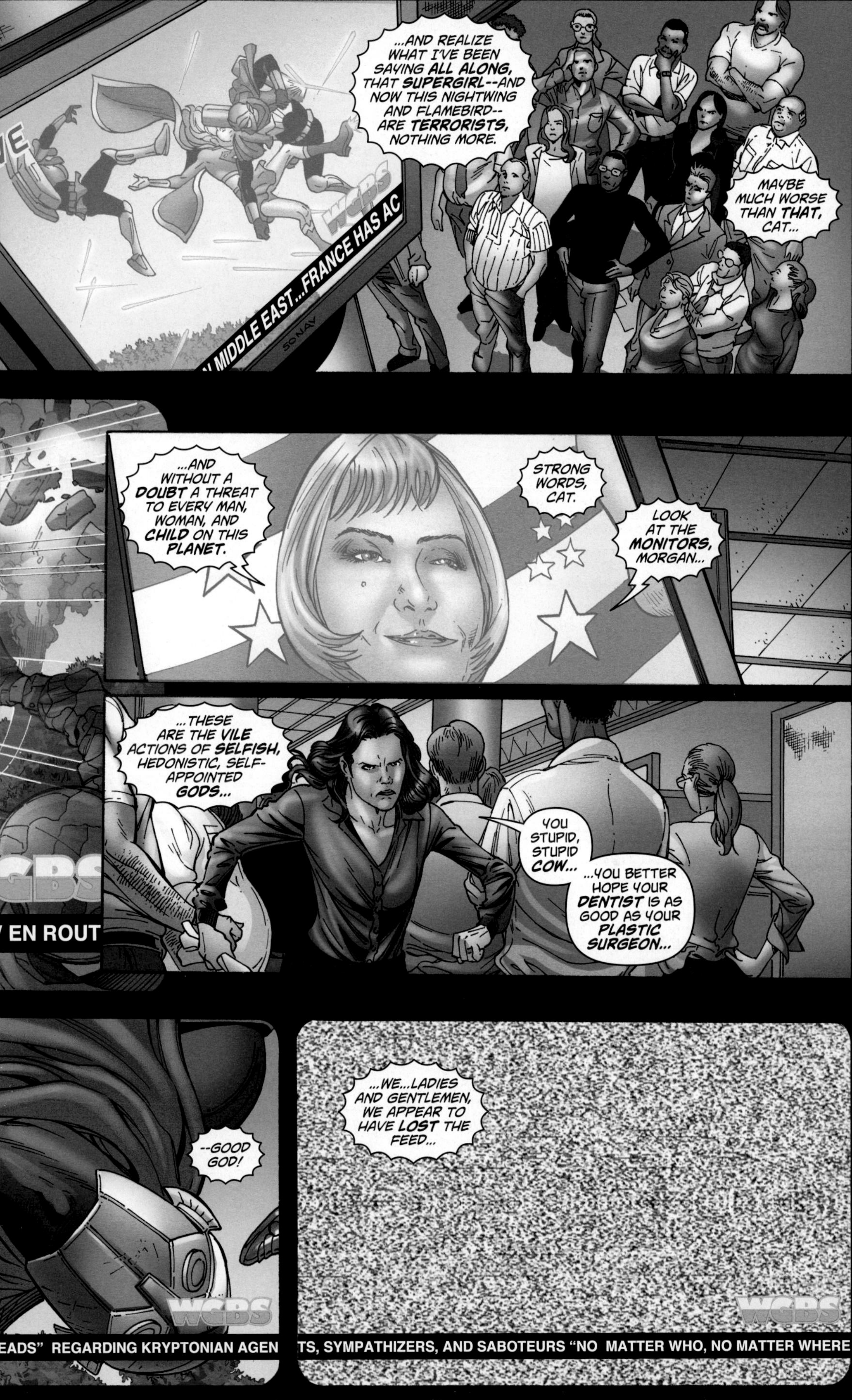

...AND REALIZE WHAT I'VE BEEN SAYING ALL ALONG, THAT SUPERGIRL--AND NOW THIS NIGHTWING AND FLAMEBIRD--ARE TERRORISTS, NOTHING MORE.
WGBS
MIDDLE EAST...FRANCE HAS AC
MAYBE MUCH WORSE THAN THAT, CAT...
...AND WITHOUT A DOUBT A THREAT TO EVERY MAN, WOMAN, AND CHILD ON THIS PLANET.
STRONG WORDS, CAT.
LOOK AT THE MONITORS, MORGAN...
...THESE ARE THE VILE ACTIONS OF SELFISH, HEDONISTIC, SELF-APPOINTED GODS...
WGBS
EN ROUT
YOU STUPID, STUPID COW...
...YOU BETTER HOPE YOUR DENTIST IS AS GOOD AS YOUR PLASTIC SURGEON...
--GOOD GOD!
WGBS
EADS" REGARDING KRYPTONIAN AGEN
...WE...LADIES AND GENTLEMEN, WE APPEAR TO HAVE LOST THE FEED...
WGBS
TS, SYMPATHIZERS, AND SABOTEURS "NO MATTER WHO, NO MATTER WHERE

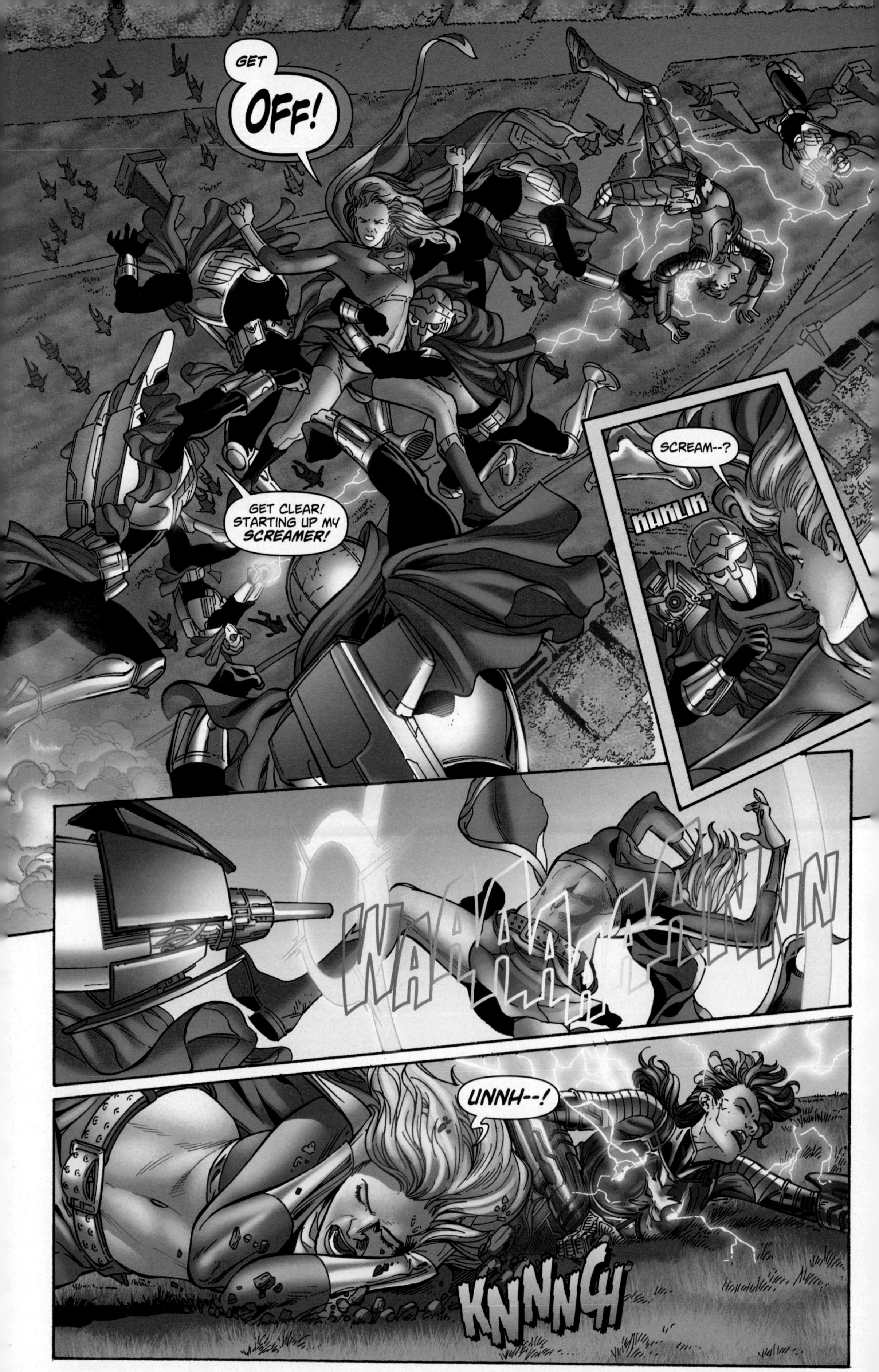
GET OFF!
GET CLEAR! STARTING UP MY SCREAMER!
SCREAM--?
KAKLIK
UNNH--!
KNNNGH

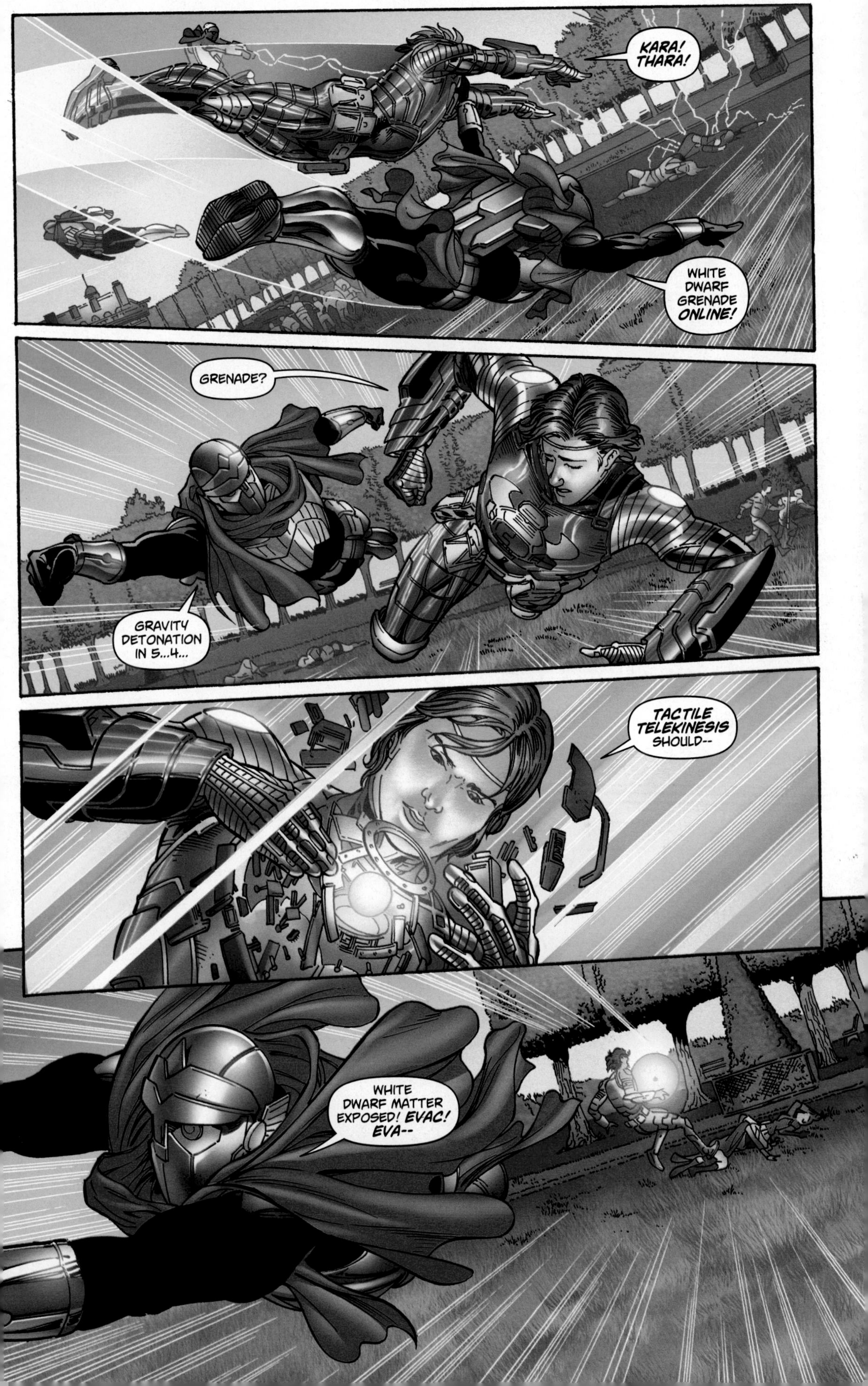
KARA! THARA!
WHITE DWARF GRENADE ONLINE!
GRENADE?
GRAVITY DETONATION IN 5...4...
TACTILE TELEKINESIS SHOULD--
WHITE DWARF MATTER EXPOSED! EVAC! EVA--

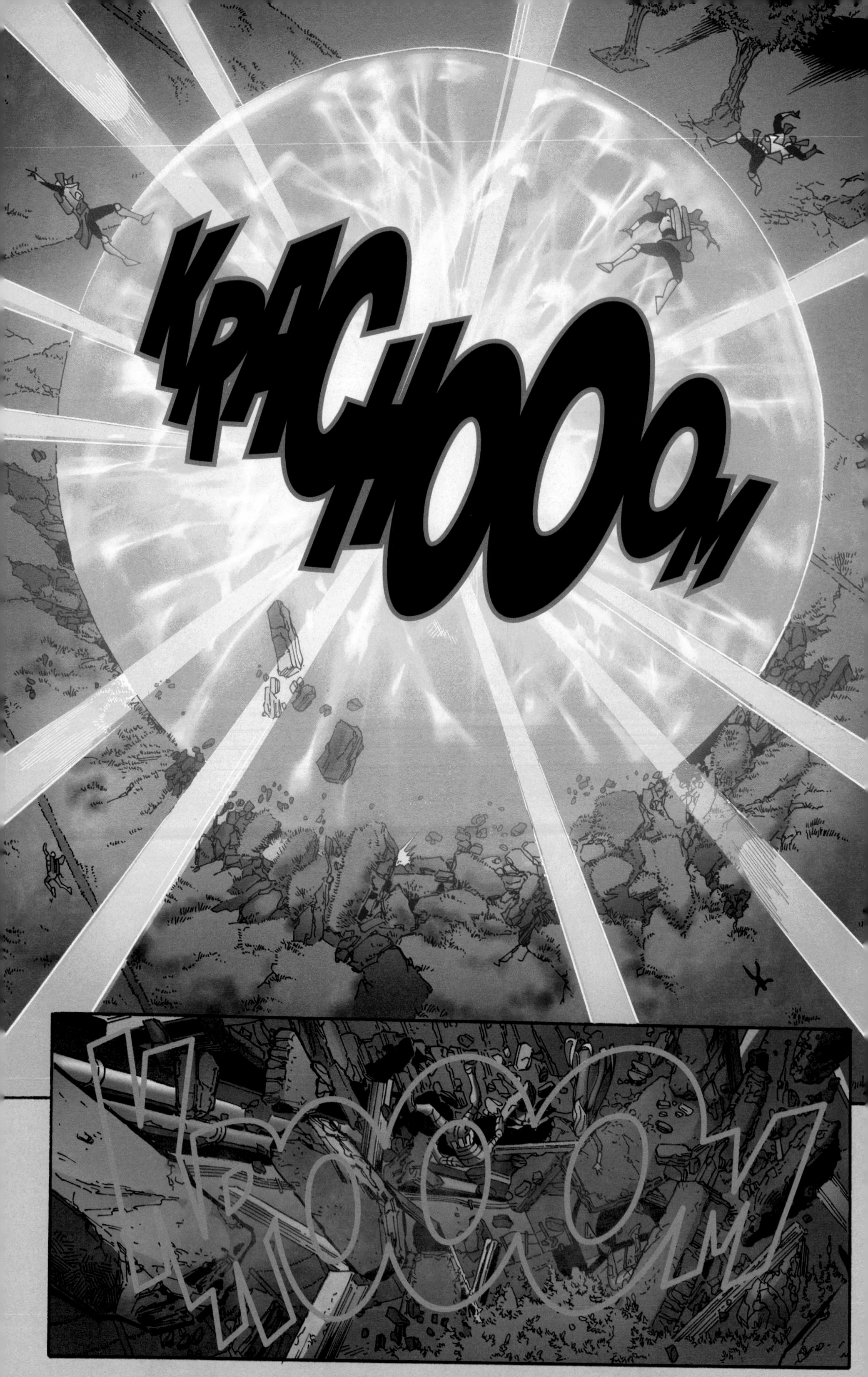
KRACHOOOM
VROOOM

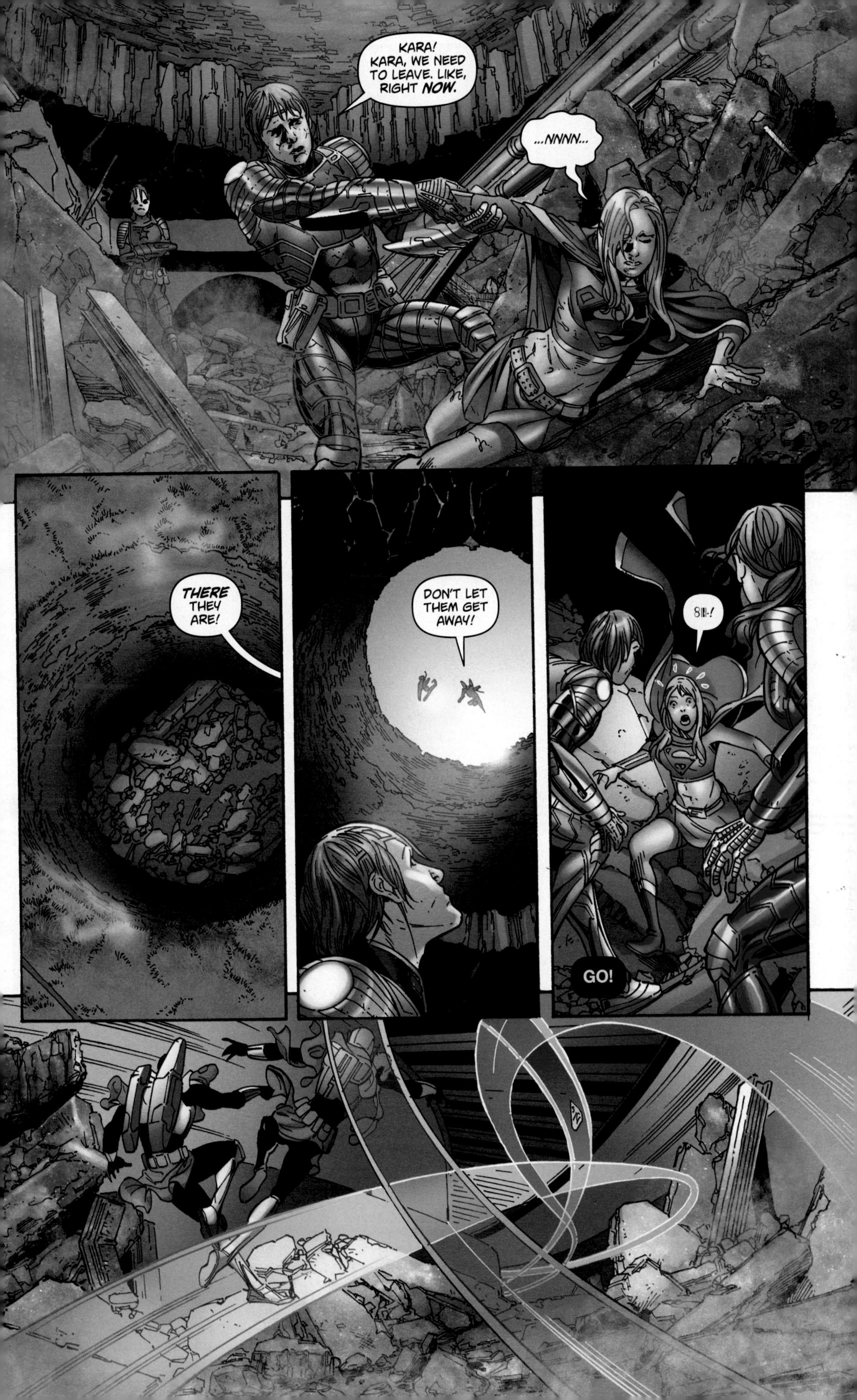
KARA! KARA, WE NEED TO LEAVE. LIKE, RIGHT **NOW**.
...NNNN...
*THERE* THEY ARE!
DON'T LET THEM GET AWAY!
GO!

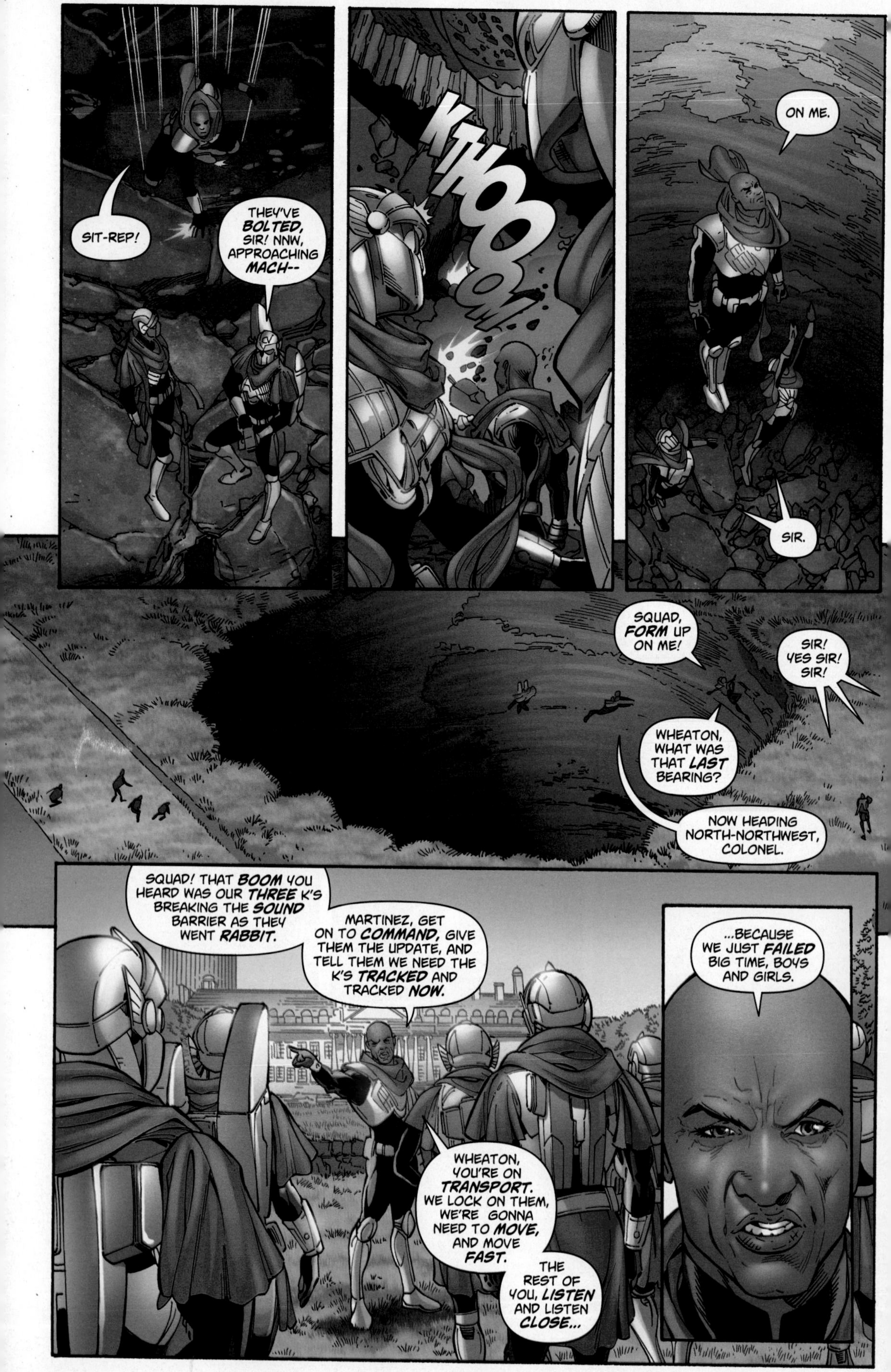
SIT-REP!
THEY'VE BOLTED, SIR! NNW, APPROACHING MACH--
KTHOOOOM!
ON ME.
SIR.
SQUAD, FORM UP ON ME!
SIR! YES SIR! SIR!
WHEATON, WHAT WAS THAT LAST BEARING?
NOW HEADING NORTH-NORTHWEST, COLONEL.
SQUAD! THAT BOOM YOU HEARD WAS OUR THREE K'S BREAKING THE SOUND BARRIER AS THEY WENT RABBIT.
MARTINEZ, GET ON TO COMMAND, GIVE THEM THE UPDATE, AND TELL THEM WE NEED THE K'S TRACKED AND TRACKED NOW.
WHEATON, YOU'RE ON TRANSPORT. WE LOCK ON THEM, WE'RE GONNA NEED TO MOVE, AND MOVE FAST.
THE REST OF YOU, LISTEN AND LISTEN CLOSE...
...BECAUSE WE JUST FAILED BIG TIME, BOYS AND GIRLS.

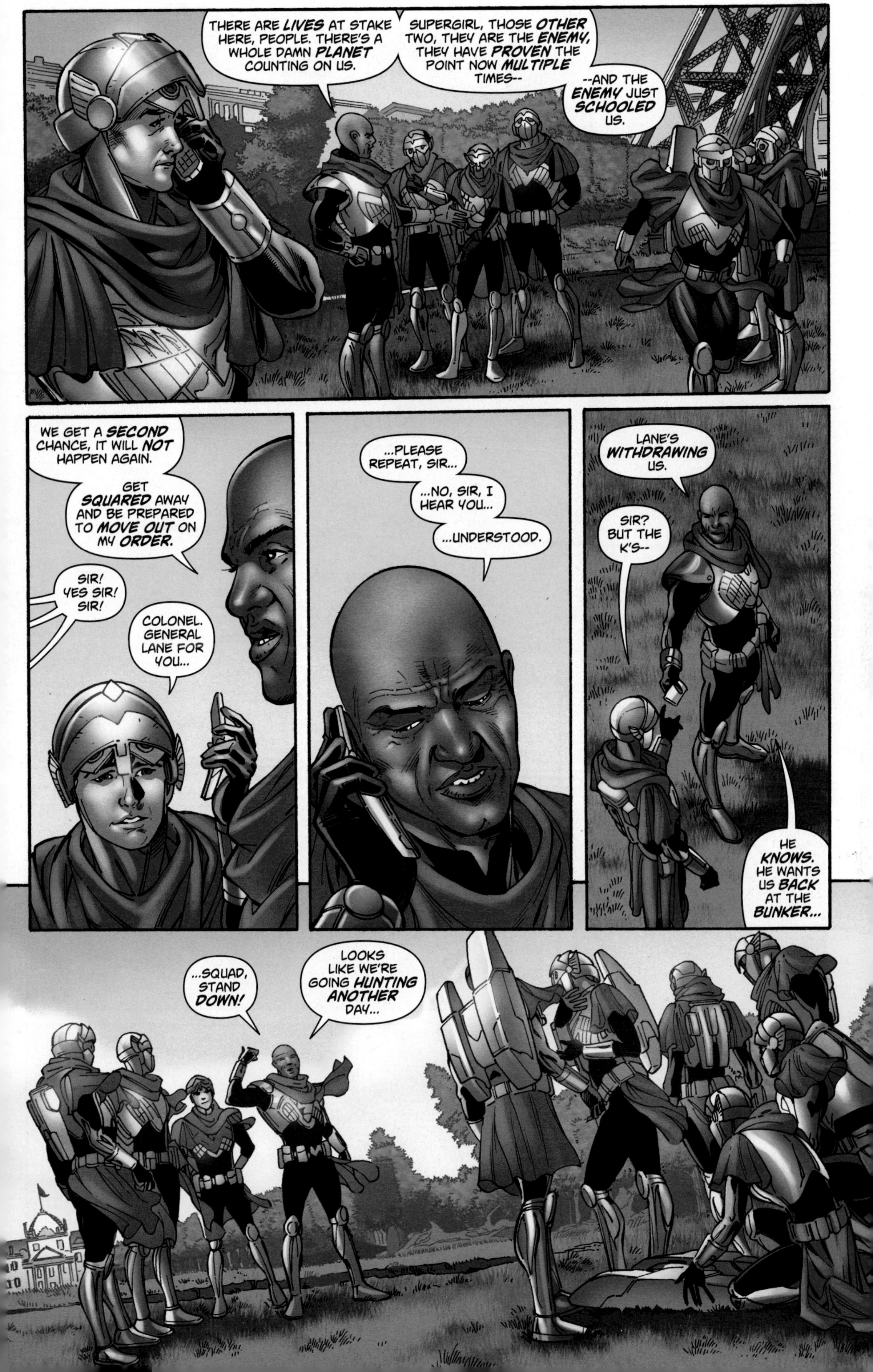
THERE ARE LIVES AT STAKE HERE, PEOPLE. THERE'S A WHOLE DAMN PLANET COUNTING ON US.
SUPERGIRL, THOSE OTHER TWO, THEY ARE THE ENEMY, THEY HAVE PROVEN THE POINT NOW MULTIPLE TIMES--
--AND THE ENEMY JUST SCHOOLED US.
WE GET A SECOND CHANCE, IT WILL NOT HAPPEN AGAIN.
GET SQUARED AWAY AND BE PREPARED TO MOVE OUT ON MY ORDER.
SIR! YES SIR! SIR!
COLONEL. GENERAL LANE FOR YOU...
...PLEASE REPEAT, SIR...
...NO, SIR, I HEAR YOU...
...UNDERSTOOD.
LANE'S WITHDRAWING US.
SIR? BUT THE K'S--
HE KNOWS. HE WANTS US BACK AT THE BUNKER...
...SQUAD, STAND DOWN!
LOOKS LIKE WE'RE GOING HUNTING ANOTHER DAY...

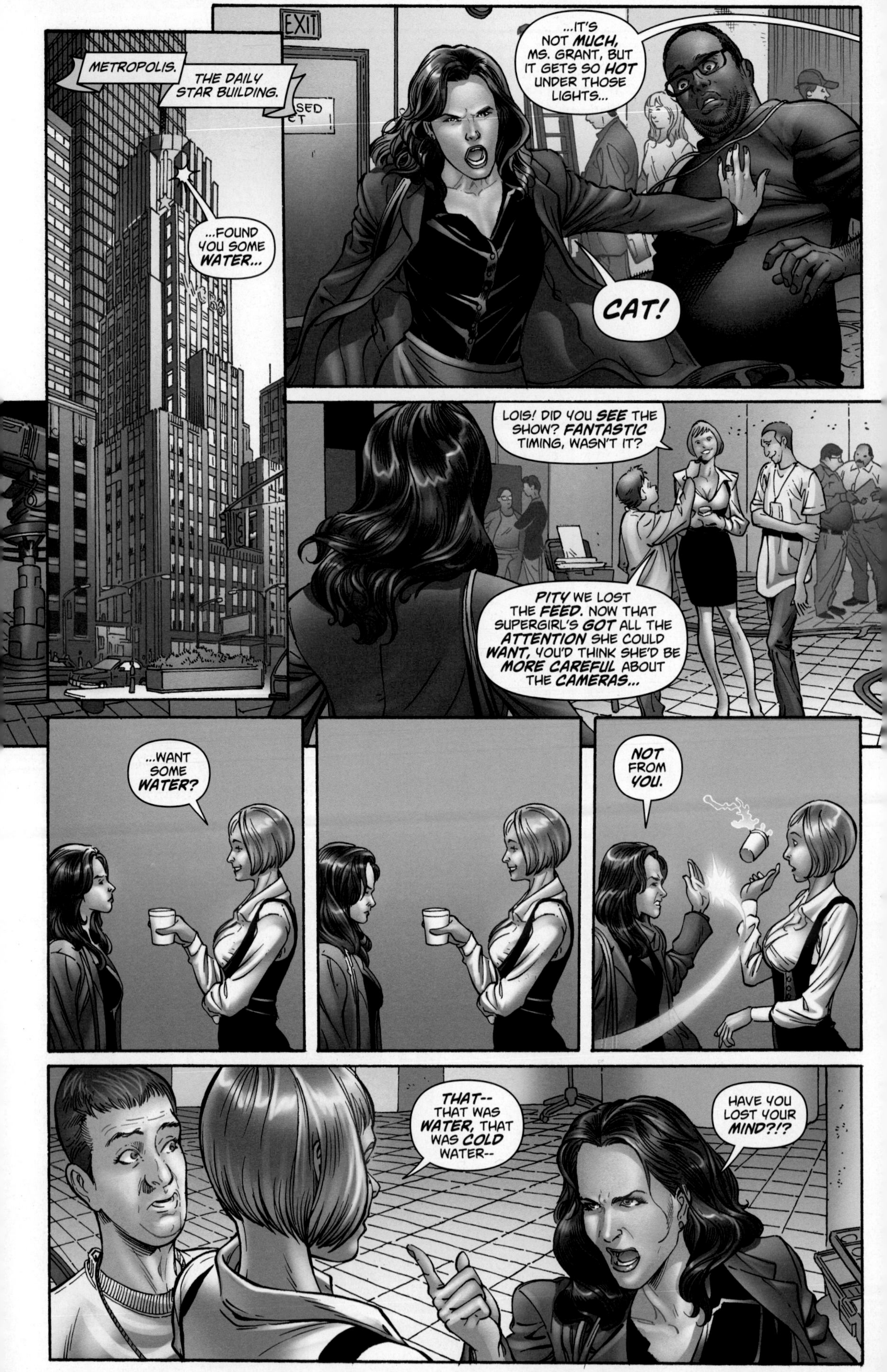
METROPOLIS.
THE DAILY STAR BUILDING.
...FOUND YOU SOME WATER...
...IT'S NOT MUCH, MS. GRANT, BUT IT GETS SO HOT UNDER THOSE LIGHTS...
CAT!
LOIS! DID YOU SEE THE SHOW? FANTASTIC TIMING, WASN'T IT?
PITY WE LOST THE FEED. NOW THAT SUPERGIRL'S GOT ALL THE ATTENTION SHE COULD WANT, YOU'D THINK SHE'D BE MORE CAREFUL ABOUT THE CAMERAS...
...WANT SOME WATER?
NOT FROM YOU.
THAT-- THAT WAS WATER, THAT WAS COLD WATER--
HAVE YOU LOST YOUR MIND?!?

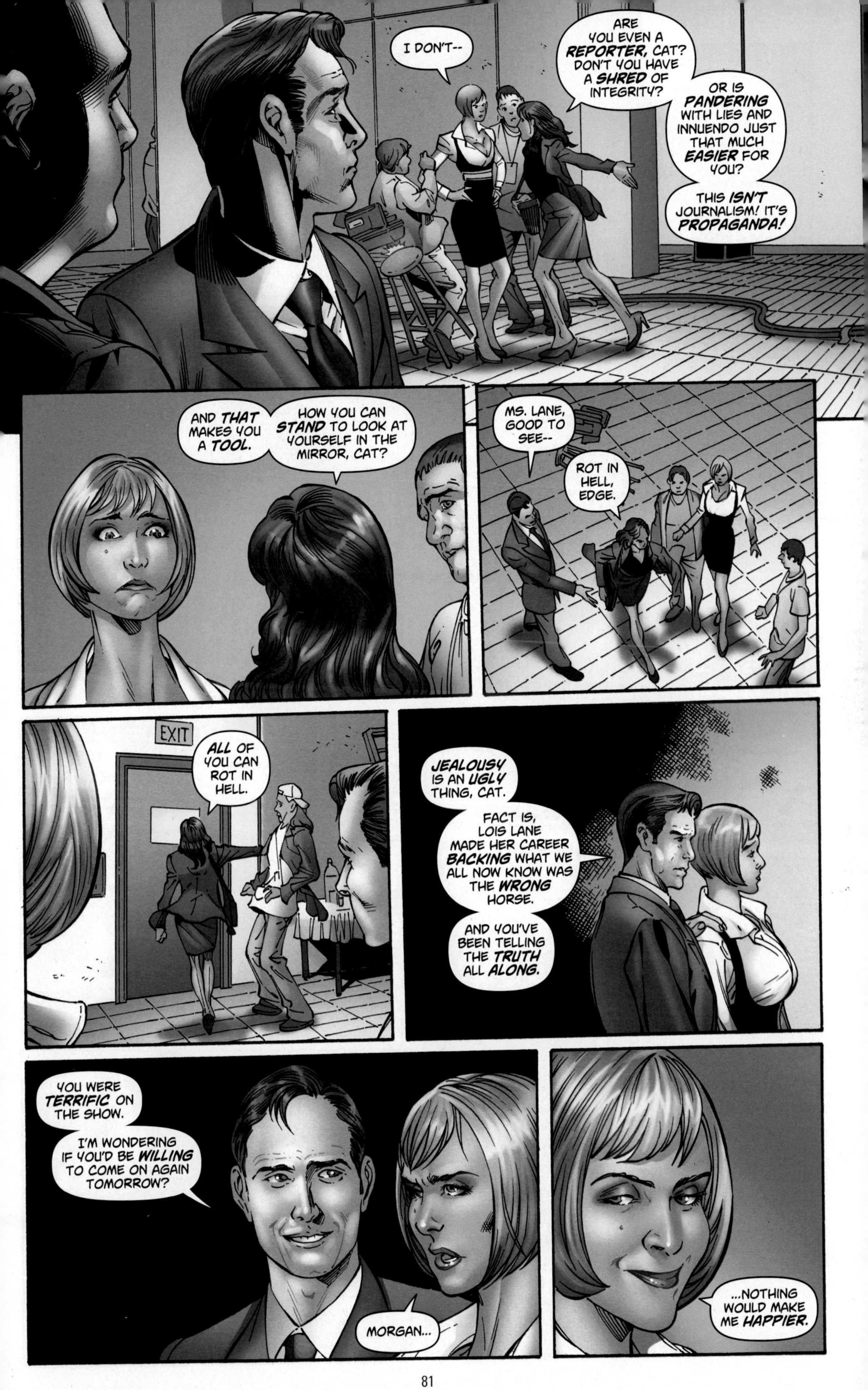
I DON'T--
ARE YOU EVEN A REPORTER, CAT? DON'T YOU HAVE A SHRED OF INTEGRITY?
OR IS PANDERING WITH LIES AND INNUENDO JUST THAT MUCH EASIER FOR YOU?
THIS ISN'T JOURNALISM! IT'S PROPAGANDA!
HOW YOU CAN STAND TO LOOK AT YOURSELF IN THE MIRROR, CAT?
AND THAT MAKES YOU A TOOL.
MS. LANE, GOOD TO SEE--
ROT IN HELL, EDGE.
EXIT
ALL OF YOU CAN ROT IN HELL.
JEALOUSY IS AN UGLY THING, CAT.
FACT IS, LOIS LANE MADE HER CAREER BACKING WHAT WE ALL NOW KNOW WAS THE WRONG HORSE.
AND YOU'VE BEEN TELLING THE TRUTH ALL ALONG.
YOU WERE TERRIFIC ON THE SHOW.
I'M WONDERING IF YOU'D BE WILLING TO COME ON AGAIN TOMORROW?
MORGAN...
...NOTHING WOULD MAKE ME HAPPIER.

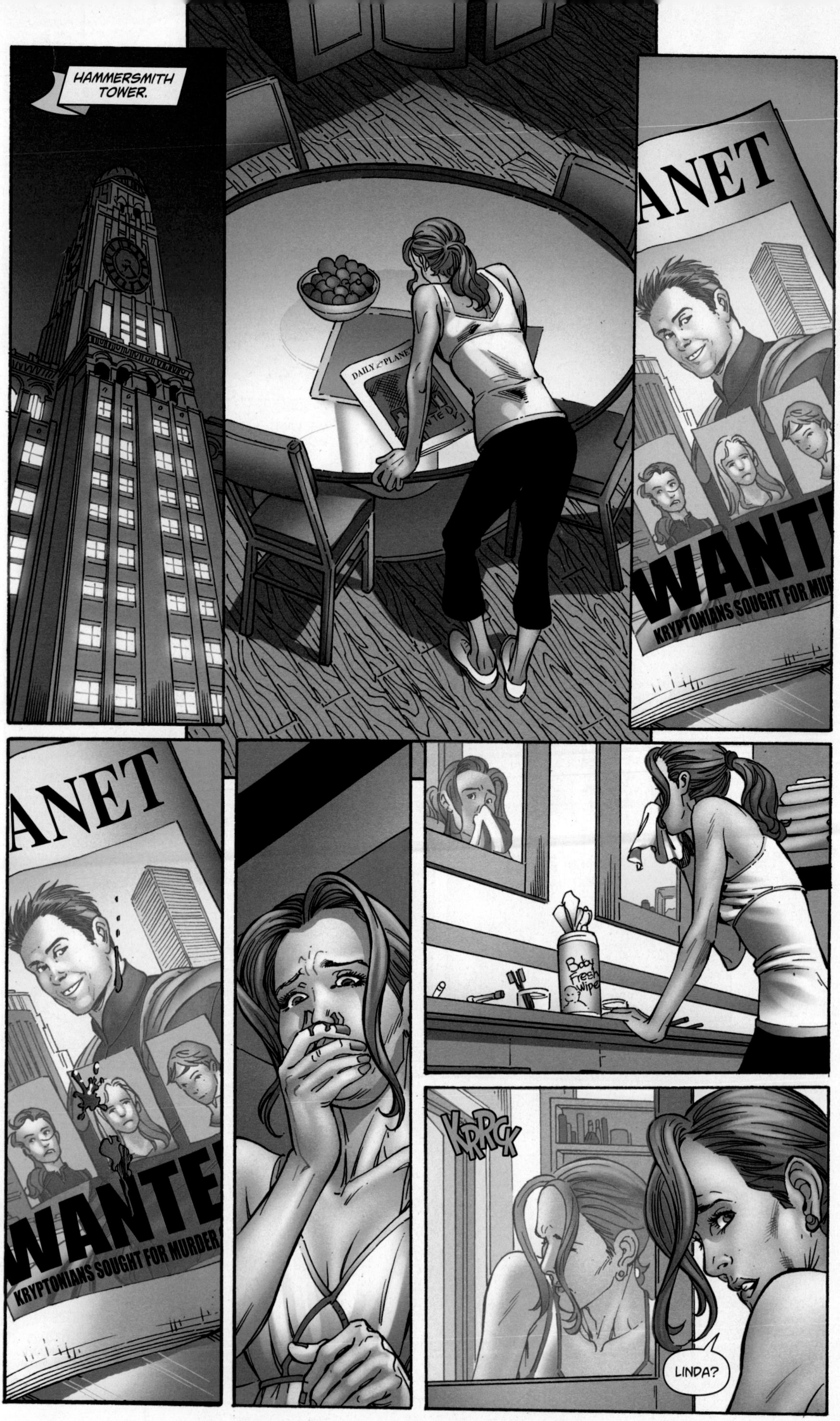
HAMMERSMITH TOWER.
DAILY PLANET
ANET
WANTE
KRYPTONIANS SOUGHT FOR MU
ANET
WANTE
KRYPTONIANS SOUGHT FOR MURDER
Baby Fresh Wipes
KRRCK
LINDA?

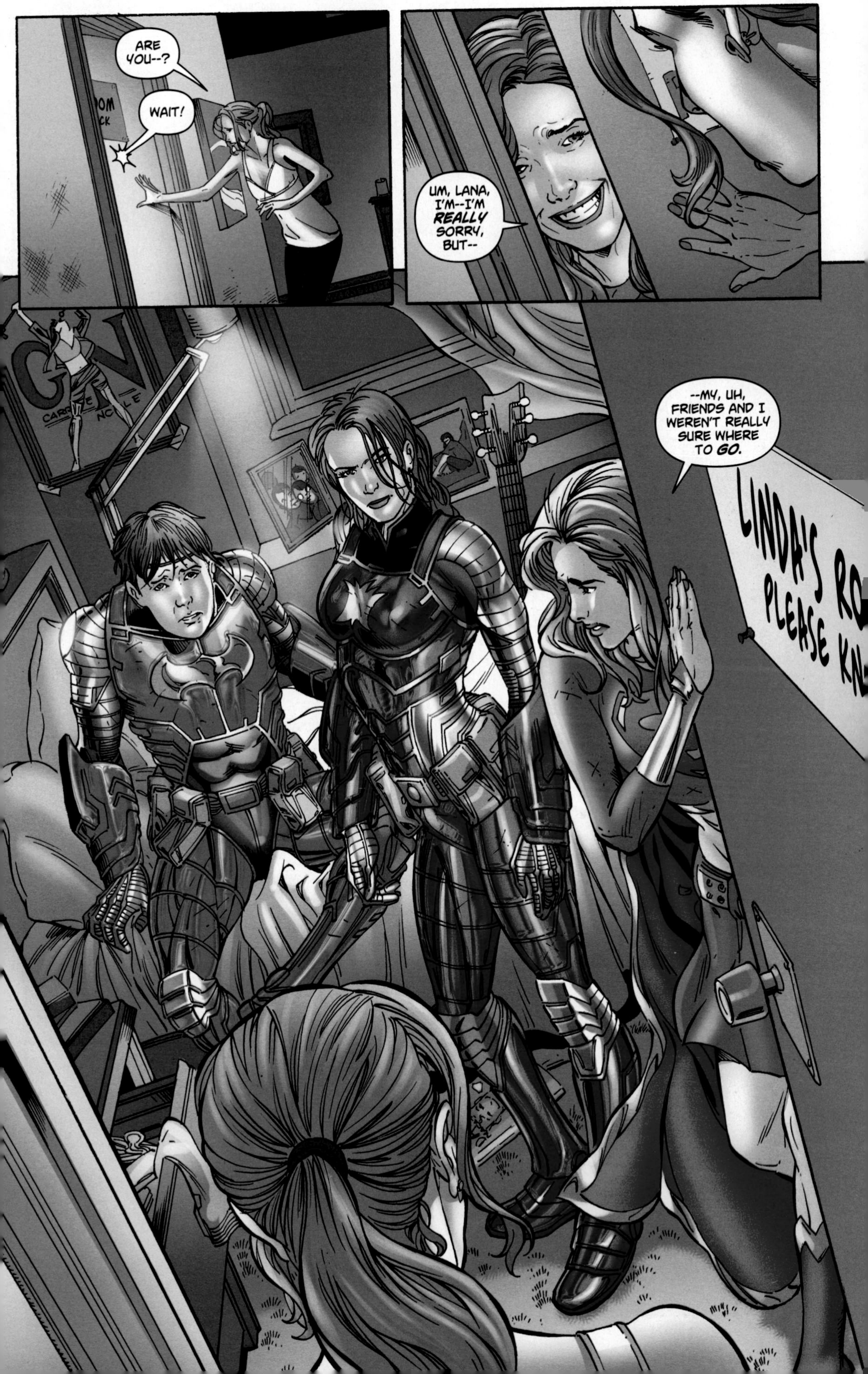
ARE YOU--?
WAIT!
ROOM
KNOCK
UM, LANA, I'M--I'M REALLY SORRY, BUT--
--MY, UH, FRIENDS AND I WEREN'T REALLY SURE WHERE TO GO.
LINDA'S RO
PLEASE KN

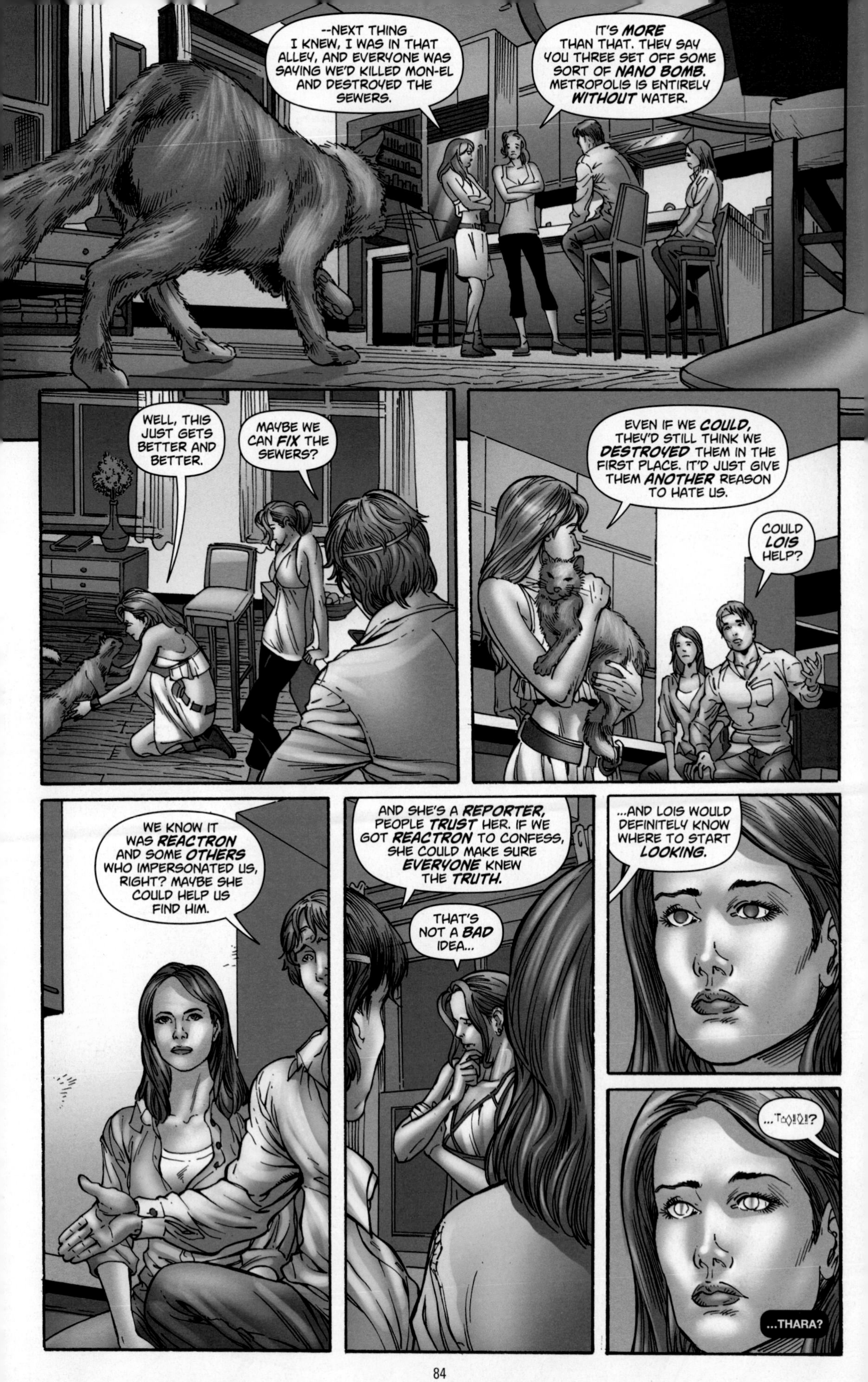
--NEXT THING I KNEW, I WAS IN THAT ALLEY, AND EVERYONE WAS SAYING WE'D KILLED MON-EL AND DESTROYED THE SEWERS.
IT'S MORE THAN THAT. THEY SAY YOU THREE SET OFF SOME SORT OF NANO BOMB. METROPOLIS IS ENTIRELY WITHOUT WATER.
WELL, THIS JUST GETS BETTER AND BETTER.
MAYBE WE CAN FIX THE SEWERS?
EVEN IF WE COULD, THEY'D STILL THINK WE DESTROYED THEM IN THE FIRST PLACE. IT'D JUST GIVE THEM ANOTHER REASON TO HATE US.
COULD LOIS HELP?
WE KNOW IT WAS REACTRON AND SOME OTHERS WHO IMPERSONATED US, RIGHT? MAYBE SHE COULD HELP US FIND HIM.
AND SHE'S A REPORTER, PEOPLE TRUST HER. IF WE GOT REACTRON TO CONFESS, SHE COULD MAKE SURE EVERYONE KNEW THE TRUTH.
THAT'S NOT A BAD IDEA...
...AND LOIS WOULD DEFINITELY KNOW WHERE TO START LOOKING.
...THARA?

◇◎▣!!T?

'▣▩◦! ▣◈◎!T?

WHAT?

YOU OKAY?

◇▣◎.

'T◇◇▣◇*'◇
▩▣◎◇◇◦T◇◇◇◦8
◦◇▣◎◇8 ◦◦◦◦T◇◇
◇2◦◇▢◦◎.

NO.
THERE'S SOMETHING *WRONG* WITH KARA'S FRIEND.

YOU *PROBABLY* HAVEN'T HEARD--

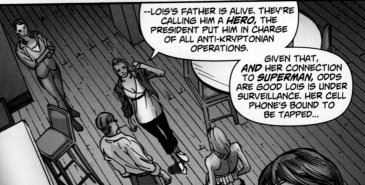

--LOIS'S FATHER IS ALIVE. THEY'RE CALLING HIM A *HERO*, THE PRESIDENT PUT HIM IN CHARGE OF ALL ANTI-KRYPTONIAN OPERATIONS.

GIVEN THAT, *AND* HER CONNECTION TO *SUPERMAN*, ODDS ARE GOOD LOIS IS UNDER SURVEILLANCE. HER CELL PHONE'S BOUND TO BE TAPPED...

...SO WE'RE GONNA HAVE TO BE SNEAKY ABOUT TALKING TO HER.

KARA, THARA, STAY HERE. TWO OF US APPROACHING HER WILL RAISE *LESS* SUSPICION THAN *FOUR*.

CHRIS, I'D LOSE THAT HEADBAND BEFORE WE GET DOWNSTAIRS.

AND HONEY, I LIKE THIS APARTMENT. *TRY* TO GET ALONG WITH HER.

WE'LL BE BACK SHORTLY.

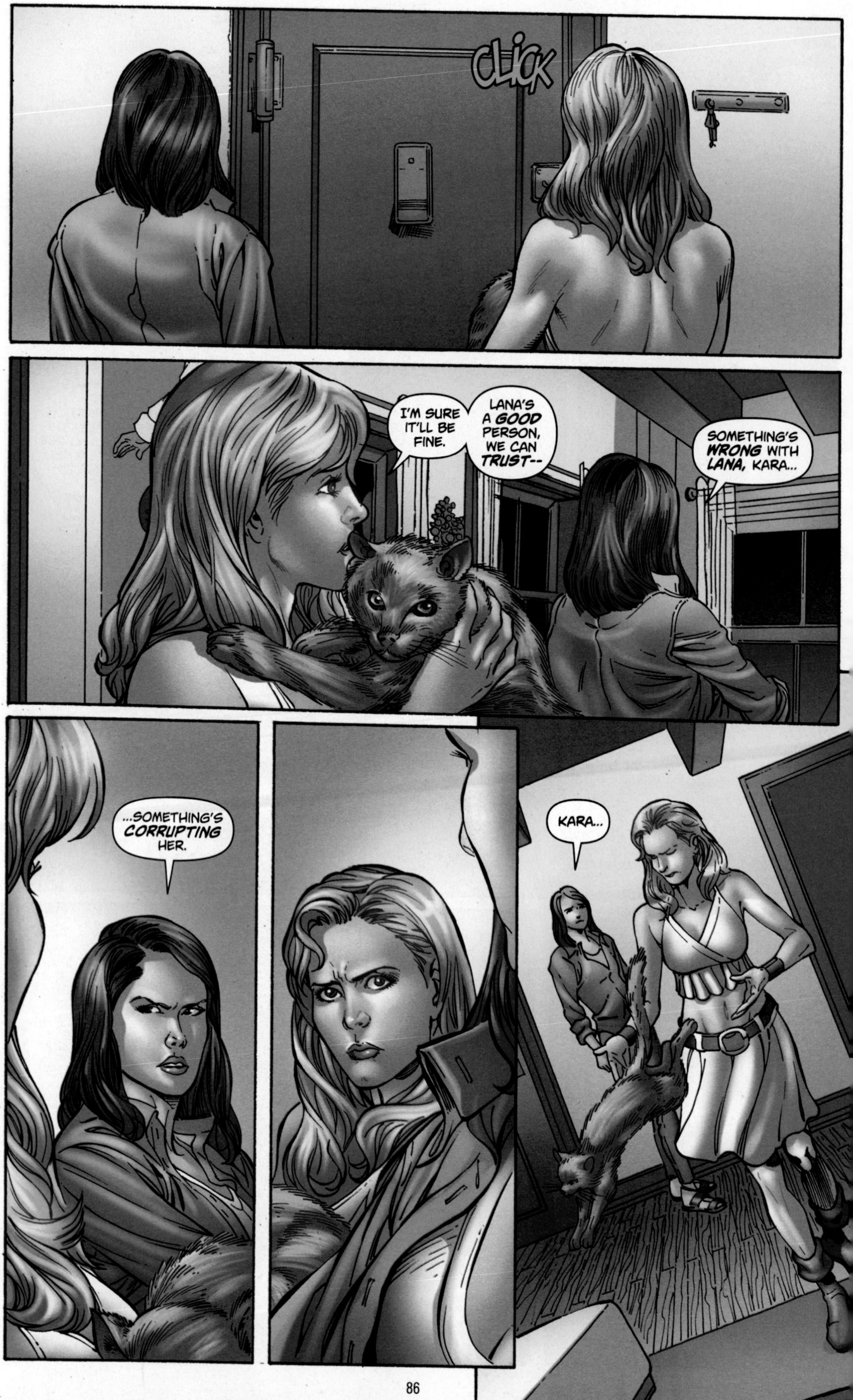
CLICK
I'M SURE IT'LL BE FINE.
LANA'S A GOOD PERSON, WE CAN TRUST--
SOMETHING'S WRONG WITH LANA, KARA...
...SOMETHING'S CORRUPTING HER.
KARA...

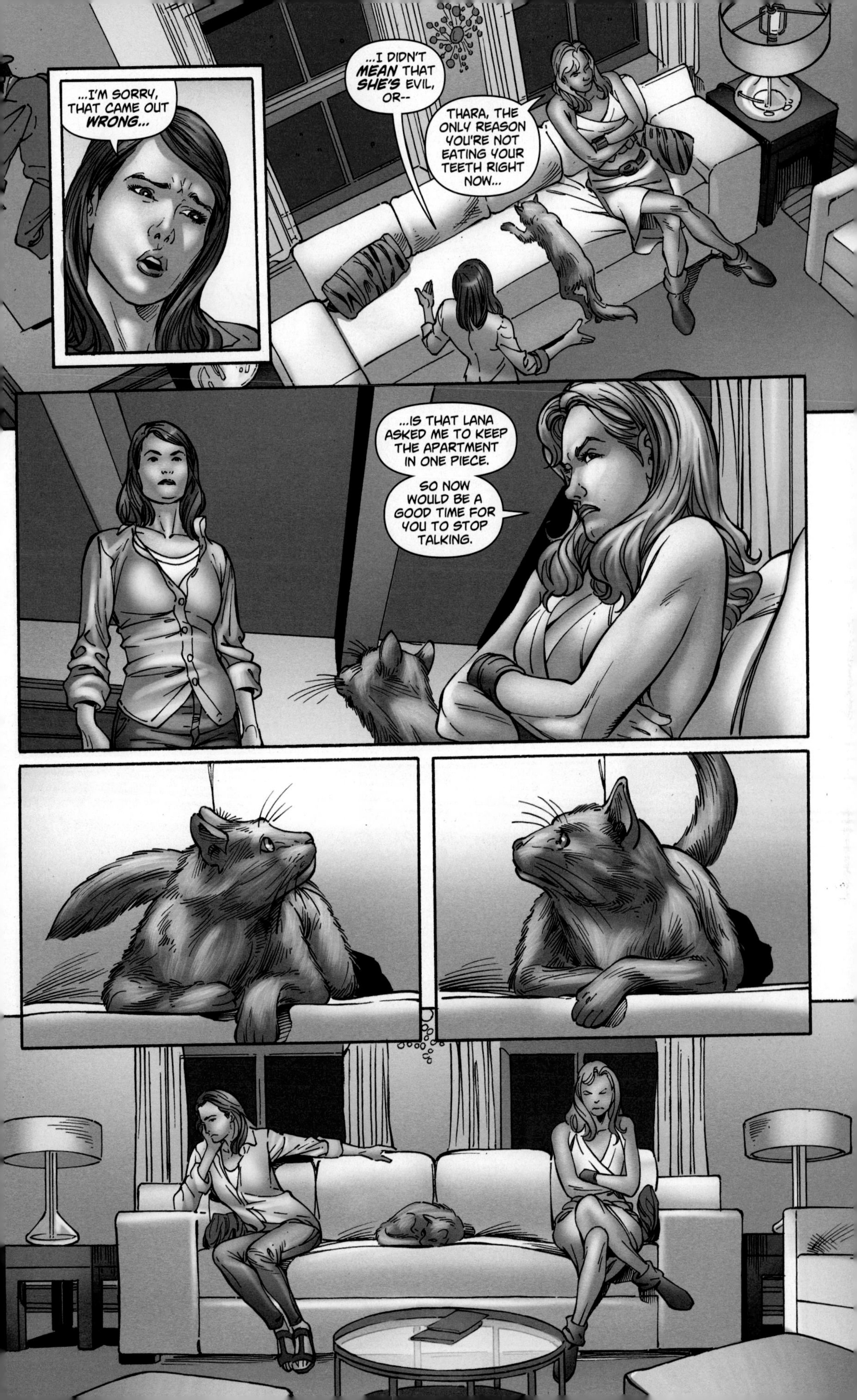
...I'M SORRY, THAT CAME OUT WRONG...
...I DIDN'T MEAN THAT SHE'S EVIL, OR--
THARA, THE ONLY REASON YOU'RE NOT EATING YOUR TEETH RIGHT NOW...
...IS THAT LANA ASKED ME TO KEEP THE APARTMENT IN ONE PIECE.
SO NOW WOULD BE A GOOD TIME FOR YOU TO STOP TALKING.

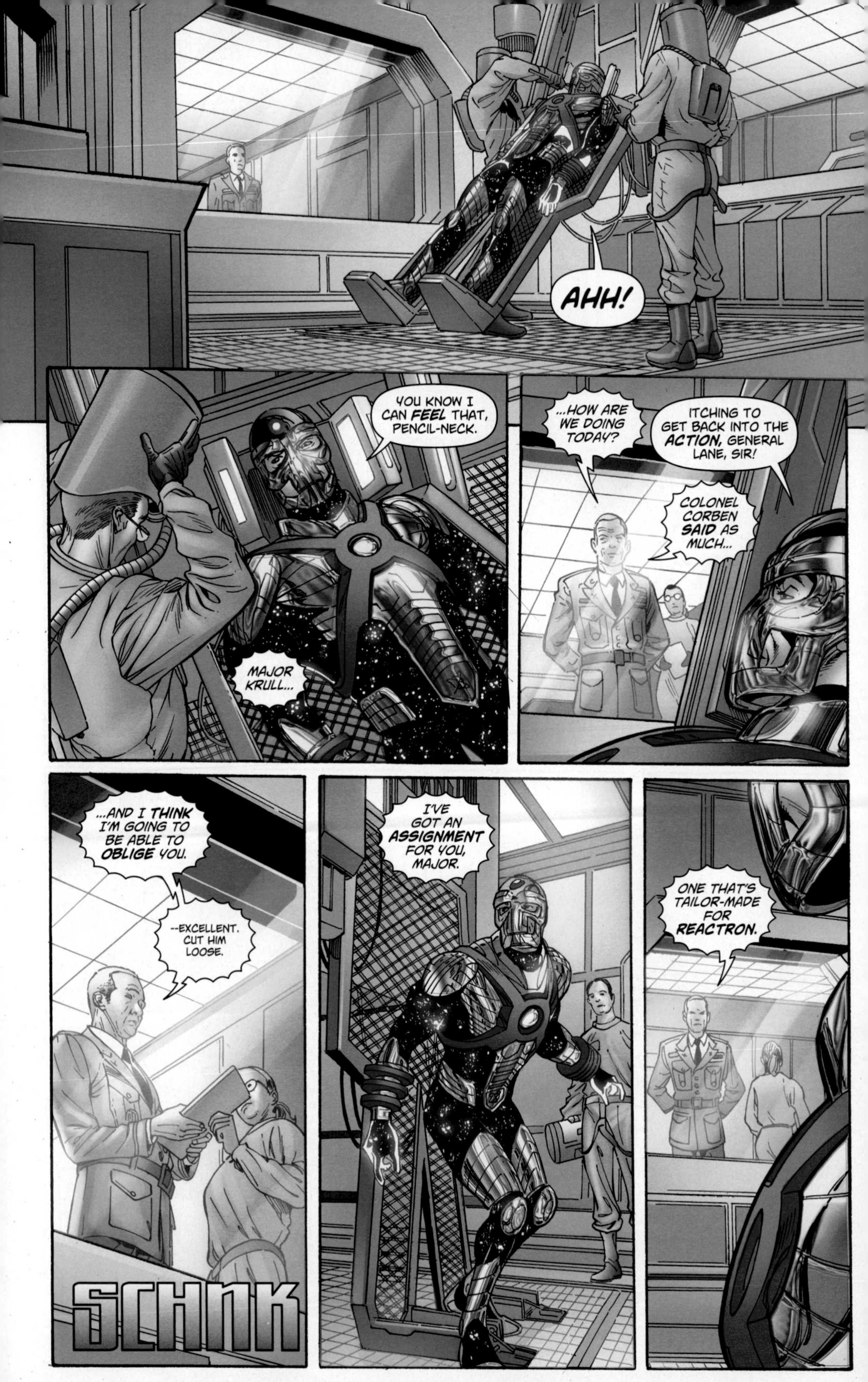
AHH!
YOU KNOW I CAN FEEL THAT, PENCIL-NECK.
MAJOR KRULL...
...HOW ARE WE DOING TODAY?
ITCHING TO GET BACK INTO THE ACTION, GENERAL LANE, SIR!
COLONEL CORBEN SAID AS MUCH...
...AND I THINK I'M GOING TO BE ABLE TO OBLIGE YOU.
--EXCELLENT. CUT HIM LOOSE.
SCHNK
I'VE GOT AN ASSIGNMENT FOR YOU, MAJOR.
ONE THAT'S TAILOR-MADE FOR REACTRON.

I *HATE* LOOSE *ENDS*, MAJOR, AND *THOSE* THREE ARE A *LOOSE* END.

RIGHT *NOW*, THE *WHOLE* WORLD BELIEVES THEY *MURDERED* MON-EL, THAT THEY *SABOTAGED* METROPOLIS'S WATER SUPPLY.

WE NEED TO *KEEP* IT THAT WAY.

THE *ONLY* MOVE LEFT TO THEM IS TO *PROVE* THEIR *INNOCENCE*.

THEY'RE GOING TO TRY TO *HUNT* THE *HUNTERS*, TRY TO GET A *CONFESSION* THAT'LL *CLEAR* THEIR NAMES.

NOT FROM *ME*.

I'M NOT WORRIED ABOUT *YOUR* LOYALTY, MAJOR.

BUT THE ENEMY IS *RESOURCEFUL*, AND WE'VE COME *TOO FAR* TO TAKE ANY *UNNECESSARY* RISKS.

NOW'S THE *TIME* TO FINISH WHAT YOU'VE *STARTED*. NOW, WHILE THEY'RE *HUNTED* AND *HATED*.

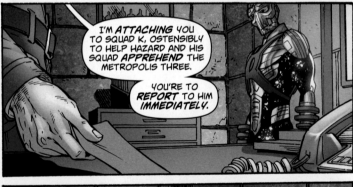

I'M *ATTACHING* YOU TO SQUAD K, OSTENSIBLY TO HELP HAZARD AND HIS SQUAD *APPREHEND* THE METROPOLIS THREE.

YOU'RE TO *REPORT* TO HIM *IMMEDIATELY*.

BUT YOU *UNDERSTAND* I AM *NOW* GIVING YOU *SEPARATE* ORDERS, AND YOU ARE ANSWERABLE TO *ME* AND ME *ALONE*.

ARE WE *CLEAR*, SOLDIER?

PERFECTLY CLEAR, GENERAL LANE, SIR...

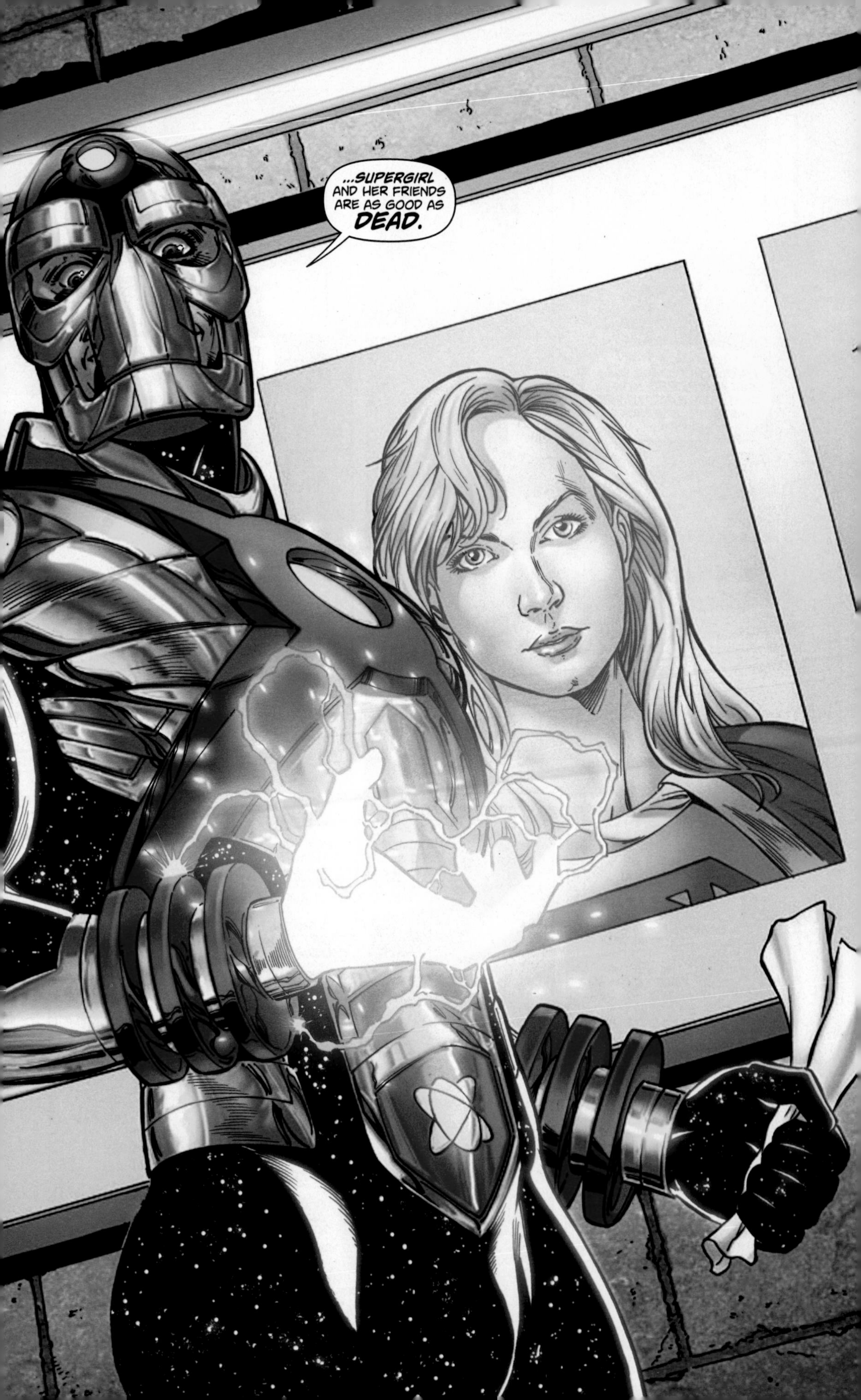
...SUPERGIRL AND HER FRIENDS ARE AS GOOD AS DEAD.

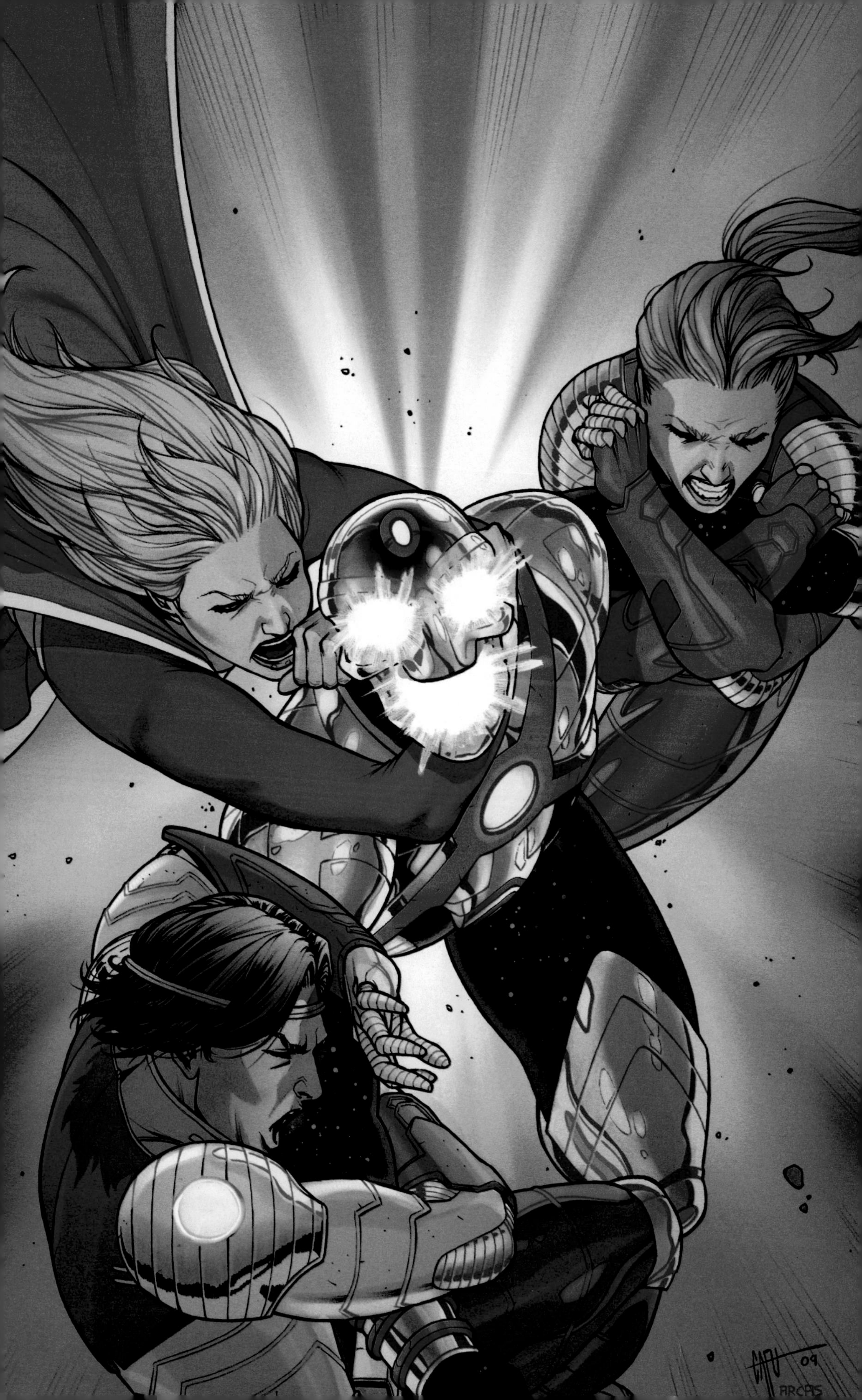

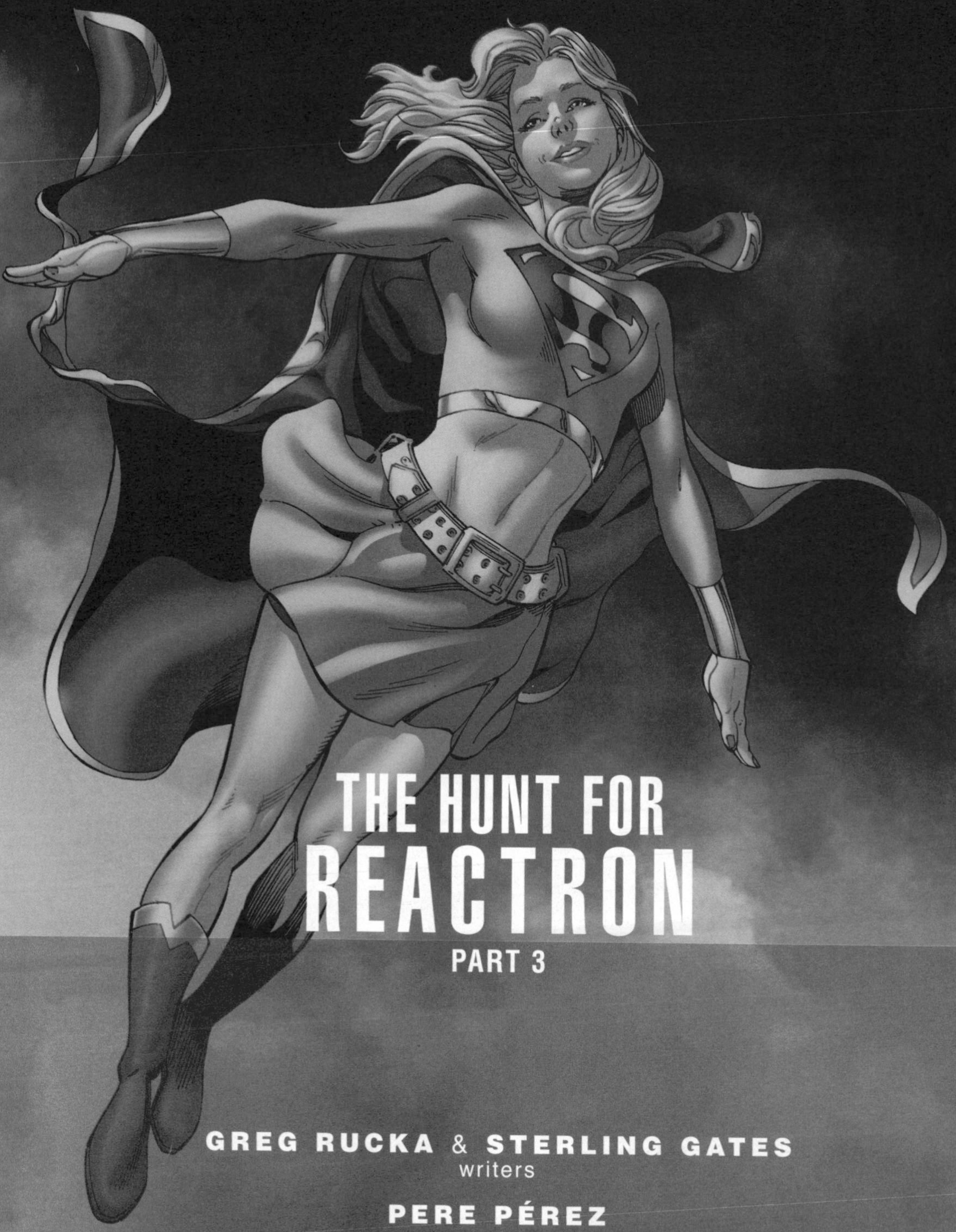

# THE HUNT FOR REACTRON

## PART 3

**GREG RUCKA** & **STERLING GATES**
writers

**PERE PÉREZ**
artist

**JAVIER MENA**
colorist

**ROB LEIGH**
letterer

**CAFU** with **SANTIAGO ARCAS**
cover

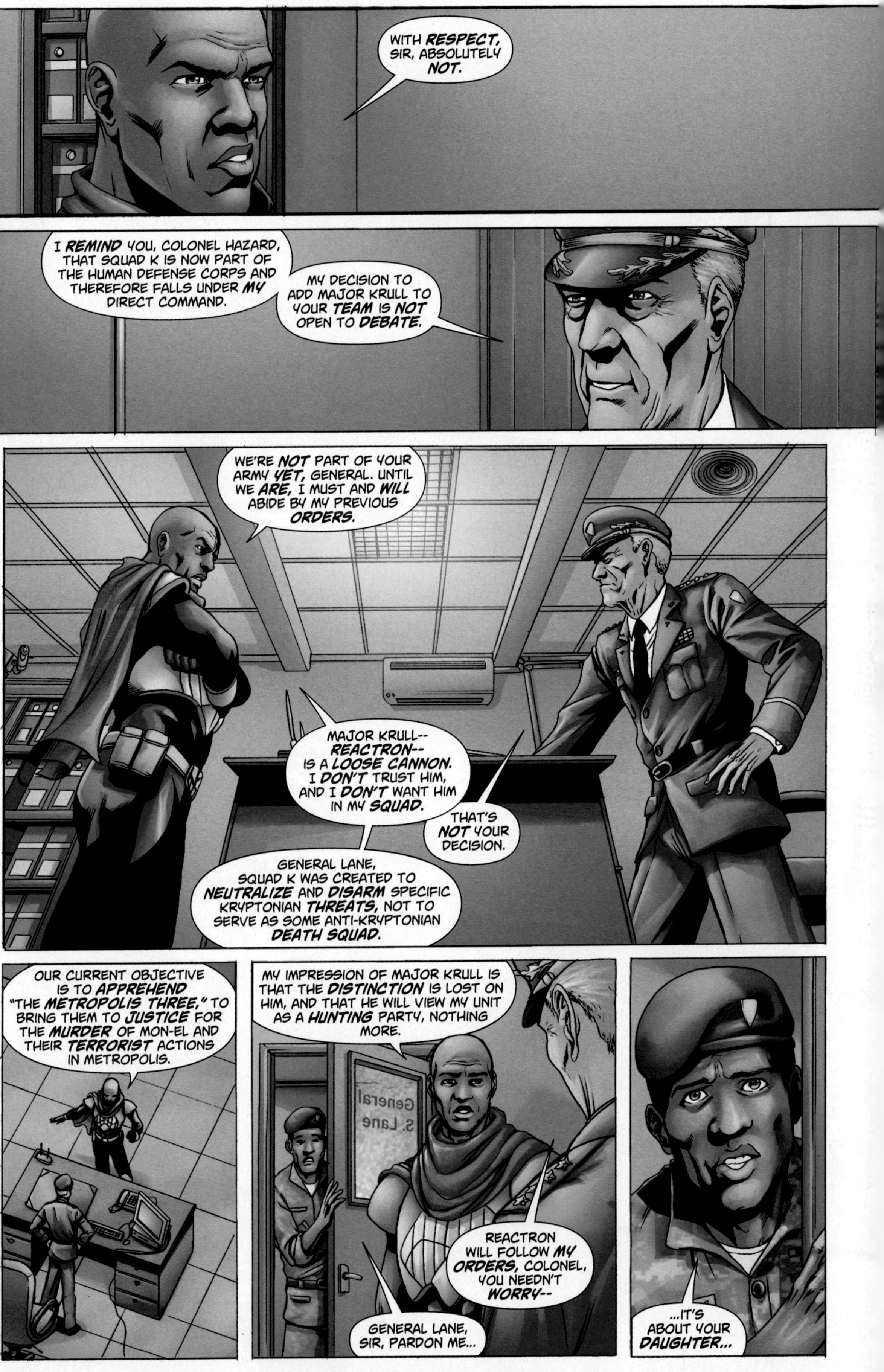
WITH RESPECT, SIR, ABSOLUTELY NOT.
I REMIND YOU, COLONEL HAZARD, THAT SQUAD K IS NOW PART OF THE HUMAN DEFENSE CORPS AND THEREFORE FALLS UNDER MY DIRECT COMMAND.
MY DECISION TO ADD MAJOR KRULL TO YOUR TEAM IS NOT OPEN TO DEBATE.
WE'RE NOT PART OF YOUR ARMY YET, GENERAL. UNTIL WE ARE, I MUST AND WILL ABIDE BY MY PREVIOUS ORDERS.
MAJOR KRULL-- REACTRON-- IS A LOOSE CANNON. I DON'T TRUST HIM, AND I DON'T WANT HIM IN MY SQUAD.
THAT'S NOT YOUR DECISION.
GENERAL LANE, SQUAD K WAS CREATED TO NEUTRALIZE AND DISARM SPECIFIC KRYPTONIAN THREATS, NOT TO SERVE AS SOME ANTI-KRYPTONIAN DEATH SQUAD.
OUR CURRENT OBJECTIVE IS TO APPREHEND "THE METROPOLIS THREE," TO BRING THEM TO JUSTICE FOR THE MURDER OF MON-EL AND THEIR TERRORIST ACTIONS IN METROPOLIS.
MY IMPRESSION OF MAJOR KRULL IS THAT THE DISTINCTION IS LOST ON HIM, AND THAT HE WILL VIEW MY UNIT AS A HUNTING PARTY, NOTHING MORE.
General S. Lane
REACTRON WILL FOLLOW MY ORDERS, COLONEL, YOU NEEDN'T WORRY--
GENERAL LANE, SIR, PARDON ME...
...IT'S ABOUT YOUR DAUGHTER...

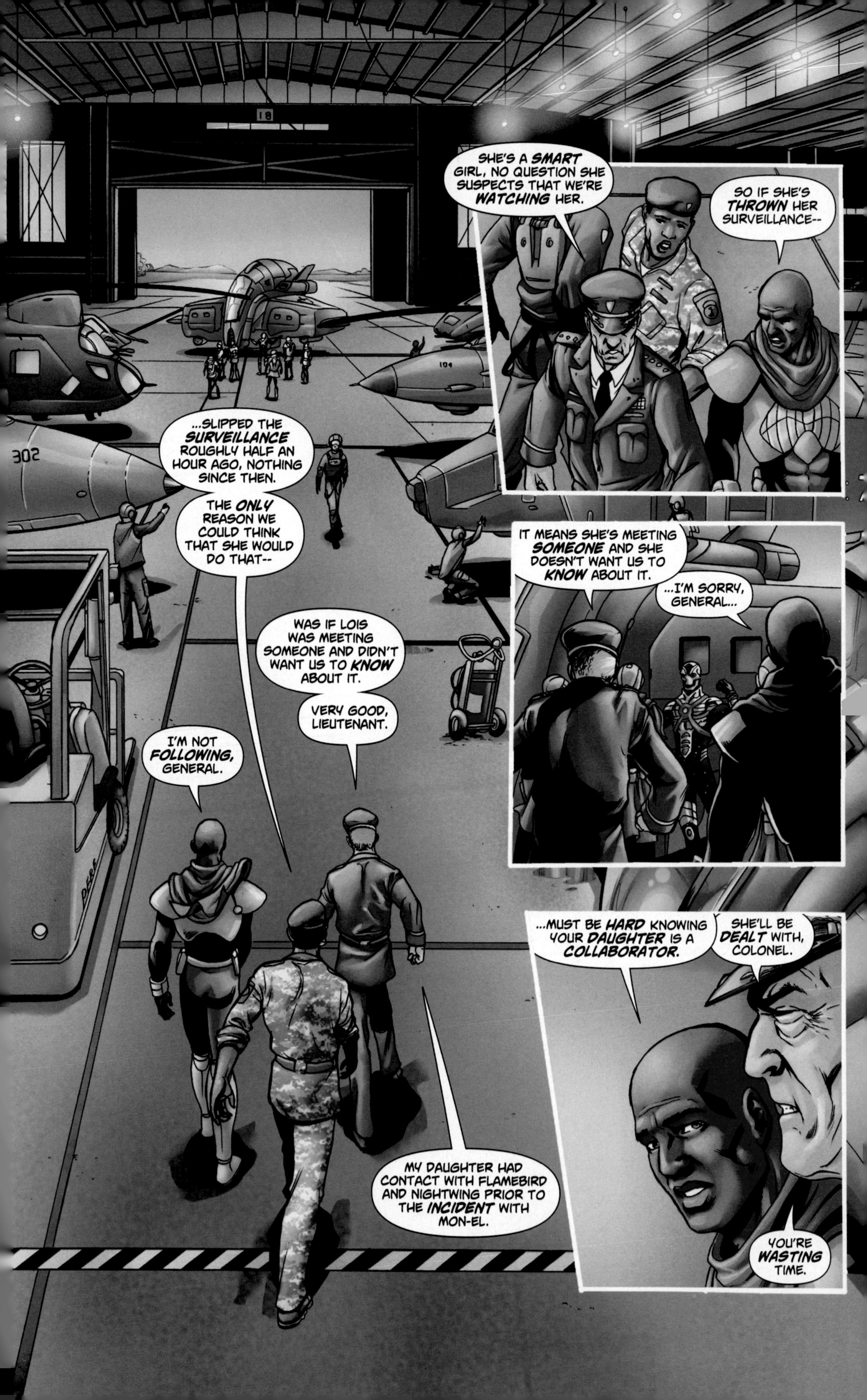
...SLIPPED THE SURVEILLANCE ROUGHLY HALF AN HOUR AGO, NOTHING SINCE THEN.
THE ONLY REASON WE COULD THINK THAT SHE WOULD DO THAT--
WAS IF LOIS WAS MEETING SOMEONE AND DIDN'T WANT US TO KNOW ABOUT IT.
VERY GOOD, LIEUTENANT.
I'M NOT FOLLOWING, GENERAL.
MY DAUGHTER HAD CONTACT WITH FLAMEBIRD AND NIGHTWING PRIOR TO THE INCIDENT WITH MON-EL.
SHE'S A SMART GIRL, NO QUESTION SHE SUSPECTS THAT WE'RE WATCHING HER.
SO IF SHE'S THROWN HER SURVEILLANCE--
IT MEANS SHE'S MEETING SOMEONE AND SHE DOESN'T WANT US TO KNOW ABOUT IT.
...I'M SORRY, GENERAL...
...MUST BE HARD KNOWING YOUR DAUGHTER IS A COLLABORATOR.
SHE'LL BE DEALT WITH, COLONEL.
YOU'RE WASTING TIME.

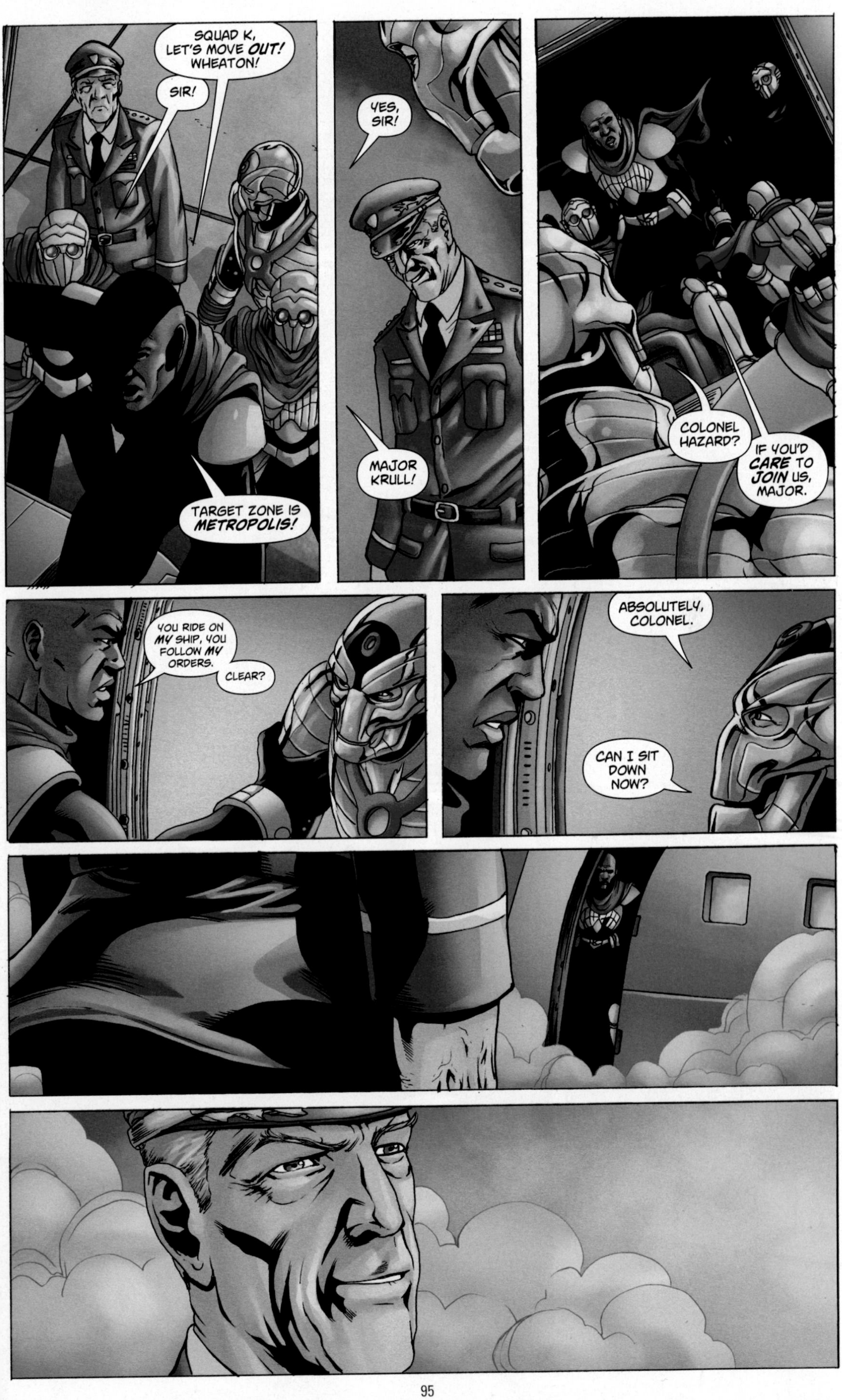
SQUAD K, LET'S MOVE OUT! WHEATON!
SIR!
TARGET ZONE IS METROPOLIS!
YES, SIR!
MAJOR KRULL!
COLONEL HAZARD?
IF YOU'D CARE TO JOIN US, MAJOR.
YOU RIDE ON MY SHIP, YOU FOLLOW MY ORDERS.
CLEAR?
ABSOLUTELY, COLONEL.
CAN I SIT DOWN NOW?

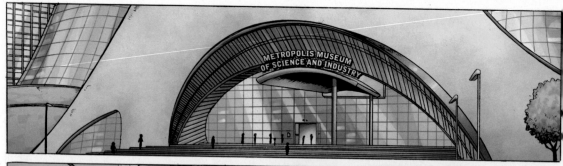

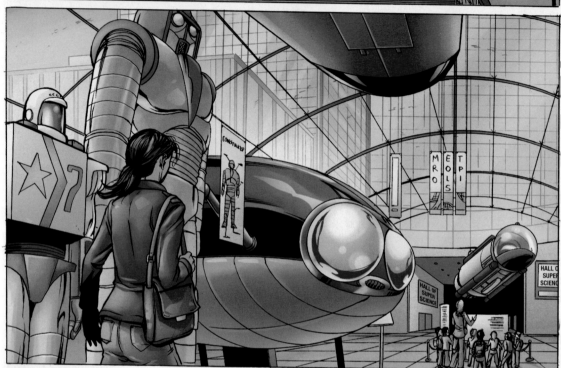

METROPOLIS MUSEUM OF SCIENCE AND INDUSTRY
HALL OF SUPER SCIENCE
MOM!
UP HERE!
REPLICA OF THE BLUE BEETLE'S BATTLE BUG! WATCH YOUR STEP!
"MOM"?
KARA CAN EXPLAIN IT.

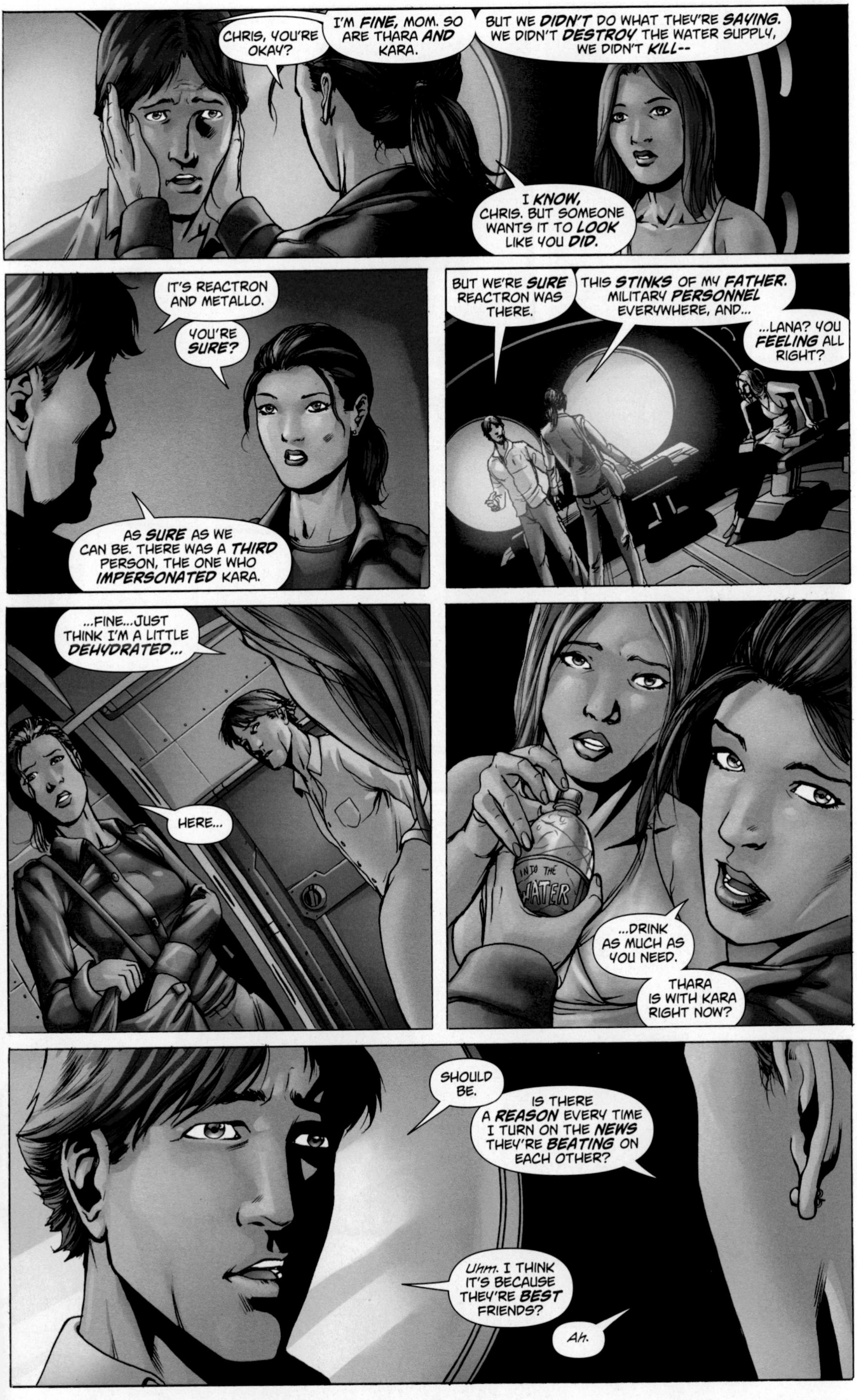
CHRIS, YOU'RE OKAY?
I'M FINE, MOM. SO ARE THARA AND KARA.
BUT WE DIDN'T DO WHAT THEY'RE SAYING. WE DIDN'T DESTROY THE WATER SUPPLY, WE DIDN'T KILL--
I KNOW, CHRIS. BUT SOMEONE WANTS IT TO LOOK LIKE YOU DID.
IT'S REACTRON AND METALLO.
YOU'RE SURE?
AS SURE AS WE CAN BE. THERE WAS A THIRD PERSON, THE ONE WHO IMPERSONATED KARA.
BUT WE'RE SURE REACTRON WAS THERE.
THIS STINKS OF MY FATHER. MILITARY PERSONNEL EVERYWHERE, AND...
...LANA? YOU FEELING ALL RIGHT?
...FINE...JUST THINK I'M A LITTLE DEHYDRATED...
HERE...
INTO THE WATER
...DRINK AS MUCH AS YOU NEED.
THARA IS WITH KARA RIGHT NOW?
SHOULD BE.
IS THERE A REASON EVERY TIME I TURN ON THE NEWS THEY'RE BEATING ON EACH OTHER?
Uhm. I THINK IT'S BECAUSE THEY'RE BEST FRIENDS?
Ah.

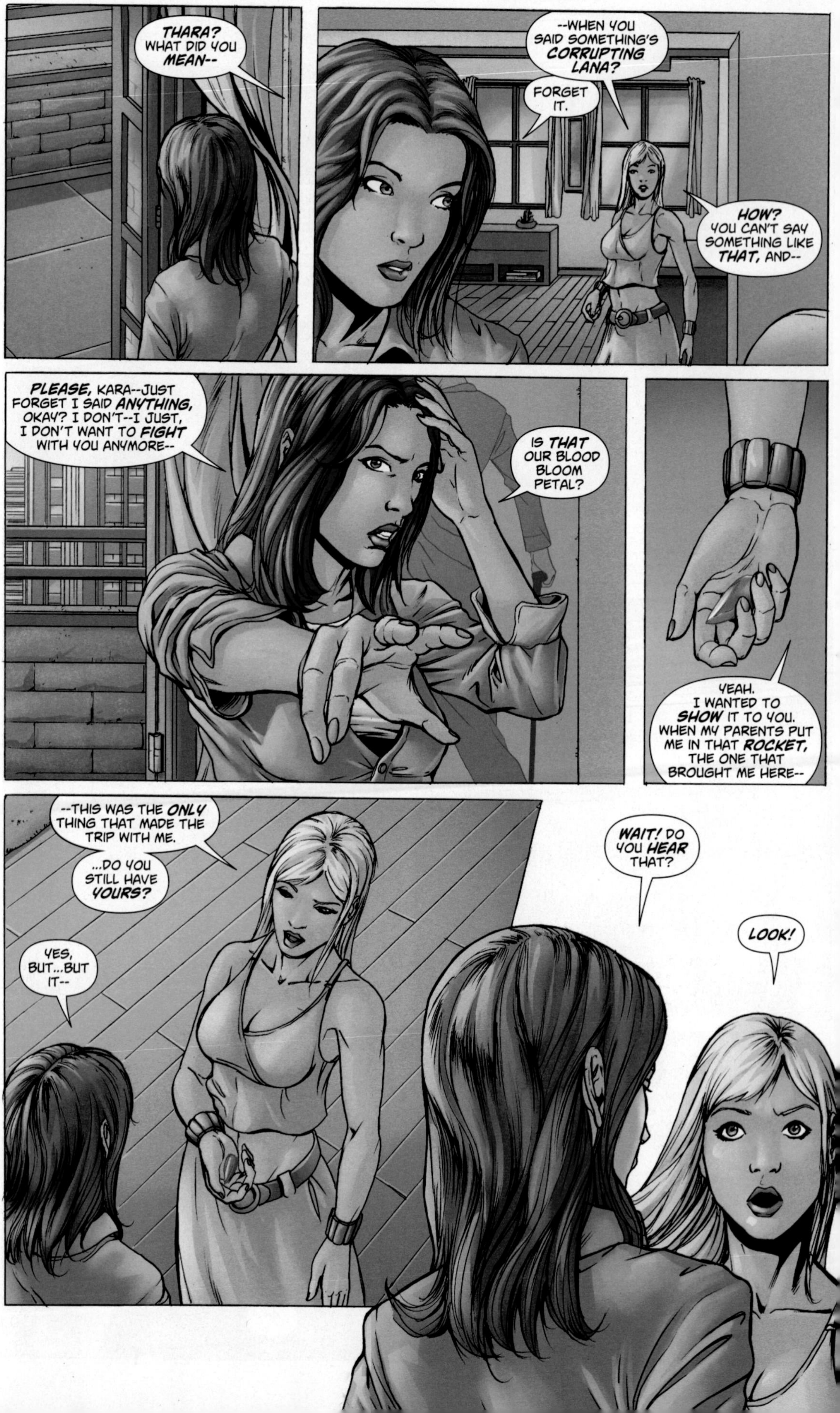
THARA? WHAT DID YOU MEAN--
--WHEN YOU SAID SOMETHING'S CORRUPTING LANA?
FORGET IT.
HOW? YOU CAN'T SAY SOMETHING LIKE THAT, AND--
PLEASE, KARA--JUST FORGET I SAID ANYTHING, OKAY? I DON'T--I JUST, I DON'T WANT TO FIGHT WITH YOU ANYMORE--
IS THAT OUR BLOOD BLOOM PETAL?
YEAH. I WANTED TO SHOW IT TO YOU. WHEN MY PARENTS PUT ME IN THAT ROCKET, THE ONE THAT BROUGHT ME HERE--
--THIS WAS THE ONLY THING THAT MADE THE TRIP WITH ME.
...DO YOU STILL HAVE YOURS?
YES, BUT...BUT IT--
WAIT! DO YOU HEAR THAT?
LOOK!

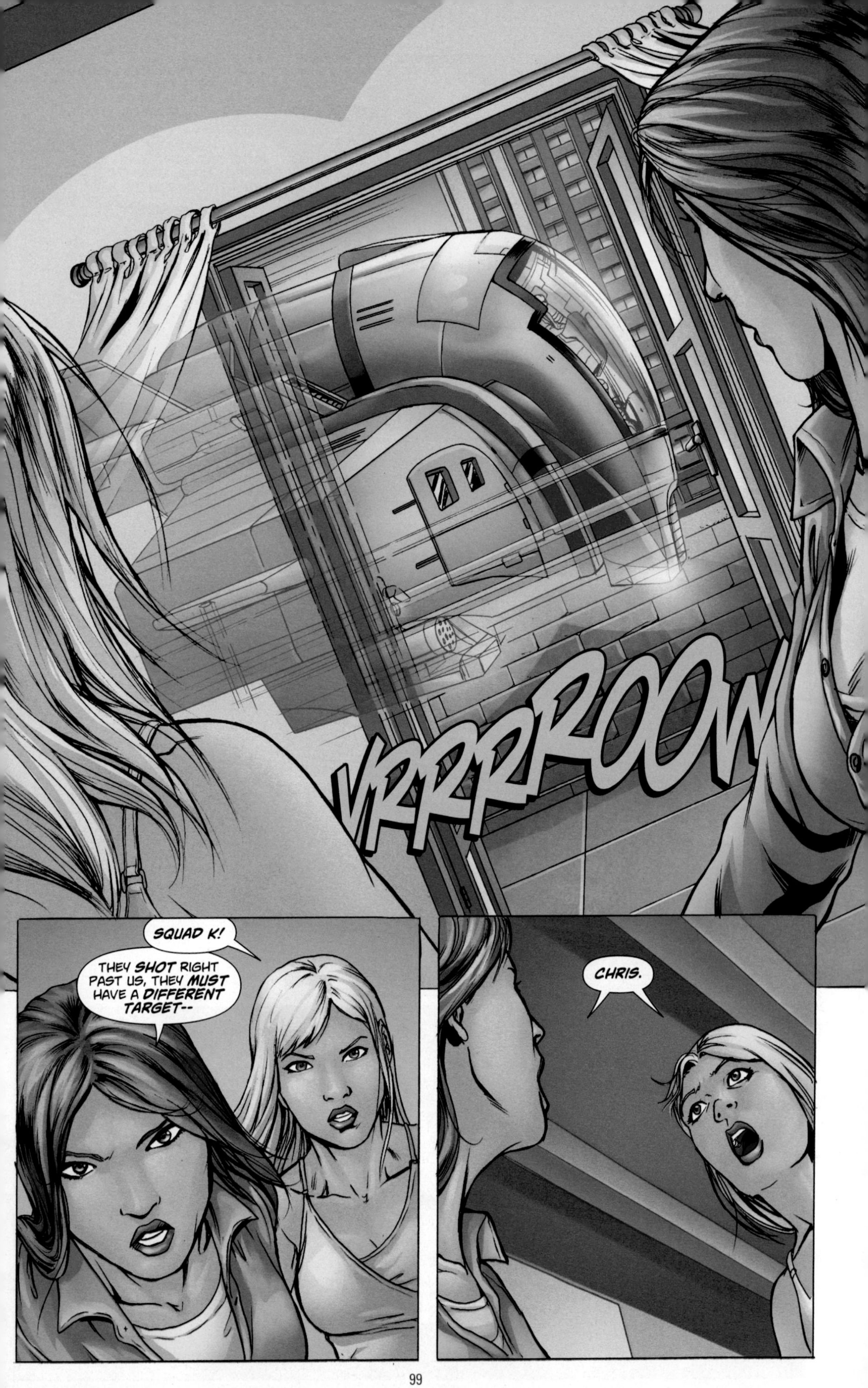
VRRRROOOW
SQUAD K!
THEY SHOT RIGHT PAST US, THEY MUST HAVE A DIFFERENT TARGET--
CHRIS.

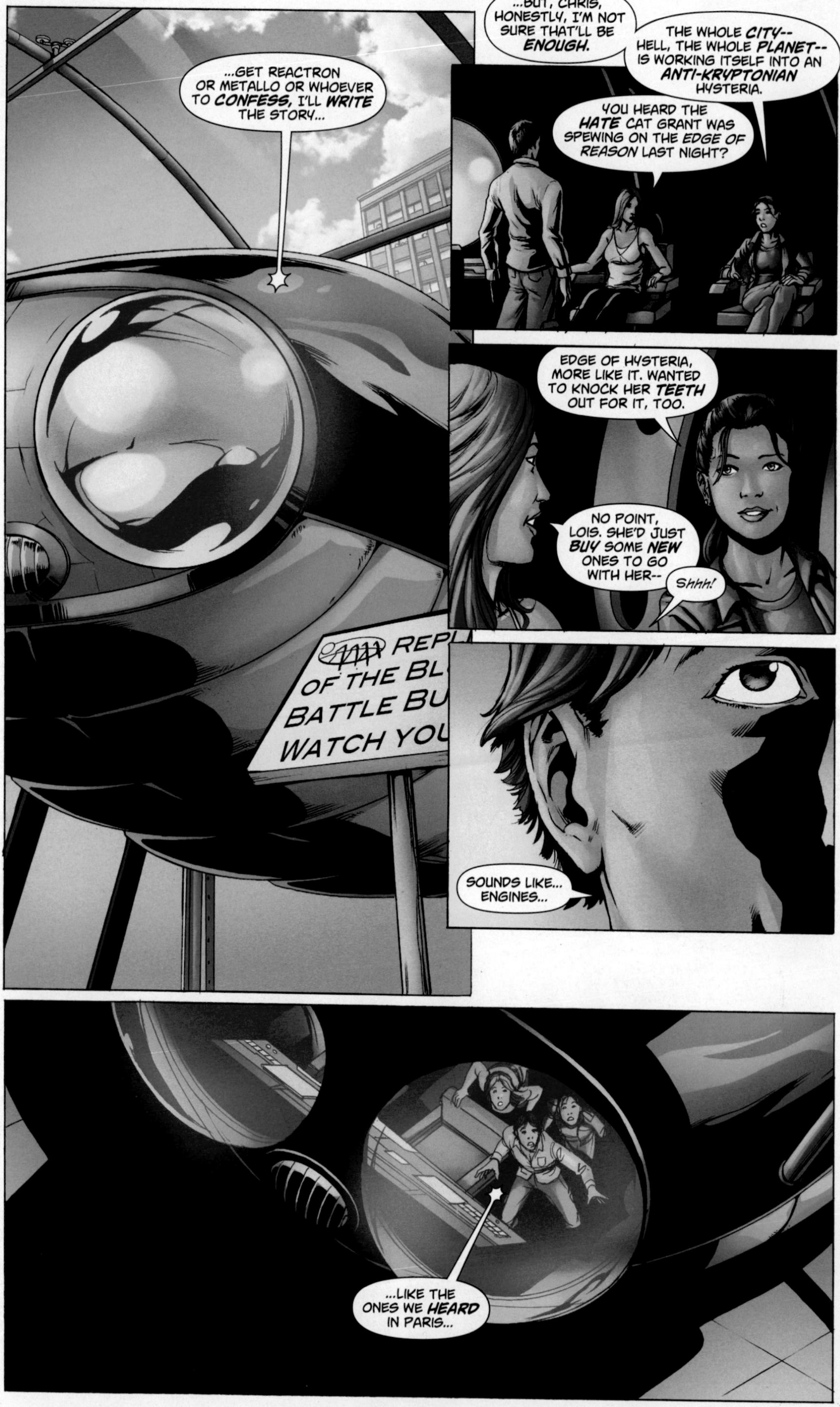
...GET REACTRON OR METALLO OR WHOEVER TO CONFESS, I'LL WRITE THE STORY...
...BUT, CHRIS, HONESTLY, I'M NOT SURE THAT'LL BE ENOUGH.
THE WHOLE CITY-- HELL, THE WHOLE PLANET-- IS WORKING ITSELF INTO AN ANTI-KRYPTONIAN HYSTERIA.
YOU HEARD THE HATE CAT GRANT WAS SPEWING ON THE EDGE OF REASON LAST NIGHT?
EDGE OF HYSTERIA, MORE LIKE IT. WANTED TO KNOCK HER TEETH OUT FOR IT, TOO.
NO POINT, LOIS. SHE'D JUST BUY SOME NEW ONES TO GO WITH HER--
Shhh!
REPL
OF THE BL
BATTLE BU
WATCH YOU
SOUNDS LIKE... ENGINES...
...LIKE THE ONES WE HEARD IN PARIS...

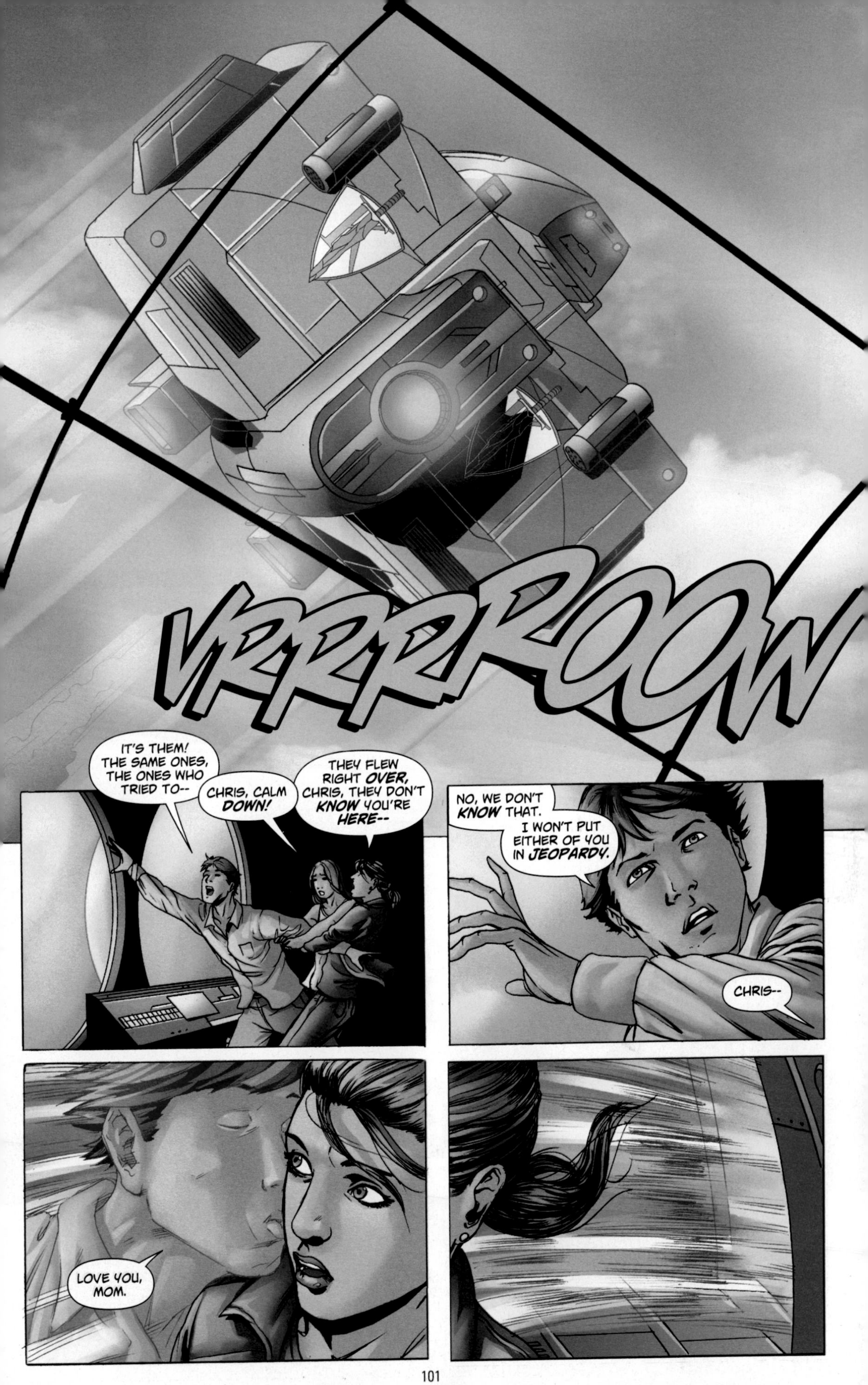
VRRRROOOW
IT'S THEM! THE SAME ONES, THE ONES WHO TRIED TO--
CHRIS, CALM DOWN!
THEY FLEW RIGHT OVER, CHRIS, THEY DON'T KNOW YOU'RE HERE--
NO, WE DON'T KNOW THAT.
I WON'T PUT EITHER OF YOU IN JEOPARDY.
CHRIS--
LOVE YOU, MOM.

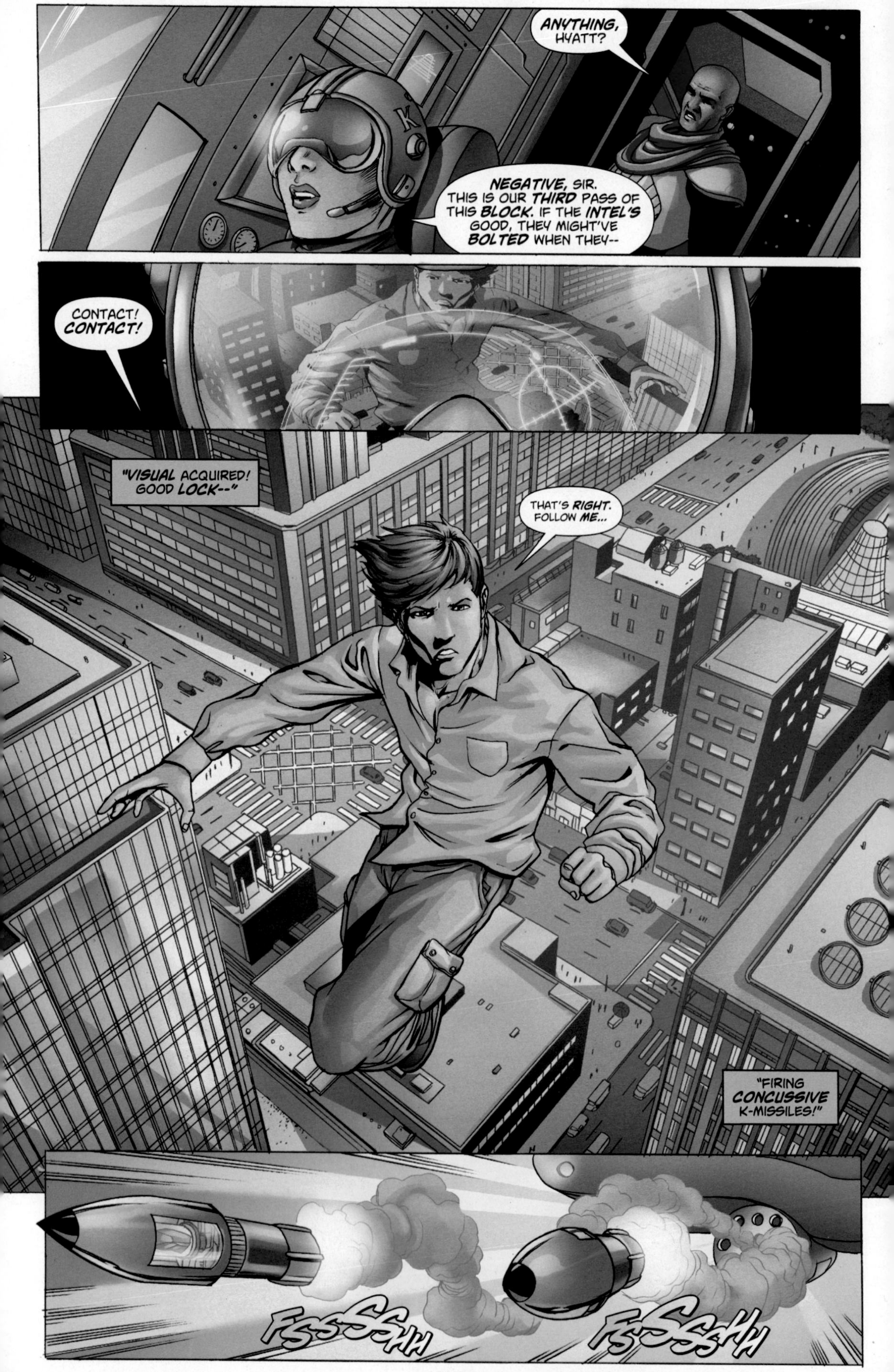
ANYTHING, HYATT?
NEGATIVE, SIR. THIS IS OUR THIRD PASS OF THIS BLOCK. IF THE INTEL'S GOOD, THEY MIGHT'VE BOLTED WHEN THEY--
CONTACT! CONTACT!
"VISUAL ACQUIRED! GOOD LOCK--"
THAT'S RIGHT. FOLLOW ME...
"FIRING CONCUSSIVE K-MISSILES!"
FSSSSSHH
FSSSSSHH

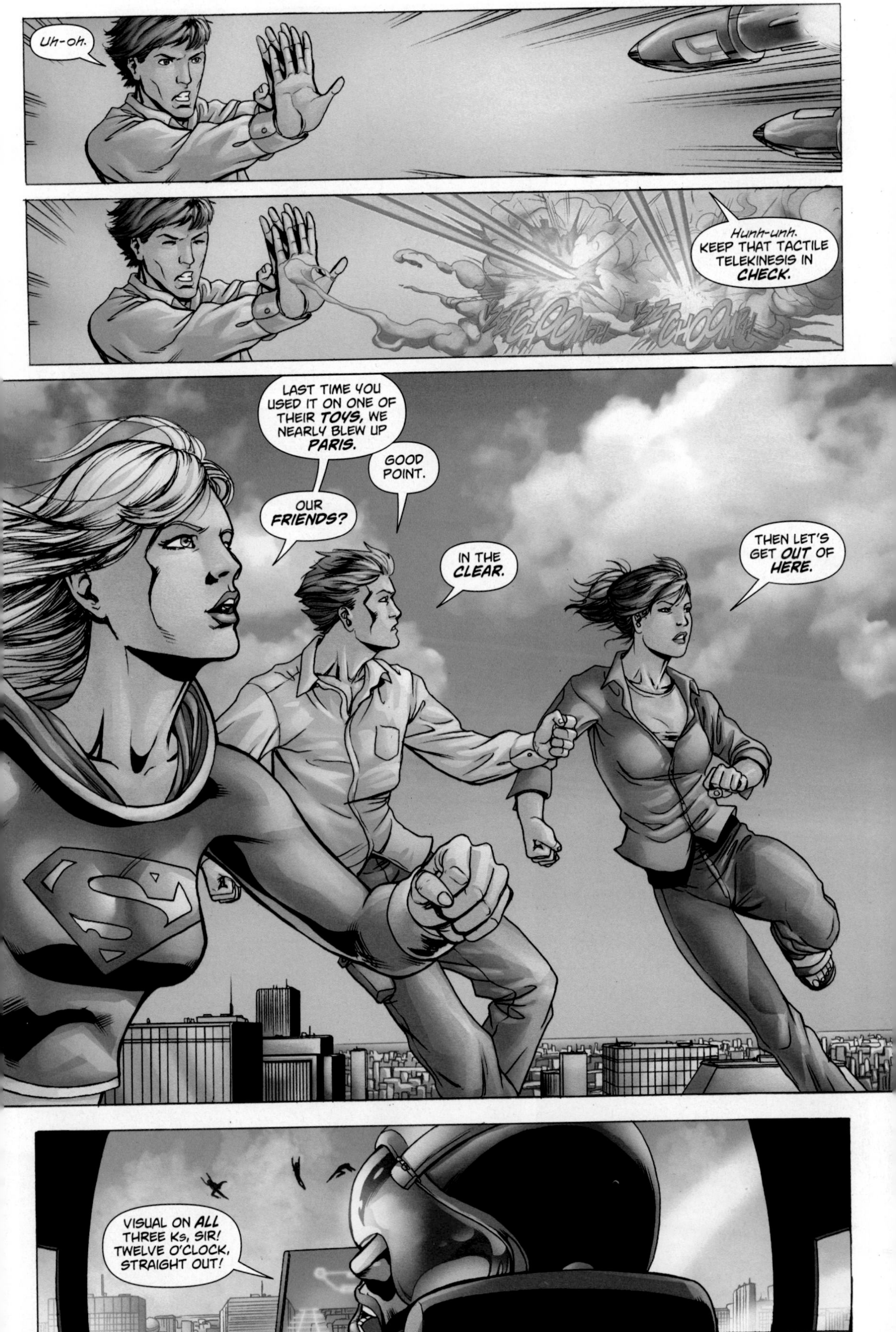
Uh-oh.
Hunh-unh. KEEP THAT TACTILE TELEKINESIS IN CHECK.
LAST TIME YOU USED IT ON ONE OF THEIR TOYS, WE NEARLY BLEW UP PARIS.
GOOD POINT.
OUR FRIENDS?
IN THE CLEAR.
THEN LET'S GET OUT OF HERE.
VISUAL ON ALL THREE Ks, SIR! TWELVE O'CLOCK, STRAIGHT OUT!

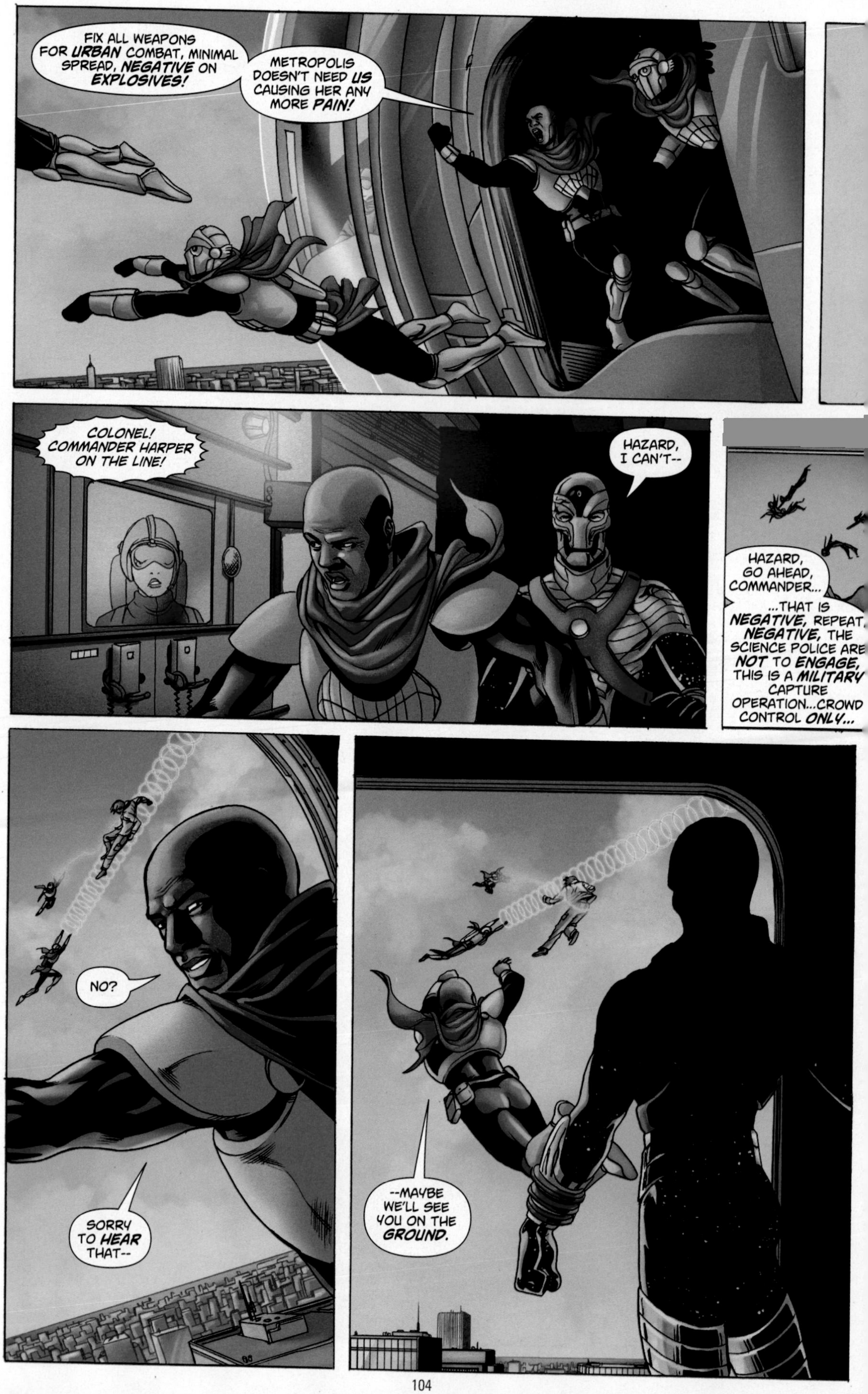
FIX ALL WEAPONS FOR URBAN COMBAT, MINIMAL SPREAD, NEGATIVE ON EXPLOSIVES!
METROPOLIS DOESN'T NEED US CAUSING HER ANY MORE PAIN!
COLONEL! COMMANDER HARPER ON THE LINE!
HAZARD, I CAN'T--
HAZARD, GO AHEAD, COMMANDER...
...THAT IS NEGATIVE, REPEAT, NEGATIVE, THE SCIENCE POLICE ARE NOT TO ENGAGE, THIS IS A MILITARY CAPTURE OPERATION...CROWD CONTROL ONLY...
NO?
SORRY TO HEAR THAT--
--MAYBE WE'LL SEE YOU ON THE GROUND.

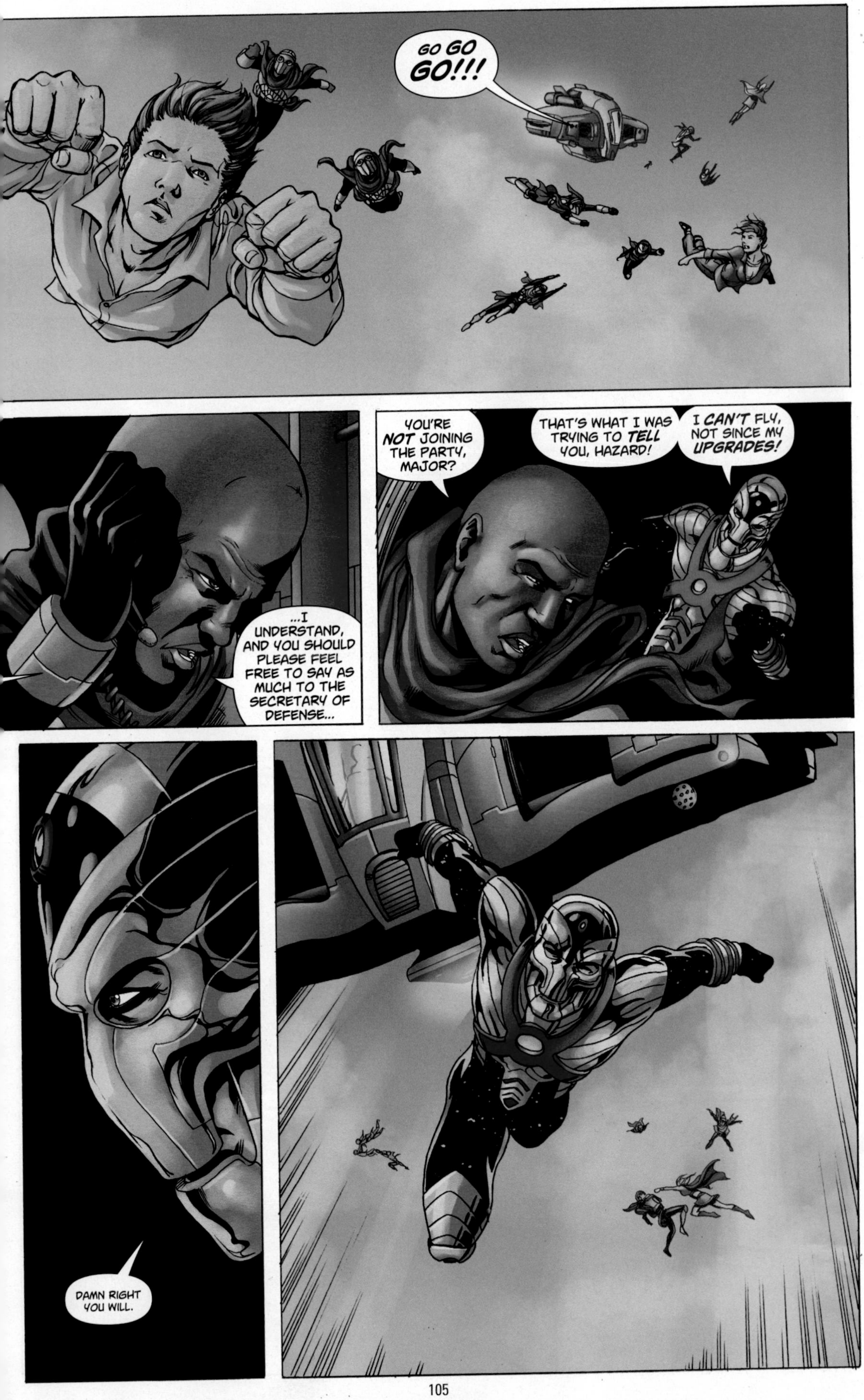
GO GO GO!!!
...I UNDERSTAND, AND YOU SHOULD PLEASE FEEL FREE TO SAY AS MUCH TO THE SECRETARY OF DEFENSE...
YOU'RE NOT JOINING THE PARTY, MAJOR?
THAT'S WHAT I WAS TRYING TO TELL YOU, HAZARD!
I CAN'T FLY, NOT SINCE MY UPGRADES!
DAMN RIGHT YOU WILL.

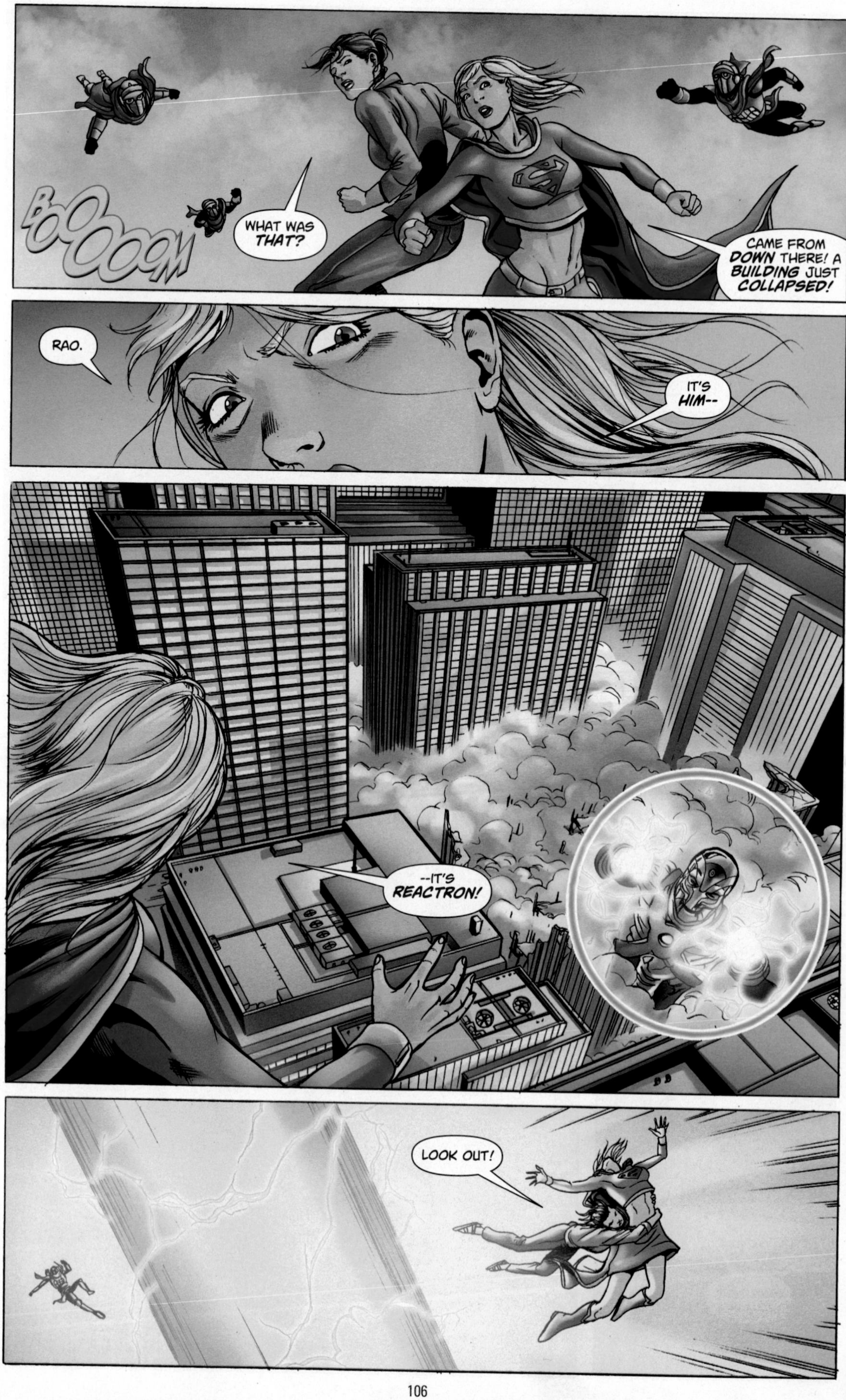
BOOOOOM
WHAT WAS THAT?
CAME FROM DOWN THERE! A BUILDING JUST COLLAPSED!
RAO.
IT'S HIM--
--IT'S REACTRON!
LOOK OUT!

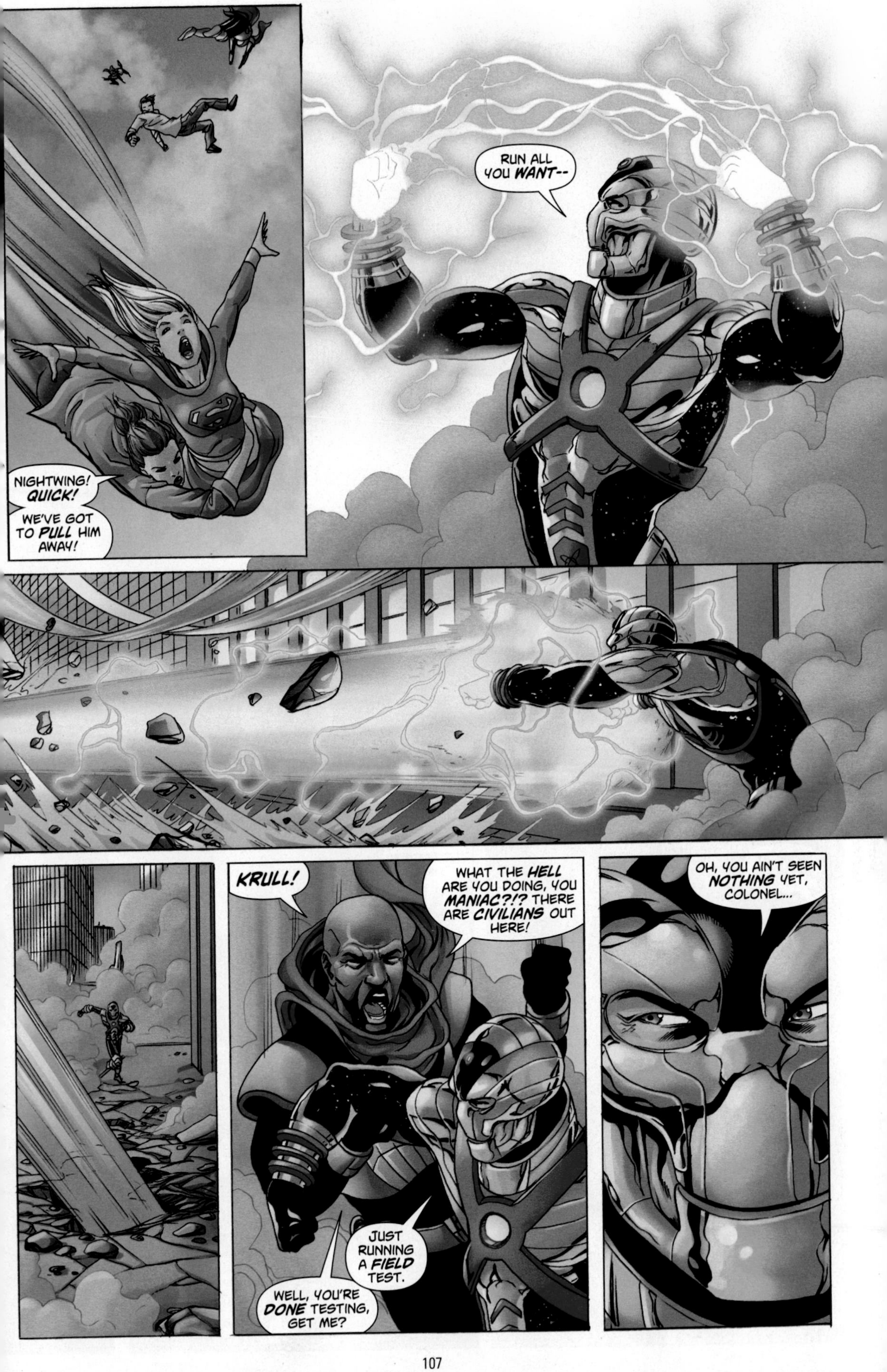
RUN ALL YOU WANT--
NIGHTWING! QUICK!
WE'VE GOT TO PULL HIM AWAY!
KRULL!
WHAT THE HELL ARE YOU DOING, YOU MANIAC?!? THERE ARE CIVILIANS OUT HERE!
JUST RUNNING A FIELD TEST.
WELL, YOU'RE DONE TESTING, GET ME?
OH, YOU AIN'T SEEN NOTHING YET, COLONEL...

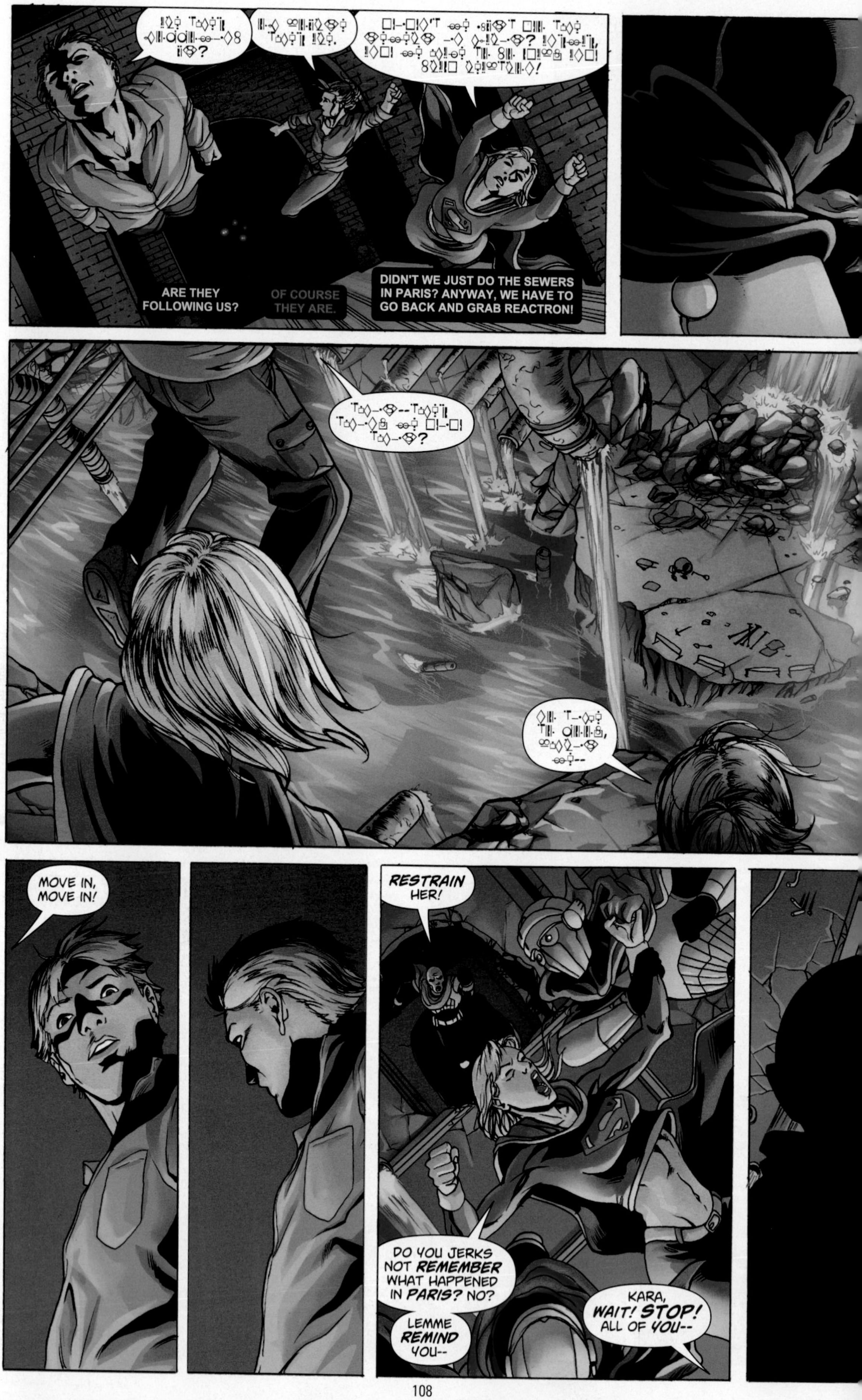
ARE THEY FOLLOWING US?
OF COURSE THEY ARE.
DIDN'T WE JUST DO THE SEWERS IN PARIS? ANYWAY, WE HAVE TO GO BACK AND GRAB REACTRON!
MOVE IN, MOVE IN!
RESTRAIN HER!
DO YOU JERKS NOT REMEMBER WHAT HAPPENED IN PARIS? NO?
LEMME REMIND YOU--
KARA, WAIT! STOP! ALL OF YOU--

LOST THE VISUAL!
SWITCH O THERMAL TRACKING.
ADJUSTING SENSORS...GOT THEIR TRAIL!
OH, NO...
WE NEED AN EXIT. AND FAST, THEY'LL BE ON US--
THIS--THEY THINK WE DID THIS?
NO TIME TO LOOK, CHRIS, WE--
ENGAGING TARGETS!
NAAARNGH--!
WE SURRENDER.
WE...WE WHAT?
"YOU'D BETTER KNOW WHAT YOU'RE DOING, CHRIS."

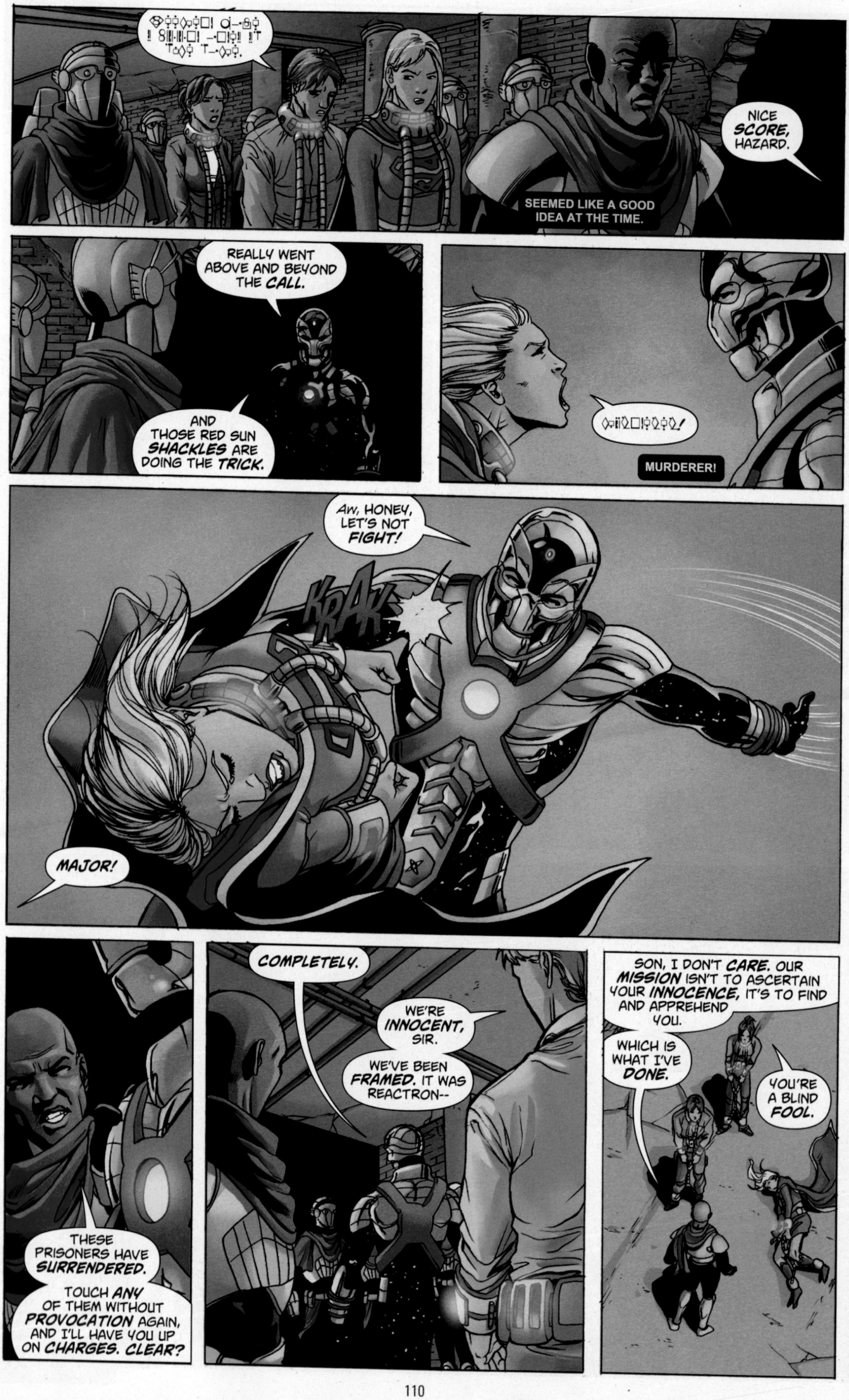
NICE SCORE, HAZARD.
SEEMED LIKE A GOOD IDEA AT THE TIME.
REALLY WENT ABOVE AND BEYOND THE CALL.
AND THOSE RED SUN SHACKLES ARE DOING THE TRICK.
MURDERER!
AW, HONEY, LET'S NOT FIGHT!
KRAK
MAJOR!
THESE PRISONERS HAVE SURRENDERED.
TOUCH ANY OF THEM WITHOUT PROVOCATION AGAIN, AND I'LL HAVE YOU UP ON CHARGES. CLEAR?
COMPLETELY.
WE'RE INNOCENT, SIR.
WE'VE BEEN FRAMED. IT WAS REACTRON--
SON, I DON'T CARE. OUR MISSION ISN'T TO ASCERTAIN YOUR INNOCENCE, IT'S TO FIND AND APPREHEND YOU.
WHICH IS WHAT I'VE DONE.
YOU'RE A BLIND FOOL.

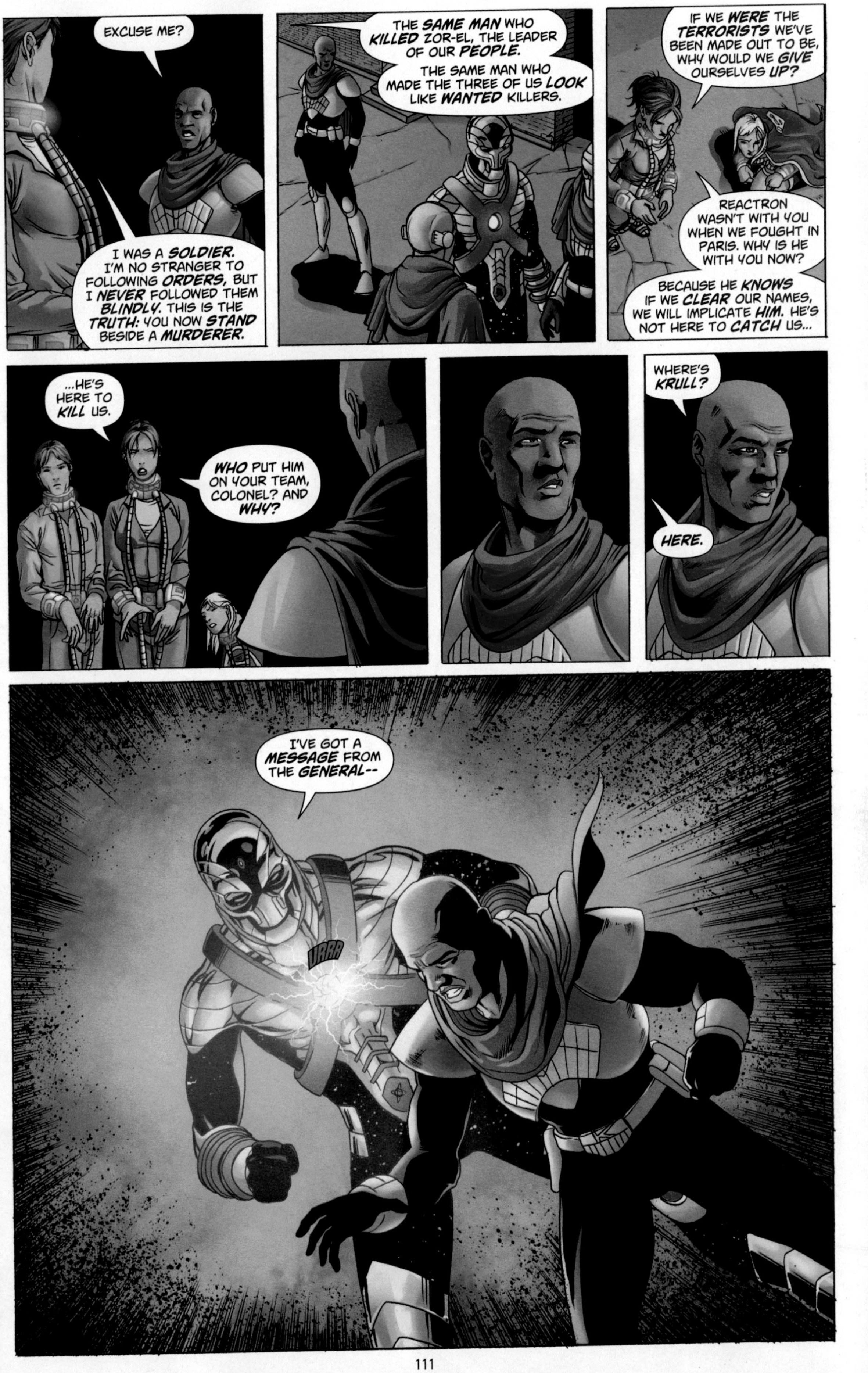
EXCUSE ME?
I WAS A SOLDIER. I'M NO STRANGER TO FOLLOWING ORDERS, BUT I NEVER FOLLOWED THEM BLINDLY. THIS IS THE TRUTH: YOU NOW STAND BESIDE A MURDERER.
THE SAME MAN WHO KILLED ZOR-EL, THE LEADER OF OUR PEOPLE.
THE SAME MAN WHO MADE THE THREE OF US LOOK LIKE WANTED KILLERS.
IF WE WERE THE TERRORISTS WE'VE BEEN MADE OUT TO BE, WHY WOULD WE GIVE OURSELVES UP?
REACTRON WASN'T WITH YOU WHEN WE FOUGHT IN PARIS. WHY IS HE WITH YOU NOW?
BECAUSE HE KNOWS IF WE CLEAR OUR NAMES, WE WILL IMPLICATE HIM. HE'S NOT HERE TO CATCH US...
...HE'S HERE TO KILL US.
WHO PUT HIM ON YOUR TEAM, COLONEL? AND WHY?
WHERE'S KRULL?
HERE.
I'VE GOT A MESSAGE FROM THE GENERAL--

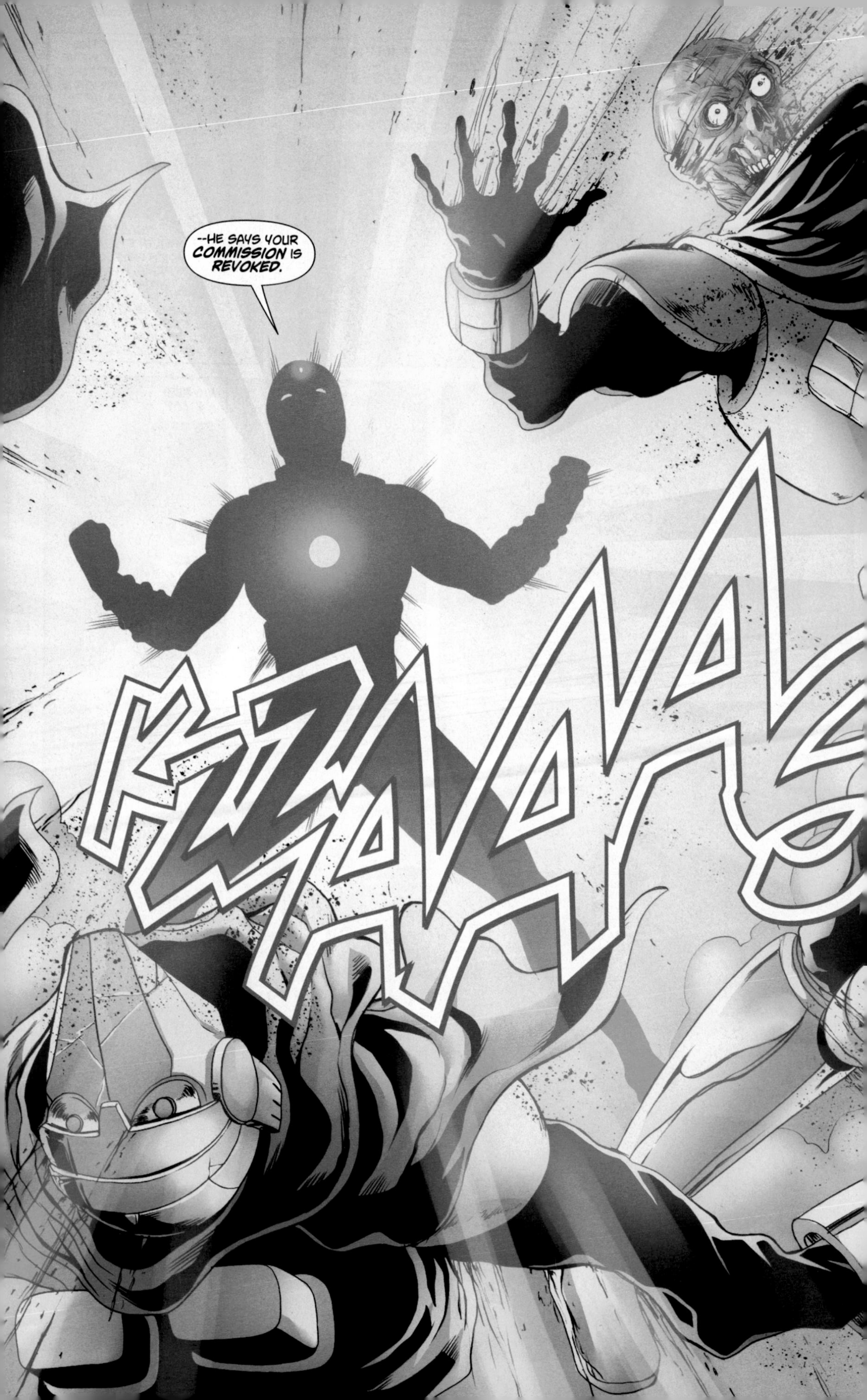
--HE SAYS YOUR COMMISSION IS REVOKED.

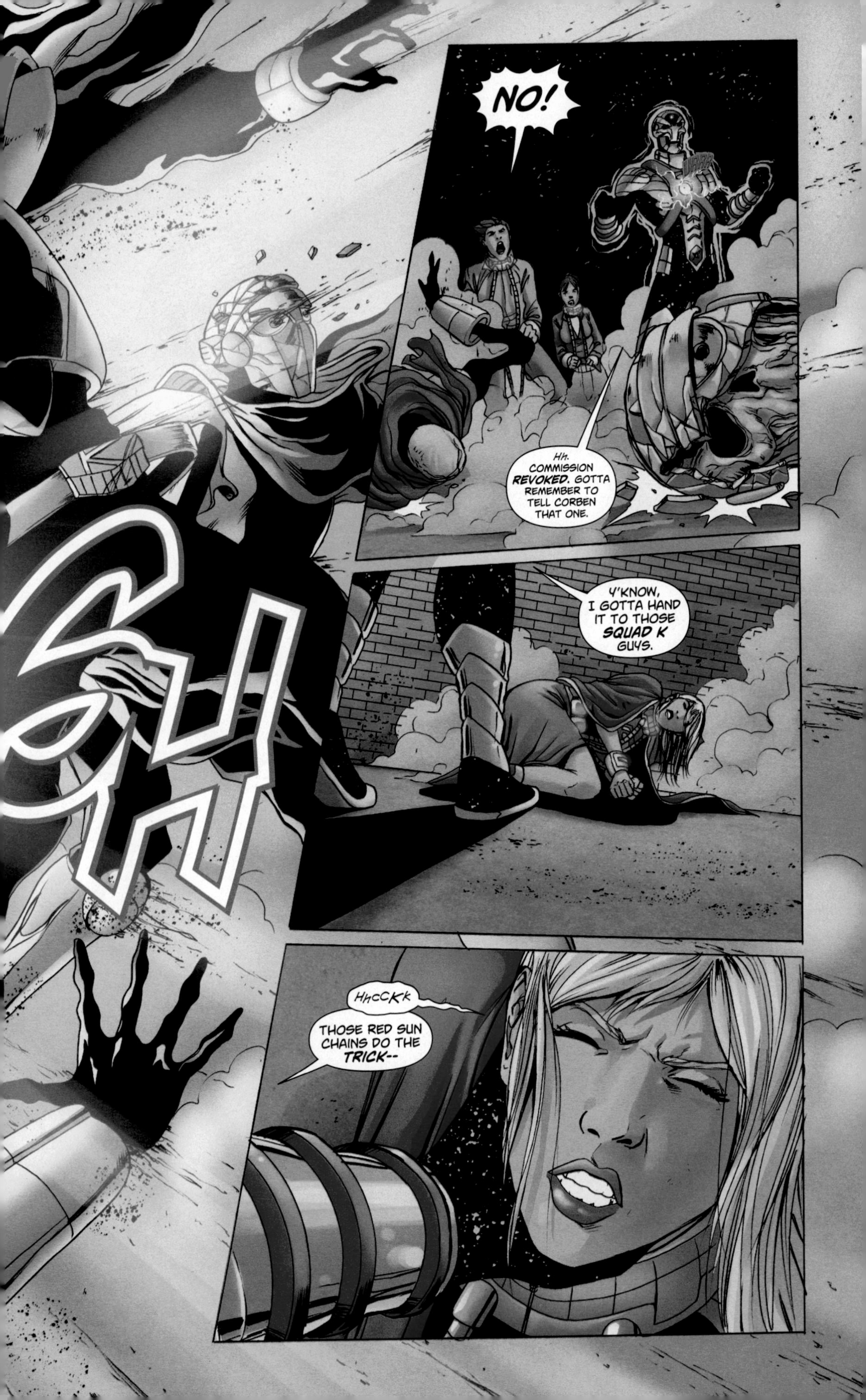
NO!
Hh. COMMISSION REVOKED. GOTTA REMEMBER TO TELL CORBEN THAT ONE.
SH
Y'KNOW, I GOTTA HAND IT TO THOSE SQUAD K GUYS.
HhcCKk
THOSE RED SUN CHAINS DO THE TRICK--

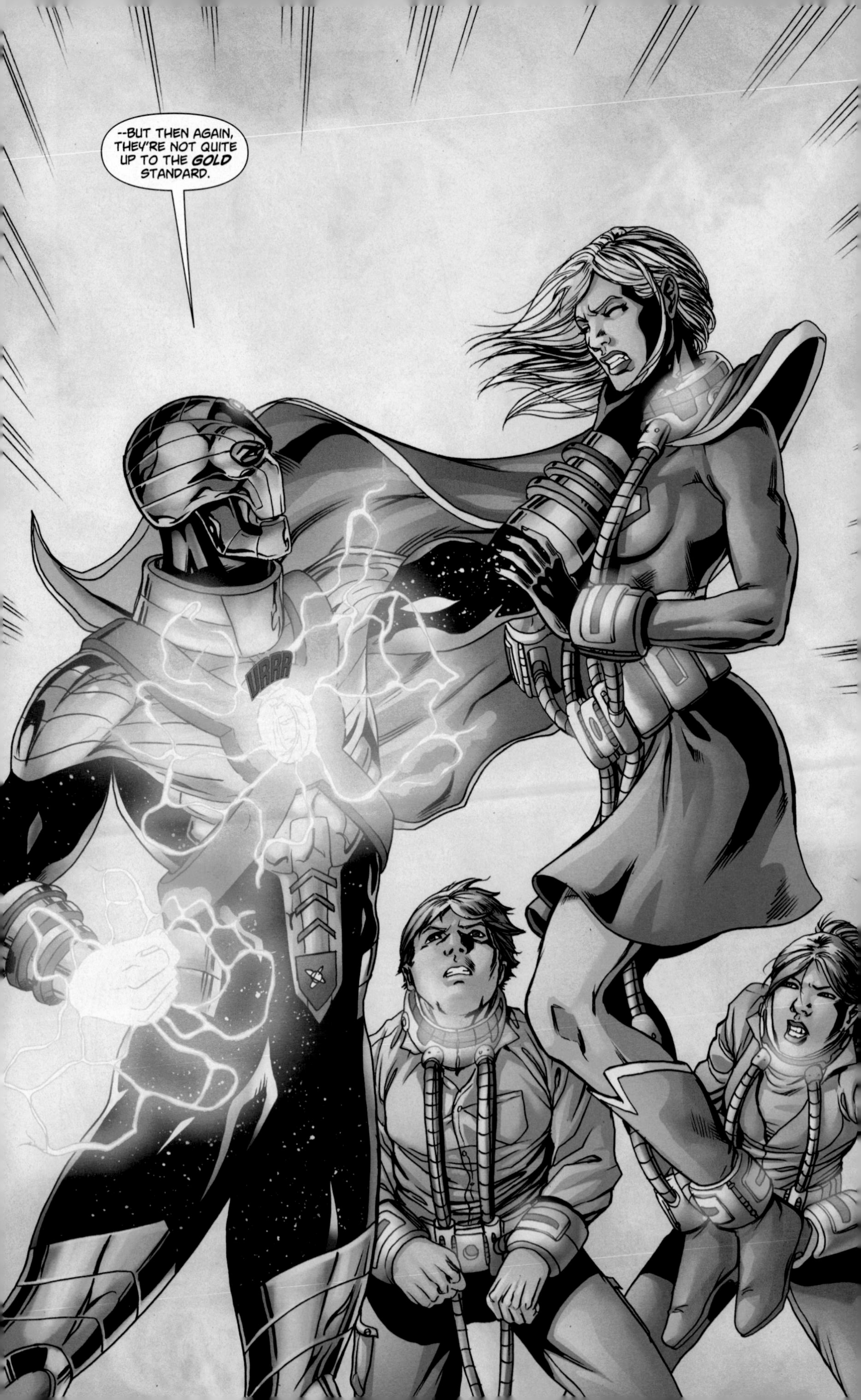
--BUT THEN AGAIN, THEY'RE NOT QUITE UP TO THE GOLD STANDARD.

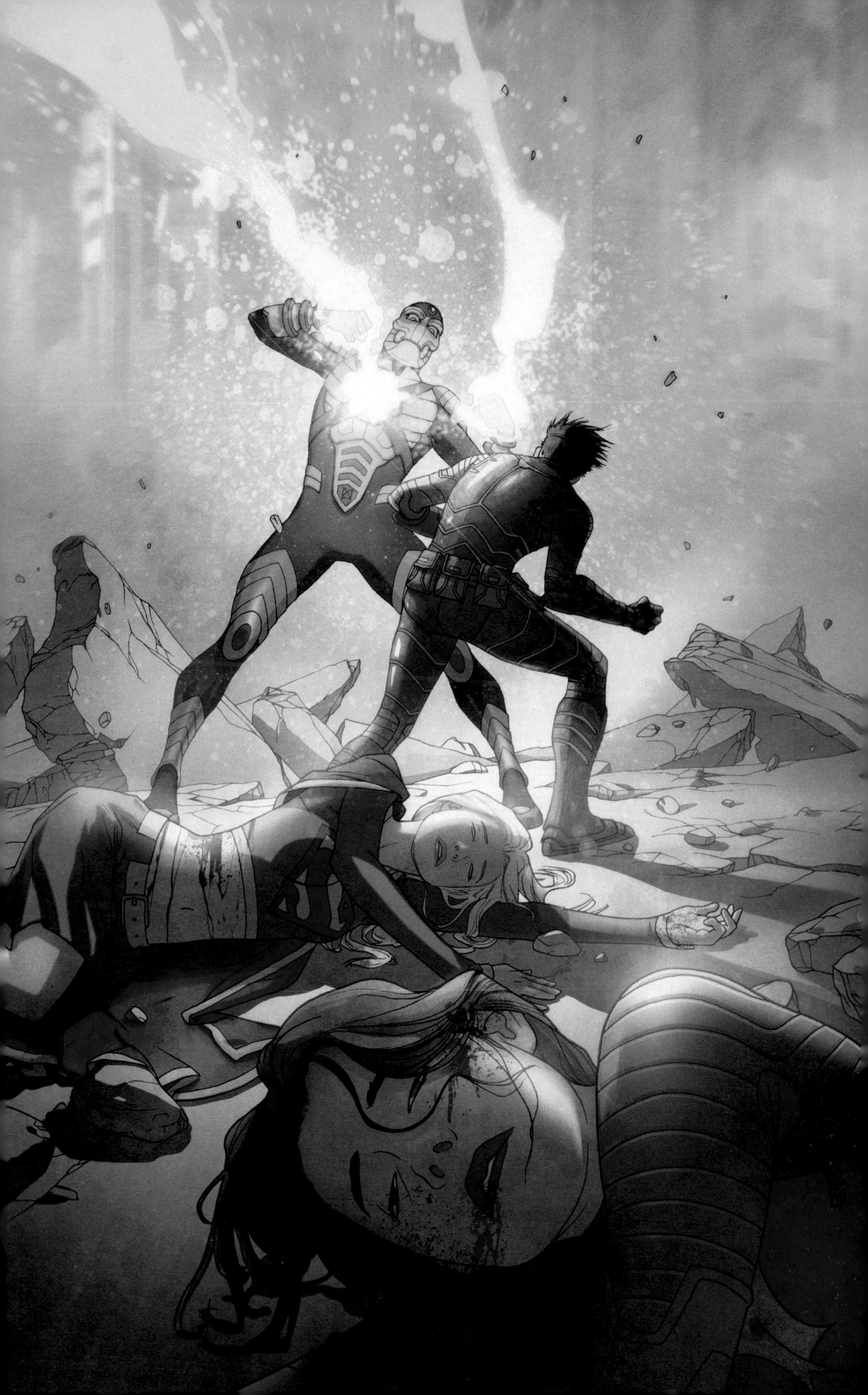

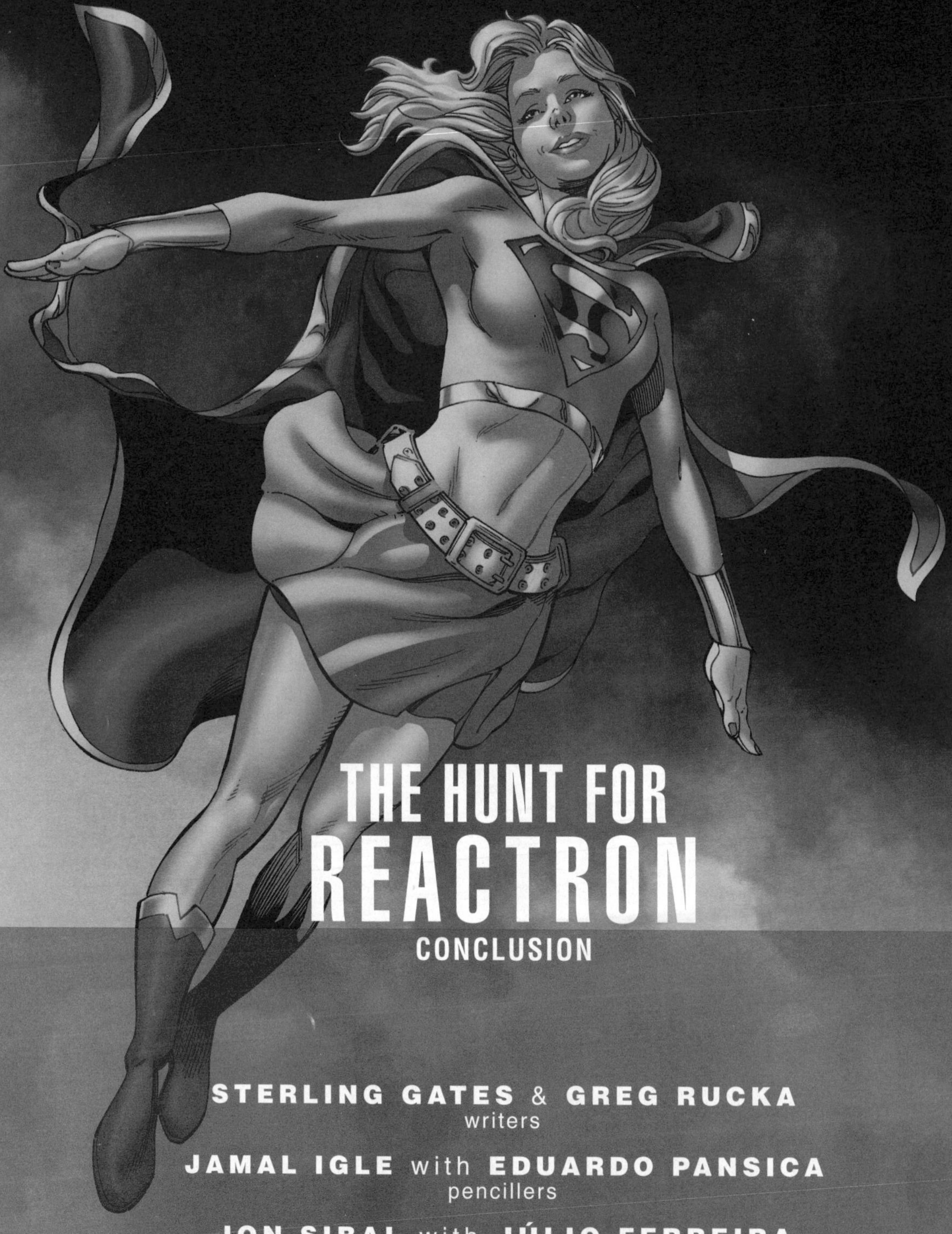

# THE HUNT FOR REACTRON

## CONCLUSION

**STERLING GATES** & **GREG RUCKA**
writers

**JAMAL IGLE** with **EDUARDO PANSICA**
pencillers

**JON SIBAL** with **JÚLIO FERREIRA**
inkers

**NEI RUFFINO** with **PETE PANTAZIS**
colorist

**JARED K. FLETCHER**
letterer

**JOSHUA MIDDLETON**
cover

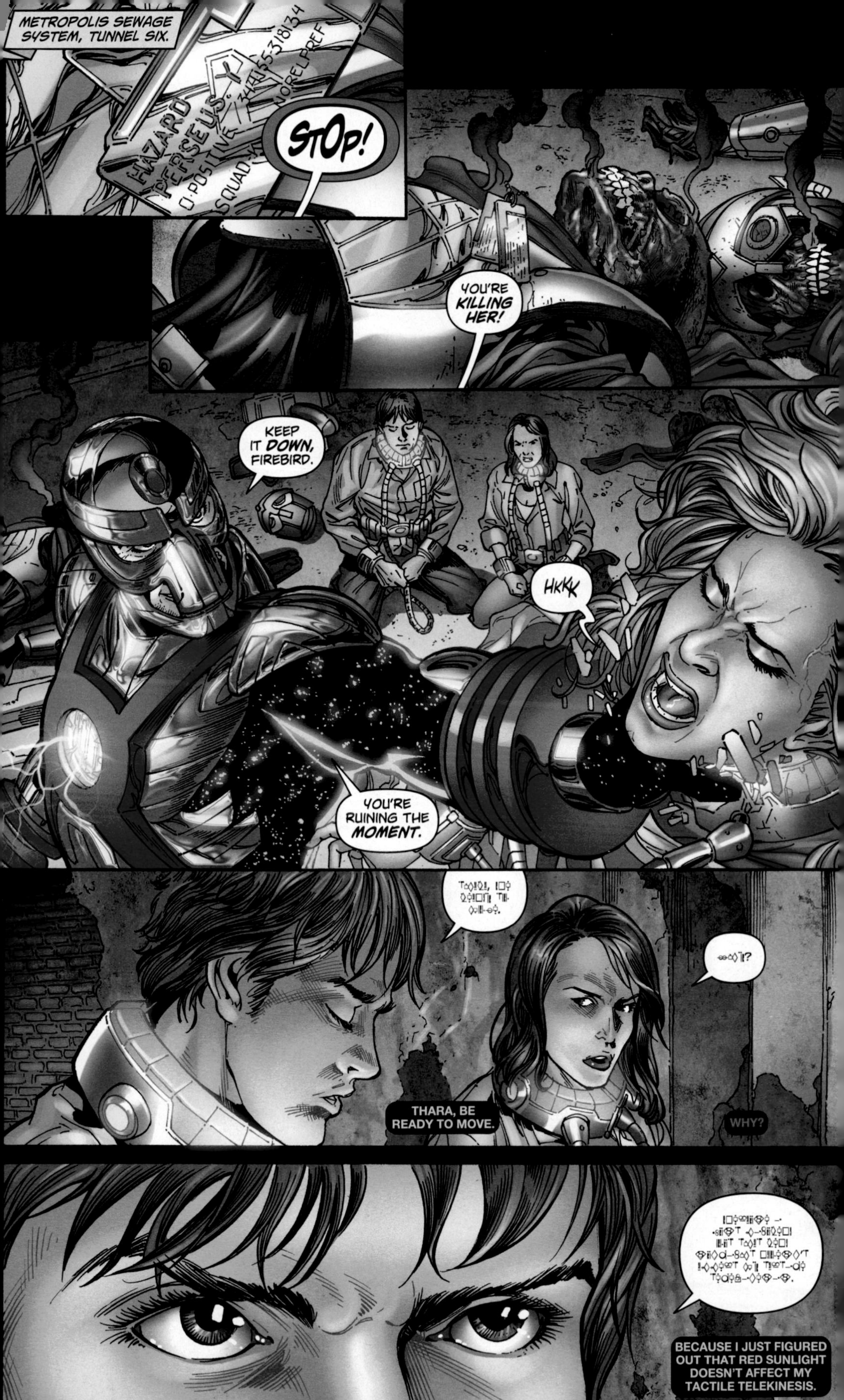
METROPOLIS SEWAGE SYSTEM, TUNNEL SIX.
STOP!
YOU'RE KILLING HER!
KEEP IT DOWN, FIREBIRD.
HKKK
YOU'RE RUINING THE MOMENT.
THARA, BE READY TO MOVE.
WHY?
BECAUSE I JUST FIGURED OUT THAT RED SUNLIGHT DOESN'T AFFECT MY TACTILE TELEKINESIS.

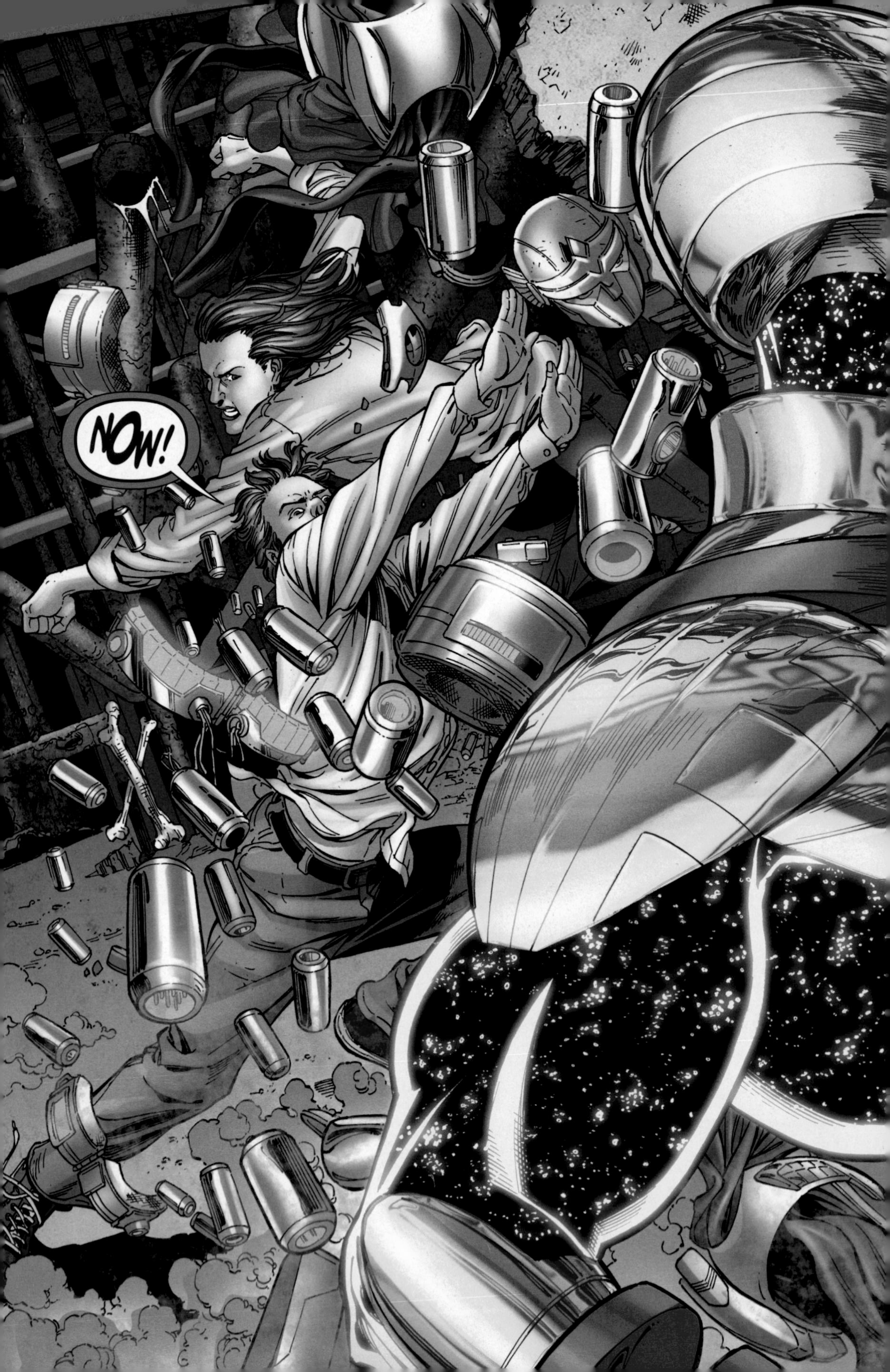
NOW!

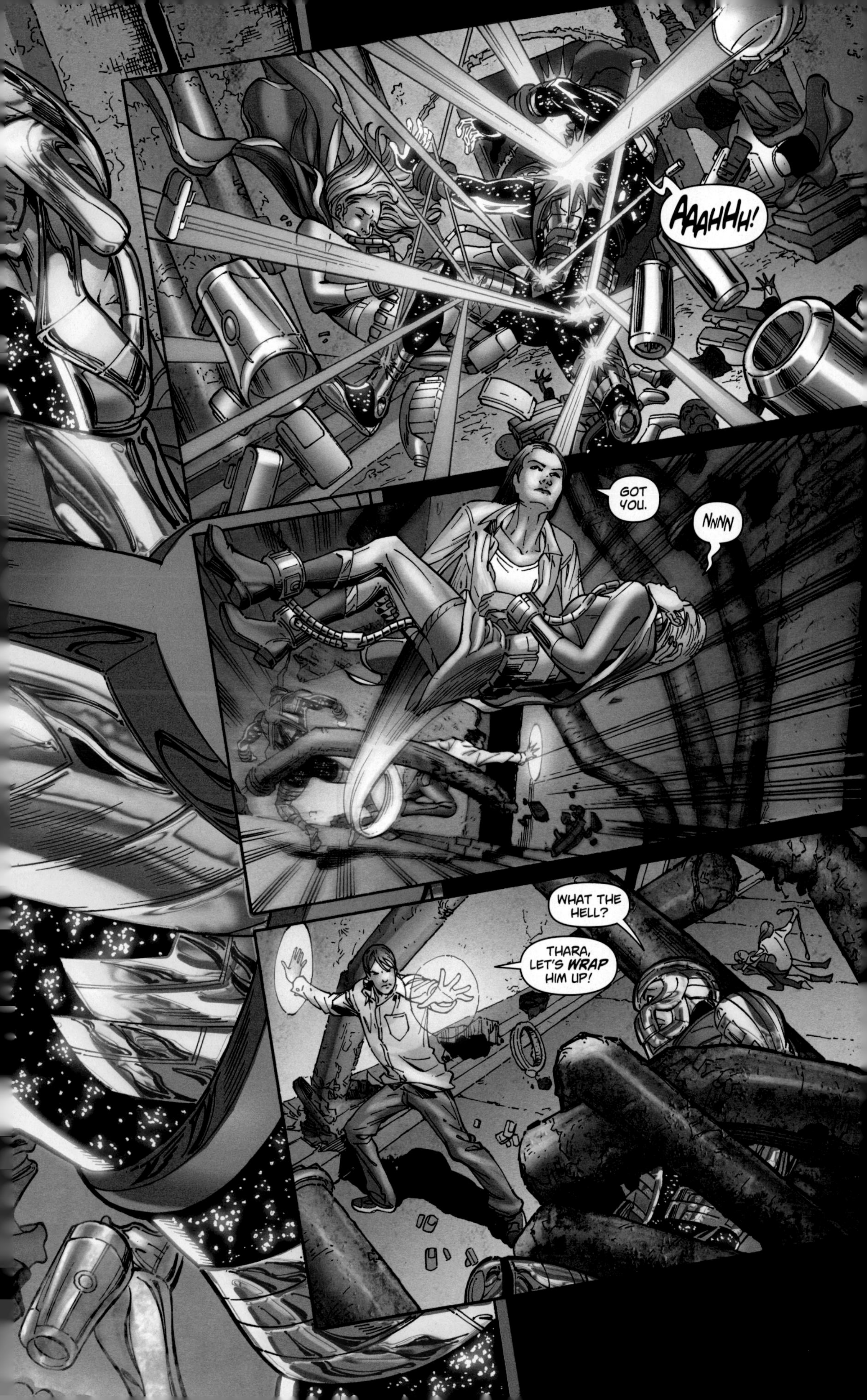
AAAHHH!
GOT YOU.
NNNN
WHAT THE HELL?
THARA, LET'S WRAP HIM UP!

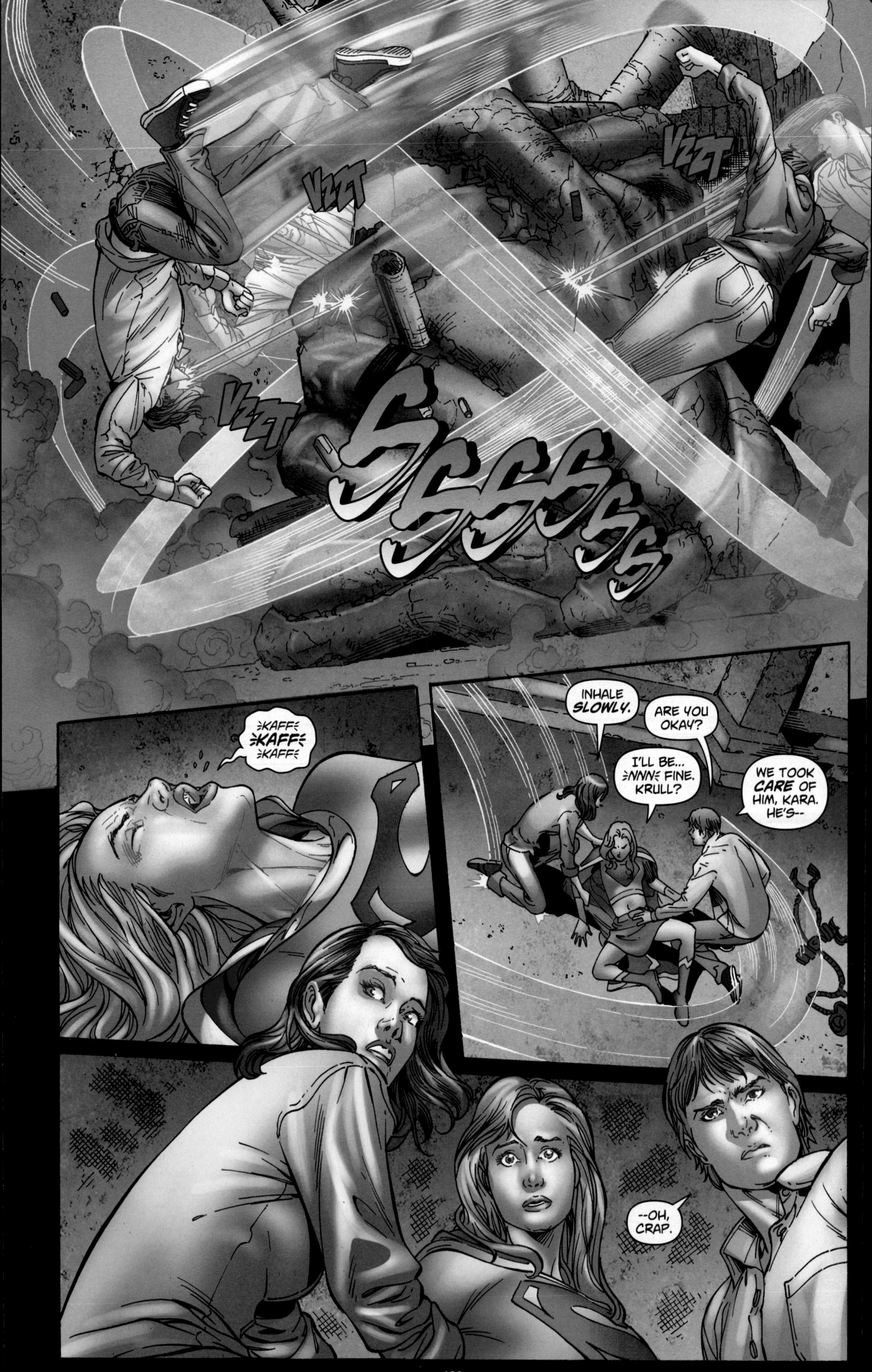
VZZT
VZZT
VZZT
SSSSSS
KAFF KAFF KAFF
INHALE SLOWLY.
ARE YOU OKAY?
I'LL BE... NNN FINE. KRULL?
WE TOOK CARE OF HIM, KARA. HE'S--
--OH, CRAP.

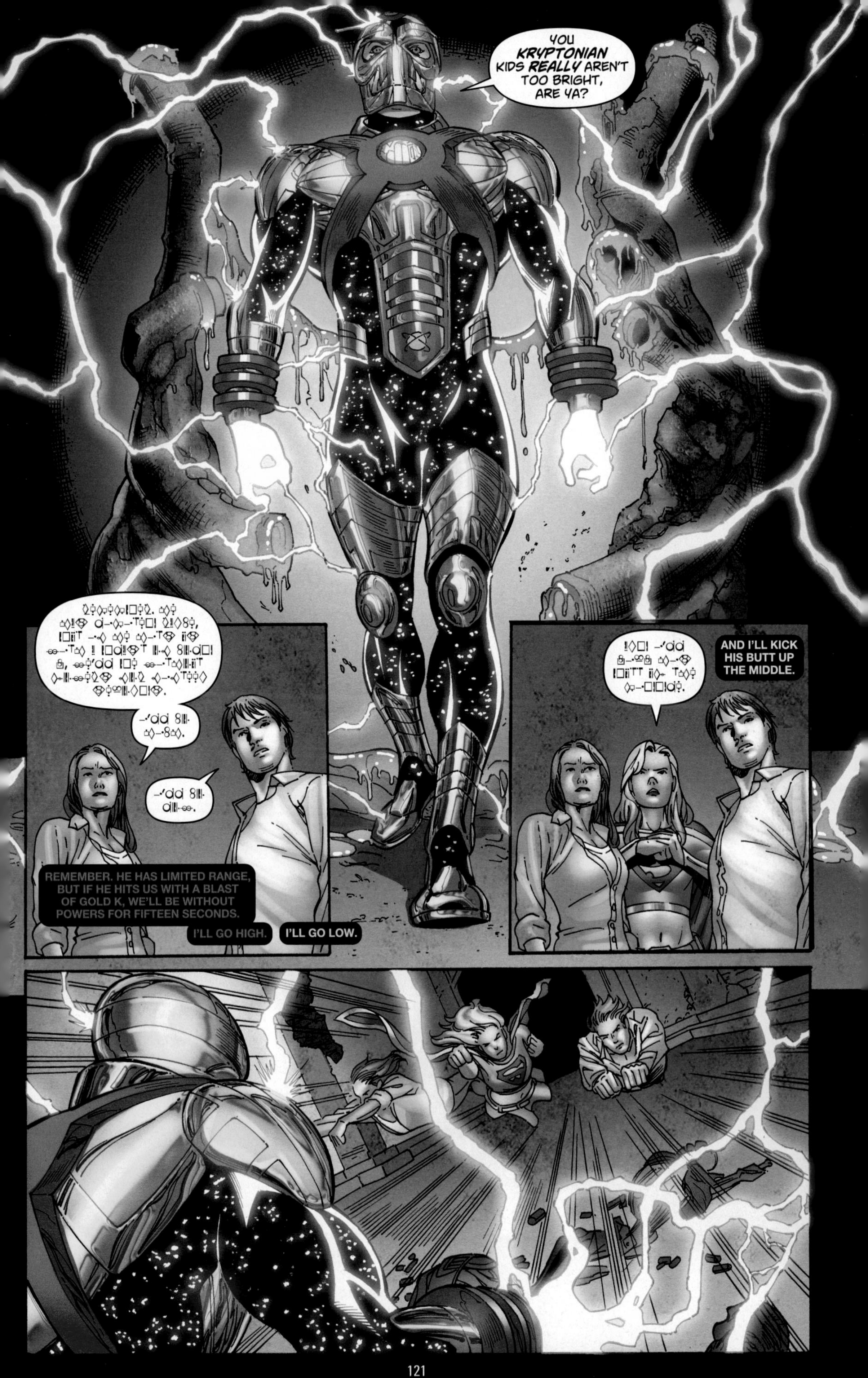
YOU KRYPTONIAN KIDS REALLY AREN'T TOO BRIGHT, ARE YA?
REMEMBER. HE HAS LIMITED RANGE, BUT IF HE HITS US WITH A BLAST OF GOLD K, WE'LL BE WITHOUT POWERS FOR FIFTEEN SECONDS.
I'LL GO HIGH.
I'LL GO LOW.
AND I'LL KICK HIS BUTT UP THE MIDDLE.

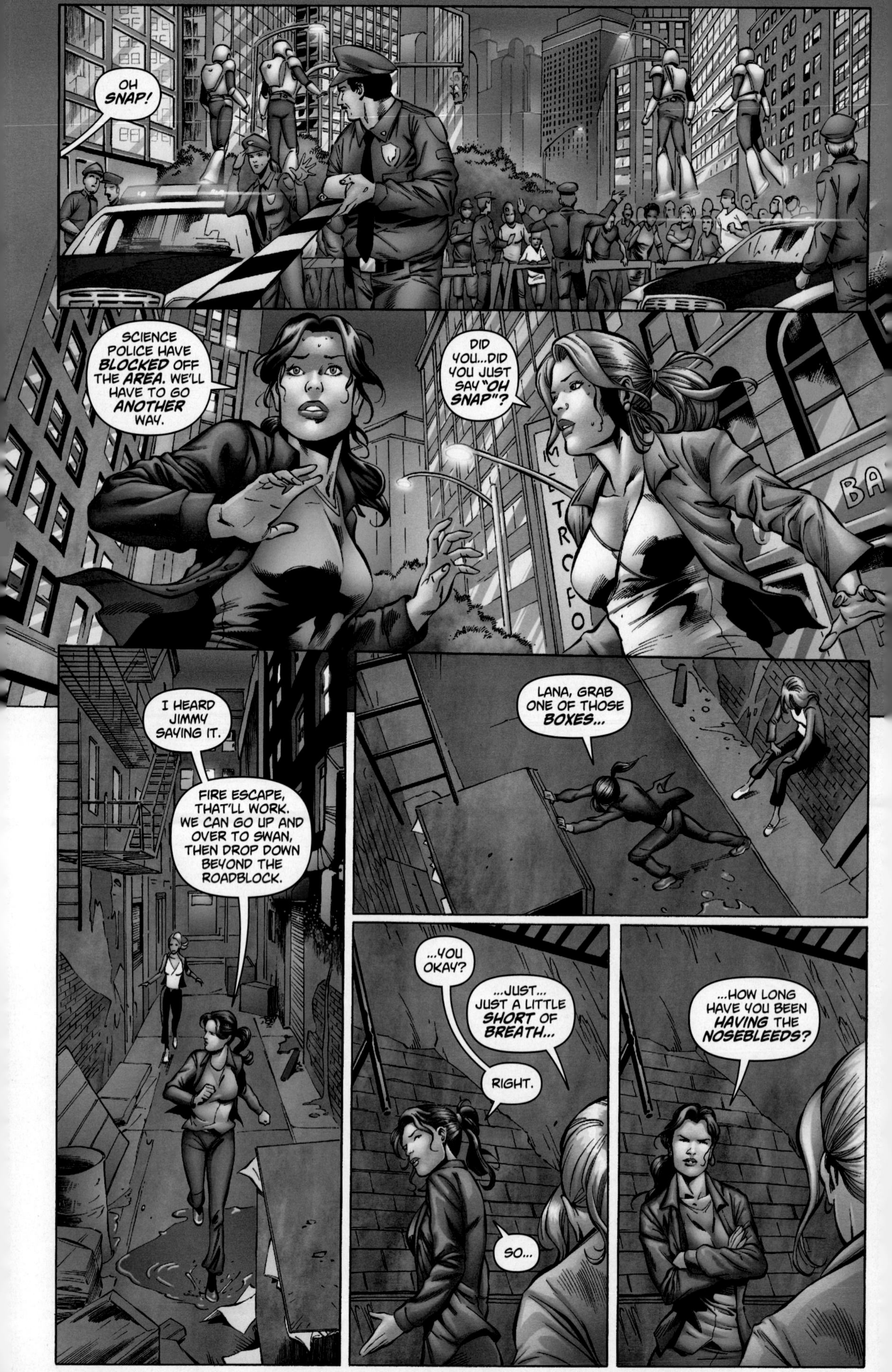
OH SNAP!
SCIENCE POLICE HAVE BLOCKED OFF THE AREA. WE'LL HAVE TO GO ANOTHER WAY.
DID YOU...DID YOU JUST SAY "OH SNAP"?
METROPO
I HEARD JIMMY SAYING IT.
FIRE ESCAPE, THAT'LL WORK. WE CAN GO UP AND OVER TO SWAN, THEN DROP DOWN BEYOND THE ROADBLOCK.
LANA, GRAB ONE OF THOSE BOXES...
...YOU OKAY?
...JUST... JUST A LITTLE SHORT OF BREATH...
RIGHT.
SO...
...HOW LONG HAVE YOU BEEN HAVING THE NOSEBLEEDS?

OH, GOD--

YEAH, I *THOUGHT* I SAW *DRIED BLOOD* BACK AT THE *MUSEUM.* PROBLEM WITH *NO* RUNNING WATER, YOU'VE GOT NO WAY TO *CLEAN UP.*

I'VE BEEN USING THOSE WET TOWLETTES, YOU KNOW.

BEEN USING THEM A *LOT?*

MORE THAN I'D *LIKE.*

I'VE BEEN GETTING *HEADACHES,* TOO.

HAVING A *HARD* TIME KEEPING *FOOD* DOWN.

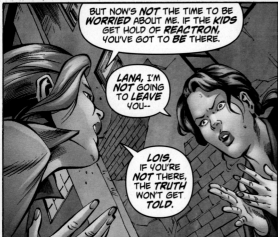

BUT NOW'S *NOT* THE TIME TO BE *WORRIED* ABOUT ME. IF THE *KIDS* GET HOLD OF *REACTRON,* YOU'VE GOT TO BE THERE.

LANA, I'M *NOT* GOING TO *LEAVE* YOU--

*LOIS,* IF YOU'RE *NOT* THERE, THE *TRUTH* WON'T GET *TOLD.*

I'LL GO BACK TO MY PLACE, I'LL BE *FINE.*

YOU'RE SURE?

POSITIVE. *GO.*

I'LL BE FINE.

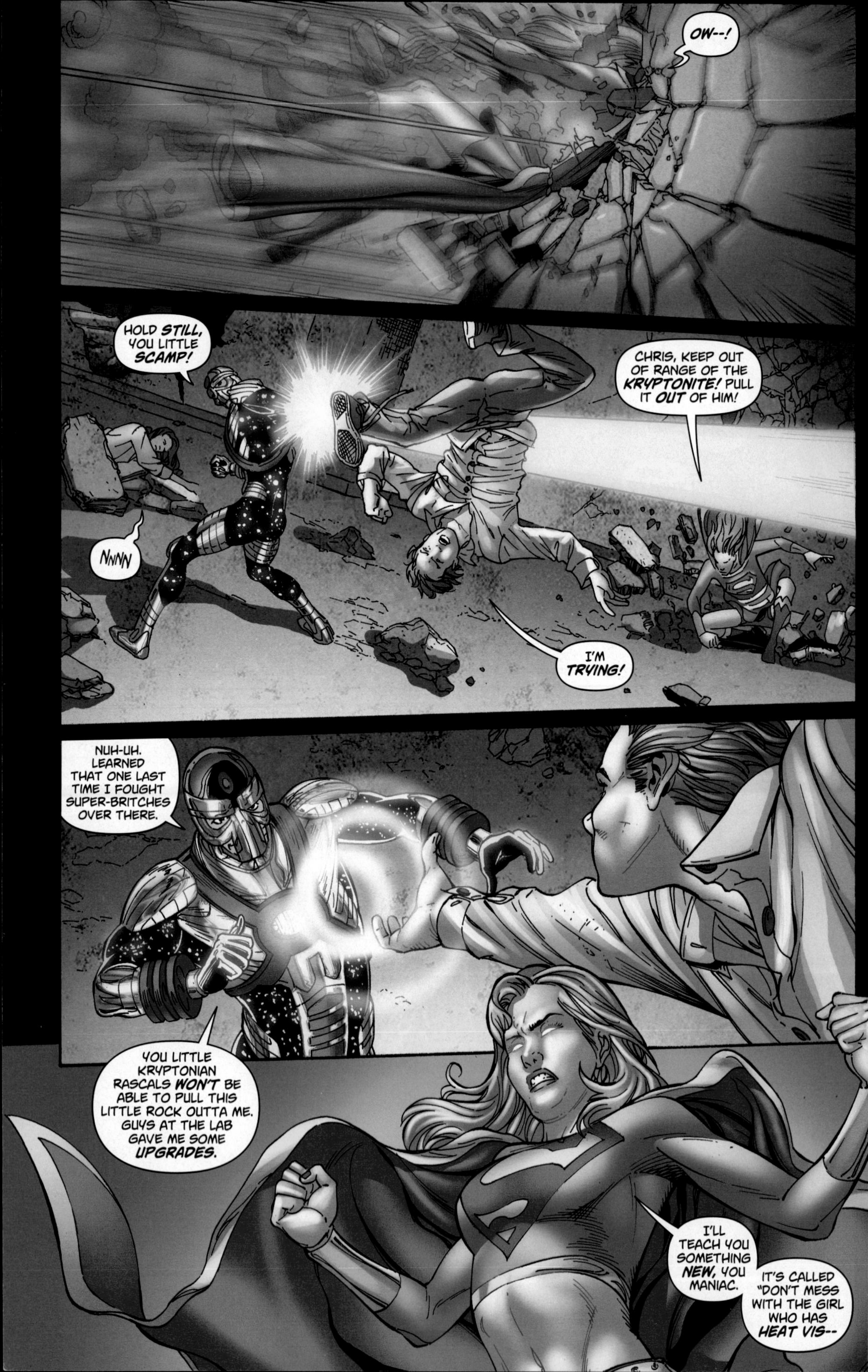

OW--!
HOLD STILL, YOU LITTLE SCAMP!
CHRIS, KEEP OUT OF RANGE OF THE KRYPTONITE! PULL IT OUT OF HIM!
NNNN
I'M TRYING!
NUH-UH. LEARNED THAT ONE LAST TIME I FOUGHT SUPER-BRITCHES OVER THERE.
YOU LITTLE KRYPTONIAN RASCALS WON'T BE ABLE TO PULL THIS LITTLE ROCK OUTTA ME. GUYS AT THE LAB GAVE ME SOME UPGRADES.
I'LL TEACH YOU SOMETHING NEW, YOU MANIAC.
IT'S CALLED "DON'T MESS WITH THE GIRL WHO HAS HEAT VIS--

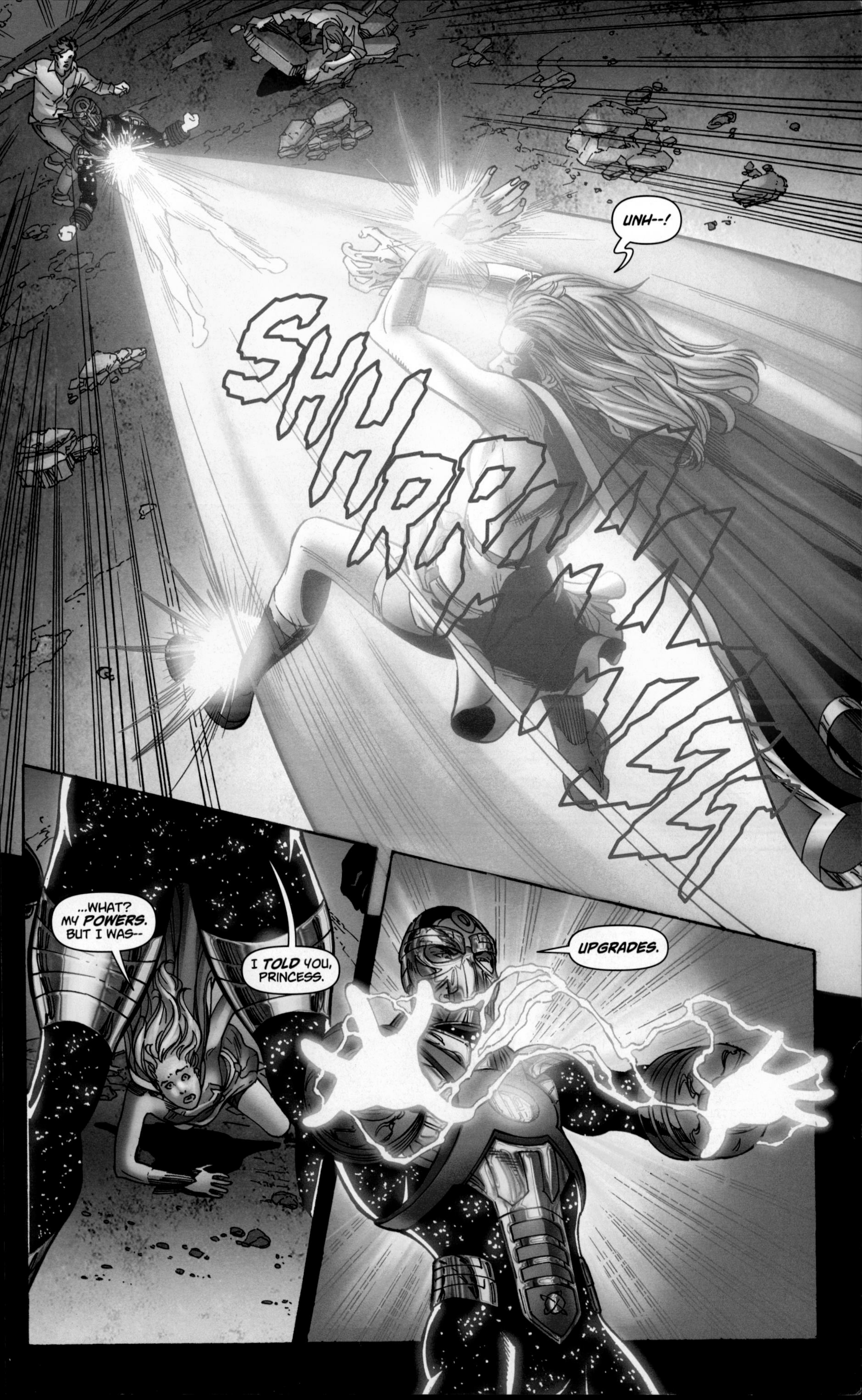
UNH--!
SHHRRMM-MMSST
...WHAT? MY POWERS. BUT I WAS--
I TOLD YOU, PRINCESS.
UPGRADES.

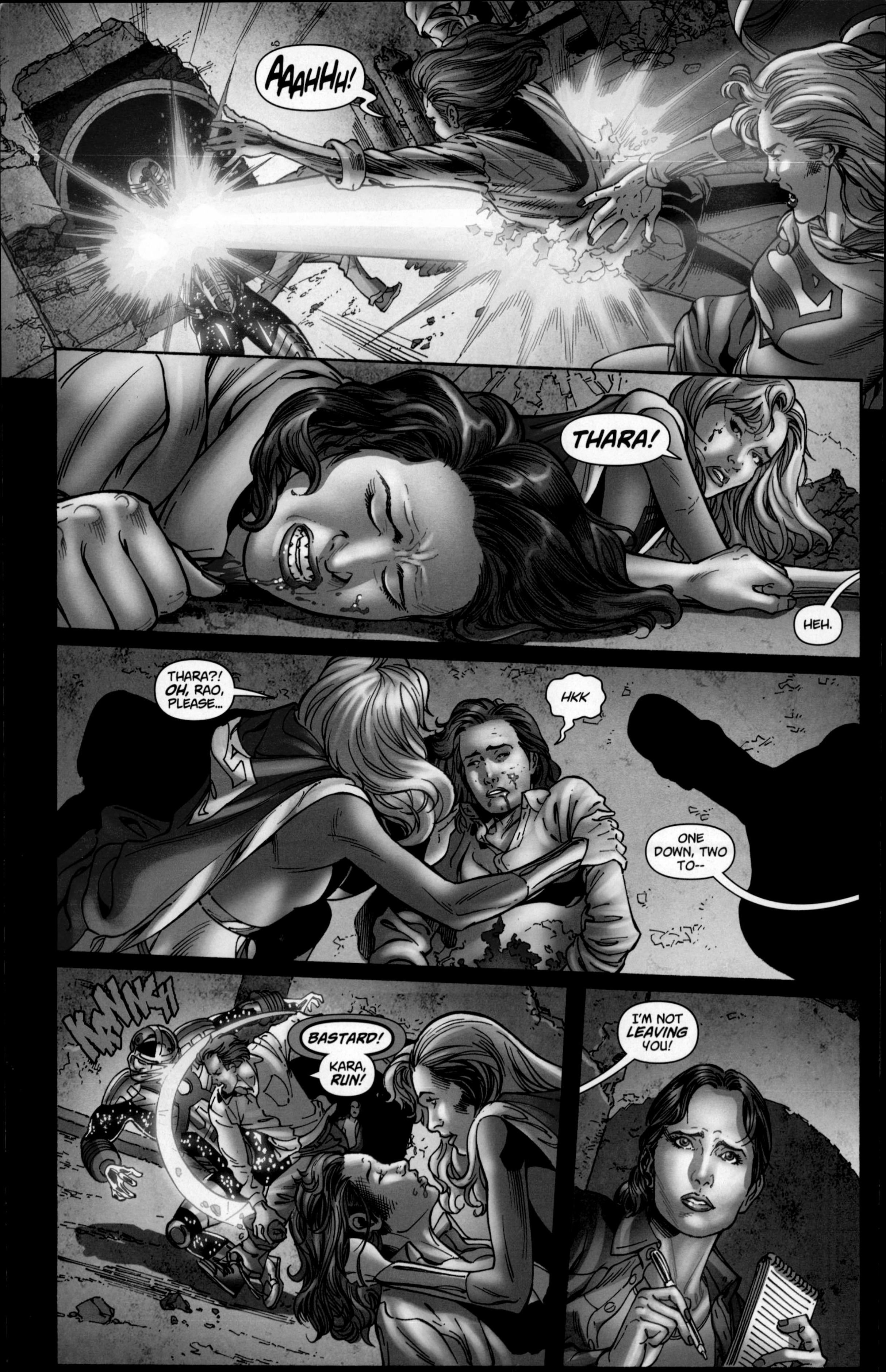
AAAHHH!
THARA!
HEH.
THARA?! OH, RAO, PLEASE...
HKK
ONE DOWN, TWO TO--
BASTARD!
KARA, RUN!
I'M NOT LEAVING YOU!

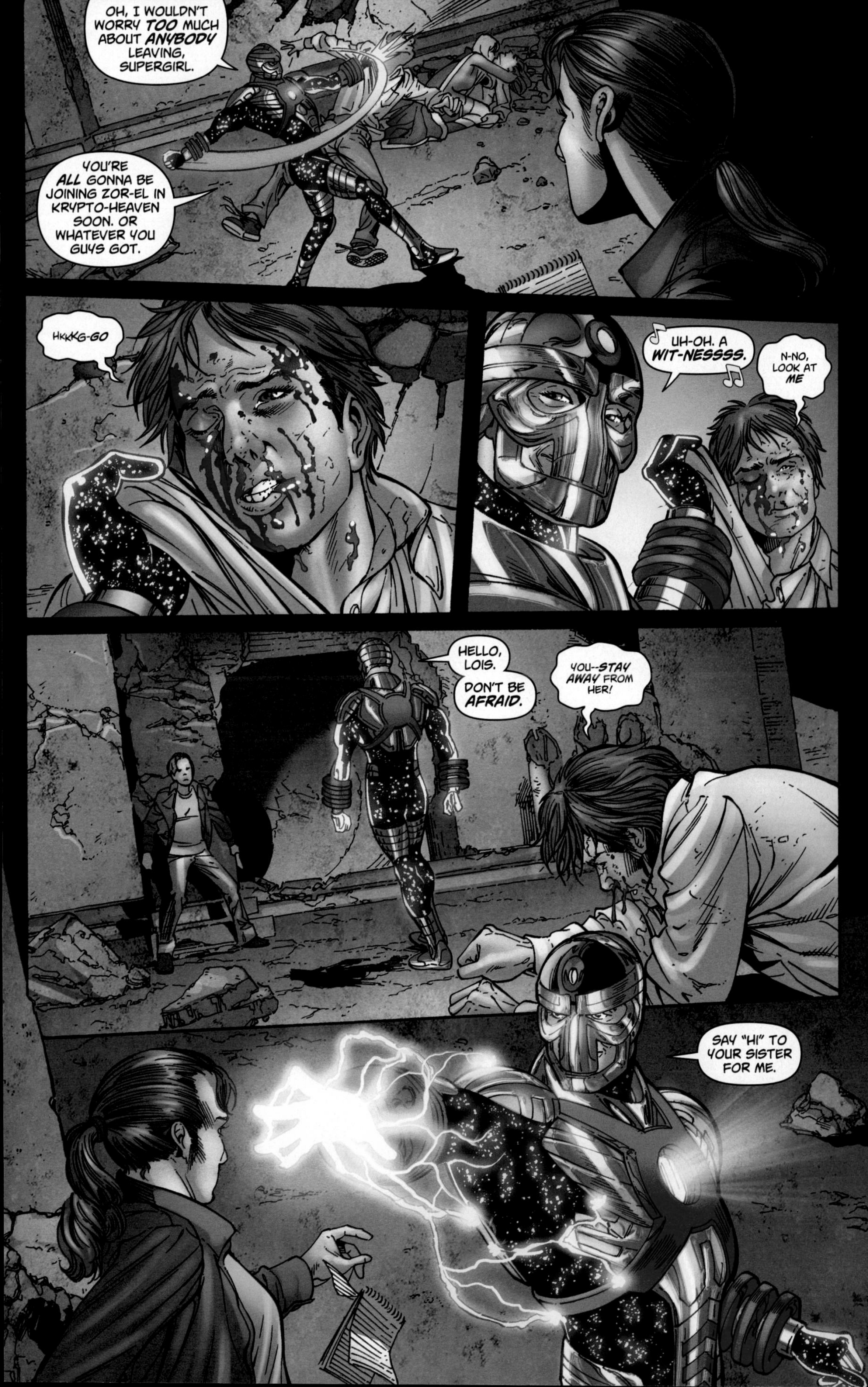
OH, I WOULDN'T WORRY TOO MUCH ABOUT ANYBODY LEAVING, SUPERGIRL.
YOU'RE ALL GONNA BE JOINING ZOR-EL IN KRYPTO-HEAVEN SOON. OR WHATEVER YOU GUYS GOT.
HKKKG-GO
UH-OH. A WIT-NESSSS.
N-NO, LOOK AT ME
HELLO, LOIS.
DON'T BE AFRAID.
YOU--STAY AWAY FROM HER!
SAY "HI" TO YOUR SISTER FOR ME.

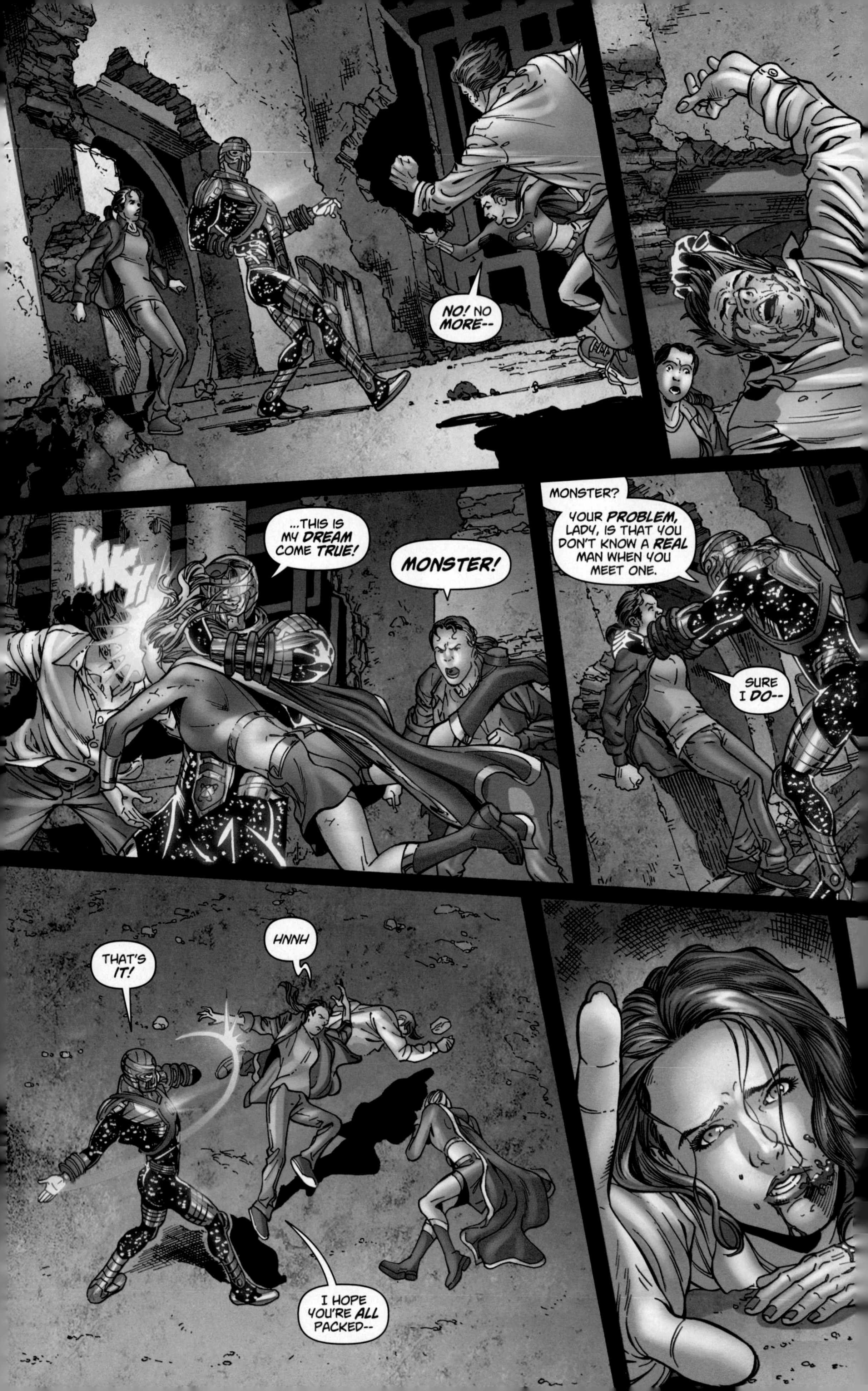
NO! NO MORE--
KAKSH
...THIS IS MY DREAM COME TRUE!
MONSTER!
MONSTER?
YOUR PROBLEM, LADY, IS THAT YOU DON'T KNOW A REAL MAN WHEN YOU MEET ONE.
SURE I DO--
THAT'S IT!
HNNH
I HOPE YOU'RE ALL PACKED--

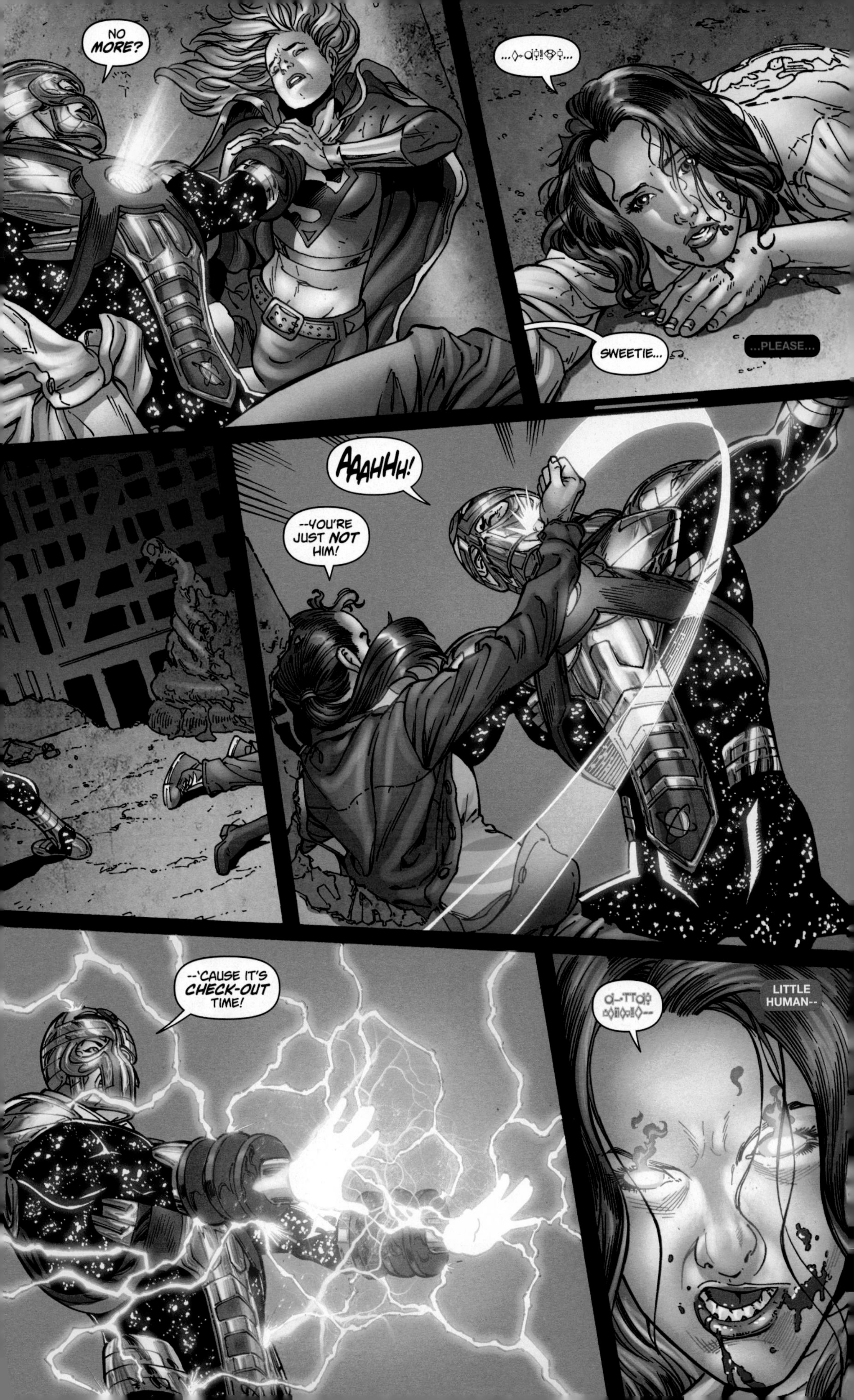
NO MORE?
SWEETIE...
...PLEASE...
AAAHHH!
--YOU'RE JUST NOT HIM!
--'CAUSE IT'S CHECK-OUT TIME!
LITTLE HUMAN--

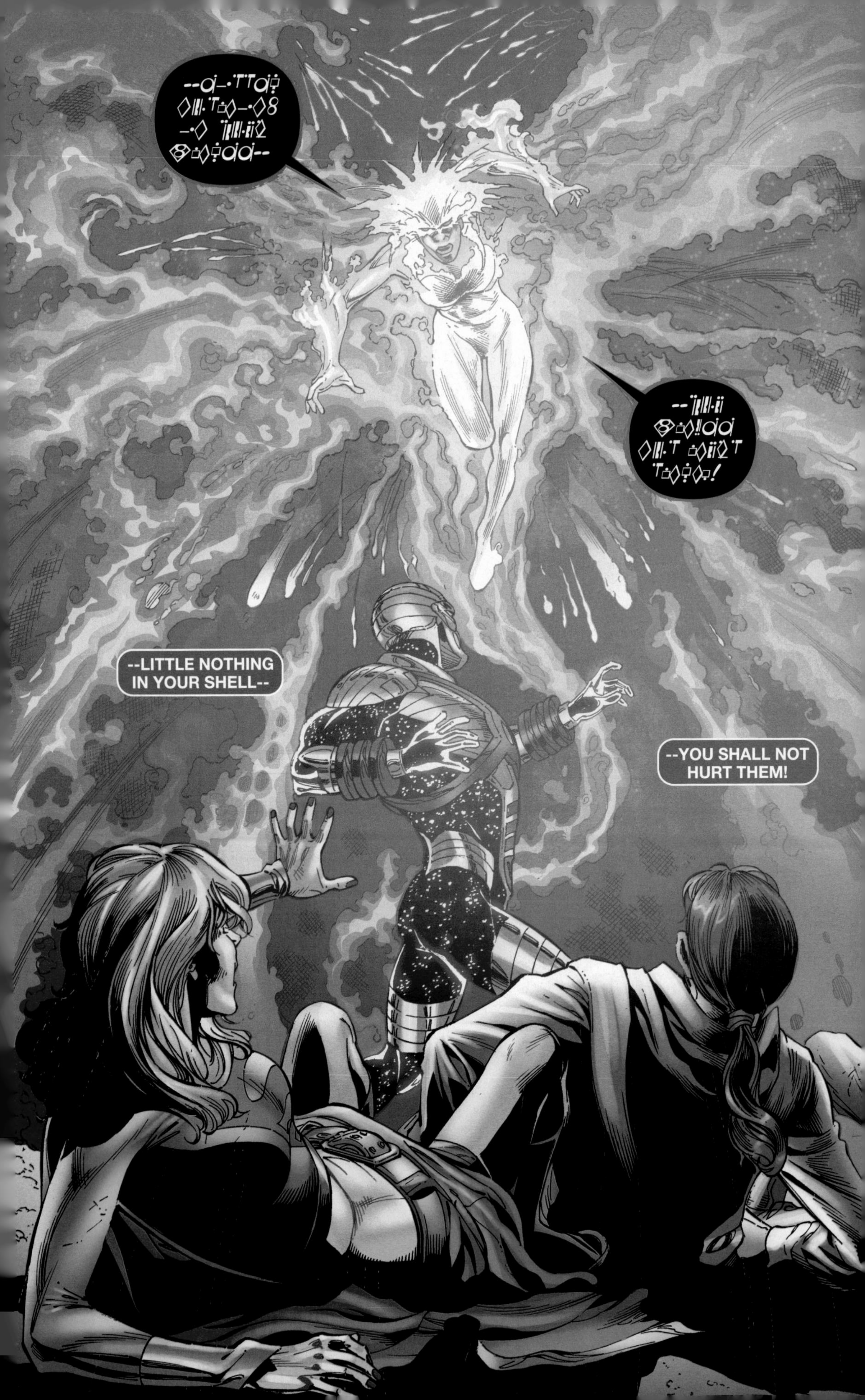
--LITTLE NOTHING IN YOUR SHELL--
--YOU SHALL NOT HURT THEM!

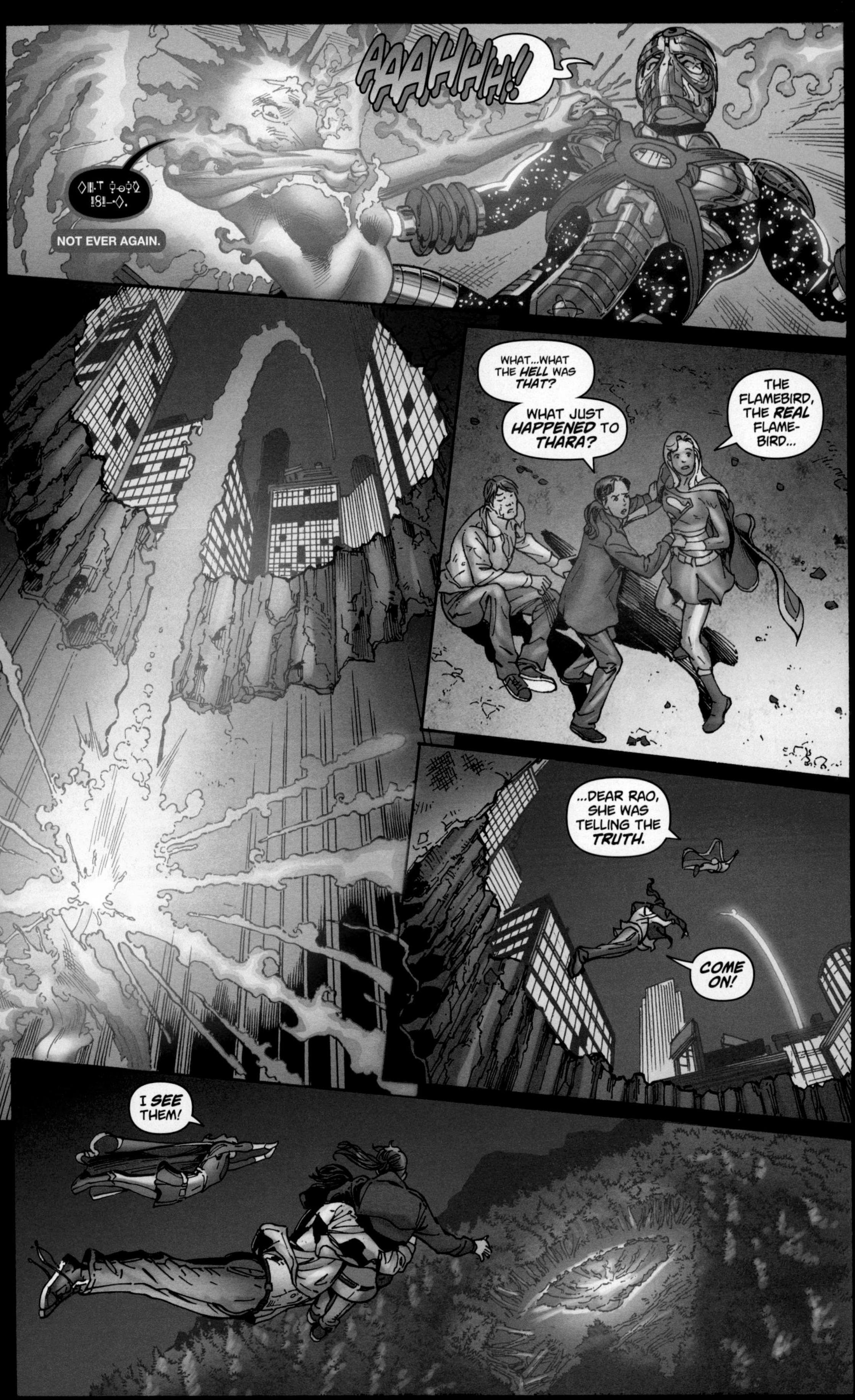
AAAHHHH!
NOT EVER AGAIN.
WHAT...WHAT THE HELL WAS THAT?
WHAT JUST HAPPENED TO THARA?
THE FLAMEBIRD, THE REAL FLAME-BIRD...
...DEAR RAO, SHE WAS TELLING THE TRUTH.
COME ON!
I SEE THEM!

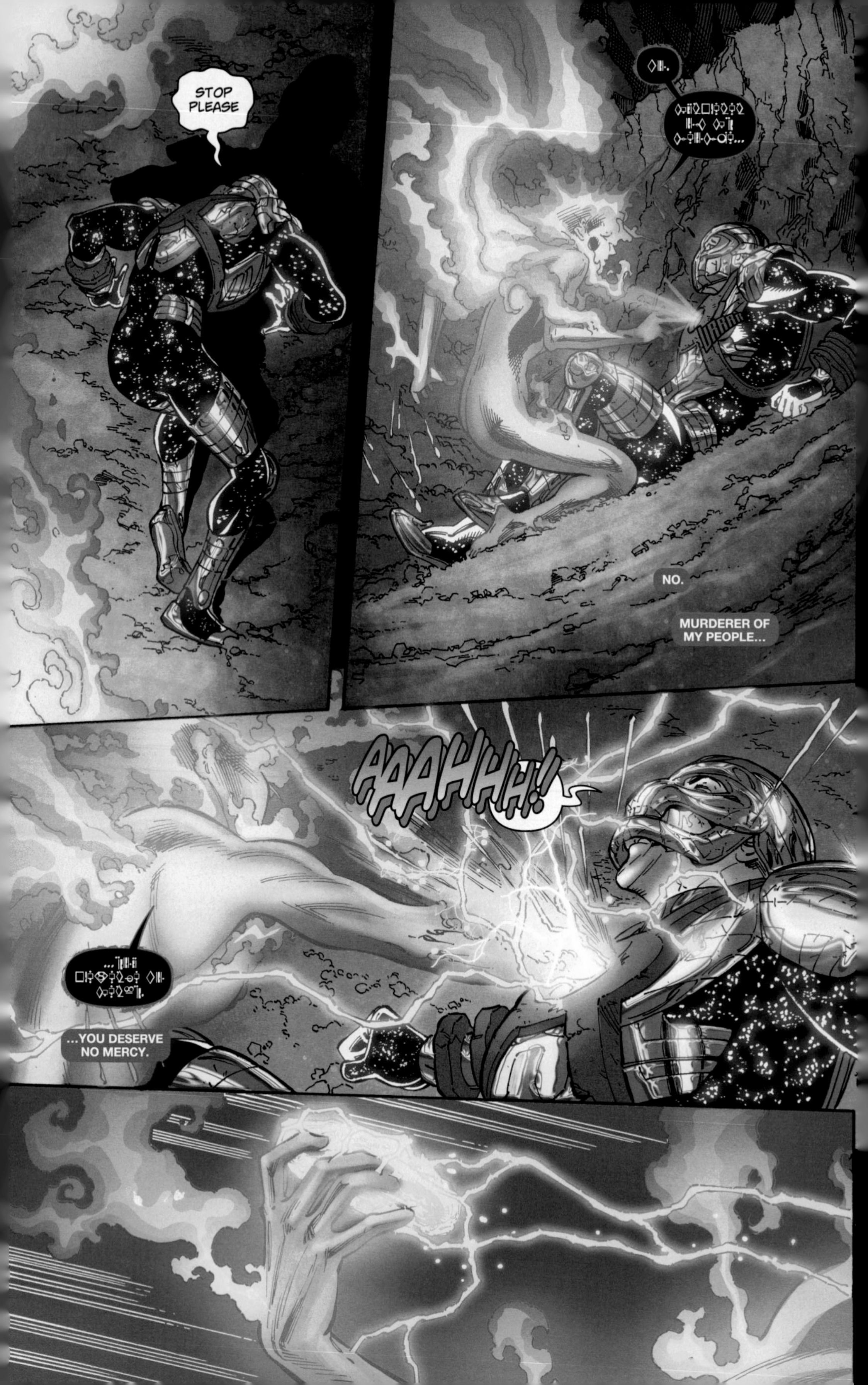
STOP PLEASE
NO.
MURDERER OF MY PEOPLE...
AAAHHHH!
...YOU DESERVE NO MERCY.

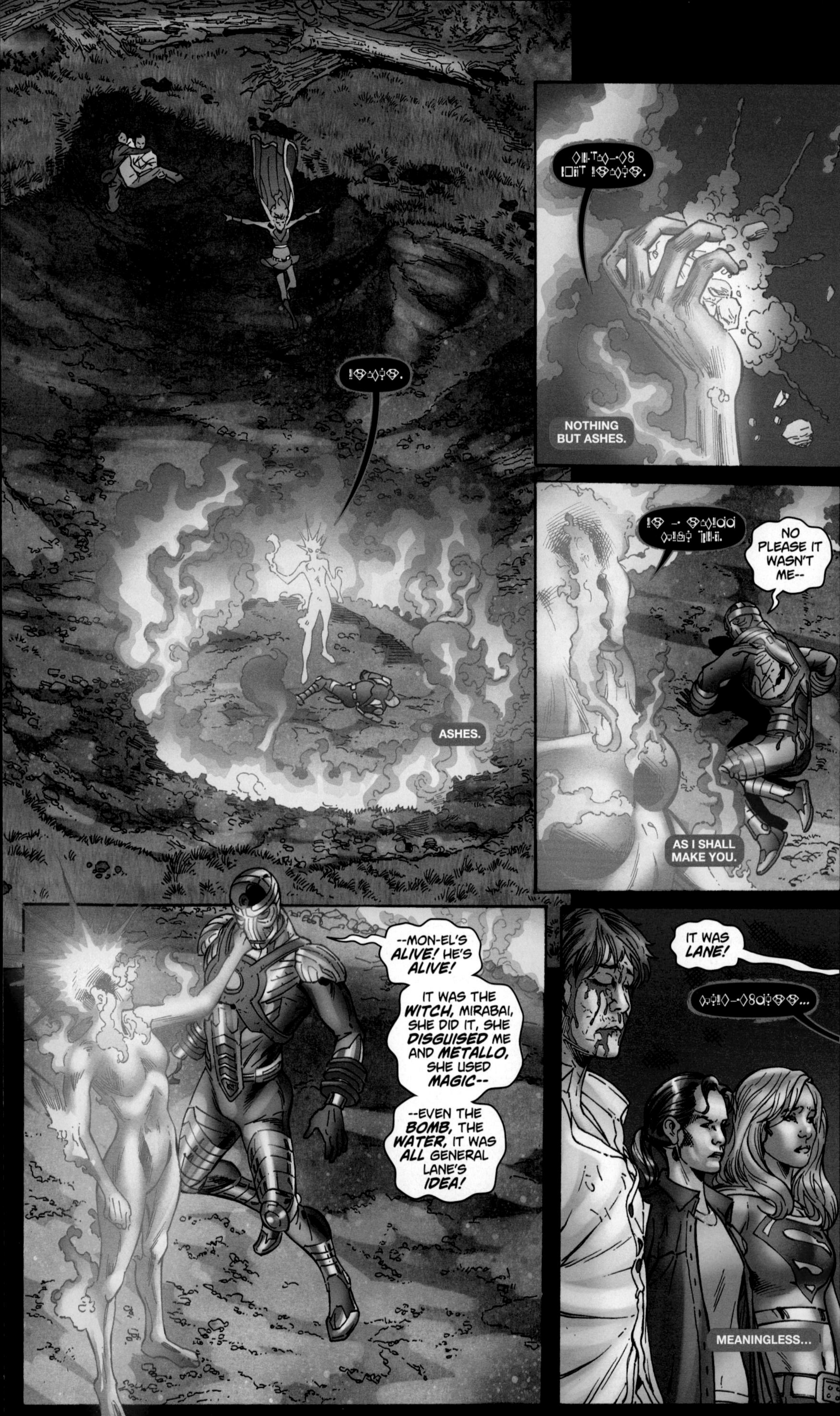
ASHES.
NOTHING BUT ASHES.
NO PLEASE IT WASN'T ME--
AS I SHALL MAKE YOU.
--MON-EL'S ALIVE! HE'S ALIVE!
IT WAS THE WITCH, MIRABAI, SHE DID IT, SHE DISGUISED ME AND METALLO, SHE USED MAGIC--
--EVEN THE BOMB, THE WATER, IT WAS ALL GENERAL LANE'S IDEA!
IT WAS LANE!
MEANINGLESS...

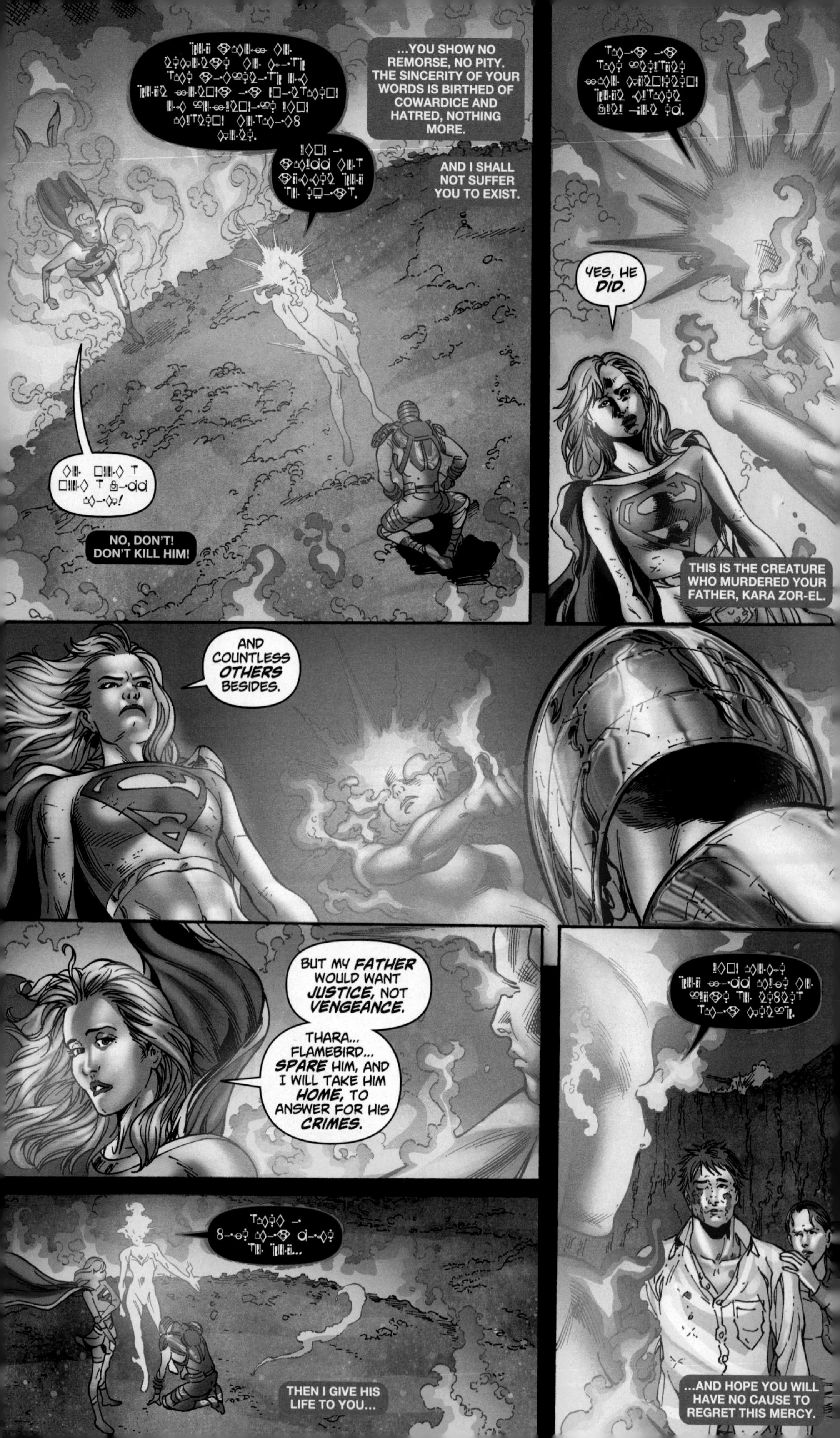
...YOU SHOW NO REMORSE, NO PITY. THE SINCERITY OF YOUR WORDS IS BIRTHED OF COWARDICE AND HATRED, NOTHING MORE.
AND I SHALL NOT SUFFER YOU TO EXIST.
NO, DON'T! DON'T KILL HIM!
THIS IS THE CREATURE WHO MURDERED YOUR FATHER, KARA ZOR-EL.
YES, HE DID.
AND COUNTLESS OTHERS BESIDES.
BUT MY FATHER WOULD WANT JUSTICE, NOT VENGEANCE.
THARA... FLAMEBIRD... SPARE HIM, AND I WILL TAKE HIM HOME, TO ANSWER FOR HIS CRIMES.
THEN I GIVE HIS LIFE TO YOU...
...AND HOPE YOU WILL HAVE NO CAUSE TO REGRET THIS MERCY.

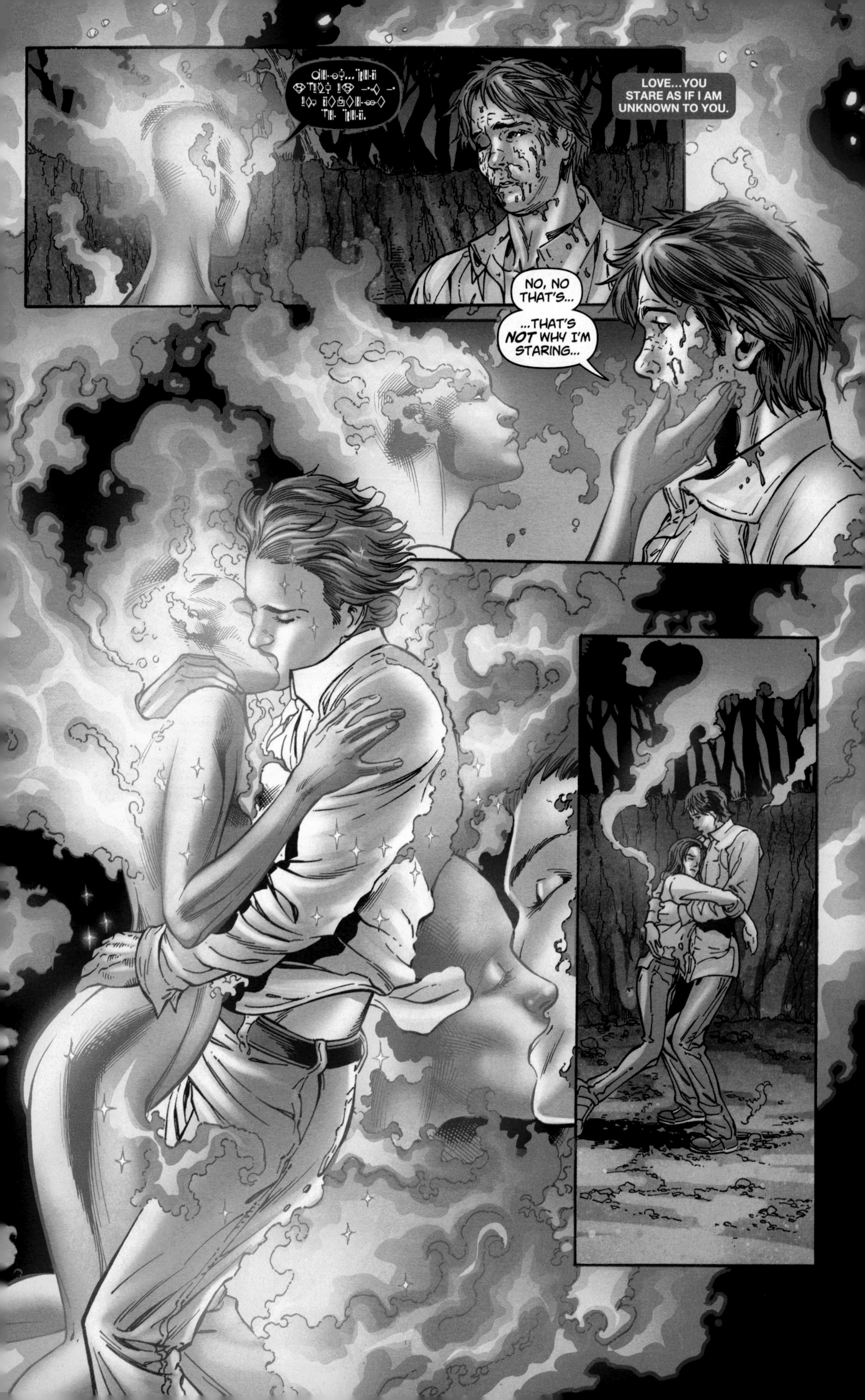
LOVE...YOU STARE AS IF I AM UNKNOWN TO YOU.
NO, NO THAT'S...
...THAT'S *NOT* WHY I'M STARING...

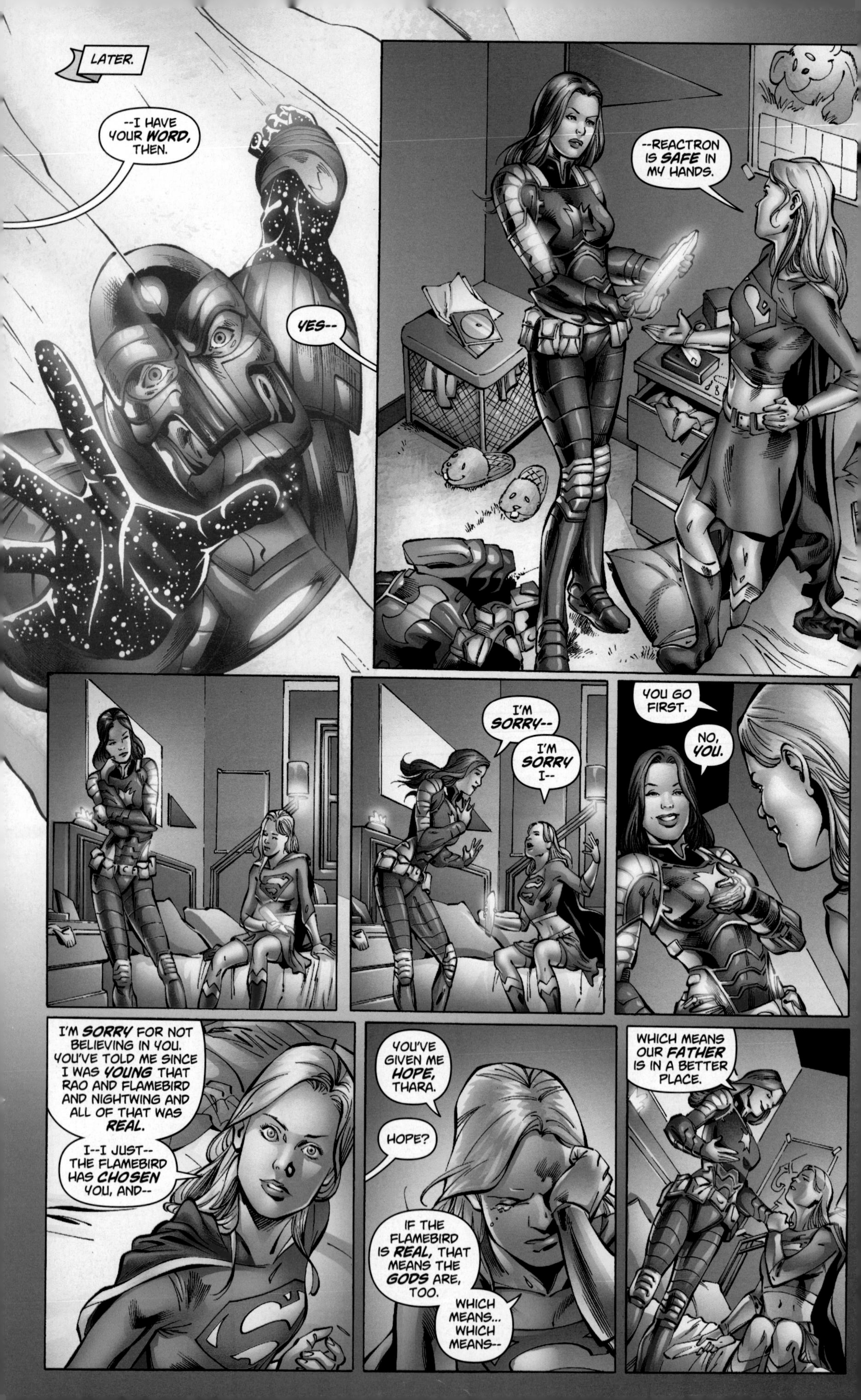
LATER.
--I HAVE YOUR WORD, THEN.
YES--
--REACTRON IS SAFE IN MY HANDS.
I'M SORRY--
I'M SORRY I--
YOU GO FIRST.
NO, YOU.
I'M SORRY FOR NOT BELIEVING IN YOU. YOU'VE TOLD ME SINCE I WAS YOUNG THAT RAO AND FLAMEBIRD AND NIGHTWING AND ALL OF THAT WAS REAL.
I--I JUST-- THE FLAMEBIRD HAS CHOSEN YOU, AND--
YOU'VE GIVEN ME HOPE, THARA.
HOPE?
IF THE FLAMEBIRD IS REAL, THAT MEANS THE GODS ARE, TOO.
WHICH MEANS... WHICH MEANS--
WHICH MEANS OUR FATHER IS IN A BETTER PLACE.

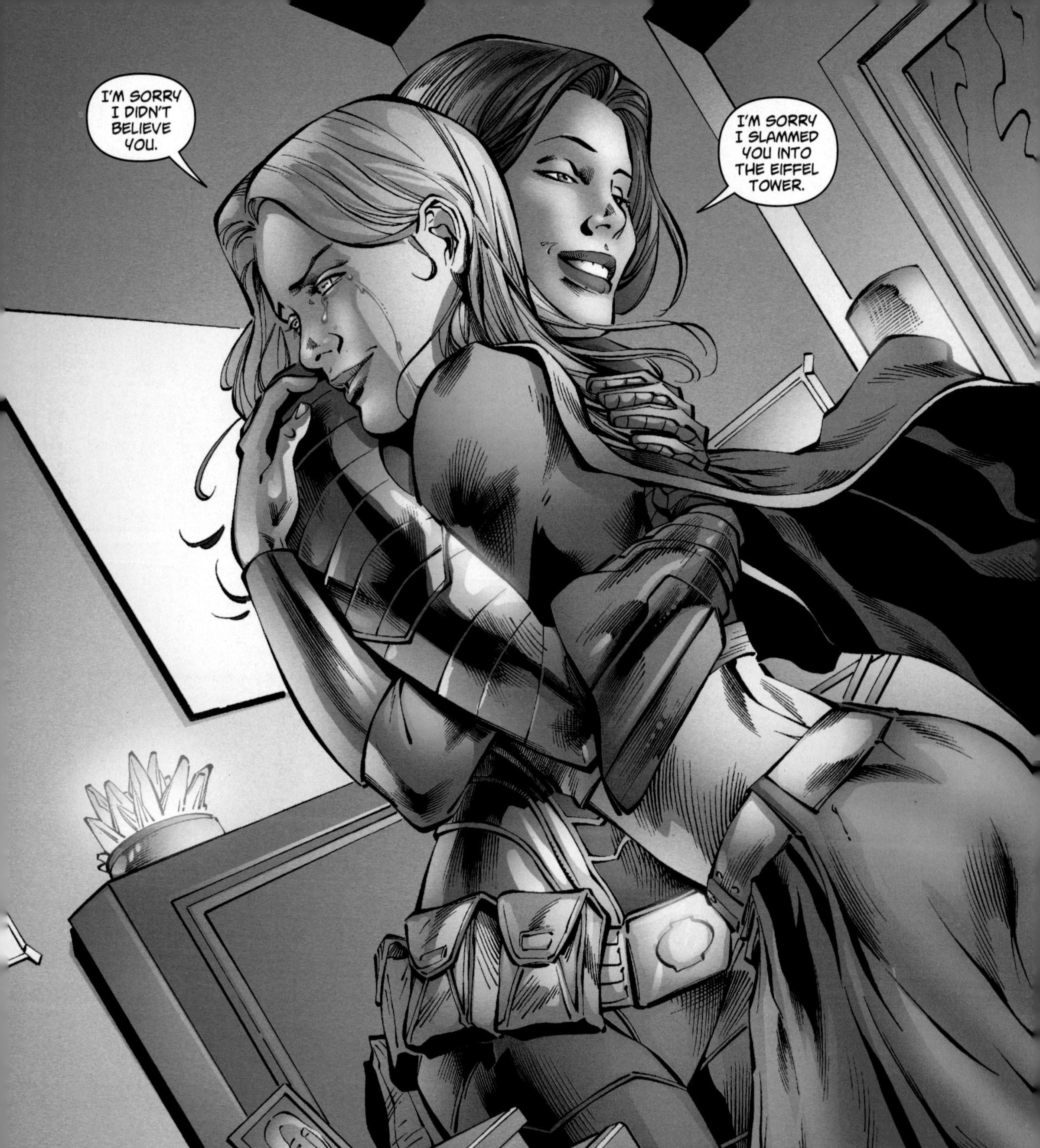
I'M SORRY I DIDN'T BELIEVE YOU.
I'M SORRY I SLAMMED YOU INTO THE EIFFEL TOWER.

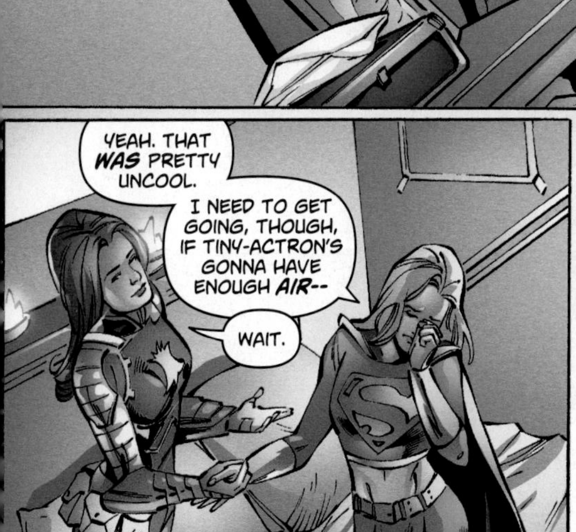
YEAH. THAT **WAS** PRETTY UNCOOL.
I NEED TO GET GOING, THOUGH, IF TINY-ACTRON'S GONNA HAVE ENOUGH **AIR**--
WAIT.

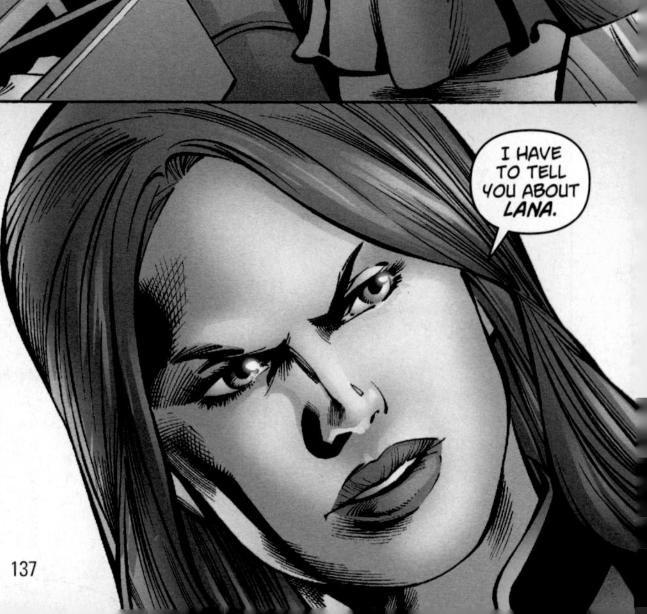
I HAVE TO TELL YOU ABOUT **LANA**.

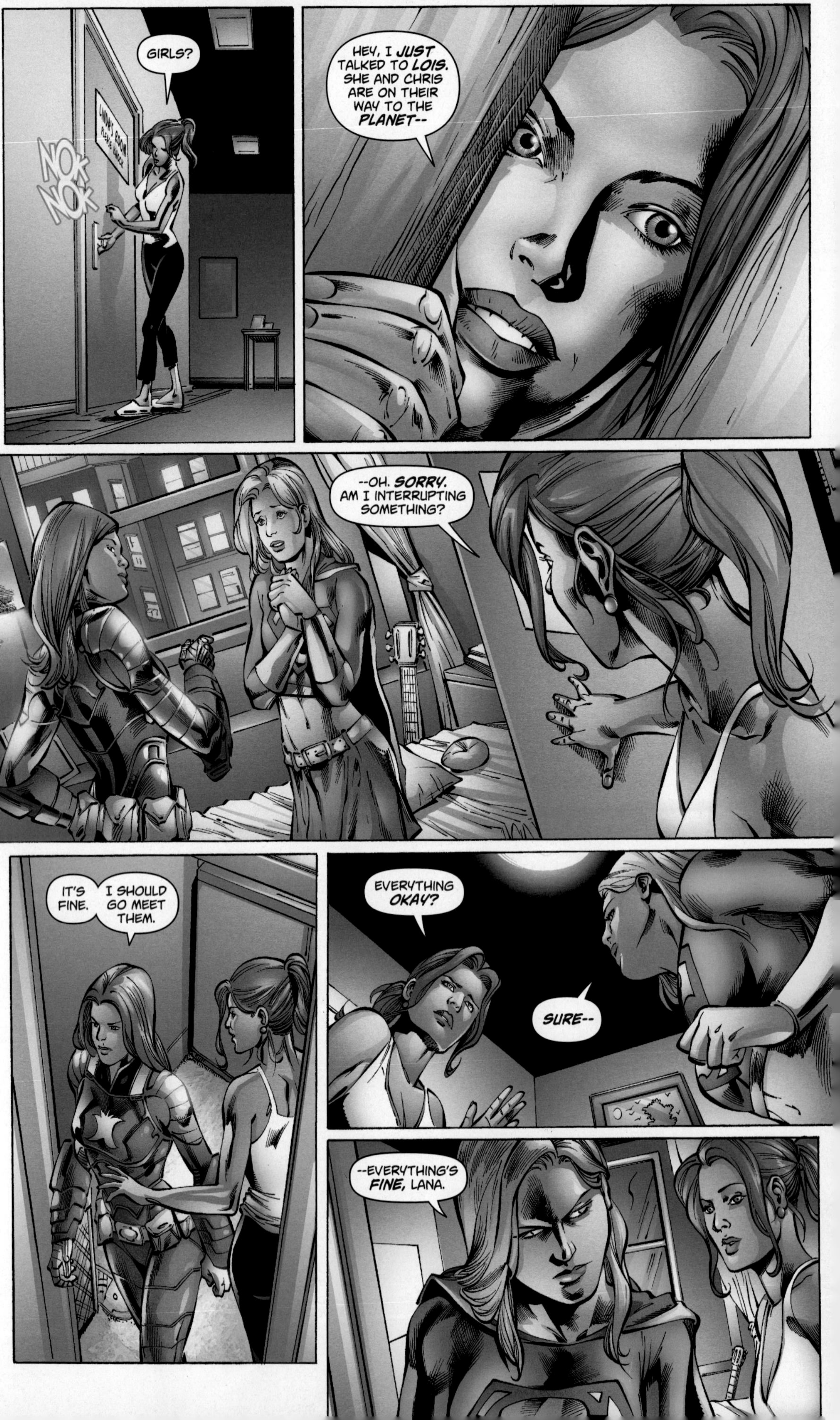
GIRLS?
NOK NOK
HEY, I JUST TALKED TO LOIS. SHE AND CHRIS ARE ON THEIR WAY TO THE PLANET--
--OH. SORRY. AM I INTERRUPTING SOMETHING?
IT'S FINE.
I SHOULD GO MEET THEM.
EVERYTHING OKAY?
SURE--
--EVERYTHING'S FINE, LANA.

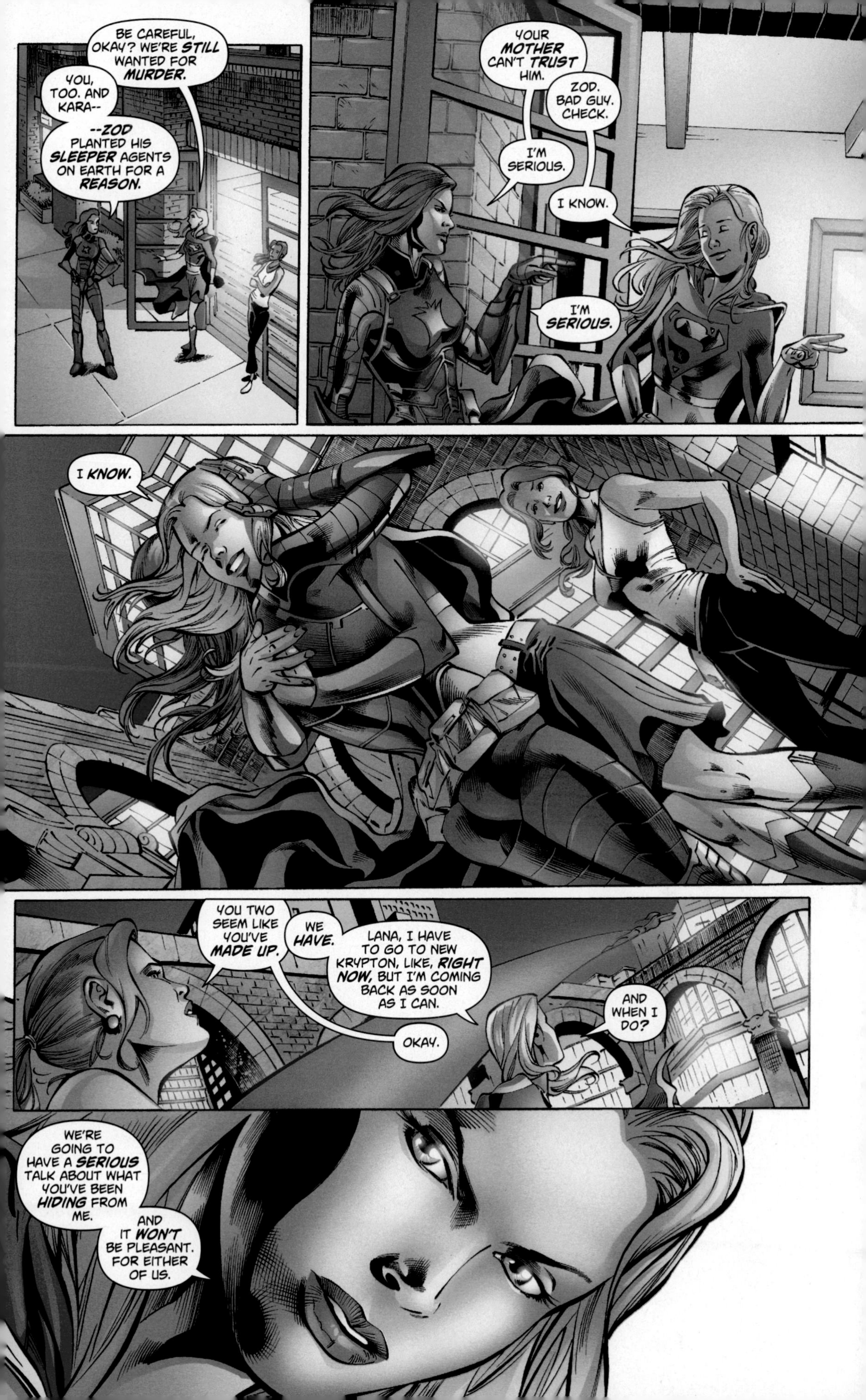

BE CAREFUL, OKAY? WE'RE STILL WANTED FOR MURDER.
YOU, TOO. AND KARA--
--ZOD PLANTED HIS SLEEPER AGENTS ON EARTH FOR A REASON.
YOUR MOTHER CAN'T TRUST HIM.
ZOD. BAD GUY. CHECK.
I'M SERIOUS.
I KNOW.
I'M SERIOUS.
I KNOW.
YOU TWO SEEM LIKE YOU'VE MADE UP.
WE HAVE.
LANA, I HAVE TO GO TO NEW KRYPTON, LIKE, RIGHT NOW, BUT I'M COMING BACK AS SOON AS I CAN.
OKAY.
AND WHEN I DO?
WE'RE GOING TO HAVE A SERIOUS TALK ABOUT WHAT YOU'VE BEEN HIDING FROM ME.
AND IT WON'T BE PLEASANT. FOR EITHER OF US.

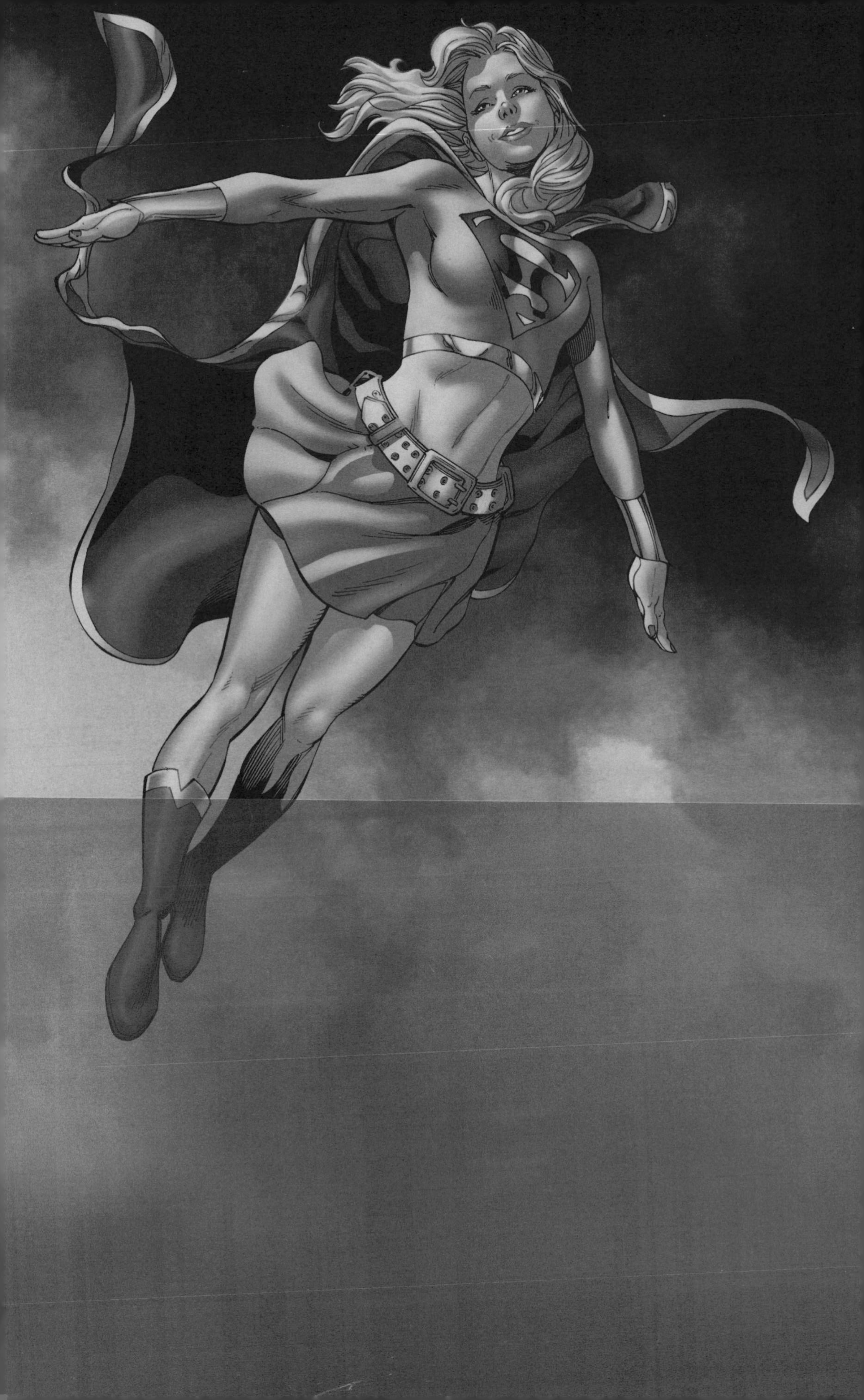

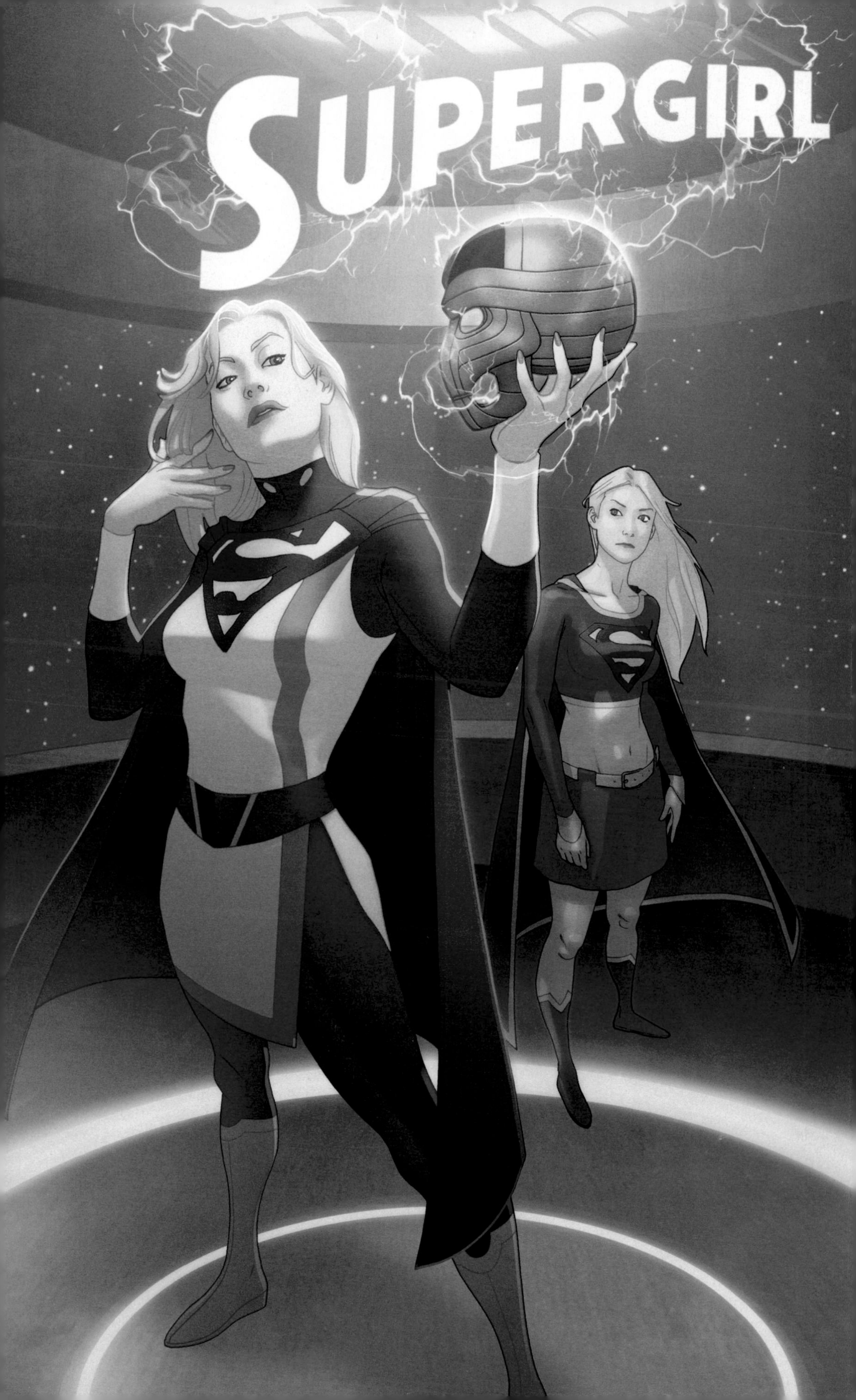
SUPERGIRL

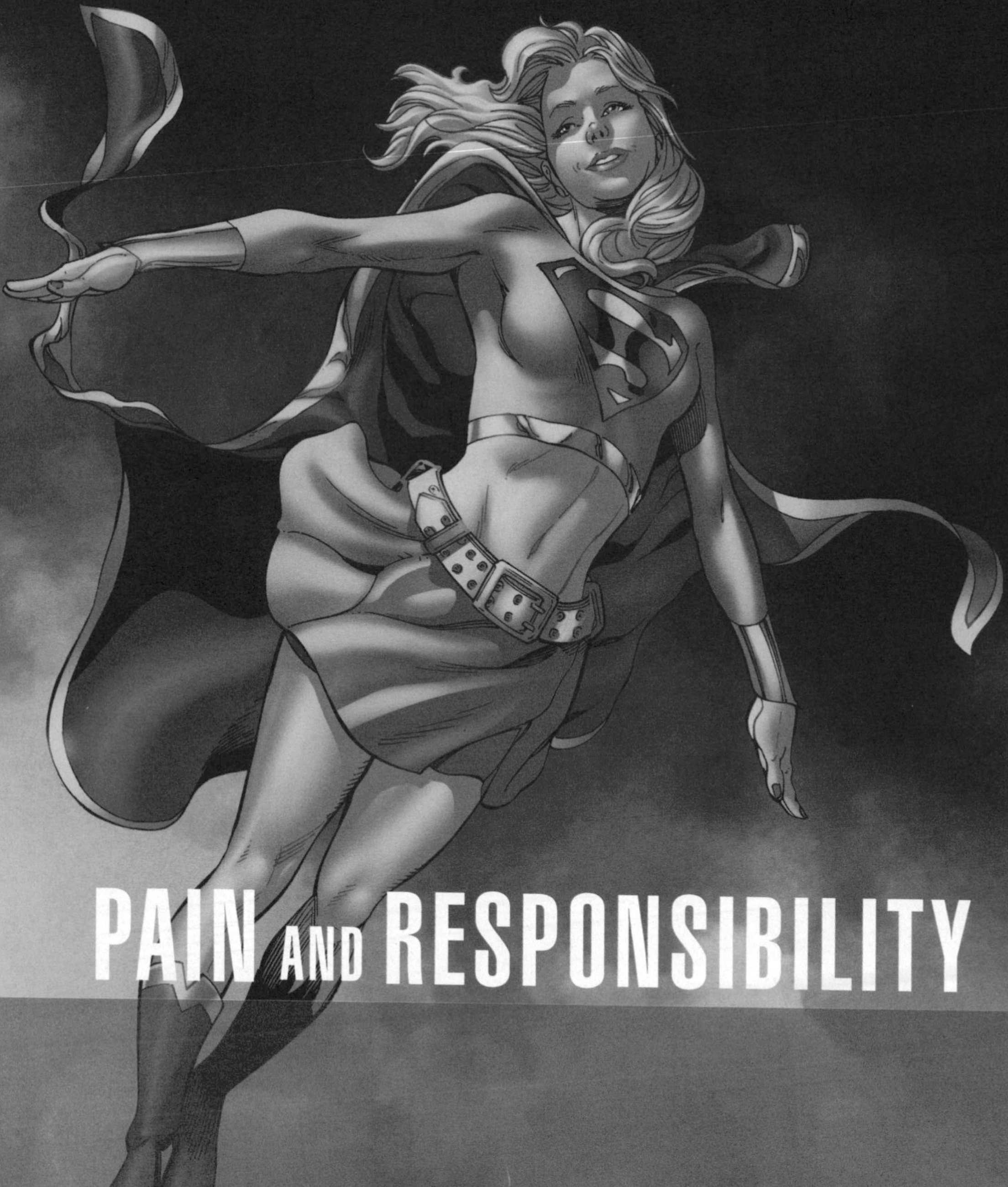

# PAIN AND RESPONSIBILITY

**STERLING GATES**
writer

**MATT CAMP**
artist

**NEI RUFFINO**
colorist

**JARED K. FLETCHER**
letterer

**JOSHUA MIDDLETON**
cover

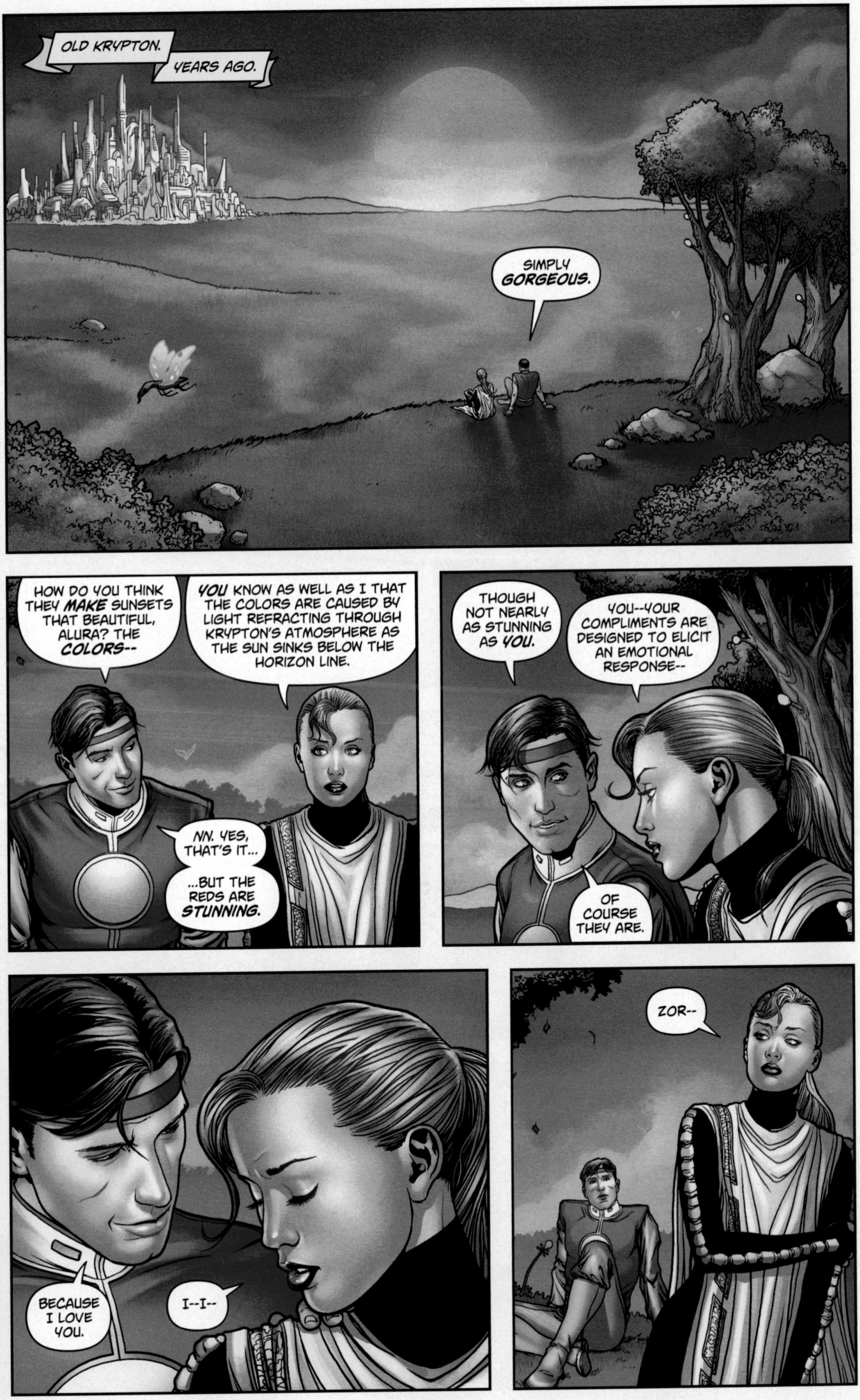
OLD KRYPTON.
YEARS AGO.
SIMPLY GORGEOUS.
HOW DO YOU THINK THEY MAKE SUNSETS THAT BEAUTIFUL, ALURA? THE COLORS--
YOU KNOW AS WELL AS I THAT THE COLORS ARE CAUSED BY LIGHT REFRACTING THROUGH KRYPTON'S ATMOSPHERE AS THE SUN SINKS BELOW THE HORIZON LINE.
NN. YES, THAT'S IT...
...BUT THE REDS ARE STUNNING.
THOUGH NOT NEARLY AS STUNNING AS YOU.
YOU--YOUR COMPLIMENTS ARE DESIGNED TO ELICIT AN EMOTIONAL RESPONSE--
OF COURSE THEY ARE.
BECAUSE I LOVE YOU.
I--I--
ZOR--

...*STILL?* WE'VE BEEN SEEING EACH OTHER FOR MONTHS, ALURA, AND STILL YOU WON'T SAY WHAT IT IS YOU *FEEL* FOR ME.

DO YOU THINK *SO* LITTLE OF ME YOU CAN'T BEAR TO OPEN UP? WHY EVEN BOTHER TO KEEP *SEEING* ME?

WHAT'S THE *POINT?*

NO, IT'S...

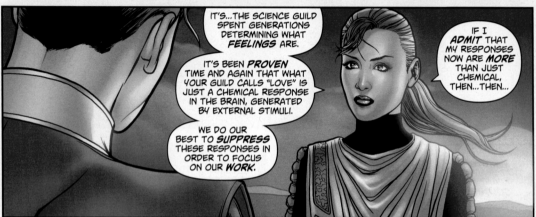

IT'S...THE SCIENCE GUILD SPENT GENERATIONS DETERMINING WHAT *FEELINGS* ARE.

IT'S BEEN *PROVEN* TIME AND AGAIN THAT WHAT YOUR GUILD CALLS "LOVE" IS JUST A CHEMICAL RESPONSE IN THE BRAIN, GENERATED BY EXTERNAL STIMULI.

WE DO OUR BEST TO *SUPPRESS* THESE RESPONSES IN ORDER TO FOCUS ON OUR *WORK.*

IF I *ADMIT* THAT MY RESPONSES NOW ARE *MORE* THAN JUST CHEMICAL, THEN...THEN...

THEN *WHAT?*

THEN I WILL HAVE BECOME SOMEONE *DIFFERENT.* *CHANGED* MY LIFE, MY THOUGHTS, MY WHOLE *EXISTENCE* COMPLETELY. FOR YOU.

NO. FOR *US.*

144

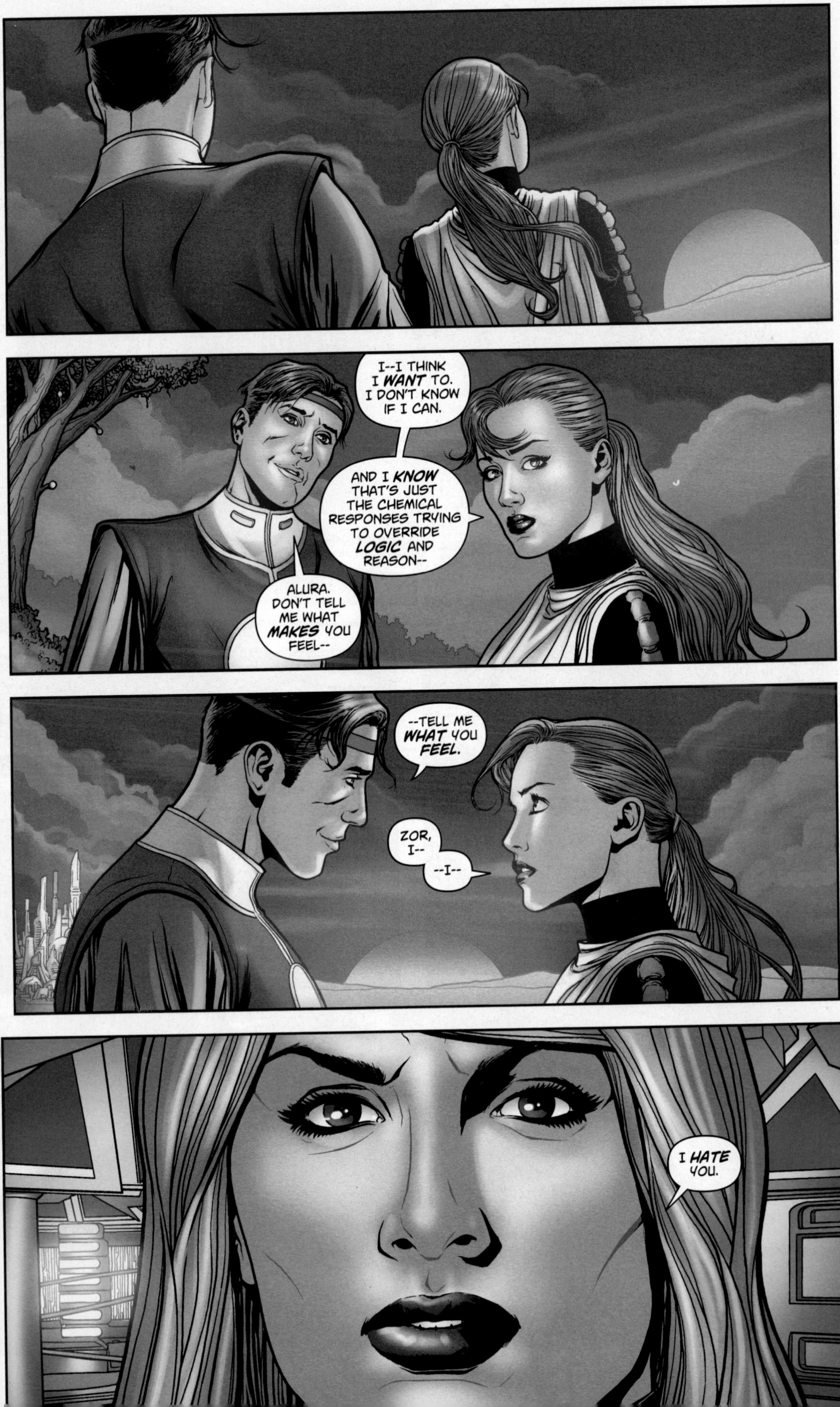
I--I THINK I WANT TO. I DON'T KNOW IF I CAN.
AND I KNOW THAT'S JUST THE CHEMICAL RESPONSES TRYING TO OVERRIDE LOGIC AND REASON--
ALURA. DON'T TELL ME WHAT MAKES YOU FEEL--
--TELL ME WHAT YOU FEEL.
ZOR, I--
--I--
I HATE YOU.

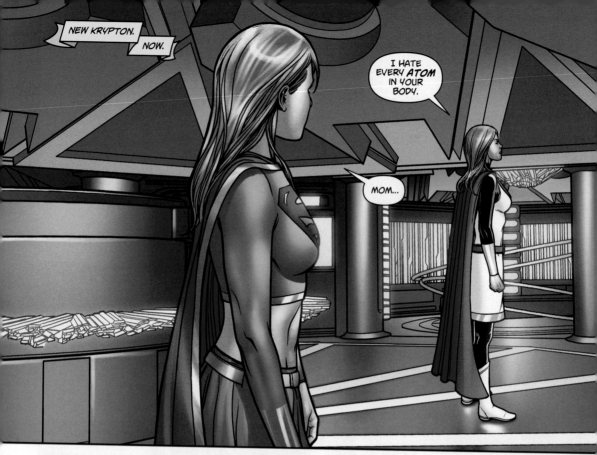

NEW KRYPTON. NOW.

I HATE EVERY *ATOM* IN YOUR BODY.

MOM...

HH. SO THIS IS YOUR *MOM*, HUH?

LOOKS LIKE ZOR-EL HAD GOOD TA--

DON'T YOU *DARE*.

AAAAHH!!

MOM!

HEH. YEAH, BUT-- *WHEN* DO WE *EAT*?

YOU *MOCK* ME?

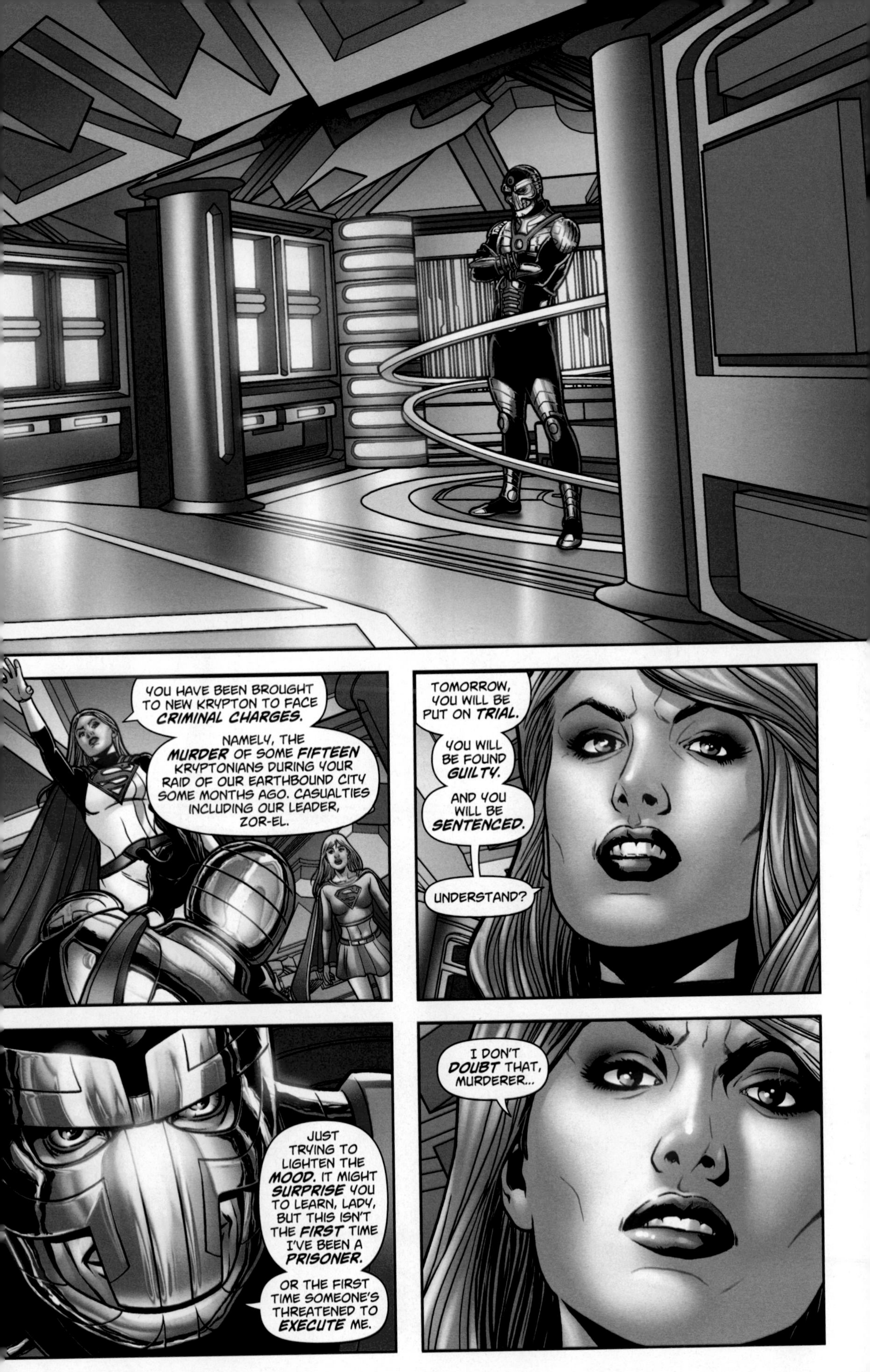
YOU HAVE BEEN BROUGHT TO NEW KRYPTON TO FACE CRIMINAL CHARGES.
NAMELY, THE MURDER OF SOME FIFTEEN KRYPTONIANS DURING YOUR RAID OF OUR EARTHBOUND CITY SOME MONTHS AGO. CASUALTIES INCLUDING OUR LEADER, ZOR-EL.
TOMORROW, YOU WILL BE PUT ON TRIAL.
YOU WILL BE FOUND GUILTY.
AND YOU WILL BE SENTENCED.
UNDERSTAND?
JUST TRYING TO LIGHTEN THE MOOD. IT MIGHT SURPRISE YOU TO LEARN, LADY, BUT THIS ISN'T THE FIRST TIME I'VE BEEN A PRISONER.
OR THE FIRST TIME SOMEONE'S THREATENED TO EXECUTE ME.
I DON'T DOUBT THAT, MURDERER...

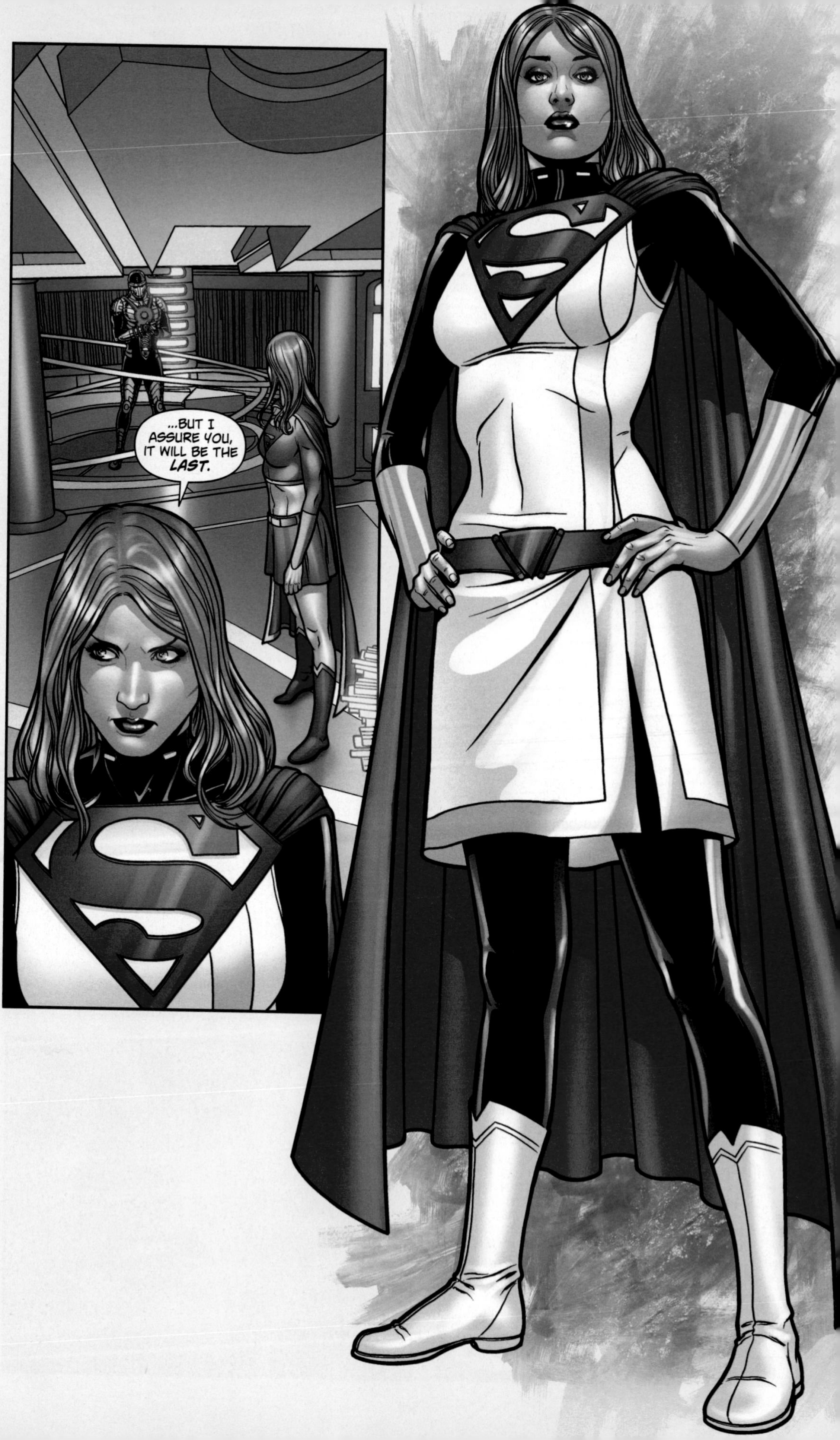
...BUT I ASSURE YOU, IT WILL BE THE LAST.

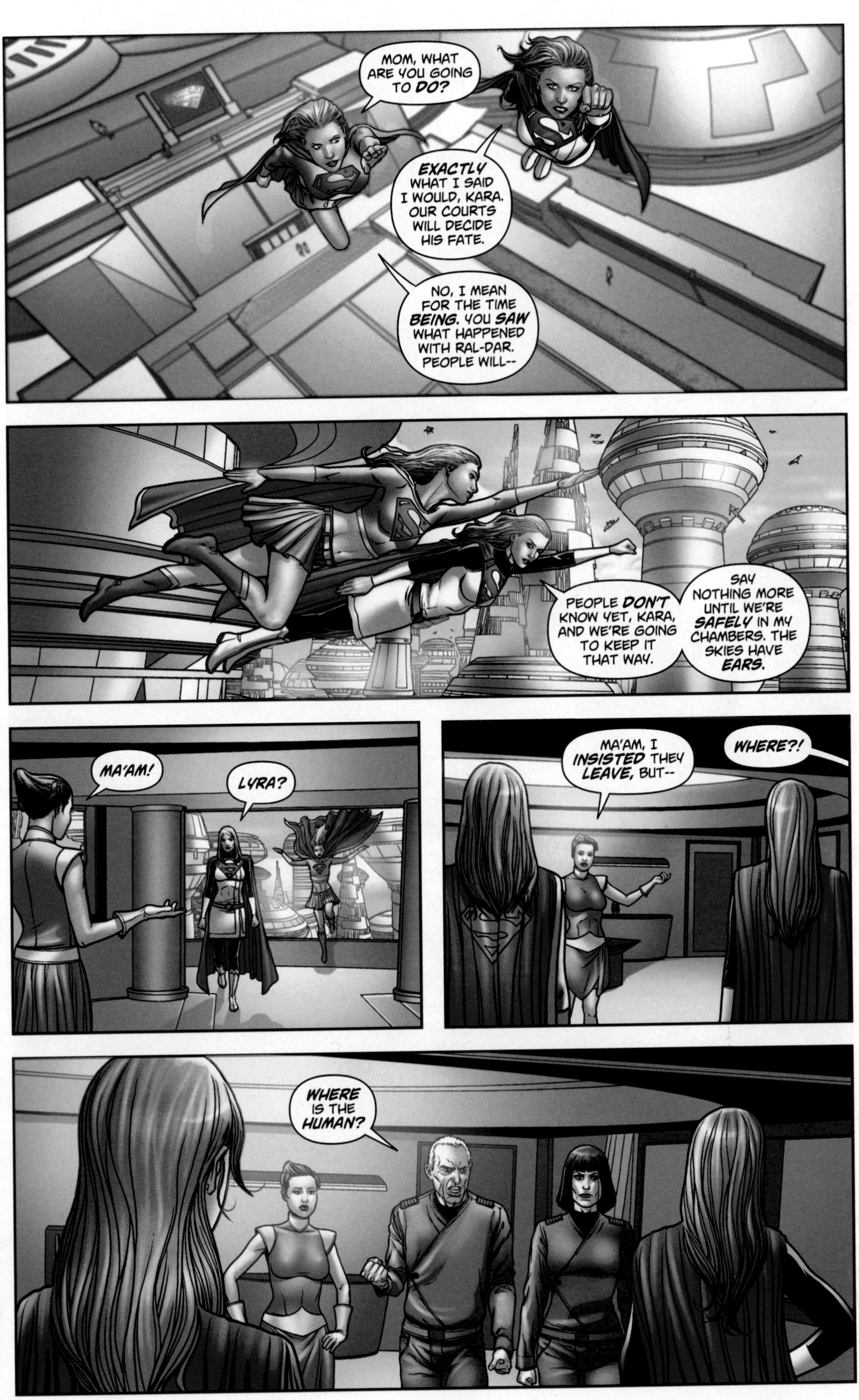
MOM, WHAT ARE YOU GOING TO DO?
EXACTLY WHAT I SAID I WOULD, KARA. OUR COURTS WILL DECIDE HIS FATE.
NO, I MEAN FOR THE TIME BEING. YOU SAW WHAT HAPPENED WITH RAL-DAR. PEOPLE WILL--
PEOPLE DON'T KNOW YET, KARA, AND WE'RE GOING TO KEEP IT THAT WAY.
SAY NOTHING MORE UNTIL WE'RE SAFELY IN MY CHAMBERS. THE SKIES HAVE EARS.
MA'AM!
LYRA?
MA'AM, I INSISTED THEY LEAVE, BUT--
WHERE?!
WHERE IS THE HUMAN?

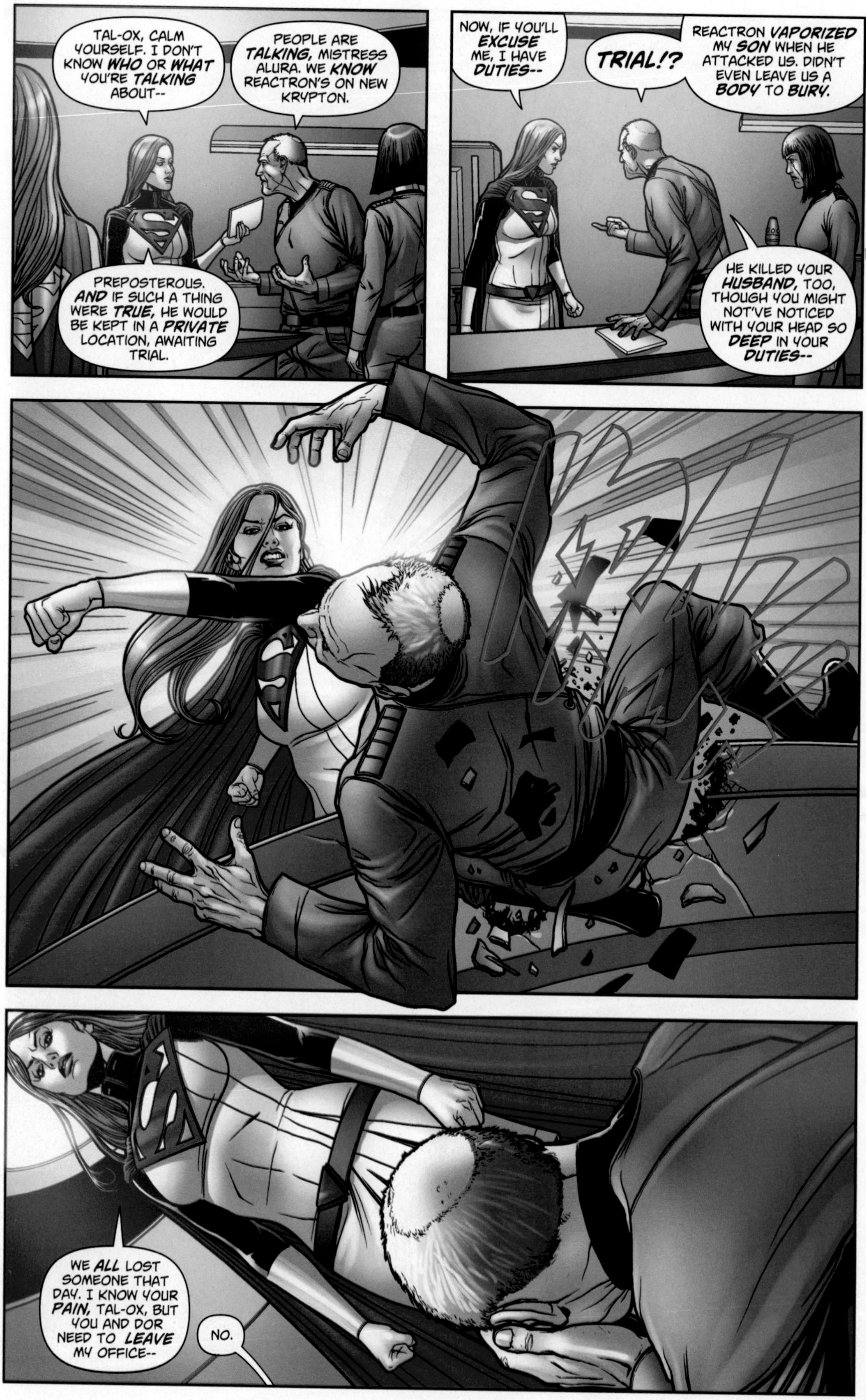
TAL-OX, CALM YOURSELF. I DON'T KNOW WHO OR WHAT YOU'RE TALKING ABOUT--
PEOPLE ARE TALKING, MISTRESS ALURA. WE KNOW REACTRON'S ON NEW KRYPTON.
PREPOSTEROUS. AND IF SUCH A THING WERE TRUE, HE WOULD BE KEPT IN A PRIVATE LOCATION, AWAITING TRIAL.
NOW, IF YOU'LL EXCUSE ME, I HAVE DUTIES--
TRIAL!?
REACTRON VAPORIZED MY SON WHEN HE ATTACKED US. DIDN'T EVEN LEAVE US A BODY TO BURY.
HE KILLED YOUR HUSBAND, TOO, THOUGH YOU MIGHT NOT'VE NOTICED WITH YOUR HEAD SO DEEP IN YOUR DUTIES--
WE ALL LOST SOMEONE THAT DAY. I KNOW YOUR PAIN, TAL-OX, BUT YOU AND DOR NEED TO LEAVE MY OFFICE--
NO.

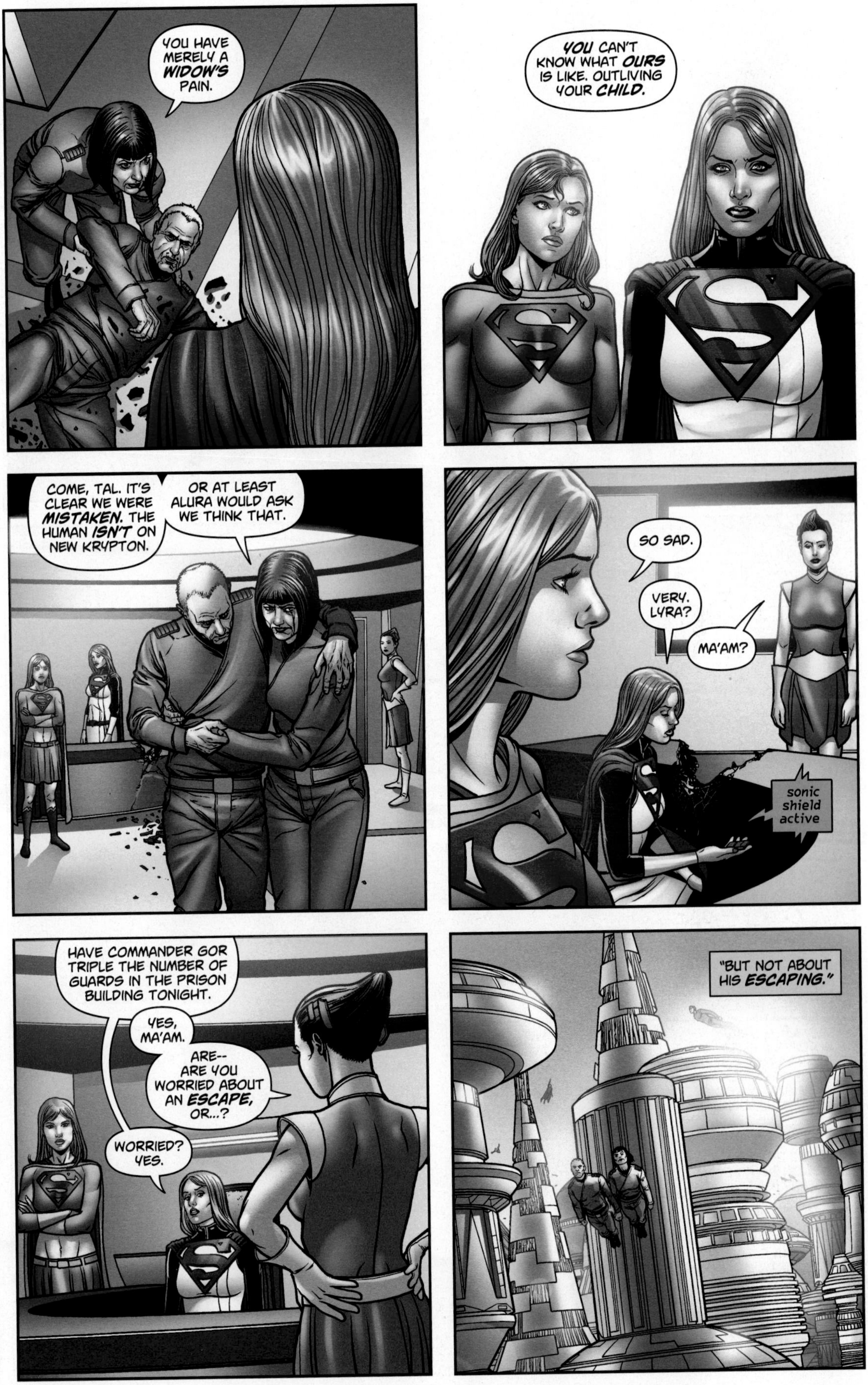
YOU HAVE MERELY A WIDOW'S PAIN.
YOU CAN'T KNOW WHAT OURS IS LIKE. OUTLIVING YOUR CHILD.
COME, TAL. IT'S CLEAR WE WERE MISTAKEN. THE HUMAN ISN'T ON NEW KRYPTON.
OR AT LEAST ALURA WOULD ASK WE THINK THAT.
SO SAD.
VERY. LYRA?
MA'AM?
sonic shield active
HAVE COMMANDER GOR TRIPLE THE NUMBER OF GUARDS IN THE PRISON BUILDING TONIGHT.
YES, MA'AM.
ARE-- ARE YOU WORRIED ABOUT AN ESCAPE, OR...?
WORRIED? YES.
"BUT NOT ABOUT HIS ESCAPING."

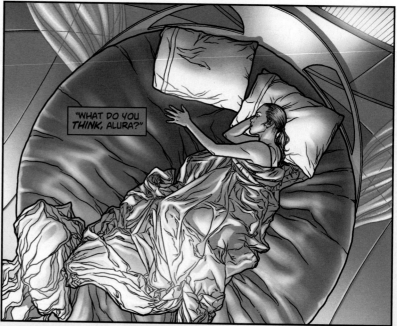

"WHAT DO YOU *THINK*, ALURA?"

ABOUT OUR GETTING *MARRIED?*

I THINK YOU'VE *LOST* YOUR *MIND.*

*LOST* IT? HM.

WELL, I *HAVE* HEARD THAT THE SCIENCE GUILD HAS A MACHINE THAT CAN *SAP* MEN'S WILLS, TURNING THEM INTO MINDLESS, MARRIED *SLAVES.*

*YOU* ARTISTS HAVE SUCH WONDERFULLY *VIVID* IMAGINATIONS.

WE *LIVE* TO IMAGINE. AND I'M IMAGINING A LIFE SPENT WITH *YOU.* WHAT DO YOU THINK?

*I* THINK, ZOR, THAT ONCE WE TAKE A MARRIAGE OATH BEFORE OUR *GODS,* WE'RE *PERMANENT.*

FOREVER.

ARE YOU... ARE YOU *POSITIVE* THAT'S WHAT YOU *WANT?*

HERE. FEEL.

WHAT? WHY--

YOUR HEARTBEAT *SKIPS* WHEN YOU LIE. KEEP YOUR HAND THERE.

*WE* ARE WHAT I WANT, ALURA. I WANT US TO BE *TOGETHER* AS HUSBAND AND WIFE.

FOREVER.

NOW. WHAT DID MY *HEART* SAY?

...THE SAME THING *MINE* SAYS.

WHICH *IS?*

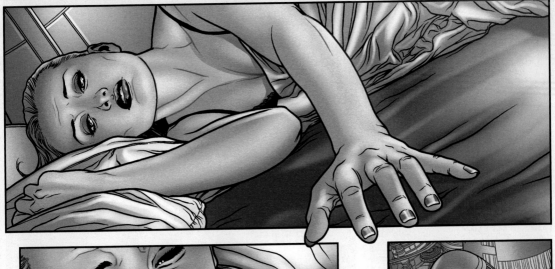

"ARBITRATORS OF THE *COURT*--"

153

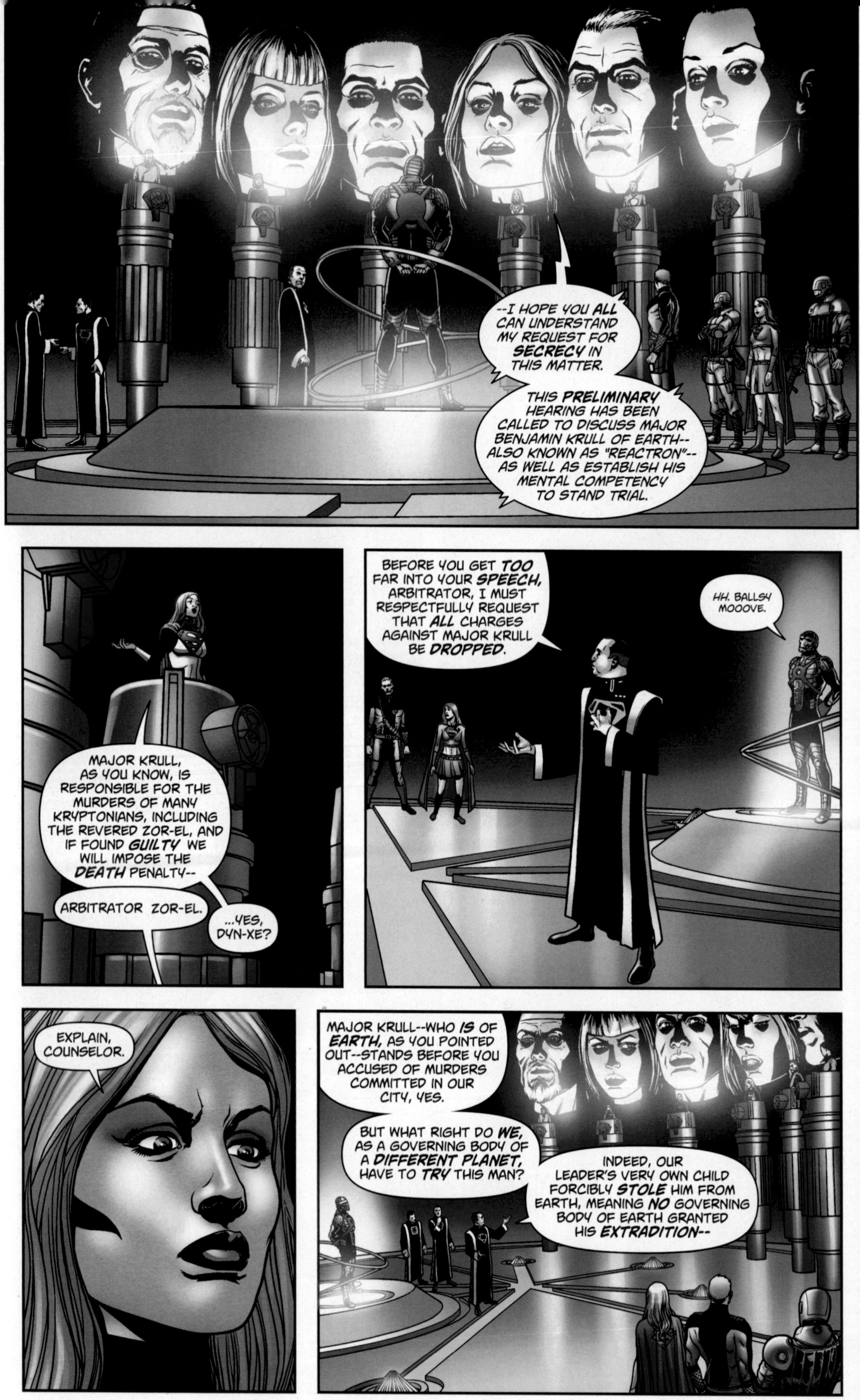
--I HOPE YOU ALL CAN UNDERSTAND MY REQUEST FOR SECRECY IN THIS MATTER.
THIS PRELIMINARY HEARING HAS BEEN CALLED TO DISCUSS MAJOR BENJAMIN KRULL OF EARTH--ALSO KNOWN AS "REACTRON"--AS WELL AS ESTABLISH HIS MENTAL COMPETENCY TO STAND TRIAL.
MAJOR KRULL, AS YOU KNOW, IS RESPONSIBLE FOR THE MURDERS OF MANY KRYPTONIANS, INCLUDING THE REVERED ZOR-EL, AND IF FOUND GUILTY WE WILL IMPOSE THE DEATH PENALTY--
ARBITRATOR ZOR-EL.
...YES, DYN-XE?
BEFORE YOU GET TOO FAR INTO YOUR SPEECH, ARBITRATOR, I MUST RESPECTFULLY REQUEST THAT ALL CHARGES AGAINST MAJOR KRULL BE DROPPED.
HH. BALLSY MOOOVE.
EXPLAIN, COUNSELOR.
MAJOR KRULL--WHO IS OF EARTH, AS YOU POINTED OUT--STANDS BEFORE YOU ACCUSED OF MURDERS COMMITTED IN OUR CITY, YES.
BUT WHAT RIGHT DO WE, AS A GOVERNING BODY OF A DIFFERENT PLANET, HAVE TO TRY THIS MAN?
INDEED, OUR LEADER'S VERY OWN CHILD FORCIBLY STOLE HIM FROM EARTH, MEANING NO GOVERNING BODY OF EARTH GRANTED HIS EXTRADITION--

I UNDERSTAND YOUR RESERVATIONS, DYN-XE, BUT I DO NOT AGREE.

WITH ALL DUE RESPECT, ARBITRATOR, OF *COURSE* YOU DON'T. YOU WANT TO SEE YOUR HUSBAND'S KILLER BROUGHT *LOW* BEFORE THE COURT AND *EXECUTED*.

I'M SURE HIS DAUGHTER DOES AS WELL.

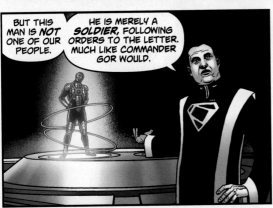

BUT THIS MAN IS *NOT* ONE OF OUR PEOPLE.

HE IS MERELY A *SOLDIER*, FOLLOWING ORDERS TO THE LETTER. MUCH LIKE COMMANDER GOR WOULD.

≥HNN≤

OR EVEN YOUR NEPHEW, GENERAL EL, WHOM I NOTICE IS *CONSPICUOUSLY* ABSENT FROM TODAY'S PROCEEDINGS. MIGHT HE *OBJECT* TO OUR TREATMENT OF MAJOR KRULL?

DOES HE EVEN *KNOW* MAJOR KRULL IS *ON* NEW KRYPTON?

GENERAL EL IS ATTENDING TO OUR NEW *MOON*, DYN-XE, AND REGRETFULLY COULD NOT BE HERE.

NOW, ARE YOU COMING TO A *POINT*, OR--?

MY POINT IS THAT MAJOR KRULL ISN'T BEING GIVEN A *FAIR* AND JUST TRIAL, ARBITRATOR. NOT BY ANY *KRYPTONIAN* STANDARD.

PERHAPS YOU'VE LET YOUR HUSBAND'S DEATH *CLOUD* YOUR JUDGM--

ENOUGH!

I AM *TIRED* OF THESE REMARKS, DYN-XE, AS I GROW TIRED OF PEOPLE *ASSUMING* MY JUDGMENT IMPAIRED.

MAJOR KRULL *MUST* BE HELD *ACCOUNTABLE* FOR HIS ACTIONS--

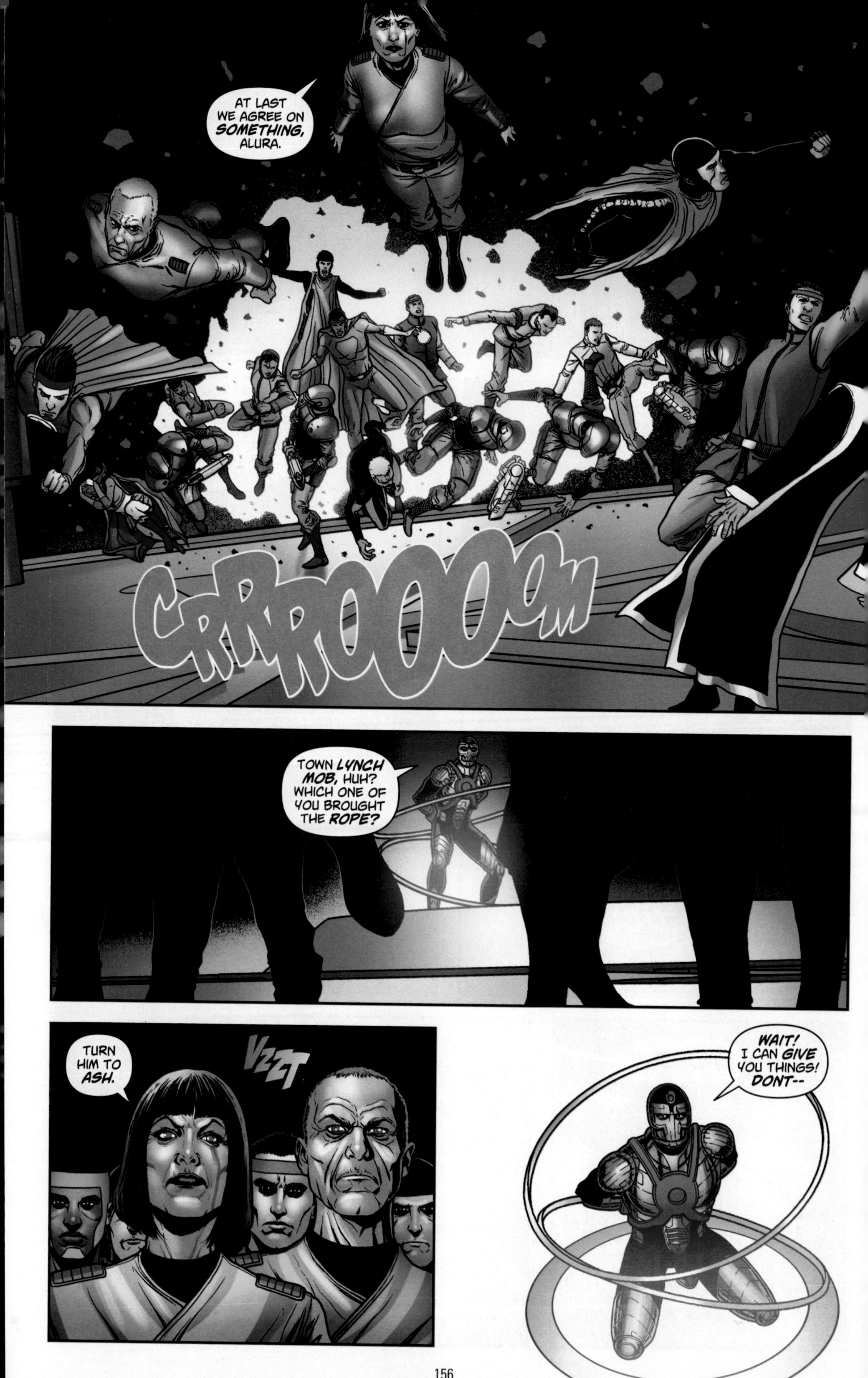
AT LAST WE AGREE ON SOMETHING, ALURA.
CRRROOOOOM
TOWN LYNCH MOB, HUH? WHICH ONE OF YOU BROUGHT THE ROPE?
TURN HIM TO ASH.
VZZT
WAIT! I CAN GIVE YOU THINGS! DONT--

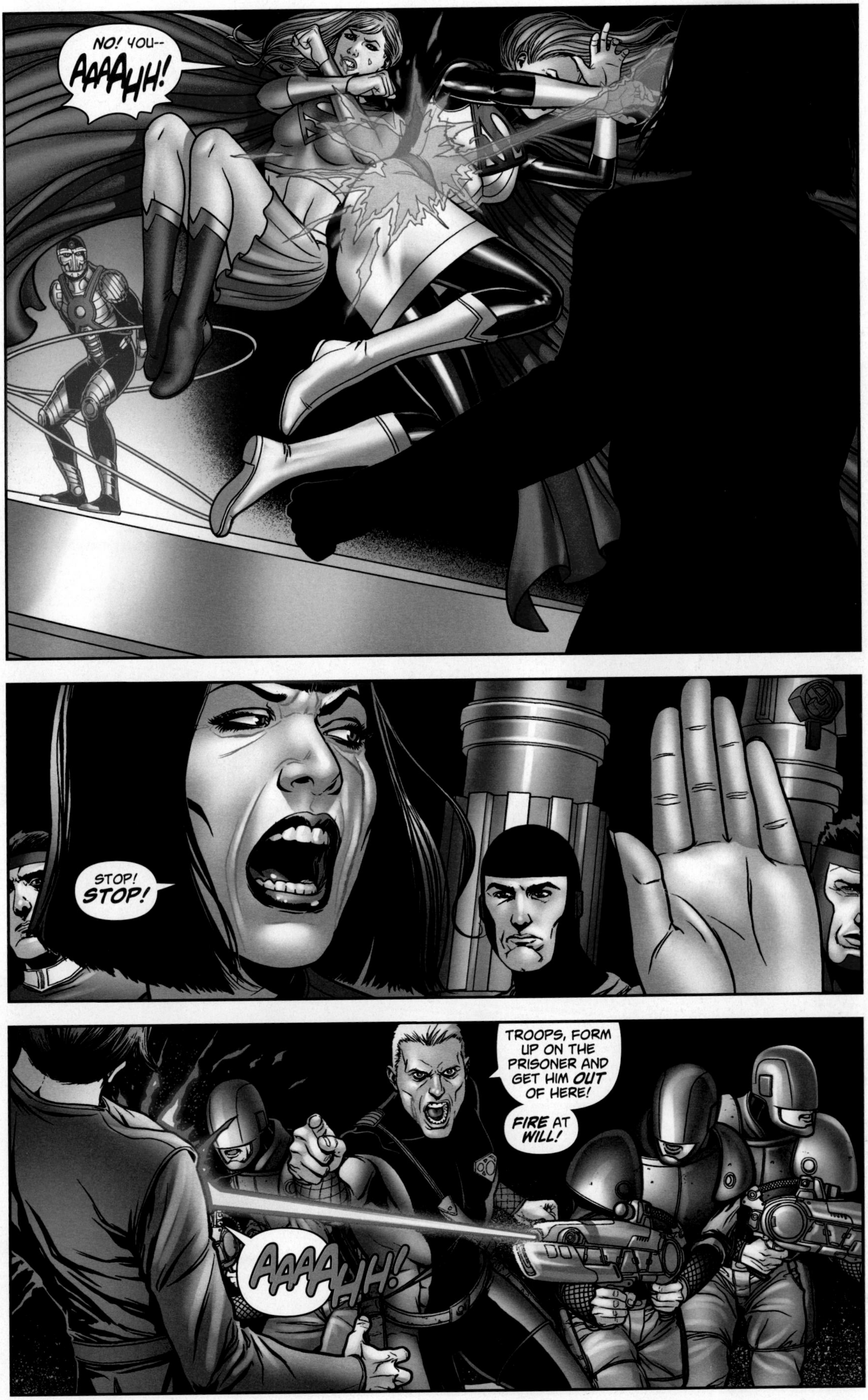
NO! YOU--
AAAAHH!
STOP!
STOP!
TROOPS, FORM UP ON THE PRISONER AND GET HIM OUT OF HERE!
FIRE AT WILL!
AAAAHH!

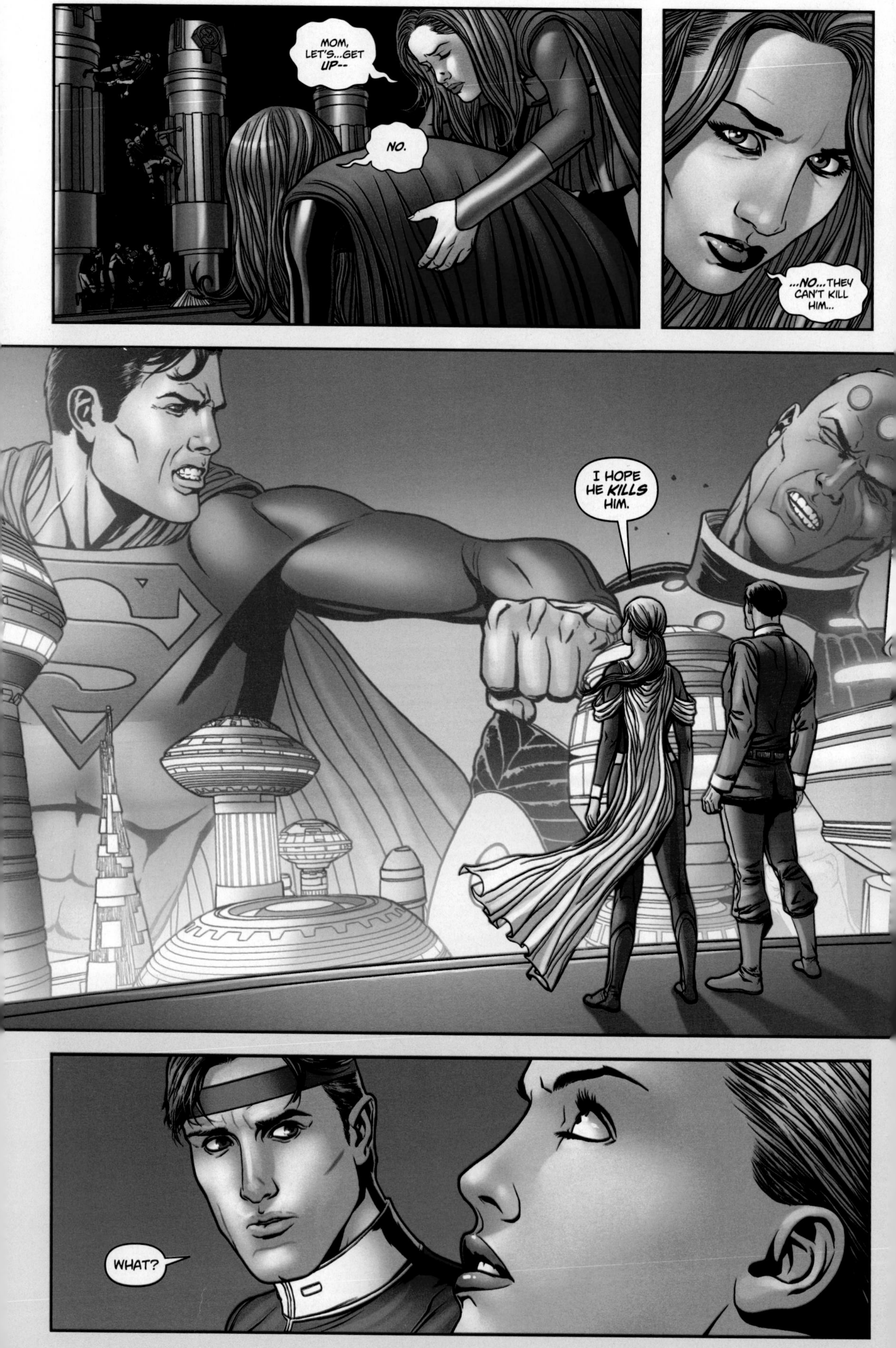
MOM, LET'S...GET UP--
NO.
...NO...THEY CAN'T KILL HIM...
I HOPE HE KILLS HIM.
WHAT?

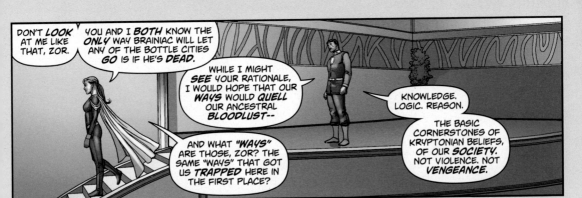

DON'T *LOOK* AT ME LIKE THAT, ZOR.

YOU AND I *BOTH* KNOW THE *ONLY* WAY BRAINIAC WILL LET ANY OF THE BOTTLE CITIES *GO* IS IF HE'S *DEAD.*

WHILE I MIGHT *SEE* YOUR RATIONALE, I WOULD HOPE THAT OUR *WAYS* WOULD *QUELL* OUR ANCESTRAL *BLOODLUST*--

AND WHAT *"WAYS"* ARE THOSE, ZOR? THE SAME *"WAYS"* THAT GOT US *TRAPPED* HERE IN THE FIRST PLACE?

KNOWLEDGE. LOGIC. REASON.

THE BASIC CORNERSTONES OF KRYPTONIAN BELIEFS, OF OUR *SOCIETY.* NOT VIOLENCE. NOT *VENGEANCE.*

THIS, COMING FROM *YOU,* THE "ARTIST"?

YOU'RE ASKING ME TO BE *LESS* EMOTIONAL? *FEEL* LESS *HATE?* HE *KILLED* MOST OF ARGO CITY WHEN HE CLAIMED US HIS OWN.

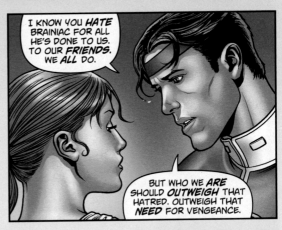

I KNOW YOU *HATE* BRAINIAC FOR ALL HE'S DONE TO US. TO OUR *FRIENDS.* WE *ALL* DO.

BUT WHO WE *ARE* SHOULD *OUTWEIGH* THAT HATRED. OUTWEIGH THAT *NEED* FOR VENGEANCE.

WE SHOULD BE *ABOVE* IT, AS LEADERS.

WE ARE *KRYPTONIANS.*

"REMEMBER THAT, ALURA."

DOR TAL-OX!

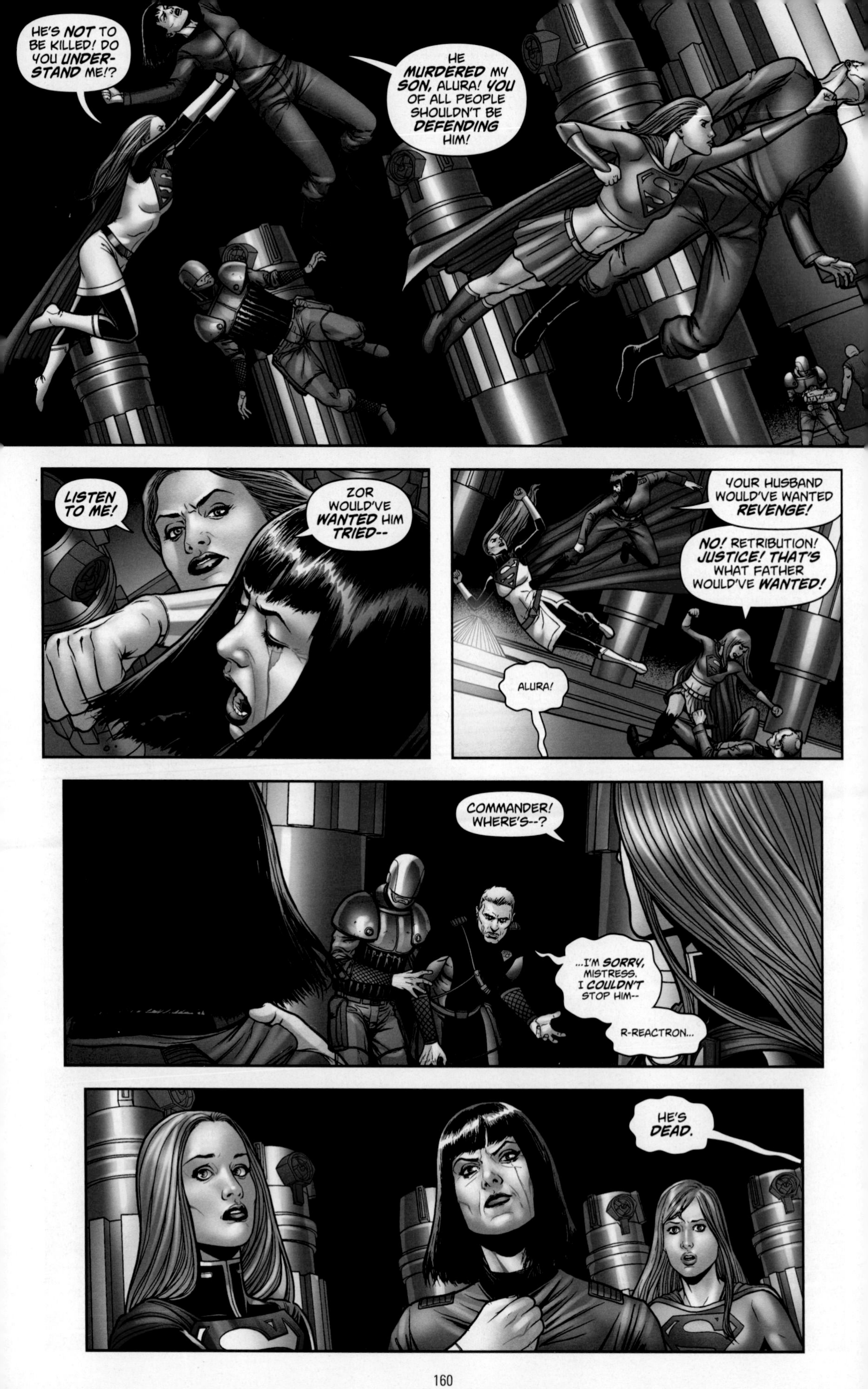
HE'S NOT TO BE KILLED! DO YOU UNDERSTAND ME!?
HE MURDERED MY SON, ALURA! YOU OF ALL PEOPLE SHOULDN'T BE DEFENDING HIM!
LISTEN TO ME!
ZOR WOULD'VE WANTED HIM TRIED--
YOUR HUSBAND WOULD'VE WANTED REVENGE!
NO! RETRIBUTION! JUSTICE! THAT'S WHAT FATHER WOULD'VE WANTED!
ALURA!
COMMANDER! WHERE'S--?
...I'M SORRY, MISTRESS. I COULDN'T STOP HIM--
R-REACTRON...
HE'S DEAD.

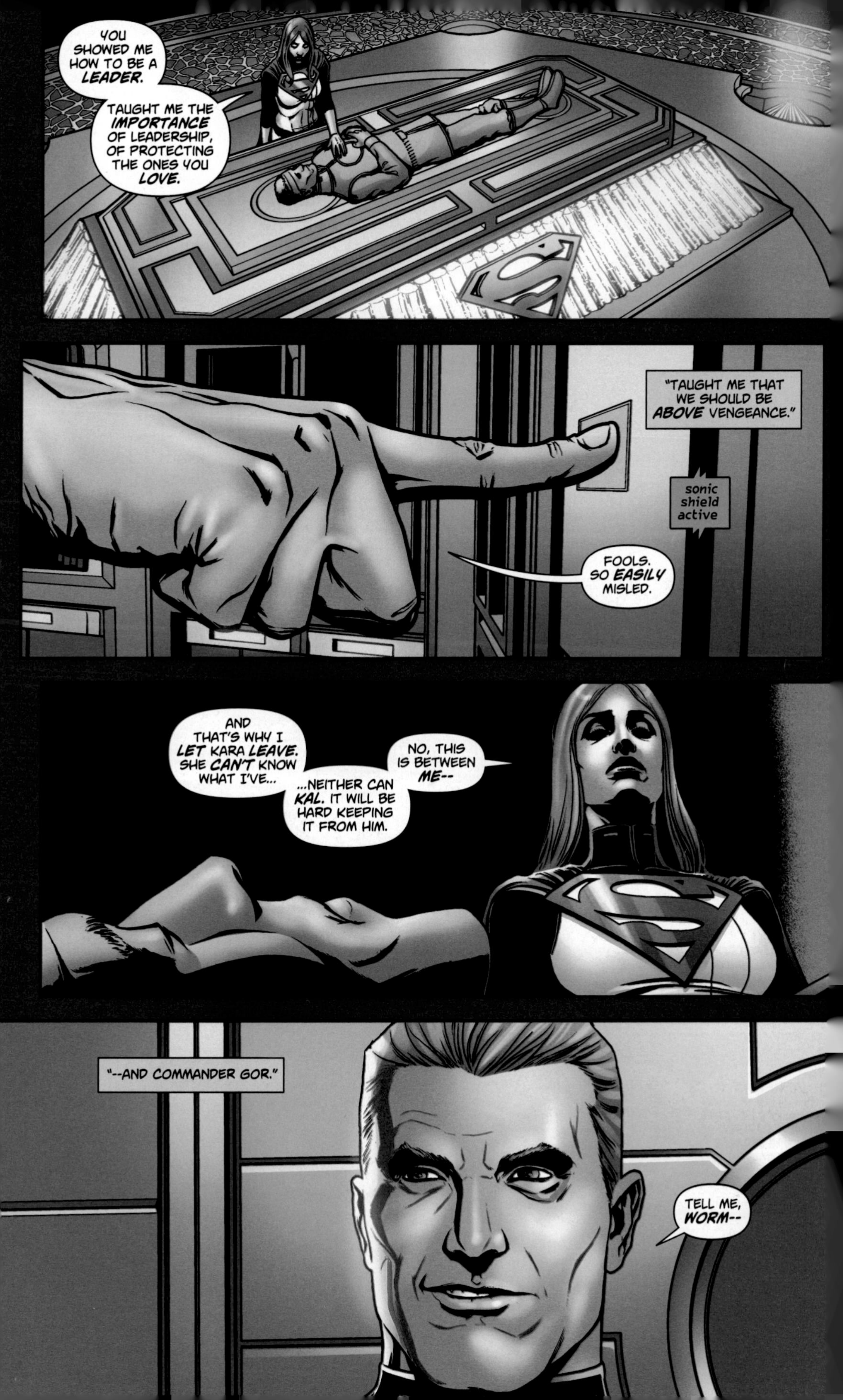
YOU SHOWED ME HOW TO BE A LEADER.
TAUGHT ME THE IMPORTANCE OF LEADERSHIP, OF PROTECTING THE ONES YOU LOVE.
"TAUGHT ME THAT WE SHOULD BE ABOVE VENGEANCE."
sonic shield active
FOOLS. SO EASILY MISLED.
AND THAT'S WHY I LET KARA LEAVE. SHE CAN'T KNOW WHAT I'VE...
...NEITHER CAN KAL. IT WILL BE HARD KEEPING IT FROM HIM.
NO, THIS IS BETWEEN ME--
"--AND COMMANDER GOR."
TELL ME, WORM--

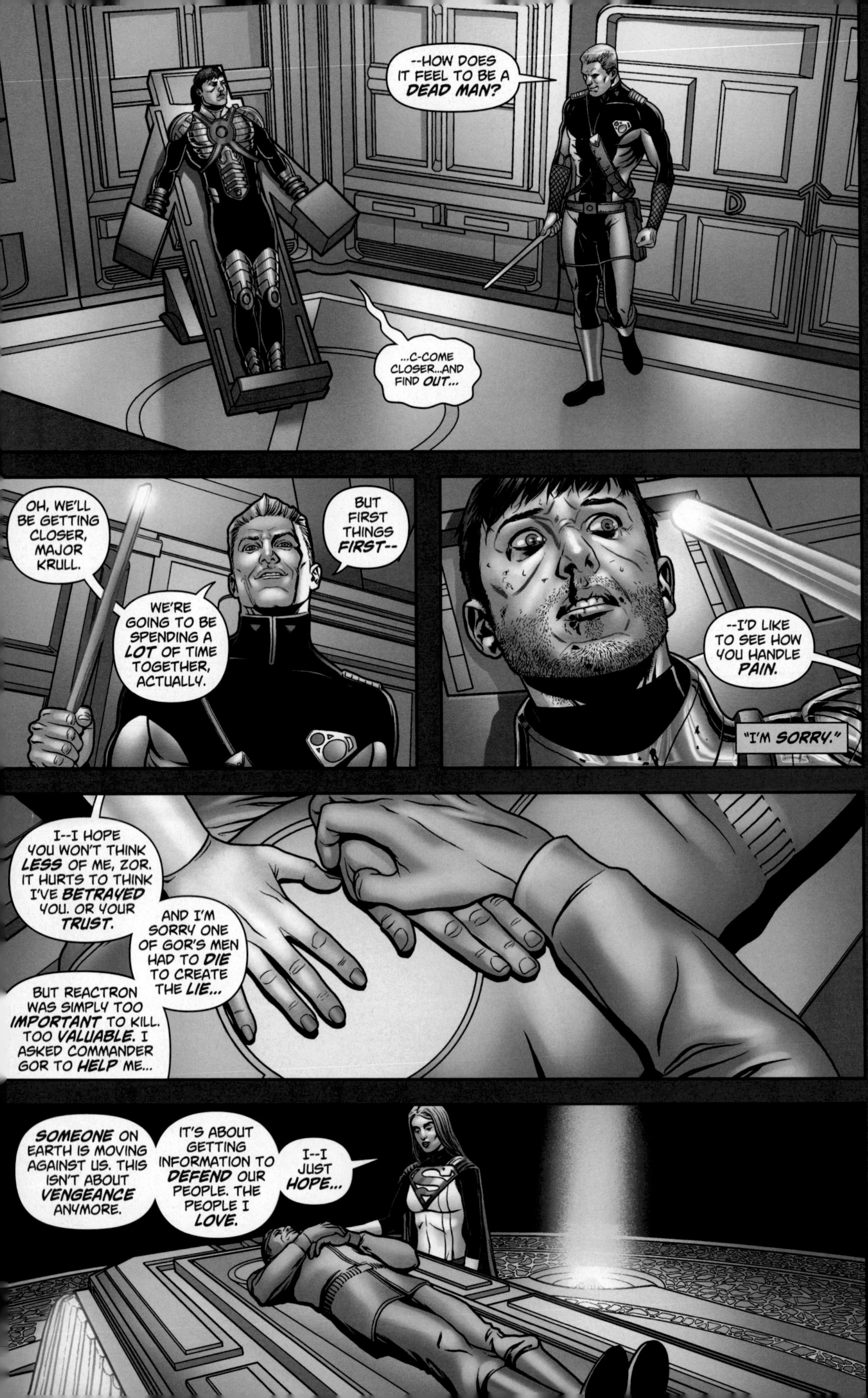
--HOW DOES IT FEEL TO BE A DEAD MAN?
...C-COME CLOSER...AND FIND OUT...
OH, WE'LL BE GETTING CLOSER, MAJOR KRULL.
WE'RE GOING TO BE SPENDING A LOT OF TIME TOGETHER, ACTUALLY.
BUT FIRST THINGS FIRST--
--I'D LIKE TO SEE HOW YOU HANDLE PAIN.
"I'M SORRY."
I--I HOPE YOU WON'T THINK LESS OF ME, ZOR. IT HURTS TO THINK I'VE BETRAYED YOU. OR YOUR TRUST.
AND I'M SORRY ONE OF GOR'S MEN HAD TO DIE TO CREATE THE LIE...
BUT REACTRON WAS SIMPLY TOO IMPORTANT TO KILL. TOO VALUABLE. I ASKED COMMANDER GOR TO HELP ME...
SOMEONE ON EARTH IS MOVING AGAINST US. THIS ISN'T ABOUT VENGEANCE ANYMORE.
IT'S ABOUT GETTING INFORMATION TO DEFEND OUR PEOPLE. THE PEOPLE I LOVE.
I--I JUST HOPE...

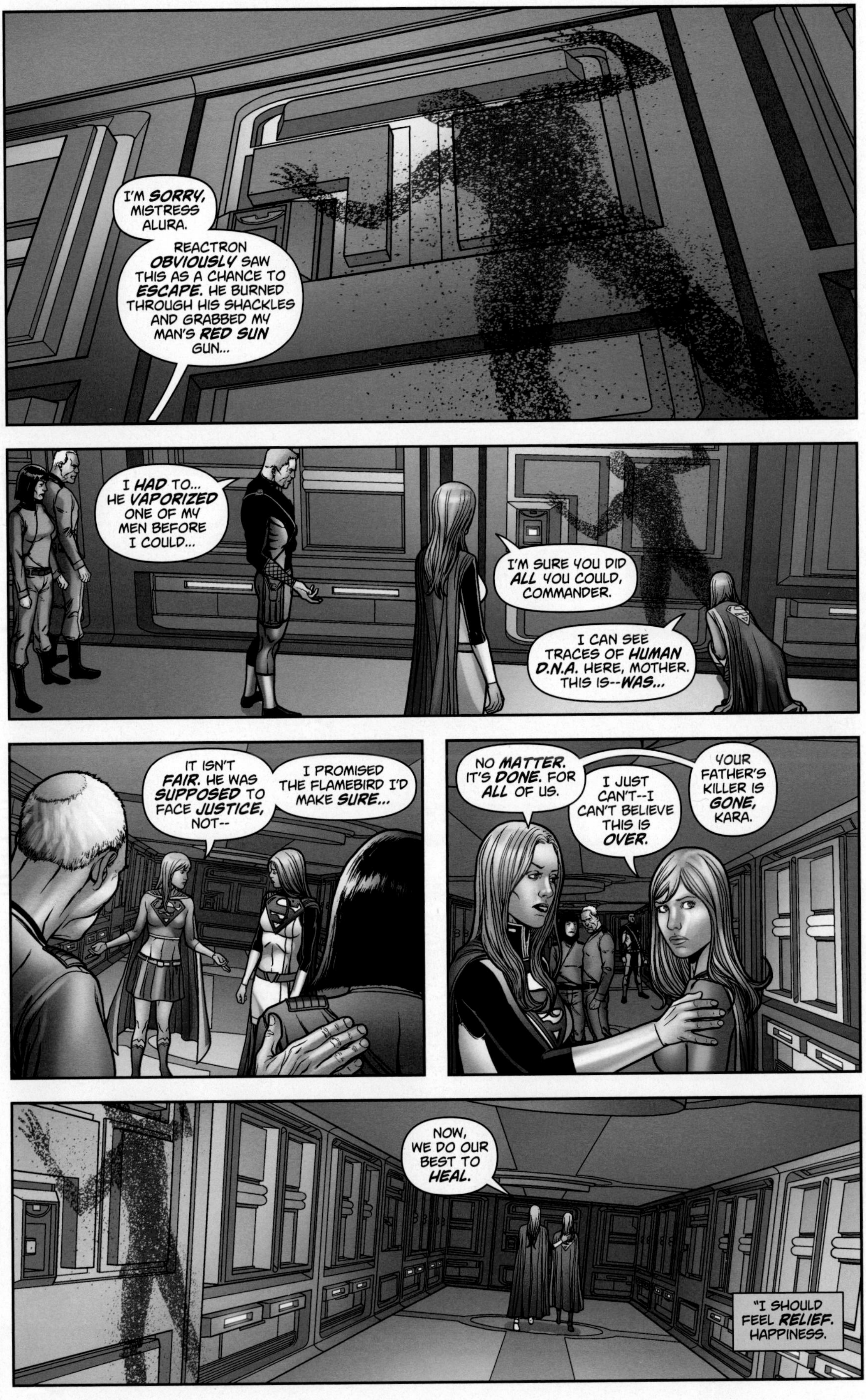
I'M SORRY, MISTRESS ALURA.
REACTRON OBVIOUSLY SAW THIS AS A CHANCE TO ESCAPE. HE BURNED THROUGH HIS SHACKLES AND GRABBED MY MAN'S RED SUN GUN...
I HAD TO... HE VAPORIZED ONE OF MY MEN BEFORE I COULD...
I'M SURE YOU DID ALL YOU COULD, COMMANDER.
I CAN SEE TRACES OF HUMAN D.N.A. HERE, MOTHER. THIS IS--WAS...
IT ISN'T FAIR. HE WAS SUPPOSED TO FACE JUSTICE, NOT--
I PROMISED THE FLAMEBIRD I'D MAKE SURE...
NO MATTER. IT'S DONE. FOR ALL OF US.
YOUR FATHER'S KILLER IS GONE, KARA.
I JUST CAN'T--I CAN'T BELIEVE THIS IS OVER.
NOW, WE DO OUR BEST TO HEAL.
"I SHOULD FEEL RELIEF. HAPPINESS.

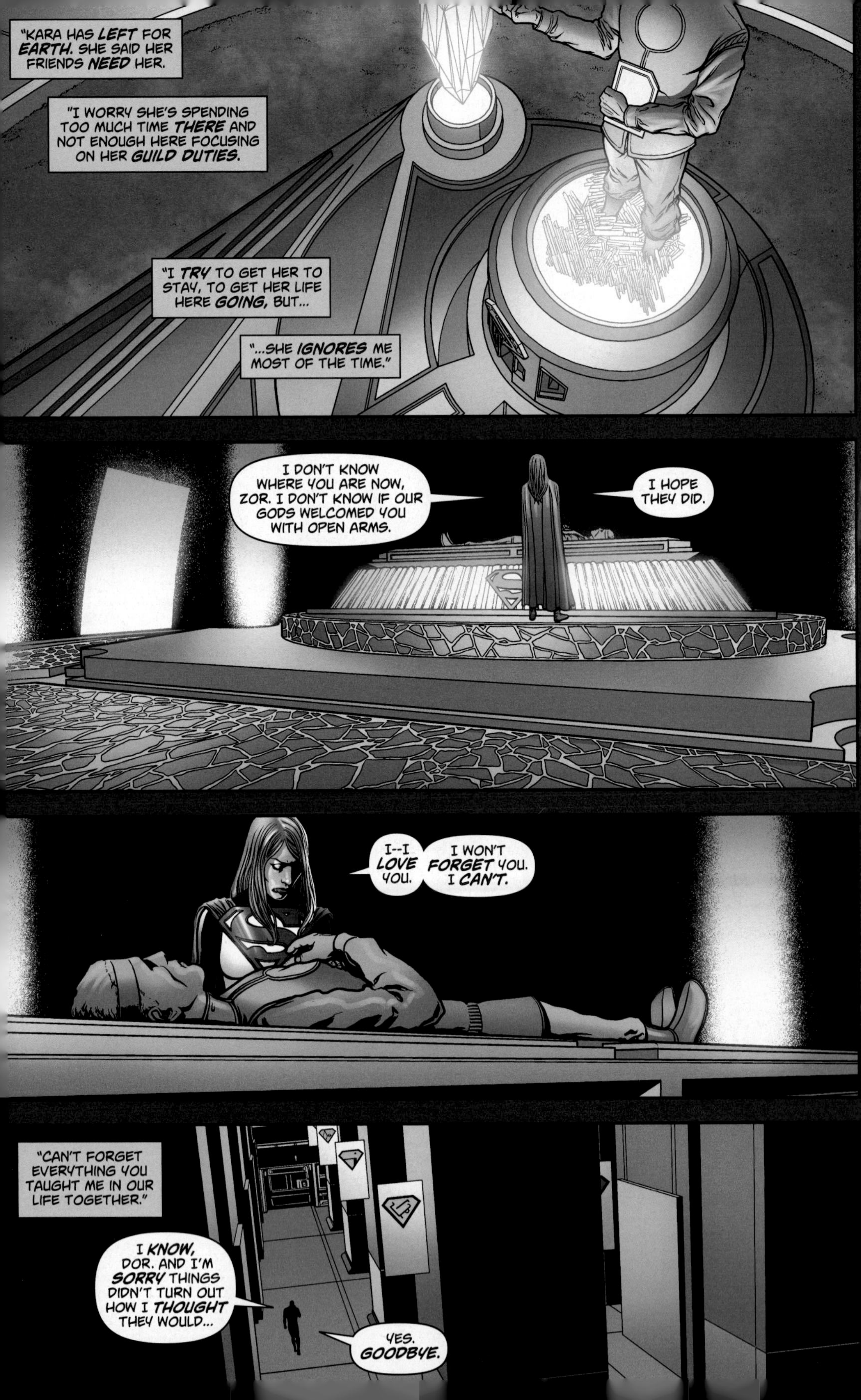
"KARA HAS LEFT FOR EARTH. SHE SAID HER FRIENDS NEED HER.
"I WORRY SHE'S SPENDING TOO MUCH TIME THERE AND NOT ENOUGH HERE FOCUSING ON HER GUILD DUTIES.
"I TRY TO GET HER TO STAY, TO GET HER LIFE HERE GOING, BUT...
"...SHE IGNORES ME MOST OF THE TIME."
I DON'T KNOW WHERE YOU ARE NOW, ZOR. I DON'T KNOW IF OUR GODS WELCOMED YOU WITH OPEN ARMS.
I HOPE THEY DID.
I--I LOVE YOU.
I WON'T FORGET YOU. I CAN'T.
"CAN'T FORGET EVERYTHING YOU TAUGHT ME IN OUR LIFE TOGETHER."
I KNOW, DOR. AND I'M SORRY THINGS DIDN'T TURN OUT HOW I THOUGHT THEY WOULD...
YES. GOODBYE.

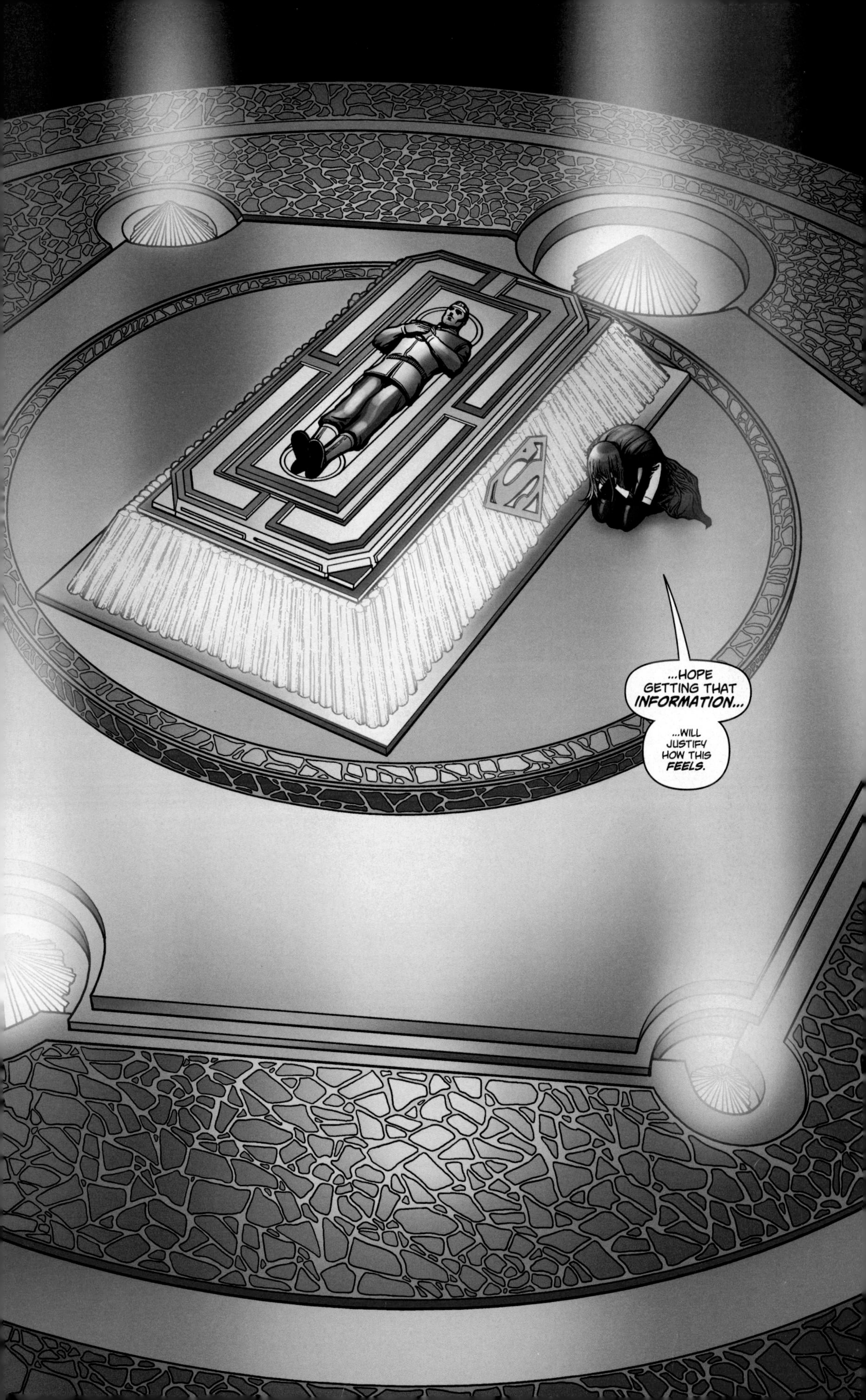
...HOPE GETTING THAT INFORMATION...
...WILL JUSTIFY HOW THIS FEELS.

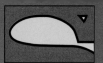

# SUPERGIRL

**ALTER EGOS:** Kara Zor-El, Linda Lang

**BASE OF OPERATIONS:** New Krypton; Metropolis; formerly New York City

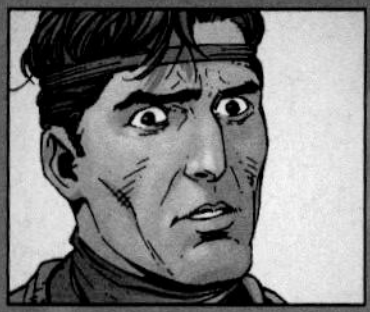
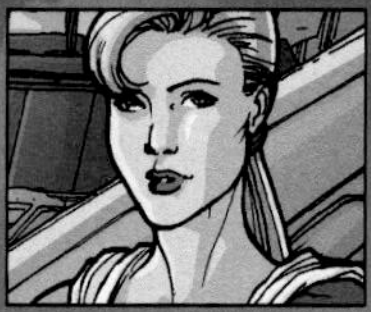
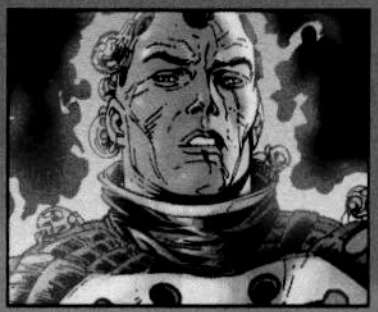
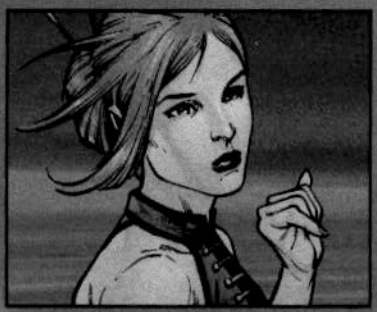
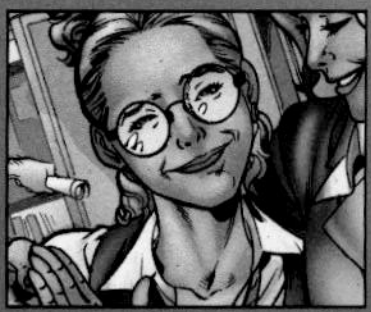

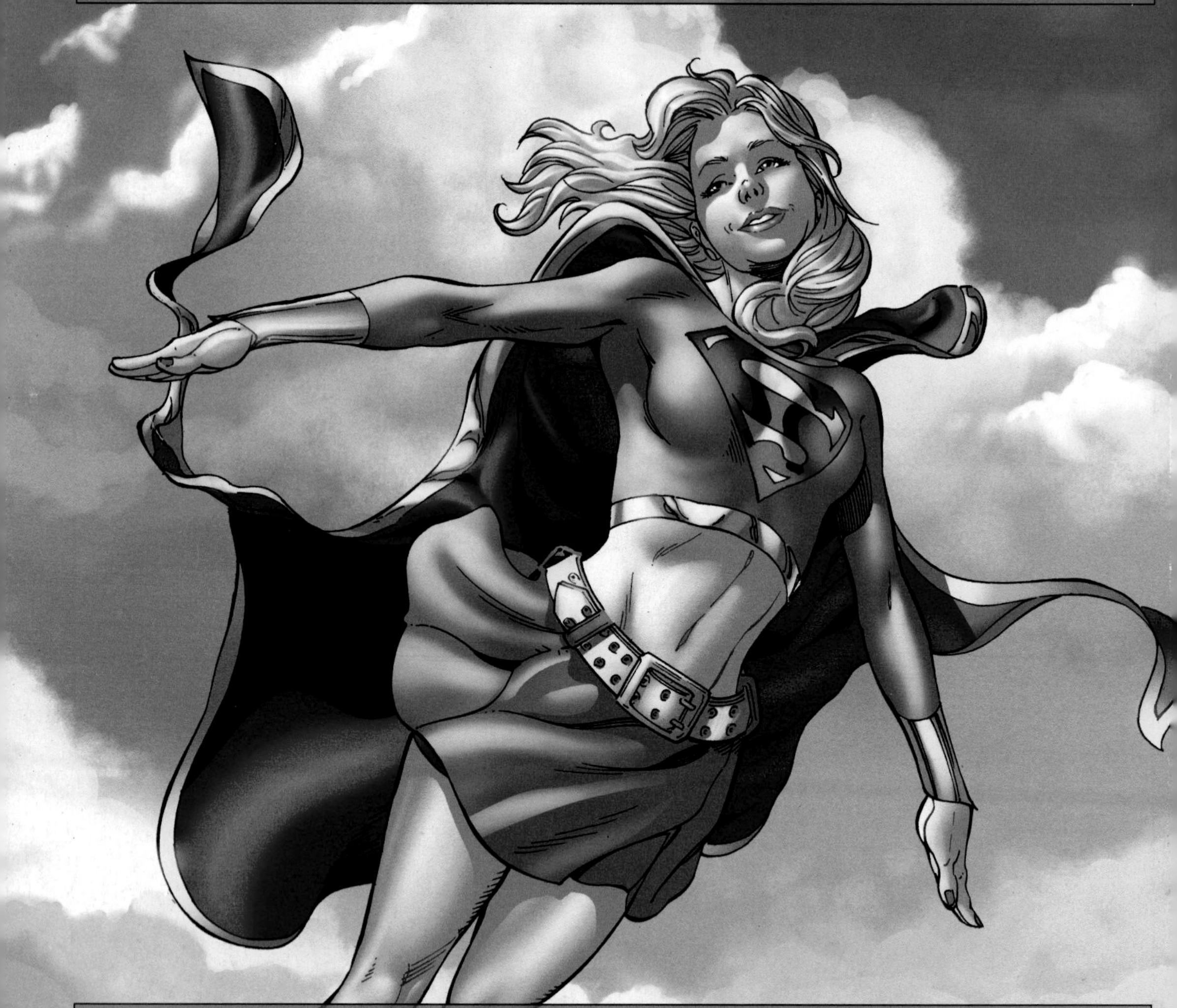

**POWERS/ABILITIES:** Supergirl possesses all of the powers of a Kryptonian under a yellow sun: flight, super strength, X-ray vision, heat vision, telescopic vision, invulnerability, and super speed. The full extent of some of these powers remains untested.

**HISTORY:** Kara Zor-El was living happily with her parents **ZOR-EL** and **ALURA** in Argo City when **BRAINIAC** attacked Krypton and stole the city of Kandor. Within weeks, her uncle Jor-El declared the planet doomed, and her father Zor-El was working on a way to save Argo City in the event of Krypton's destruction. Krypton exploded weeks later.

Using Brainiac-based force field technology, Zor-El was able to keep Argo City intact, and the city floated adrift in space. Knowing the force field would one day fail, Zor began constructing a prototype rocket, with plans for mass-producing escape rockets for his people. His attempts were cut short when Brainiac discovered Argo and attacked. Alura and Zor-El quickly programmed the prototype rocket with the same coordinates Jor-El had used for his own son, Kal-El, and sent Kara off into space.

Unfortunately, Kara's rocket was struck by a massive piece of the exploding Argo City and was knocked off course. Arriving on Earth 30 years later, Kara found that her cousin was Superman, one of Earth's greatest heroes. Kara took on his heroic mantle to become Supergirl, and eventually took the secret identity of **LANA LANG'S** niece, **LINDA**.

During a fight on Brainiac's ship, Superman discovered Kara's parents were alive and well, living along with 100,000 other Kryptonians in the Bottle City of Kandor. Superman returned them to Earth. Kara's joyous reunion with her parents was short-lived, however, as the villain Reactron used his Gold Kryptonite-powered blasts to kill Zor-El.

Distraught, Alura created a new planet, which she dubbed New Krypton, and moved the displaced Kryptonians there. Kara elected to move to New Krypton, but her Earth ties keep pulling her back, even in light of the United Nations' decision to ban all Kryptonians.

Now, whenever Kara is on Earth, she spends time searching for Reactron. When she finds him, she will return him to New Krypton to face Kryptonian justice.

Supergirl has undergone extensive hand-to-hand training with Batman and the Amazonian warriors. Reunited with her people, Supergirl has also begun studying the Kryptonian martial art Klurkor, testing as high as first-degree badge.

Text by STERLING GATES, art by JAMAL IGLE & JON SIBAL, color by NEI RUFFINO

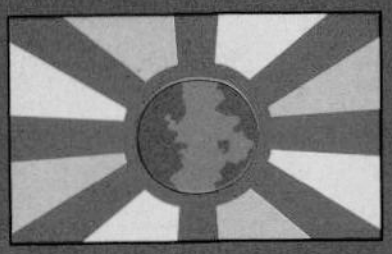

# ALURA AND THE GUILDS OF NEW KRYPTON

**BASE OF OPERATIONS:** Kandor, New Krypton

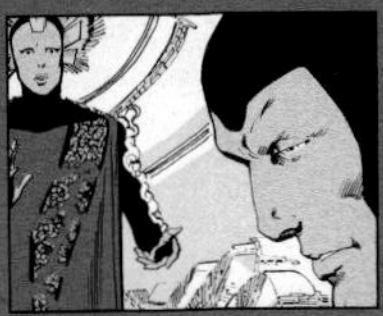
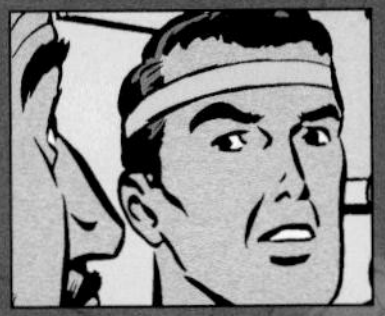
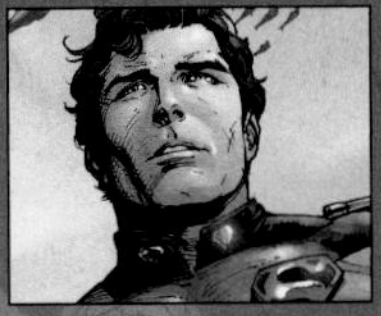
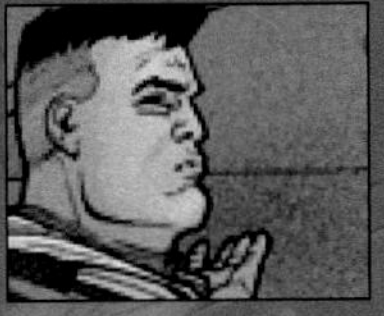
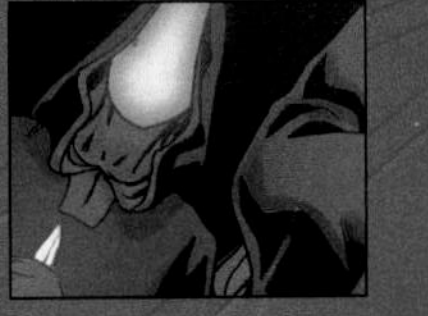

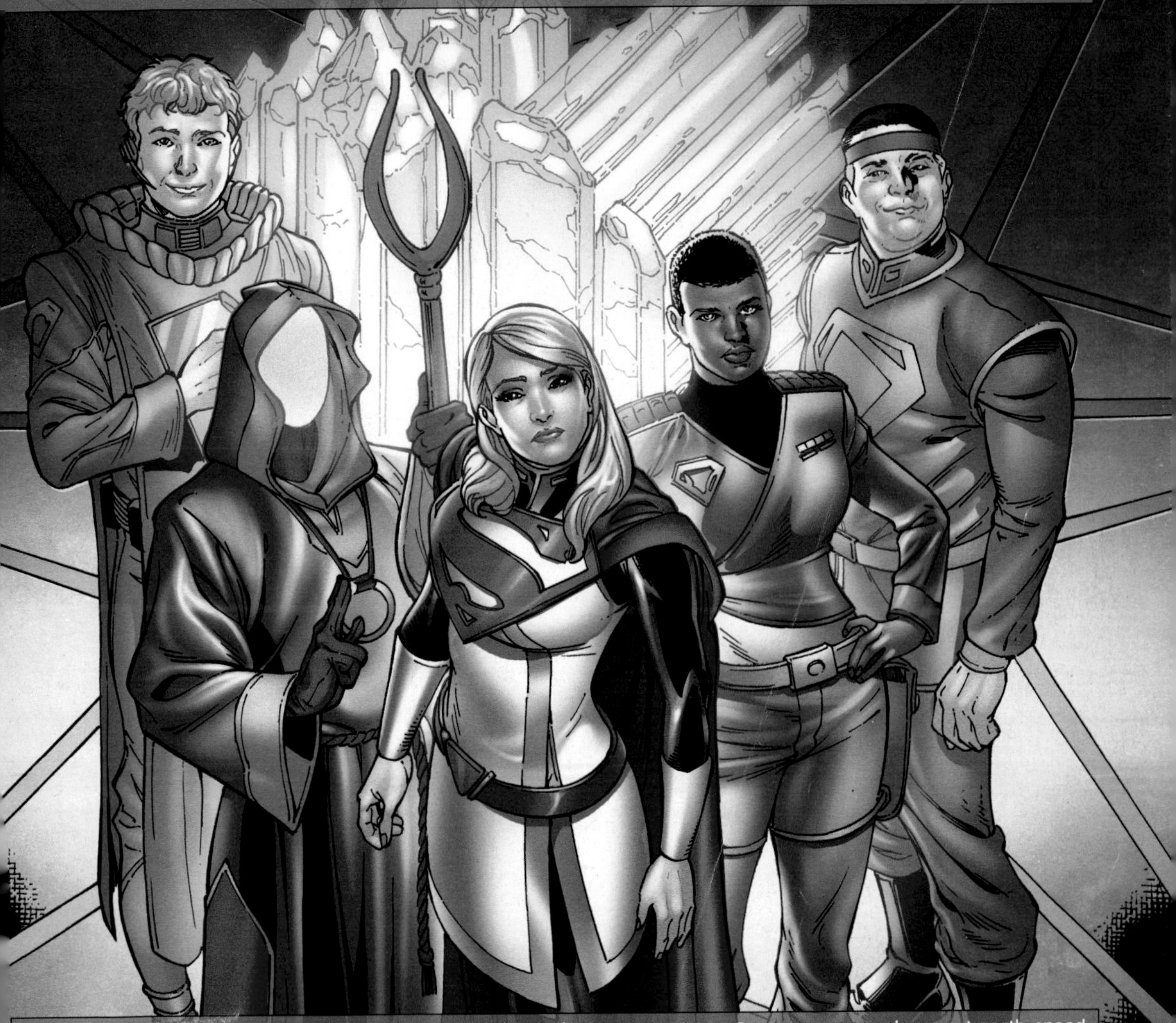

**POWERS/ABILITIES:** Alura Zor-El and all Kryptonians have the same powers as Superman — superhuman strength, speed, flight, stamina, freezing breath, super hearing, heat vision and X-ray vision — but they lack his lifetime of experience with these powers, making them less adept at using them.

**HISTORY:** As one of Brainiac's bottled cities and afterward while residing on Earth's Arctic tundra, Kandor was governed by Zor-El, Superman's uncle and father of Supergirl. When Reactron assassinated him, Zor's wife Alura became the city's leader. Initially overcome with grief, Alura made rash, hostile decisions based on her distrust and hatred of humanity, most importantly Kandor's relocation to a new Planet Krypton where she made Zod head of the Kryptonian military. As time has passed, Alura's grief has ebbed and she seems to act more sagely, and she's beginning to heal the rift with her daughter as well.

She endeavors to preserve Kryptonian life — its culture, arts, science, military might and theology, these being the things that divide the citizens into their respective guilds:

**THE SCIENCE GUILD** (Alura's own guild) governs most forms of science and technology on the planet. Their ways are sometimes seen as emotionless, decrying all aesthetics. Nevertheless, this ethic has made Krypton into a mighty technological power.

**THE ARTISTS GUILD** (Zor's guild), while involved with science, also handles all forms of art, design and creativity. They more strongly believe in the religions of Krypton and seek to find the hand of Rao at work in all things.

**THE MILITARY GUILD** believes in its own might. Under Zod's leadership, it strives to maintain the martial glory of Krypton.

**THE LABOR GUILD** keeps the planet running, taking on any and all manual jobs. They are the unseen masses, going all but unnoticed by other guilds. Indeed, they are the only guild without Council representation.

**THE RELIGIOUS GUILD** moves silently throughout Krypton. Priests represent all Kryptonian gods, each in turn representing a guild. Telle (god of wisdom/Science). Lorra (beauty/Artists). Mordo (strength/Military). Yuda (the moon/Labor). The Religious Guild itself honors the ice goddess Cythonna, while also being priests for the deity above all others — Rao, the fire god, which is seen as the wellspring of all life on Krypton.

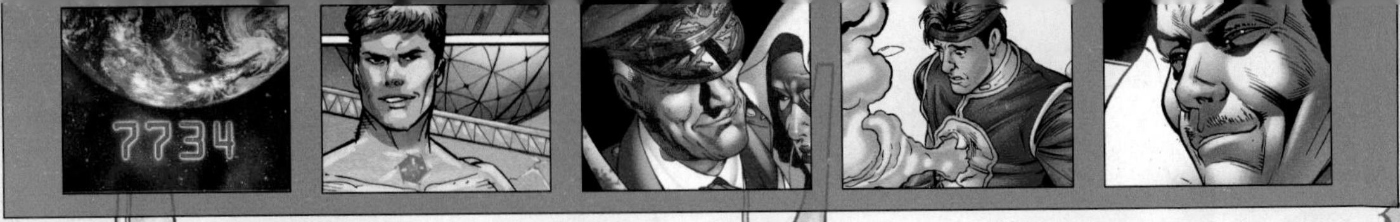
7734

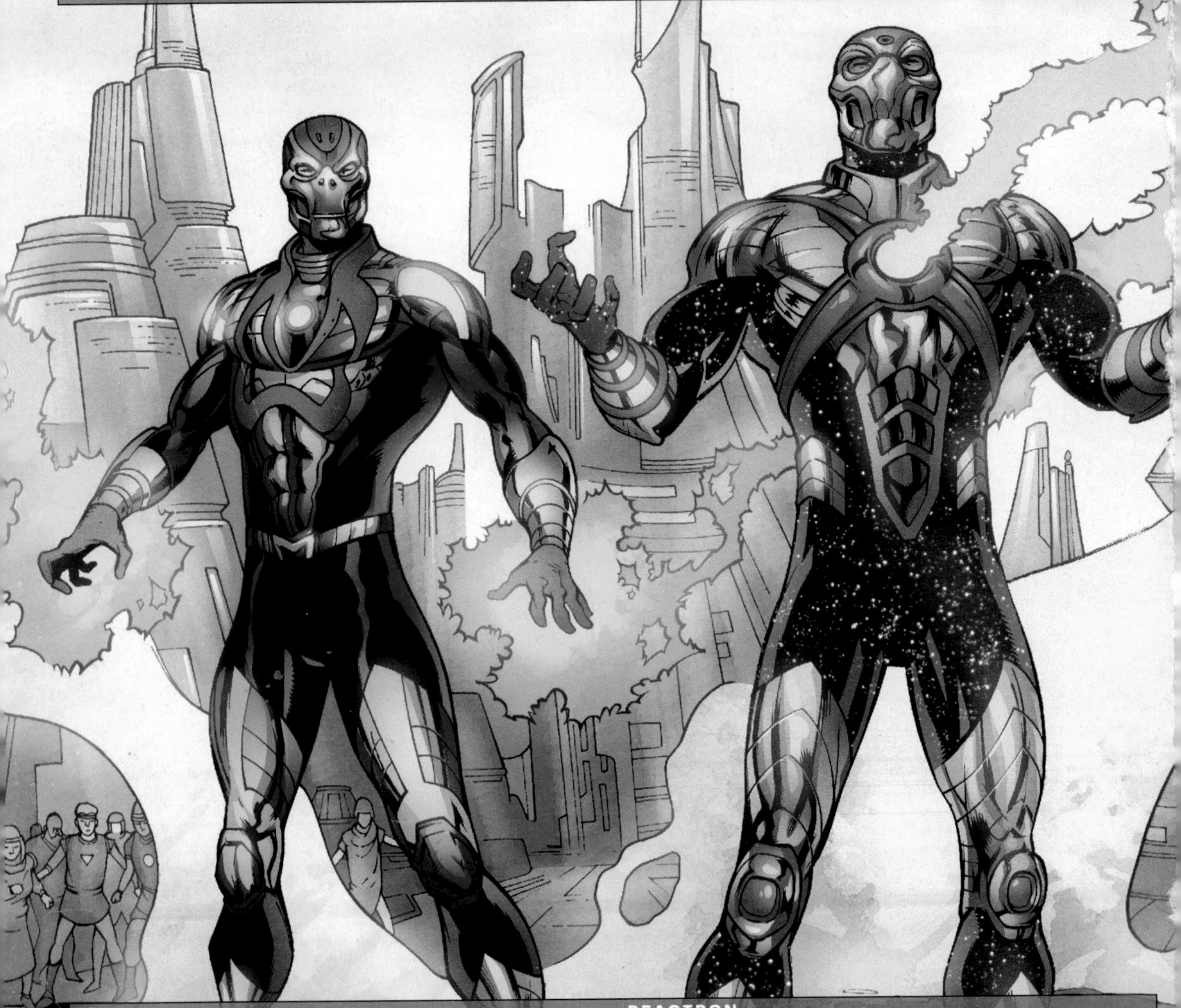

**METALLO**
**ALTER EGO:** John Corben
**BASE OF OPERATIONS:** Project 7734 Bunker (location unknown); Metropolis

**POWERS/ABILITIES:** Metallo possesses a super hard skeleton laced with metallo, the alloy from which he draws his codename. Within his chest is a piece of Green Kryptonite, giving him the ability to harm, and eventually kill, Kryptonians.

**HISTORY: JOHN CORBEN** was [REDACTED BY THE U.S. ARMY - REDACTED BY THE U.S. ARMY - REDACTED BY THE U.S. ARMY - REDACTED BY THE U.S. ARMY - REDACTED BY THE U.S. ARMY] a test subject for [REDACTED BY THE U.S. ARMY - REDACTED BY THE U.S. ARMY] Kryptonite heart and a metallic alloy lacing his chest cavity. Naming himself Metallo after the type of metal in his body, Corben [REDACTED BY THE U.S. ARMY - REDACTED BY THE U.S. ARMY] and a long history with Lois Lane.

Corben was stunned when the Green Kryptonite in his chest was able to take down the Man of Steel, but was eventually stopped by Superman. The once [REDACTED BY THE U.S. ARMY] was now a full-fledged super-villain.

Recently Metallo has been recruited into Project: 7734 by **GENERAL LANE**. He and Reactron were part of an elite team that infiltrated Kandor after its enlargement. They murdered several Kryptonians, including the Kryptonian leader **ZOR-EL**, before being evacuated from the city by Superwoman. Now a man wanted by the Kryptonian government, Metallo is smart enough to lie low before showing his face again.

**REACTRON**
**ALTER EGO:** Major Benjamin Krull
**BASE OF OPERATIONS:** Project 7734 Bunker (location unknown); Metropolis

**POWERS/ABILITIES:** Reactron has a piece of Gold Kryptonite embedded in his chest, giving him the ability to neutralize a Kryptonian's powers for approximately fifteen seconds. He's also able to fire blasts of energy from his hands.

**HISTORY: BENJAMIN KRULL** was a loser who didn't know what to do with his life until he joined the U.S. Army. One night, while guarding an experimental [REDACTED BY THE U.S. ARMY], Krull was injured. Knowing he was going to die, Dr. [REDACTED BY THE U.S. ARMY], the man in charge of Project [REDACTED BY THE U.S. ARMY], decided Krull needed a new uniform, one that they hoped would prolong his life: the StarSuit.

Soon after his initial defeat at the hands of Supergirl, Krull was approached by General Lane with an offer to join Project 7734. Krull accepted, and he was fitted for a new suit — one with a piece of Gold Kryptonite in the middle.

Reactron was part of an elite team that infiltrated Kandor when it appeared on Earth, and was directly responsible for the death of the Kryptonian leader Zor-El. It is unknown what the ramifications will be once a Kryptonian finally gets hold of him. Fortunately for him, the piece of Gold Kryptonite in his chest will make it a fair fight.